Development Governor

Sir Geoffrey Colby

Development Governor

A Biography of Sir Geoffrey Colby

COLIN BAKER

British Academic Press
An Imprint of I.B. Tauris
London · New York

Published in 1994 by
British Academic Press
45 Bloomsbury Square
London WC1A 2HY

An imprint of I.B.Tauris & Co Ltd

In the United States of America
and Canada distributed by
St Martin's Press
175 Fifth Avenue
New York
NY 10010

A full CIP record for this book is available from the British Library

Library of Congress Catalog card number 93–61871
A full CIP record is available from the Library of Congress

ISBN 1–85043–616–9

Phototypeset by Intype, London
Printed and bound in Great Britain by
WBC Ltd, Bridgend, Mid Glamorgan

Contents

Note on Spelling and Currency

The spelling of place names follows that used at the relevant time and no attempt has been made to change them to their present form: e.g. Cholo and Mlanje are so spelled, as in colonial days, rather than Thyolo and Mulanje as in their modern form. Similarly the colonial names are used rather than the modern Malawian names: e.g. Port Herald rather than Nsanje and Fort Johnston rather than Mangochi.

The currency used is the pound sterling, undecimalized. No attempt has been made to render the monetary amounts into their Malawian equivalent in kwacha and tambala.

Acknowledgements

I owe an immense debt of gratitude to a large number of people who have helped me by providing information, views and advice over many years during the preparation of this biography. In many cases I have taxed their memory and patience most sorely, yet they have seemed always very willing to help to the fullest extent which their – as they thought – failing memories permitted. I have been much touched by those who even thanked me for having revived old, and often proud, memories. I acknowledge the help and generosity of all these people and I thank them with deep appreciation. The book owes more to them than it does to me. I will not, however, embarrass them – with one exception – by giving their names here; they are mentioned and acknowledged in the notes to the various chapters, and the frequency with which some appear is in part a measure of the debt I owe them as individuals and collectively. The one exception is Dick Kettlewell. For over a decade he has responded with an extraordinary fullness, willingness and promptness to my requests for facts, opinions and advice. If – as was inevitable at times – progress seemed to be lagging or I had not communicated with him for some time, he would, in a charming Colby-like fashion, write to me to ask how I was getting on, and it always had the desired effect: I got on rather more speedily!

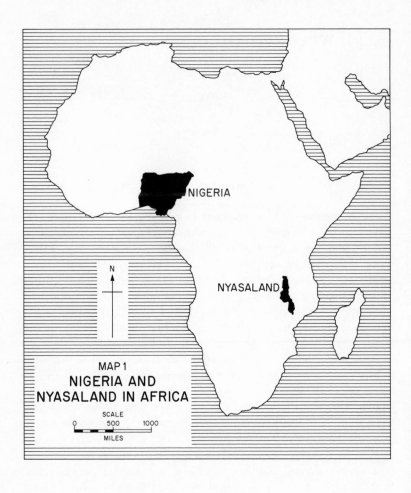

N

NIGERIA

NYASALAND

MAP 1
NIGERIA AND
NYASALAND IN AFRICA

SCALE
0   500   1000
MILES

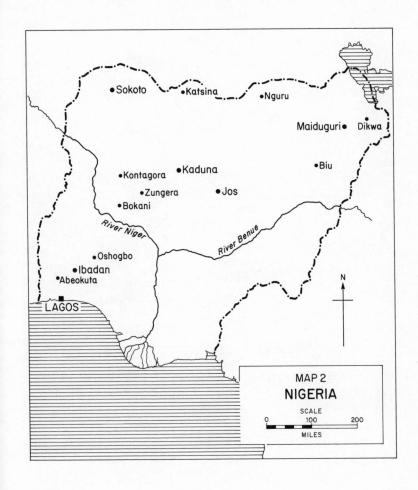

MAP 2
NIGERIA

SCALE

0   100   200

MILES

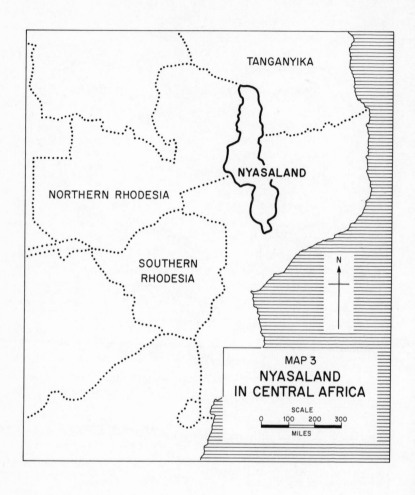

TANGANYIKA

NYASALAND

NORTHERN RHODESIA

SOUTHERN
RHODESIA

N

MAP 3
NYASALAND
IN CENTRAL AFRICA

SCALE
0   100   200   300
MILES

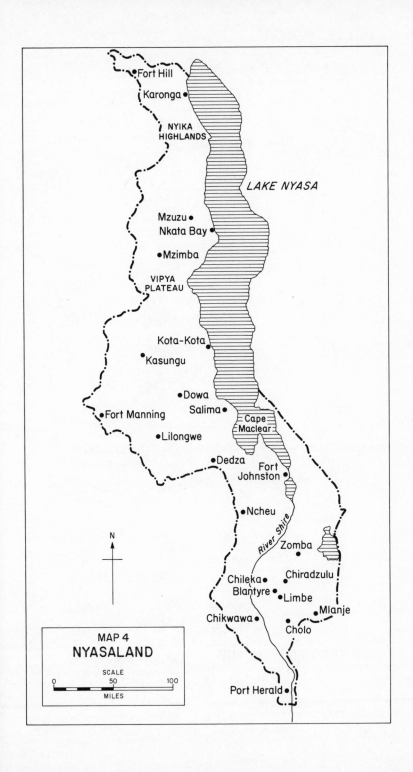

Fort Hill
Karonga

NYIKA
HIGHLANDS

LAKE NYASA

Mzuzu
Nkata Bay

Mzimba

VIPYA
PLATEAU

Kota-Kota
Kasungu

Dowa
Salima
Cape
Maclear

Fort Manning

Lilongwe

Dedza
Fort
Johnston

Ncheu

River Shire

N

Zomba

Chiradzulu
Chileka
Blantyre
Limbe
Mlanje
Chikwawa
Cholo

MAP 4
NYASALAND

Port Herald

SCALE
0   50   100
MILES

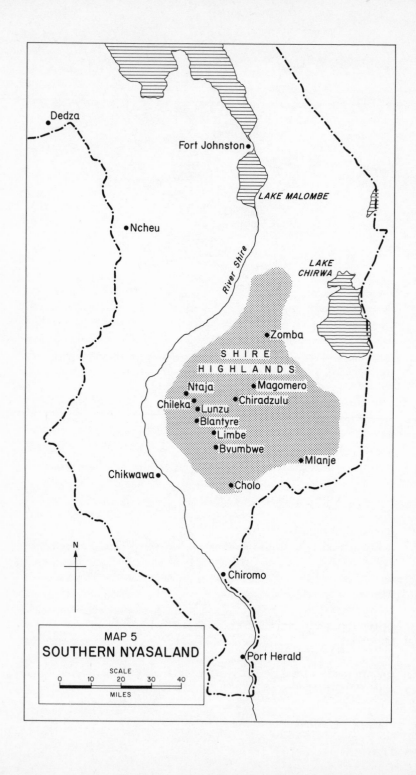

Dedza

Fort Johnston

LAKE MALOMBE

River Shire

Ncheu

LAKE CHIRWA

Zomba

S H I R E

H I G H L A N D S

Ntaja • Magomero

Chileka • Chiradzulu

• Lunzu

• Blantyre

• Limbe

• Bvumbwe

Chikwawa • • Mlanje

• Cholo

N

Chiromo

MAP 5

SOUTHERN NYASALAND

SCALE

0   10   20   30   40

MILES

Port Herald

Preface

The end of empire in Africa was breathtakingly swift and nowhere more so than in Nyasaland where, within four years of Dr Banda's return to his country of birth in 1958, (including 13 months which he spent in political detention) internal self-government was achieved; within five years the abolition of the Federation of Rhodesia and Nyasaland was accomplished; and within six years the country became the independent state of Malawi with Dr Banda as its first head.

In agreeing to Nyasaland's independence the British government needed to be reassured on two fundamental factors, the one political, the other economic, although the two were closely intertwined.

Politically, they needed to be reasonably sure that a capable leader, preferably pro-British, was emerging who could command the following of sufficient of the country's people. Such was Dr Banda's background and his popularity and standing among the vast majority of Nyasalanders that the British government had little difficulty with this political point. Indeed, in practical terms Dr Banda had no rivals.

Economically, the British government was worried about Nyasaland's ability to stand on its own feet and to pay its way without Britain having to support it massively for a long and indefinite period. The worries were acute because Nyasaland was leaving the federation which many believed had been its economic and financial salvation and of which Britain had forced Nyasaland's membership precisely in order to relieve the imperial exchequer of the dangers of a heavy and growing financial burden. Dr Banda argued that, given temporary support by Britain, his country could survive on its own and that he could accomplish this within a relatively few years.

Whilst neither Dr Banda, in pressing this argument, nor the British government in eventually deciding to risk accepting it, publicly made the point, it is the case that in the decade preceding Dr Banda's return, Sir Geoffrey Colby, governor from 1948 to 1956, had shown that the country could stand on its own feet and that achieving this highly desirable state of economic affairs could be accomplished in a relatively short period. In his eight years of gubernatorial office – precisely the time taken later by Dr Banda to relieve the British government of the need to support his revenue budget – Colby vastly increased agricultural production, improved public utilities and social services, and raised individual incomes and the general standard of living, whilst trebling his government's annual recurrent revenue.

This was the contribution which Colby made: he laid the economic foundation upon which independence was later built and showed that Nyasaland could not only flourish independently but also had the potential to do so in a relatively short period of time.

Although this book is primarily about Sir Geoffrey Colby's governorship of Nyasaland, it is essentially a biography. It is not about development theoretically or *per se*, but rather about a governor who devoted himself to development in a very practical sense. It deals in the initial chapters with his early family life in England and his early professional life in Nigeria, periods which helped to form the sort of man who became not only a distinguished colonial civil servant but also an outstanding Development Governor.

1· Early Life

'A very fine training ground for a hardworking professional career.'

The Edwardian era was but two months old when Geoffrey Francis Taylor Colby was born at 10 St James Road, Surbiton, Surrey, on Monday, 25 March 1901, a day which dawned fresh and fair but which later became unsettled and turned snowy.[1] His birth was announced, without Christian names, in *The Times* two days later.[2] When he was baptised, his first name was new to the family, his second was taken from his father and maternal uncle, and his third from his paternal grandfather. His parents' marriage the previous year had united two very different families, the one professional, the other business.[3]

On his father's side were at least three generations of medical practitioners. His paternal great-grandfather, William Colby, was born in 1802, was admitted to the Licentiateship of the Society of Apothecaries in 1821, became a Member of the Royal College of Surgeons the following year, married Mary Anne Etty in 1826 and lived at New Malton, Yorkshire, where he was senior surgeon to the Malton Dispensary and the Union medical officer. He died on 27 March 1877.[4]

One of William and Mary's children was William Taylor Colby – Geoffrey's grandfather – who was born in May 1827. In 1848, he went to Saint Thomas's Hospital Medical School, and became a Member of the Royal College of Surgeons and a Licentiate of the Society of Apothecaries in 1851. He took his Doctorate of Medicine at St Andrew's in 1878, and lived at The Mount, Malton, Yorkshire, becoming a justice of the peace of the North Riding of that county. Politically he was a staunch Conservative and took a considerable interest in military matters: he was a founder volunteer of the 2nd Volunteer Battalion of the Princess of Wales Own Yorkshire Regiment, of which he was for many years surgeon lieutenant-colonel, and for which services he was awarded the Long Service Volunteer Medal. His hobbies were gardening and sport; he was an excellent shot and, despite his advanced age of 85, was out with his gun only a month before his death on 22 December 1912, which was believed to have been hastened by anxiety over the illness of his eldest son, Ernest. He had three sons and two daughters.[5]

William and Mary may have had another son, George, born about 1840 who also became a doctor, going to St Thomas's in 1857 and qualifying MRCS there in 1860. George Colby, who lived at New Malton, died in the early 1920s.[6]

Two of William Taylor Colby's sons also became medical practitioners. The elder of these, James George Ernest, known as Ernest – Geoffrey's uncle – was born at Malton in 1861, went to King Edward VI Grammar School, Old Malton, and matriculated on 24 January 1879 as a science exhibitioner at Wadham College, Oxford, where he took his BA in natural science in 1882, and his MA in 1885. In 1883, he gained the Open Entrance Scholarship in science to St Bartholomew's Hospital, London, where he obtained the junior scholarship in anatomy and physiology in 1884, and the Brackenbury scholarship in surgery in 1888, the year he qualified MB, BCh, MRCS and LRCP. When he left St Bartholomew's (where he was house surgeon and ophthalmic house surgeon) he studied at Wurzburg, was appointed FRCS in 1890, and took the Cambridge diploma in public health in 1894. He joined his father in practice at The Mount, Malton, in 1890. Ernest Colby was the chief promoter of the Malton Cottage Hospital, and he was appointed its first surgeon. He was also medical officer of health to the Malton Union Sanitary Authority, and became president of the Yorkshire Medical Society for the year 1905–6. He married Grace – known invariably as Gracie – daughter of the Rev J. H. Mandell, vicar of Haydon Bridge, Northumberland, in 1899, and they had two sons and three daughters. In August 1912, only a few months before his father's death, Ernest had a severe attack of septicaemia, which his constitution, undermined by constant hard work, was unable to withstand. Although his illness was long and trying, his health seemed to improve for a time after treatment at Leeds, and he went to Colwyn Bay to convalesce, but, despite being attended by a number of leading doctors, he did not recover, and died aged 52 on 5 March 1913, less than three months after his father's death. He was known as an able, skilful, thorough man of initiative, who never spared himself.[7]

William Taylor Colby's second son – Geoffrey's father – was born at

The Mount, Malton, on 27 January 1865, was baptised Francis Edward
Albert, and was known throughout his life as Frank.[8] He went to school
at Malton Grammar and then in January 1881 (when he was 16) to St
Peter's at York, as a day boy. He won an open scholarship in science to
King's College, Cambridge, in January 1889, and received an exhibition
in 1890 and a scholarship in 1891, during which latter year he secured
a class one in part one of the natural science tripos. He was also a
prizeman. He graduated BA in 1891 and – like his brother Ernest –
went on to become a student at St Bartholomew's Hospital in 1892. His
career at Bart's was outstanding and although he narrowly missed the
Brackenbury Medical Scholarship for 1892–3, he qualified MB, BCh,
MRCS and LRCP in 1894. He became junior house surgeon in March
1894, and senior ophthalmic house surgeon in September 1894, both
with Henry Trentham Butlin, with whom he published a joint paper in
the hospital records in 1895. To work with Butlin was itself a mark of
Frank's ability, because Butlin was a distinguished surgeon in several
fields but specialized in ear, nose and throat surgery, in which field he
was a leading pioneer. After his housemanship, Frank became assistant
electrician at Bart's in the electricity department, a treatment and diag-
nostic department founded in 1883 and the forerunner of the x-ray
department. He became FRCS on 12 December 1895, and later was
clinical assistant at the Great Ormond Street Hospital for Sick Children.
He married Elizabeth Ann Carkeet Bryant – known as Elsie – on 1 May
1900, and they lived at 10 St James Road, (with consulting rooms, shared
with his partner, Dr Coleman, at 5 Victoria Terrace, Surbiton) until
shortly after the birth of their first child, Geoffrey, in 1901, when they
moved to Woking. He was appointed honorary medical officer at the
Woking Victoria Cottage Hospital in Chobham Road, and had a large
and expanding private practice at his home, Hill View, Guildford Road,
from (at the latest) 1909 to well into the 1920s. At Woking he did not
have a partner but worked by himself with a number of wealthy patients,
including members of the Guiness family. The Colbys' sons were
brought up at Hill View, although later Frank and Elsie moved to
Littlewood, Sutton Green, Woking, and later still to Meadow Cottage,
White Rose Lane. Frank was a delightful, rather eccentric and nervy
person. He was a not very tall man, shrewd, alert and friendly, and
retained his Yorkshire accent throughout his life. He died on 20 January
1933, suddenly dropping dead whilst out shooting snipe at Woking, and
was cremated at Brookwood Crematorium. His widow, Elsie – who was
described as 'very fascinating when young, very vivacious and always

laughing' and whose 'liveliness remained with her always' – survived him for over 20 years, and died at Bournemouth on 11 November 1954. She was cremated privately with the request that there should be no mourning, no letters and no flowers.[9]

Whereas on his father's side, Geoffrey's recent ancestors were professional men, on his mother's side they were businessmen.[10] His maternal great-great-grandfather was James Bryant, a starch-maker at Tiverton, Devon, who had four children, one of whom was Geoffrey's great-grandfather, William Bryant, a man of forceful personality who was born in 1804 shortly before James and his family moved to Plymouth to set up a starch factory in Mill Lane. Between the ages of 15 and 28, he was employed as an official in the Excise Department at Plymouth, before going into business as a soap and grease maker and sugar refiner. In the same year as he went into business, William – brought up in a family of Wesleyan Methodists – joined the Society of Friends on marriage. In 1835, he went into partnership with Edward James and started a general merchants' firm in Woolster Street. They were joined in 1844 by a partner, Burnell, and started a soap factory in Coxside, Plymouth. In 1843 William entered into partnership with a fellow Quaker, Francis May (1803–85), the fourth son of a wealthy London merchant, who owned a prosperous grocer's shop in Bishopsgate Without, and who had been Bryant and James's London agent from the early 1840s. Bryant and May established themselves as provision merchants at 133–4 Tooley Street and 5 Philpot Lane, London, and began to manufacture matches in Bow, London, in 1861. The friction match had been invented by John Walker in Stockton-on-Tees in 1827, and independently by Isaac Holden, a latin, chemistry and English teacher at the Castle Street Academy, Reading, in 1829. Neither patented his invention, in Isaac Holden's case because a pupil of his had told his father of the invention and the father, a chemist in London, had begun manufacturing matches commercially. It fell to Francis May to take out the first British patent in 1855. William Bryant died in 1874.

William Bryant married Anne Jago Carkeet (1804–79), a member of an old and well-known Quaker family, in 1832 and they had four sons: Wilberforce (1837–1906); Arthur Charles – Geoffrey's grandfather – (1841–84); Frederick Carkeet (1843–88); and Theodore Henry (1843–1913). All of them became partners with their father in 1868.

Wilberforce became senior partner when his father died and persuaded May to be bought out. He then masterminded a number of important developments in the firm which included a programme of mechanization, the introduction of new products, mergers with rival firms, a campaign of intensive advertising, diversification, and expansion into export markets. In 1876, Wilberforce married Margaret, the daughter of William Lawson of Perth, and they had a son (who died in infancy) and three daughters. Although he remained on the register of the Society of Friends, he became a staunch churchman and a patron of the Church of England Temperance Society. He was a Conservative, became a justice of the peace and high sheriff of Buckinghamshire in 1892, and was president of local agricultural shows which he held in his grounds at Stoke Poges. He 'was fond of driving and was an excellent whip', a keen gardener, president of the local horticultural society, and a good amateur photographer.[11]

Arthur married, first, Emily Lucas who bore him two sons, Arthur and Charles, and then in 1872, his late wife's cousin, Elizabeth Lucas (1848–1928). Elizabeth – Geoffrey's grandmother – was a woman of very strong character and views which were markedly puritanical. Although she was brought up as a Quaker, she became a member of the Church of England on marriage. She was a fundamentalist in religious matters and disapproved of frivolity and alcohol; indeed, when her husband died she poured the contents of his wine cellar down the sink. She made no attempt to launch either of her two daughters socially and when one of them broke off an engagement to become betrothed to another man – whom she then married – Elizabeth was furious and disapproving, saying that her daughter's behaviour set such a bad example to the servants. Her grandchildren found her a formidable character, feeling uneasy in her presence lest she enquire into the state of their souls. She did, however, mellow with age, and had a jolly laugh. When Arthur Bryant died, his brothers persuaded his widow to sell her shares in Bryant and May to one or more of his brothers, and she lost heavily on the transaction.[12]

Arthur and Elizabeth Bryant had five sons (Francis, George, Gilbert, Harold and Edward) and two daughters (Mary and Elizabeth Ann Carkeet – Geoffrey's mother). Edward Bryant emigrated to the USA as a young man and in 1923 began operating the first sugar mill in south Florida. He was one of the leaders in the Florida Sugar and Food Products Company, an imaginative and progressive set of promoters, and was seen as 'a symbol of the rising sugar industry'. By the early 1940s, he was superintendent of the eastern field division of the United States Sugar Corporation. The town which he founded around his sugar mill is today a very small unincorporated settlement, called Bryant, where the major employer is still the 'Bryant Sugar House'. Edward's sister, Elizabeth Ann Carkeet Bryant – Elsie – married Frank Colby in 1900.[13]

Although their father, paternal grandfather, great-grandfather, uncle, and possibly great-uncle, were medical men, none of Frank and Elsie Colby's three children – all sons – entered that profession. Geoffrey, the eldest, did specialize in science at Charterhouse and read natural science at Cambridge, and at an early stage may have had a medical career in mind, but became a colonial administrator; William Marcus (1903–) read English Literature at Christ Church, Oxford, graduating in 1925, and became a successful member of the Stock Exchange, which he attended regularly even as an octogenarian; and Reginald Edward (1906–69) went to Wadham College, Oxford, where he graduated in 1926 and became a much-travelled and successful journalist and author, dying from cancer on 13 August 1969 after a long illness.[14]

Geoffrey spent his early childhood at Woking in a professional, middle-class, Church of England, fairly close, conservative environment: the son of a doctor with a large and flourishing private practice with sufficient leisure to indulge his liking for shooting. The three brothers generally spent their holidays with their grandmother, Elizabeth Lucas Bryant, at Fir Grove, Claygate, near Esher in Surrey: a large Victorian house (with a billiards room, four tennis courts and a nearby golf course) where their cousins, Nancy and Jack Beevor, were also frequent visitors. These meetings of infant cousins were often exciting and occasionally unruly affairs, the Colby boys being known to fling pats of butter up to the ceiling where they stuck during nursery tea-time, presumably without the knowledge, and certainly without the approval, of their puritanical grandmother. Geoffrey was a particularly popular cousin and considered to be great fun. Games played – and in Geoffrey's case continued to play – an important part in the Colby boys' upbringing. All three brothers were very keen on all sorts of games – as were their mother's brothers – and they had a good grass tennis court at the Woking house, kept to the highest possible standards – 'as good as the centre court at Wimbledon' – by the head greenkeeper of the Woking golf club, a patient of Dr Colby's.[15]

At the age of seven, in 1908, Geoffrey was sent to preparatory school at Bexhill, where a large number of independent schools were playing an important role in promoting the town's prosperity and indeed in forming its character. St Wilfred's School, which Geoffrey attended, was but one of more than 30 such schools founded there in the late Victorian and Edwardian era:

> Not only was the time favourable to their commencement, with its emphasis on strict principles and manly games – a healthy mind in a healthy body – but the still rural nature of the town gave room for expansive playing fields around the large premises . . . Though not necessarily sectarian, most exerted a strong Christian influence . . .
>
> Many schools took boarders, children whose parents were often abroad, the father usually in one of the armed or administrative services of the Crown.

St Wilfred's was opened some three years before Geoffrey's arrival there, by a Mr and Mrs Clark who remained owners, with Mr Clark as headmaster, for 25 years. The school buildings were formerly Birchington House, a three-storeyed, elegant, red-brick, late Victorian house, the home of Mr Ebenezer Howard, first mayor of Bexhill (1902), who organized cricket festivals there in the early years of the twentieth century. On one occasion, 1100 runs were recorded in a two-day match, and one innings was declared at more than 600 runs for half the wickets, with an individual score of 239 not out. There was a strong tradition of cricket at Bexhill, early matches (of four a side) being played in the 1820s, and Viscount Cantelope laying out a private ground in 1894 to entertain the South African tourists and, two years later, the Australian test team. The headmaster of the first independent school at Bexhill, Holmwood, was the Warwickshire cricketer, A. F. Bryan. Several of the girls' schools also had cricket teams, and one, the Beehive, had a professional coach.[16]

Geoffrey spent his preparatory school years, from the age of seven to the age of 13 in this environment with its 'emphasis on strict principles and manly games', its strong and distinguished cricketing tradition, its Christian influences and its association with the offspring of parents in 'the armed or administrative services of the Crown' overseas.

In October 1914, at the beginning of the oration quarter, he went to Charterhouse where his time coincided with the First World War.[17] He was joined by his brother, Marcus, in 1917 and his other brother, Reginald, went to Charterhouse in 1919. Geoffrey, now 13, entered Robinites, one of the school's eleven houses, and was one of nine new boys entering the house that year.[18] Robinites' housemaster was O. H.

Latter, a notable figure in the history of the teaching of biology in the public schools – whose place was taken by Major F. W. F. Smart when Latter resigned at the end of the oration quarter, 1918 – and there were just over 40 boys in his house, out of 600 in the school altogether. The headmaster, who had some three dozen masters with him, was Frank Fletcher (later Sir Frank) who:

> took over Charterhouse, as he had taken over Marlborough . . . at a time when it stood very low in public estimation . . . He left it, as he had left Marlborough, at the top of the tree. And much that [became] good in the life of the school [was] directly due to his influence and his inspiration.[19]

R. C. Robertson-Glasgow, a contemporary of Colby, has said of Fletcher:

> he was great; an idealist with the will and the power to turn dreams into fact. Also, he was . . . utterly unselfish . . . in that Pauline attitude of attack which willingly, and without counting the cost, makes a host of enemies in battling to an appointed end; and Fletcher's end . . . was a Charterhouse that was free but disciplined. In his quest he was inflexible . . . So Fletcher went to it, and, within a month, the first batch of boys took single tickets for home.
>
> Certainly he lacked the grace of conciliation; and he was often rude to those whom he had decided to regard as opposed to his system and ideal. He made enemies of some who, more graciously and deftly handled, were ready to have been important friends . . . He often broke opposition, less often converted it . . . Yet, for those who found it, his kindness was as warm as fire.[20]

At Charterhouse Geoffrey played a full part in school life. He began his academic career well by being first in the Upper IV in his second term, the long quarter of 1915, and fourth and third respectively in the other two terms of that year. Although this level of achievement was not maintained, he progressed well, was regularly promoted, and after specializing in biology, chemistry and physics in the science sixth form, which then had about 20 members, he was awarded an open scholarship to Clare College, Cambridge, in the oration quarter of 1918 and a leaving exhibition in the summer quarter of 1919 – one of normally only five, but occasionally six, such awards at Charterhouse, valued at £80 a year. In securing these awards he followed his uncle, Ernest, who had been a science exhibitioner at Wadham, Oxford, in 1879, and his father, Frank, who had won an open scholarship in science to King's, Cambridge, in 1889. In his final year at Charterhouse, he was second out of four in biology, a liking for which subject he had early acquired from his housemaster, Latter, seventh out of 31 in chemistry, and seventh out of 24 in physics.[21]

He was made house monitor during the second half of the long quarter of 1918 when two senior monitors were called up to join the army. As with a successor a few years later this was:

an appointment which meant an interview with the Headmaster in his study. After a few words . . . he handed [over] the informal badge of office, a small, blue leather wallet of good quality and of a size to hold the School and House lists. It bore the School crest in gold. At the same time he gave . . . his parting advice 'Have confidence in yourself: but not too much'.[22]

As house monitor he was entitled to two study fags, selected from members of the lower school by himself by mutual arrangement, whose duties were 'minimal consisting mainly of making toast for their master's breakfast and tea and other such tasks'.[23] Yet fulfilling the duties of monitor was not the easiest of tasks, as a near-contemporary of Geoffrey has indicated:

One of the first and potentially nerve-racking moments in the life of a new house monitor was when he first 'took' banco [prep] . . . which meant walking into a crowded and noisy [room] of fellows engaged in diverse activities, and reducing them to silence and order by a, one hoped, commanding shout. Everyone was agog to hear how the new monitor acquitted himself.[24]

Geoffrey spent a good deal of his time at games and did particularly well at cricket. Afternoons at Charterhouse were devoted to games and practically every boy was expected to play. Charterhouse is one of the football, as opposed to the rugby, schools and it has a long history of achievement in this game. Geoffrey played football for his house from 1917 onwards, usually at inside forward, at both inside right and inside left, and although he did not particularly distinguish himself – his brother, Marcus, recollected that Geoffrey 'only just got into the football team' – he did score the first goal against Verites House on a very wet

day early in 1919, and he did retain his interest in football much later
in his career. He was also one of the Robinites House racquets pair
(with C. W. H. Price) in 1916 and (with C. E. F. Clennel) in 1918, and
of the house fives pair (with J. W. B. Strong) in 1917. He won the school
competition for throwing the cricket ball. There were no tennis courts
at Charterhouse at that time, nor were there golfing facilities, but he
played a good deal of both these games during his vacations. He was a
strong player in both but in the case of golf was 'somewhat erratic'.[25]

It was, however, at cricket that Geoffrey particularly excelled and to
which he increasingly devoted his time whilst at Charterhouse. During
his very first summer, he was awarded his yearling (4th XI) colours and
played for his house, batting at number eight, scoring 0 in his first
innings and 4 in his second, catching and bowling a member of the
Verites House team and bowling another. The following year he batted
for his house at number five, scoring 20 (out of 102) and taking 2 wickets for 45 runs in 8 overs against Bodeites House. He also played that
year for the Charterhouse under-sixteens against Saint Paul's under-
sixteens. In 1917, he was awarded his Swallows colours – the cricket
and football club of Saunderites, Pageites and Robinites founded about
1875 – and continued to bat at number five for his house, scoring 22
and 19 against Gownboys House and taking 2 of their wickets for 9 runs
in 4 overs. In 1918, he opened the batting for his house, scoring 27
against Pageites, was awarded his second XI colours, and also played for
Charterhouse against the Royal Field Artillery Wanderers, and although
he neither batted nor bowled on that occasion this was the first of many
matches which he played with R. C. Robertson-Glasgow.

1919 was a particularly full cricketing year for Geoffrey; he was
awarded his first XI colours, captaining and opening both the batting
and the bowling (the former with his brother, Marcus) for his house,
making 8 and 23 runs and taking 4 wickets in each innings and 2
catches against Bodeites. He played for Charterhouse against Winchester,
Harrow, Eton, Pembroke College Cambridge, Free Foresters, I Zingari,
Wellington, Cryptics, Oxford Authentics, Blackwatch and Hampshire
Rovers. He was a brave player, a fast bowler and a hard hitter, being
caught more often than bowled. In 11 innings he scored 211 runs with
an average of 23.44, being sixth in batting averages after H. E. le Bas
(40.00), R. C. Robertson-Glasgow (38.36), F. H. Barnard (34.31), F. G.
Frost (29.54), and I. A. W. Gilliat (29.37). His highest score was a very
fast 67 (out of a total of 115, only one other batsman reaching double
figures) against Wellington, but he also scored 55 against Hampshire

Rovers, 44 (the top score) against I Zingari – a strong bowling side – and 28 against the Free Foresters.[26] Against Harrow he took three catches, and in a house match against Hodgeites he took six wickets and two catches, one off his own bowling. During August 1919, he played for the Young Amateurs of Surrey, batting number six, against the Young Amateurs of Middlesex at the Oval where he scored 21, and against the Australian Imperial Force team also at the Oval, batting number ten (in a 12-man team) and making the top score of 25 not out (out of a total of 95) in the first innings and two in the second.[27] It was a full and successful conclusion to his time at Charterhouse.

The Carthusian life emphasized concepts of leadership, hierarchy, empire, public service and unruffled reaction to emergencies. As for leadership, hierarchy and empire, and their accompanying privileges:

> Charterhouse is ruled on the system of an ancient empire. At the head of all is an Emperor with a few rulers beneath him of the same invading race, and beneath them are the natives ruled by their own chieftains who are responsible only to their superiors and who have a fairly free hand.

Robert Graves, an Old Carthusian, has said that the social code of Charterhouse was based on a very strict caste system: the caste-marks were slight distinctions in dress.[28] A new boy had no privileges at all; a boy in his second year was allowed to wear a knitted tie instead of a plain one; a boy in his second year could also wear coloured socks; the third year conferred most of the privileges – turned-down collars, coloured handkerchiefs, and a coat with a long roll; the fourth year a few more privileges, such as the right to organize raffles; but a number of 'very peculiar and unique distinctions' were reserved for 'the bloods'. These included light grey flannel trousers, butterfly collars, coats slit up the back, and the privilege of walking arm-in-arm.

As a member of the cricket first XI – a 'blood' – Geoffrey enjoyed these 'very peculiar and unique' privileges:

> The bloods were the members of the cricket and football elevens. They were the ruling caste at Charterhouse; the eleventh man . . . though a member of the under-fourth form, had a great deal more prestige than the most brilliant classical scholar in the sixth. Even 'Head of School' was an empty title.[29]

Carthusians, especially during the First World War, were encouraged to see themselves as leaders. Special army classes were conducted by the masters to coach those who were 'trying for Sandhurst or Woolwich', and Major Smart – who became Geoffrey's housemaster in 1918 – was in charge of 'the necessary training preparatory to commanding troops'.

The overwhelming manifestation of public service was the response of Charterhouse to military service.[30] Well over half the school belonged to the Officers Training Corps; many senior boys left the sixth form to join the army; within six months of the war starting the school's war list contained 2200 names of Old Carthusians; and a year later the list bore the names of 2639 serving in the forces – 241 killed, 182 awards and promotions in recognition of services, and 333 mentioned in despatches. Six months later still, the school took great pride in the award of Old Carthusian Ian Macnair's Victoria Cross. Month after month the school magazine carried lists of those killed, wounded or missing, and the distinguished list of obituaries and of military distinctions grew ever longer. But public service was not confined to military service nor to Old Carthusians, for the school held agricultural camps in 1917 and 1918 on the farms of Tangley Manor, 22 miles from Oxford, to help bring in the harvests and do general farm work, a service much appreciated by the farmers who initially seemed somewhat surprised by the willingness, hard work and robustness of the 60 boys who worked with them for six weeks each summer.[31]

During Geoffrey's final years at Charterhouse, there were two outstanding opportunities for the school to demonstrate its ability to react in an unruffled fashion to emergencies. In March 1918, Verites House was partially destroyed by fire and, in January 1919, Lockites House was burnt nearly to the ground.[32] Geoffrey was a member of the school fire brigade and in both emergencies the brigade reacted promptly and well:

The monotony of school life in war-time was temporarily relieved, and its difficulties greatly increased, in the early spring of 1918 when Verites . . . was partially destroyed by fire. Starting in the roof where it was discovered about 8.30 a.m. it spread rapidly . . . half an hour later . . . the school had already organized itself to deal with the situation. The boys' fire brigade were already at work, some of them plying the hose, others on the roof hacking away the wood work which connected Verites with the other buildings of the block. Relays of boys were working the hand engine to pump

up water: others were busy clearing out the furniture and contents
from the burning house . . .

By lunch-time the fire had been got under [control]. . . . The
whole [school] community showed that they could face an unexpected and unprecedented situation. [The headmaster did] not
remember having had . . . to issue any special orders: there seem[ed]
to have been instinctive co-operation on the part of all.

No school work of course was done in the morning: but at 4.00
everyone except Verites went into school as usual, and the ordinary
routine was followed.[33]

So, after five years, Geoffrey left Charterhouse. This was an important
period in his life, covering his formative years between the ages of 13
and 18, years in which significant influences were brought to bear on
him. The main elements in these influences have already been sketched:
the Carthusian emphasis on leadership, hierarchy, empire, public service,
unruffled reaction to emergencies, and a quick return to normal routine
in those emergencies. But there were other important factors. First,
there was the influential part which the great emphasis on games played:
competition, teamwork, physical accomplishment, outdoor pursuits and,
especially for one who both captained his house and was a 'blood',
leadership, status and 'the reverence, as for gods, with which young boys
regarded the outstanding athletes of the school and their own houses'.
Then there was the mental training of a classical education sharpened
and varied by specialization in the sciences, and the intellectual confidence which the award of an open scholarship and a leaving exhibition
brought. Again, appointment as a monitor brought with it not only
status, authority and privilege, but also the opportunity to learn the
lessons and develop the skills of leadership. Charterhouse also taught
the lessons of hard work and long hours for, although the afternoons
were devoted to games, classes started at 7.30 a.m. (before breakfast)
and ended at 12.30 p.m., and even part of the half-hour morning break
was devoted to physical training in the open air. There was 'banco' in
the evenings, there were compulsory classes on Saturday mornings, and
chapel had to be attended twice on Sundays – with Dr (later Sir
Reginald) Thatcher, subsequently head of the Royal Academy of Music,
directing the choir from the organ. And who knows what may have been
the influence of the headmaster who had in so few years lifted Charterhouse from the doldrums to a leading position, and of such a man as
A. F. Radcliffe, who enlivened his teaching of the classics by relating

them to his own experience in the Indian civil service and who gave such sound advice to potential civil servants as, 'Oh, my dear boys, pray cultivate the writing of charming little notes: it will be of use to you all your lives'?

Lord Pearce, a contemporary at Charterhouse, has summed up life at the school at that time:

> Charterhouse in those war years had plenty of rigours and austerity, like the rest of England, but there was plenty of inspiration too – a very fine training ground, I think, for a hardworking professional career.[34]

After half a decade of these influences, with the horror and privations of the First World War recently ended – service in which he had so narrowly escaped – with the promise and hopes of peace before him, with a full and successful final year at school behind him, and with a scholarship and exhibition in his pocket, Geoffrey left Charterhouse for Cambridge in the autumn of 1919.

The undergraduate population of Cambridge[35] during the years Geoffrey spent there, 1919 to 1922, differed markedly from that of earlier and of later years, in that it included a large number of former military and naval personnel who had gone straight into war service from school.[36] On the whole, the ex-servicemen and the younger, less mature, school-leavers did not mix a great deal, but this was not the case with Geoffrey whilst at Clare:

> Geoff's friends at Cambridge had been on war service and in reaction were 'out to paint the town (London) red' whenever possible, and some were very moneyed. Geoff, on the fringe of this set, thoroughly enjoyed all their jollifications.[37]

We shall return to these jollifications shortly. Among those who were 'moneyed' were, of course, some of the ex-servicemen with substantial gratuities. One of his close friends, not an ex-serviceman, was Eric Claude Collymore, who had been educated at Harrison College, Barbados, and was 'a very fine cricketer'.[38]

A fairly typical undergraduate day at Cambridge started with breakfast in one's rooms at about 8.00 a.m., followed by a morning from 9.00 a.m. to 1.00 p.m. attending lectures, or reading. After lunch in one's rooms, delivered by college domestic staff or more frequently purchased oneself, but occasionally in hall, the afternoon (from 2.00 p.m. to 5.00 p.m.) was devoted to games, except that science and engineering students were required to spend several afternoons a week doing laboratory work. After tea, at about 5.00 p.m., one devoted oneself to reading or the writing up of lecture notes and it was during this period, from 5.00 p.m. to 7.00 p.m., that once a week or so meetings with one's tutor were held. From 7.00 p.m. to 7.30 p.m., dinner was taken, compulsorily, in hall in gown, and thereafter the evening was spent in a great variety of pastimes: music, dramatics, clubs, bridge, union debates and, in the summer, punting on the Backs, or simply in social discourse with friends in one's rooms, over coffee, beer or cider.

It was the practice at that time for most undergraduates to live in college only in their third year because of the large number of students and the relatively small number of rooms available in college. Only the Old Court then existed and the Memorial Court had not yet been built. Occasionally scholars and secretaries of major games spent rather longer than one year resident in college. Some undergraduates spent all three years in lodgings and some, such as Ronald Aird, who later became secretary and president of the MCC, lived all three years in college.[39] Geoffrey spent his first two years in lodgings at 40 New Square, together with Alec Coulson, and they both spent their final year in college with rooms on the same staircase, Geoffrey above and Alec below the rooms occupied by the fellow, G. V. Carey.[40]

Many undergraduates preferred life in college to that in lodgings principally because, although the latter were usually very comfortable, one was more part of a community in the former. From the point of view simply of physical comfort, lodgings were often preferable because:

the college authorities had not fully caught up with the new fangled ideas about heating or bathrooms.

No outside visitors other than fellow undergraduates were allowed in one's college rooms after 6.00 p.m., nor were lady visitors allowed at any time without a chaperone.

As a scholar, Geoffrey was required to read grace at dinner in hall. This consisted of several verses of a psalm, always in Latin, starting 'Occuli omnium in te sperant Domine' ('The eyes of all wait upon thee, O Lord').[41]

Geoffrey read natural science and specialized in chemistry. Had he intended to pursue a medical career, as had his father, grandfather, great-grandfather and uncle, he would have read anatomy and physiology for his second MB, probably having taken his first MB at Charterhouse; these he did not do. He and his brothers knew what a very busy professional life their father had and how arduous a career in medicine was, and consequently they all decided not to enter the profession.[42] In the Michaelmas term of 1920, *The Clare Magazine*, in its section on awards of scholarships, exhibitions and prizes, recorded Geoffrey as receiving an award for natural science. A similar award was made at the same time to Harry Godwin, later Professor Sir Harry Godwin, FRS. Geoffrey took an active part in the affairs of the Clare Scientific Society and was its vice-president in 1922. It appears, however, that his earlier academic promise was not fulfilled – to his father's displeasure. Many scholars were expected to secure first class degrees. Geoffrey took a second class in part one of the tripos in 1921 and a third class in part two in 1922. It was his brother's belief that, as the cleverest of the three boys, Geoffrey could have attained a double first, but that he did hardly any work at Cambridge and was not interested in academic distinctions there.[43]

He does not seem to have played as much cricket as might have been expected after the intensive season which he had enjoyed immediately before going up to Cambridge. There are several possible reasons for this. First, the necessity to spend several afternoons a week in chemistry laboratories severely restricted the amount of time available for net practice and for matches. Second, many people who had been obliged to play a great deal of sport compulsorily at school found the non-compulsive attitudes at Cambridge more congenial, and in reaction either ceased to play the games which they had previously played, or did so much less frequently and diligently:

> for the first time in life one was not forced to play games [and] many people preferred to make their own amusements such as golf, tennis, squash, etc.

It is unlikely that Geoffrey himself was reacting against compulsory cricket at school since his brother, Marcus, has said that Geoffrey had a genuine liking for cricket and always enjoyed playing it. Third, Cambridge – although not Clare itself – had such a plethora of outstanding cricket talent at that time that the general chances of excelling were much diminished. Fourth, cricket took up much more time than did many other games, such as tennis and fives, and consequently ate into

the time available for other activities, including academic study. Fifth, the
Clare cricket field was somewhat distant and inconveniently placed in
relation to the college. The old King's and Clare ground – 'one of the
best as well as one of the prettiest in Cambridge' – which was con-
veniently close to the colleges, had been commandeered during the war
and upon it was built the Eastern General Hospital. After the war, the
master of Clare – not without criticism from his senior academic colleagues – agreed to the area being used as a temporary housing estate
to relieve the current housing shortage; in fact he had little choice since
the local authority possessed statutory powers of compulsory acquisition.
Consequently, Clare cricketers had to travel some distance to play on a
new ground on the Barton Road, and this must have dissuaded a number
of them from regular participation. Finally, Clare was more of a 'rowing'
college than a 'cricketing' college, and as a result there may not have
been college pressure to play cricket.

For whatever reasons, although he certainly did not drop the game
completely, Geoffrey did not play as much cricket as one might have
expected after his Charterhouse successes. He did, however, play quite
a lot of tennis, especially during the long vacations of 1920 and 1921
when a number of undergraduates who normally lived in lodgings moved
into college to take up residence: this was especially true of science
students who had special laboratory work to do then. One of those with
whom he played a good deal of tennis at that time, Dr N. T. Glynn,
recalled over six decades later:

> He had the fastest service I ever met. I played many singles with
> him and sometimes as his partner in College matches . . . As his
> tennis partner I was scared stiff that he would hit me in the back
> of the neck. He never did . . . I could only win his service (at
> singles) by 'gamesmanship'. Standing two yards behind the base
> line. Then one foot behind the service line (where it was possible
> to get a winner off the wood). The change in position upset his
> range and double faults resulted.[44]

Glynn, a medical student, observing Geoffrey's strong spectacles, had
diagnosed 'quite a degree of myopia' and taken sporting advantage of it!

To place games generally and tennis in particular in perspective, Lord
Baker, a contemporary of Geoffrey has said that: 'Most of us played
some games on six days a week – and had a long walk on Sundays.
Tennis was played by most of us – with or without particular skill.'[45]

Earlier we mentioned the light-hearted side of Geoffrey's life at Cambridge when commenting on his friendship with former members of the armed forces – rather than with school-leavers – and on the way in which he 'thoroughly enjoyed all their jollifications'. In returning to this, mention must be made of five matters.

First, in later life he was an exceptionally gifted bridge player and clearly showed a liking for cards since at Clare there were 'protracted poker sessions in his rooms on "A" staircase':

> Cards of some sort, usually bridge, were played by most men most nights of the week after dinner.

It is likely that he played poker with his ex-service friends because a Clare man who went up in the year that Geoffrey graduated has said:

> I heard very little of poker playing. Colby's generation, more than mine, however, included quite a number of ex-service men from the first war, who would have been older and more sophisticated, so perhaps there was more playing then.[46]

The degree of acceptability of poker playing is indicated in the views: 'Nobody would have been thought the worse of for his playing poker, or the better for that matter'; 'People did what they liked about playing poker and no one was considered the better or the worse for doing so'; 'There would be no feeling against poker unless the stakes were unduly high'. Many years later, his brother, Marcus, said that 'Geoffrey was always a bit of a gambler'.[47]

Second, the college regulations required all resident undergraduates to have returned to Clare by 10.00 p.m. each evening unless special permission had been obtained. Late returners were recorded by the college porter and required to pay a fee or fine of six shillings and eight pence and a larger sum after midnight:

> There is a fairly large area of grass bounded on two sides by King's College, on the third side by the unbroken outer wall of Clare, and on the south side by the river Cam. . . . A reveller, returning late and wanting to get into Clare without passing the Porter's Lodge, could make his way across the Cam and on to the ground of King's, but would then be confronted with the bare wall of Clare . . . My uncle (who was Senior Tutor) spoke with someone who was an

Alpine Climber, and showed him the wall of Clare College. The
Alpine Climber said 'I could do it, but it is about as much as I
could do'.[48]

Geoffrey was one who did do it, but only just, for in the course of so
entering the college after midnight on one occasion 'through the outer
bedroom windows of his set [he] put a wandering foot through the
fellow's bedroom panes [below] during the ascent'. It is likely, however,
that he got away with even this because a fellow has recalled that:

> once or twice, working late, he had heard sounds suggesting
> that someone might be making his way up the wall. He was in two
> minds. By looking out of the window he might be able to identify
> the intruder; or he might startle him and cause an accident; author-
> ity would be upheld at too great a cost.[49]

The contemporary views on such ingress via 'the garden route' varied
from those who found that it was 'well-known and generally amused
others' to those who 'had not heard of such a case in Clare College . . .
the master and fellows would have regarded the villains as a nuisance'.
The general view probably was that it was done 'more as a prank than
anything else, and was generally regarded with equanimity by others';
it was 'looked upon as a bit of fun by those "in statu pupillari" but not
by the College Porter or the Senior Tutor'. Marcus spent the whole of
a long vacation with Geoffrey at Clare but 'saw very little of him'
because he was out most of the time and had to climb into college
'nearly every night'.[50]

Third, Geoffrey owned a Norton motorcycle at Cambridge, which he
rode very fast and which he used for evening and weekend visits to
London (although he drove it somewhat less fast after an accident one
evening which threw him 20 yards into a field). Later he sold the
motorcycle to Marcus.[51]

Next, especially during the vacation, he played a good deal of billiards,
making tours of the Woking public houses with Marcus to play the
game.[52]

Finally, on the light-hearted side, an enigmatic, intriguing and amusing
entry in *The Clare Magazine* for the Easter term of 1922, Geoffrey's
penultimate term at Cambridge, under the heading 'Things we want to
know', sought to discover:

> Why Mr. C-lb- wears the top of his pyjama suit as a blazer? Does
> he think it matches his complexion?

In the summer it was customary to wear a 'summer amal blazer' – that
is, a blazer in the style authorized by the amalgamated clubs of the
college. This was of white or cream material with the college colours,
black and white, running down in stripes all round.[53] Undergraduates
sometimes wore strange garb, especially in going from their rooms to
the baths under the Hall, and it was probably in connection with this
that *The Clare Magazine* asked the question.

These five matters suggest that Geoffrey enjoyed a less serious, less
conventional, more light-hearted side of Cambridge life, and took full
advantage of the few years of freedom between the disciplines of public
school and the responsibilities of professional life to enjoy himself and
express his individuality. A contemporary who knew him well at Cambridge, but who recalls only the lighter side of his life there and who
thereafter completely lost touch with him, has said:

> He was very good fun and I am surprised that he took life suf-
> ficiently seriously to reach a position of such eminence . . . My
> impression [is] that he was rather a wild youth and I find it difficult
> to imagine him in plumed headgear, bearing the necessary dignity
> of a colonial governor.[54]

Rather more than today, undergraduates of the inter-war period were
expected to enjoy themselves. In 1950, the master of Clare, 'that very
great man Thirkill, who had been Senior Tutor' during Geoffrey's time,
said that 'he looked back to the 20's and 30's as the happiest of his many
years at Clare and that few of the modern undergraduates seemed to
know how to enjoy life and were inclined to be "Exam mad" '.[55] A
contemporary of Geoffrey's, looking back to his days at Clare, has
commented:

> It was a very 'gentlemanly' existence with lots of fun and good
> friends – a completely artificial existence in a sense. An eight-week
> term in Cambridge was a separate world.[56]

Geoffrey's three years in this separate world helped both to reinforce
the influences of Charterhouse and to introduce new and important
elements into his personal development.

On the one hand, 'this was an age when the non-public school undergraduate was the exception, and it was almost more glamorous to achieve greatness at sport than academically' – just as at Charterhouse where 'bloods' were 'the ruling caste'. As a house monitor and 'blood', he had enjoyed a special status and a privileged position at Charterhouse, and as a scholar at Clare he had also enjoyed a special status and privileged position: good rooms in college and reading grace in hall. Similarly, the somewhat spartan physical conditions of public school were shared by Clare College in the early 1920s, and the disruptions of the war were not entirely things of the past: during the coal strike of early 1921, the prime minister called for volunteers to join the defence force, and a number of undergraduates, including some from Clare, received temporary commissions and were away from Cambridge for two full terms.

On the other hand, there were significant differences between life at Charterhouse and life at Clare which introduced new and different elements into Geoffrey's life and personal development. Three of these are important.

First, to a large extent for the first time, he was not only encouraged but was obliged to make his own decisions as to how he was to apportion his time, especially his 'spare' time, and how, generally, he was to arrange his life and life style. Only the period of 7.00 p.m. to 7.30 p.m. daily was rigidly prescribed: dinner in hall, gown and reading grace. There was also some degree of obligation in respect of attending lectures, doing laboratory work and meeting with tutors, but the rest of the undergraduates' life was significantly in their own hands. Geoffrey was able to determine which games he would play, if any and when, how often and with whom he would play, and how much studying he would do.

Second, he was able to decide from which of his many and varied fellow undergraduates he would select his more intimate friends, and by choosing ex-servicemen he came into closer contact with men of experience and maturity who had safely come through a terrible war and might well be excused 'jollifications'.

Third, he was able to express any of the more light-hearted, unconventional and 'risky' parts which may have existed in his nature to a greater extent than at any time since his pre-school days. As a child, he and his brothers had flung pats of butter onto the ceiling at their grandmother's house and his cousin thought him 'great fun'; as an undergraduate, mysteriously, he wore his pyjama jacket as a blazer and his tennis partner thought him 'very good fun' and 'rather a wild youth', whilst Marcus says that Geoffrey was 'a wild young man' who 'lived it up' at Cambridge. He enjoyed risks – as a member of the fire brigade at school, and in playing poker, riding a fast motorcycle, and regularly climbing into college at Clare.

From Cambridge onwards he, not others, would decide how hard he would push himself at work, and he, not others, would decide how he would spend his leisure time. He now had to decide on his profession; on his father's side medicine predominated, but he himself had not turned to medical studies; on his mother's side business predominated, but his grandmother had sold her shares and severed the family's direct connection with Bryant and May 40 years earlier.

General employment prospects were not good in the early 1920s and many new graduates found difficulty in finding a satisfactory job:

> at that date, 1923, there were still a number of more mature men coming out of the forces and a schoolboy with no speciality to offer might have been up against tough opposition. On the other hand, there would be some employers who would prefer to take young material that they could mould to their own image.
>
> There were still a number of men in residence after being demobbed from the forces and who had taken shortened degree courses – and even then were coming onto a limited market. Competition for jobs was very keen.[57]

At Clare he had had to decide on the balance between work and play, and his first job on leaving Cambridge combined the two. Geoffrey's mother was a close friend of the wife of the headmaster of St Wilfred's, his old preparatory school, and through this connection he was appointed junior master, a post he sought principally in order that he should be able to play for the Cryptics cricket team whilst he was deciding on a permanent career.[58] The qualification for the Cryptics was membership of public schools, universities or services, and the club was at its peak as a touring club in the 1920s when 'there was keen competition among members of both universities to join its ranks, and in those years such names as the three Gilligans, three Naumanns, D. R. Jardine, J. L. Bryan, R. H. Bettington and R. C. Robertson-Glasgow figure frequently in the score sheets'.[59] Rex Alston recalls that during this period he 'played with Colby for Hastings at the Central Ground. We had a pretty useful club side in those days and I remember him as a big, strong fast bowler and hard-hitting left-hand bat.'[60]

After about a year at St Wilfred's, Geoffrey took a job at a textile mill in Galashiels. He secured this post as a result of his friendship with Patrick Arnold Fraser whilst at Charterhouse. Patrick was the only son of the mill's wealthy managing director, Robert Atkin Fraser, who was employed by Sanderson and Murray Ltd, fellmongers.[61] Sanderson and Murray bought in sheepskins from overseas, removed the wool from the skins and sold the two separately; their firm closed down in the early 1980s and the factory buildings were then demolished.[62] Geoffrey and Patrick were almost the same age – less than two months separated them – and they went to Charterhouse at the same time, both being in Robinites. Academically, Patrick was significantly less successful than Geoffrey, but in games there was little to choose between them and they played a great deal of sport together throughout their school careers. At that time:

> boys were not automatically promoted by year and only the top ones moved up. Some boys indeed got stuck in one form for a long time and it was not unknown for a boy to finish up in a form below the one he started in. Boys who did not move up in a reasonable period of time were liable to be 'superannuated' i.e. asked to leave.[63]

When, at the end of his second term, Geoffrey was top of form and was promoted to the remove, Patrick came twelfth and remained in the upper IVth; when Geoffrey entered the under Vth, Patrick entered the army remove and stayed there whilst his friend moved on to the Vth. Thereafter Patrick was always a form behind Geoffrey, but this in no way affected their friendship which was developed in Robinites house and on the playing fields. From 1916 they played cricket together for their house, and from 1917 they also played football together for their house. They both received their Swallows colours in 1917, Patrick for football, and Geoffrey and Patrick together for cricket in the summer quarter. Both received their second XI colours in 1918, again Patrick for football and Geoffrey for cricket. Patrick captained the Robinites football team in 1917 – when Geoffrey played for his house for the first time – and then captained Robinites at cricket in 1918, to be followed by Geoffrey as house cricket captain in 1919 when Patrick joined the army and left school, having just received his first XI football colours, as Geoffrey did for cricket two terms later. After the war Patrick went as a commoner to Exeter College, Oxford, where he played football for the university as a half back and was awarded his blue. He graduated BA in agriculture on 3 May 1923 and then took up farming in South Africa, where he died in 1960.[64]

Although he had intended the job at Fraser's to be the beginning of a permanent career in business, Geoffrey found the work and life at Galashiels most uncongenial. He worked on the factory floor in most unpleasant conditions and felt that he was being exploited; his time there, 1923–4, was far from happy and it was not long before he began to seek more satisfying, permanent career employment.[65] Perhaps because Patrick Fraser had gone to Africa, perhaps also because he recalled the boys at St Wilfred's whose fathers served overseas, or because of his friendship at Clare with Collymore from Barbados, Geoffrey's mind turned also towards the colonies and particularly towards Africa. After his sad experience in private industry he may well have been more attracted to the prospects of a career in public service – unlike his great-great-grandfather, James Bryant, who turned from a career in the public service, the excise department, to enter the business world, as a soap and grease maker and sugar refiner, a hundred years earlier. In any event, he applied to join the Colonial Administrative Service, and did so at a time when the number of appointments was beginning to increase after the slump of the early 1920s. From a post-war peak of 179 administrative appointments in 1920, the figure dropped to 18 in 1922 and then rose annually to another peak, of 133, in 1928. In 1924, when Geoffrey applied, 72 appointments were made to the Colonial Administrative Service by the Colonial Office's appointments department.[66] Members of his family were surprised by this application to join the Colonial Service since there were no family connections with the Service and Geoffrey had not previously mentioned an interest in it. He was, however, known to be of an adventurous nature and his interest was attributed to this.[67]

The leading members of the appointments department at that time were Ralph (later Sir Ralph) Furse, Francis Newbold and Greville Irby (later Lord Boston and brother-in-law of Sir Harry Johnston, first commissioner and consul-general of British Central Africa) who placed great reliance upon expert interviewing and a thorough examination of the candidate's previous record:

> While still in his twenties, a district officer might find himself in charge of a slice of Africa as big as Yorkshire, and quite possibly alone. Qualities of character and personality (not excluding physical presence and bearing, and some rather elusive facets of a man's

intelligence and temperament like imaginative sympathy) were therefore factors of prime importance. Such factors could not be adequately listed by any form of written examination yet invented ... One discovered quite a lot about his education and what he had made of it; his subsequent career, if any; his tastes and interests; what chance he had had of exercising responsibility or of showing in practice whether he possessed other qualities you were on the lookout for – self-reliance, for instance, self-sufficiency in loneliness, foresight, imaginative sympathy, or many others.[68]

Geoffrey's education and training, and his athletic accomplishments, especially at Charterhouse, and indeed his 'physical presence and bearing' stood him in good stead and his interviewers must have taken a liking to this tall, well-built, fast-serving, fast-bowling, fast-driving, hard-hitting, poker-playing, obviously intelligent, former prefect, public schoolboy and Cambridge graduate who appeared before them with a mind of his own and a distinct sense of adventure and humour, who had already moved from preparatory school teaching to fellmongering and now wished to move to the colonies. In any event, he was successful in his application, being offered an appointment in the Colonial Administrative Service in Nigeria and being required to attend a training course for junior administrative officers proceeding to tropical Africa.

The course which he attended at Imperial Institute, South Kensington, London – the last or last but one before the Tropical Africa Services course of a year's duration started at Oxford and Cambridge – lasted from early January to the middle of April and lectures were from 10 a.m. to 5 p.m. Candidates lived in lodgings, often close to South Kensington. There were some two dozen probationers to be posted to various colonies attending the course, which gave tuition in administration, criminal law, Muhammedan law, tropical diseases, phonetics, agricultural products, accounting and elementary surveying. There were oral or written examinations in all subjects except phonetics. Surveying was the most popular course of all, principally because it was very practical and because of the skills and personality of the tutor, Edward Ayearst Reeves, instructor in survey at the Royal Geographical Society. Although the Colonial Office felt that the course 'was a not very satisfactory piece of cramming and discipline was slack', most, though not all, of those attending took the course seriously and found most of the course – except phonetics, which seems to have been badly taught – interesting and useful.[69] Sir Rex Niven was one who found the course unsatisfactory:

The Services course was virtually a waste of time. It was unpractical. We were not told how to deal with practical things that would arise. The leading experts lectured – interesting usually but not for three months.[70]

Geoffrey passed the Imperial Institute course and in the early summer of 1925 prepared himself to sail for Nigeria to start a new career at an annual salary of £500 and with an advance of £60 to pay for essential equipment. His appointment was effective from the date of starting the training course – 7 January 1925 – and ten other officers were appointed to the Nigerian Administrative Service on the same date.[71]

2· Nigeria

'A lot of people would have given their eyes for a spell in the Secretariat.'

Colby travelled by mail boat from Liverpool, arriving in Nigeria in May. His journey and his arrival there were very similar to those described by A. C. G. Hastings at the same time:

> The month of May . . . saw me . . . lying off the West African coast at daylight, . . . and steaming into the lagoon of Lagos. The voyage had been a pleasant one . . . and . . . life on shipboard was a thing of gaiety, dances, fancy-dress dinners, concerts . . . and sports . . .
>
> We berthed on the Lagos side at the Customs wharf, where . . . we began the weary business of transhipping to a tender. It was six or seven hours before we were through with this, and crossing over were spilt out on Iddo wharf beside the boat-train. The getting through the Customs took other hours. As soon as possible I drove off . . . to dine and join the train at nine o'clock when it was scheduled to start.[1]

Niven, five years senior to Colby in the Service, returned to Nigeria with his bride in July 1925, two months after Colby's first arrival, and he also has written of his journey:

> We sailed in July and the journey was uneventful. With us were our full two-and-a-half tons of luggage. . . . All our clothes and personal things were in . . . steel 'uniform cases', black enamelled in the standard manner, with names in white script. . . . I had a fair idea of the kind and quantity of stores required, together with luxuries – like puddings and crystallized fruit . . . as well as a full

medicine chest and bandages and the like. Toilet articles had to be bought in quantity, bottles and jars and packets . . . All this came from Fortnum & Mason, and the linen from John Baker.[2]

Sir Bryan Sharwood-Smith, on his first arrival in 1921, brought with him 'sixty odd tin uniform cases, hessian-covered bales, wooden crates, and boxes of provisions'.[3]

Like Hastings and the Nivens, Colby took the boat train, since he was being posted to Kaduna in the Northern Provinces, and followed the route taken slightly earlier by Hastings, who has described the journey for us:

> I turned into my sleeping berth at once, for the landing day is always a long one, and passed the usual uneasy hours of partial sleep while the train thundered on through the night and the unseen tropic country of the south. Past Abeokuta . . . and Ibadan . . . we clattered and rocked on until at daylight we reached Oshogbo, and by breakfast time drew in to Offa, the boundary between north and south . . .
>
> We reached the Niger at Jebba in sixteen hours, steaming slowly across the great bridge which spans the river there. . . . Through a long hot afternoon we pulled up heavily out of the Niger valley, clattering onwards through the Nupe province, . . . passing . . . Bokani, Charati, Mokwa – and at nightfall hot, dirty and cramped, we reached Zungeru.[4]

At daybreak the train reached Kaduna, but we shall leave a description of this northern capital for the present, for Colby was to return there seven years later.

Colby's first appointment in Nigeria was as private secretary to Herbert (later Sir Herbert) Richmond Palmer, lieutenant-governor of the Northern Provinces, 'the principal executive authority' whose job it was 'to overlook the entire machinery of government in the area, whether political or departmental'.[5] Palmer was then 48 years of age and had been in the administration of the Northern Provinces for 21 years, first as assistant resident (1904–17), then as resident, Bornu Province (1917–25) and recently (15 May 1925) as the new lieutenant-governor, stationed at Kaduna.

Palmer had worked closely with, and learned much from, Lugard; was 'one of his most outstanding and most anthropologically-minded northern Residents'; he was a leading expert on Muslim Nigeria and had 'immersed [himself] in the intricacies of northern culture and government, particularly as represented by Hausa-Fulani'. He has been described as 'the strongest northerner of them all'. For 26 years before becoming governor of the Gambia (1930–33) – after which he was appointed governor of Cyprus (1933–9) – 'in various parts of Northern Nigeria, much of [his] leisure was occupied in . . . the compilation of a true history of its more important units, or ruling races'. Niven has described him as 'an able lawyer, perhaps a shade eccentric . . . He was large and kind, with a twinkle in his blue eyes'. He was a considerable scholar and an outstanding administrator. The qualities which he looked for in his officers were 'toughness, soundness of policy, and a reputation for being "solid" . . . Slowness or frivolity he particularly disapproved'.

Colby's duties combined those of an aide-de-camp with those of a private secretary and, as such, covered both the social and the professional aspects of assisting Palmer. He had a close insight into the workings of the relationships between the lieutenant-governor in the north and the governor-general in Lagos; between Government House and the secretariat in Kaduna; and between the secretariat and the provincial and district administration. He was able to observe at very close quarters the problems faced by an experienced and successful top colonial administrator and the ways in which he tackled them. Colby could hardly have had a better beginning to his professional career. 'The great advantage', Sir Alan Burns believed, 'of serving on a Governor's staff is that the junior officer meets many interesting persons he would not otherwise meet, and travels over the whole country.'[6]

Towards the end of 1926, he took his first leave and spent it with his parents in Woking. He played some cricket for Hastings as he had done during the year after he graduated.

Colby's second tour of duty, from mid-1927 to the end of 1928, was spent as assistant district officer in Bornu Province – the province of which Palmer had been resident until he became lieutenant-governor and which 'up until 1930 . . . was the recognized cradle of successful men'. He was stationed at Maiduguri, in the far north-eastern corner of Nigeria almost a thousand miles from Lagos. Maiduguri was the provincial headquarters and also a divisional headquarters under a district officer, assisted by an administrative officer at Nguru 250 miles to the north-west, by another at Dikwa 50 miles to the east, and by a third at Maiduguri itself:

The D.O.'s flat-roofed office opened on to a wide verandah, as did
the clerks' office further along . . . Senior officers had excellent
brick houses, built . . . some ten years earlier . . .

There were about fifteen European officers in the station. Apart
from the Administration we had education, doctors, agriculture
and forestry, an engineer or two, with a yard superintendent and a
mechanical foreman. . . .

The D.O.'s work was . . . complicated by the great distances and
the persistence of the Kanuri complainants, who never took no for
an answer. . . . They would come to the D.O.'s office and, if they
got no satisfaction, would set out for the Residency along the
road. . . .

As elsewhere the administration worked through the District and
Village Heads.[7]

Much of the young administrative officers' time was taken up in touring
the rural areas,[8] almost invariably on horseback and often for up to two
months at a time, during which they checked the tax figures and tax
collection, inspected the courts and court records, and kept an eye on
public works. It 'was hard, lonely and uncomfortable work. However,
they learned a lot and the people had a visible presence of Government
that they could see and talk to.'

The resident in charge of Bornu at that time was Pierre de Putron,
who had been in the Nigerian Service since 1909, and of whom an
administrative officer has said:

In a province which bulged with larger than lifesize figures in the
early days, Pierre de Putron was larger than others. A hard, nuggety
man, arrogant and domineering, much feared and usually disliked.
He could be grossly unfair to any of his administrative officers who
incurred his displeasure.[9]

And another administrative officer has added that:

the then Resident of Bornu, a compulsive horseman and polo
player himself, expected virtually every member of his staff and
particularly every administrative officer to keep at least two horses.
These had to be versatile animals serving a dual purpose – for use
both for trekking in the bush . . . and also as polo ponies. . . .

Especially if you were stationed in Maiduguri, but also if you were only passing through, staying no more than a night or two, you were expected to turn out, wet or fine, to play in at least two chukkas . . . whether you had had some experience of the game or none . . . Ignorance or lack of experience of the game was no sin in the eyes of that particular Resident, provided always there was enthusiasm to learn. To opt out was unforgivable.[10]

An interesting and revealing clash between de Putron and Colby occurred during this period. In Sir Rex Niven's words, 'In Bornu at that time polo was a fetish and a sine qua non.'[11] At Cambridge, Colby, long a hard-playing sportsman, became accustomed to deciding for himself which games he would play, with whom and how often, and it was a freedom of choice which he was deeply reluctant to forgo:

During the de Putron period, every administrative officer had been expected to play polo. New arrivals were put in a walled enclosure on a horse, with a polo stick and a ball and set to learn strokes by the hour . . . on arrival [Colby] had refused to play and had even refused to learn. He was immediately sent on tour for three months. On his return to the so-called civilisation of Maiduguri he was permitted three days in station and then sent out again for another three months. At the end of that he still refused to play polo and he was eventually accepted.[12]

In commenting on this clash well over half a century later, Niven said that it was 'a particularly brutal punishment or retaliation to impose', and he added that Colby:

obviously had considerable personal courage and the mental strength to stand against Pierre de Putron. . . . De Putron himself was a commanding personality, over six feet two, and not a man to come up against lightly. Though I agreed with his stand . . . I doubt whether I could have resisted the pressure.[13]

Scarcely anyone else did resist that pressure, although Sir John Patterson later lieutenant-governor of Northern Nigeria, had done so:

When he was posted to Bornu, [Sir John] said firmly that he didn't like polo and didn't intend to play. De Putron posted him to the furthest outstation available and forbade him to come to Maiduguri at all, except in case of serious illness.[14]

For Colby, refusal to play polo was a matter of principle because in all other games he was a tough and forceful player, and because it seems that later, when not under de Putron, he did play polo. Two contemporaries and friends, without referring to, or indeed indicating an awareness of, the de Putron incident, have said that he was 'an extremely good polo player'[15] and that 'he was outstanding as a polo player'.[16] His brother Marcus long kept a photograph of Colby in polo gear beside a polo pony in Nigeria. Another contemporary has said that Colby's refusal:

> would have entailed taking a stand against repeated efforts to persuade him to change his mind; he would have felt no qualms about responding with a categorical refusal – he was not prone to give way, once his mind was made up but he would have been aware that anything like a heated disagreement with his Resident... would not help his promotion prospects, and these would always have been important to him.[17]

Towards the end of 1928, he returned to Britain on leave after a tour which had been far from comfortable. In Bornu the climate was harsh and unforgiving. The dry season from October to June, with the temperature during April and May rarely dropping below 100°F by day or night, was named 'the season of umbrage', and the land was brown desert with hardly any vegetation, although when the rains came everything went green overnight.[18] In this climate he had spent long periods on tour in the rural areas and had to contend with the unpleasant pressures placed upon him by his resident. Even so, a colleague wrote over 50 years later, 'I retain the most vivid memories of Geoff, his joie de vivre and humour ... and the amusing times we had together in remote Bornu.' He was naturally grateful for a few months' break in Britain. Sir Donald Cameron believed that:

> while an officer is resident in [Nigeria] he can obtain no real relaxation at all from his daily unceasing round of work; he can obtain no leave locally that is of any benefit to him ... and it is this lack of relaxation and change of scene ... that impairs an officer's well-being and general condition even more than the climate of Nigeria.[19]

Early in 1929, Colby returned to Nigeria to begin his third tour of duty and he was posted again to Bornu division, this time as district officer in charge of Biu some 100 miles south-west of Maiduguri, an attractive place about 2000 feet above sea level, looking across the Hawal river 1500 feet below into the Adamwa mountains: 'It was a view you could look at by the hour without wearying; and of course all was utterly quiet.'

It was during this period that he passed the government lower standard Hausa and Arabic language examinations. Although it was quite usual for administrative officers in the north to pass the Hausa examination fairly early in their careers – indeed it was required of them – it was much less usual to study for and pass the Arabic examination because of its limited everyday use relative to Hausa. Possibly Palmer's proficiency in, and enthusiasm for, things Arabic influenced Colby in becoming interested in the language, and perhaps, too, the quiet beauty of Biu gave him an environment in which to study it.

However, despite the attractiveness of the terrain and the easier climate and 'fine air' of Biu, Colby did not enjoy good health there:

He was always of an almost jaundiced complexion. He maintained that he kept healthy by a regime of a 'gunpowder plot' at regular intervals. The fearsome compound involved, made up of Epsom salts, Enos, calomel, and I don't know what else, was legendary. We advised him to change his cook. He used to tell us of a conversation with this character. 'Cook, there will be four masters coming to lunch on Sunday. Now, what shall we have? First, soup?' 'What soup, master?' 'Why, soup!' There was only one soup: made from the carcase of the small local fowl and the local onion.[20]

Indeed, so ill did he become that he had to be admitted to the Jos hospital suffering from a serious form of jaundice and malaria. 'In the whole of Bornu, some 45,000 square miles in area, with a six figure population, there was but one government general hospital ... and seldom more than one and never more than two doctors.'[21] By the time he went on leave, late in 1930, he had somewhat recovered but was still in very bad shape. As for his 'jaundiced complexion', several of his colleagues commented that 'his complexion was always yellow', a view in which members of his family concurred, although they did not associate it with any illness. Another officer with whom he worked recalled that:

his complexion was always that of a man with jaundice; there was never a hint of redness in it. One got so used to the unchanging yellowness, reminiscent of old parchment, accentuated as it seemed by the dark shade of his horn-rimmed spectacles, that it would have been a shock to see in his face any hint of redness.

His wife much later said, 'Always, whenever he had such complaints as malaria or jaundice, it affected him very badly . . . We knew he had a low blood count and was anaemic.'

Few expatriates found Nigeria a particularly healthy place and Hastings wrote of Northern Nigeria in the 1920s:

It is not a good climate. . . . It is not merely the fever, the sun heat and the wet; it is all of these and more, some sun ray which saps the life and energy and weakens the ill-nourished blood.

The water is indifferent. Even to wash in, it is often every grade of colour and consistency and of evil smell. To drink, it is poor stuff. It must always be boiled and filtered, and . . . is best drunk with whisky. Of the smaller discomforts there are plenty. The mosquito . . . bloodsucking flies and tsetse, the tumbo fly, the mango fly and others . . . snakes . . . spitting cobra . . . scorpions, black and red . . . the flying ants . . . the chinaka, a tiny ant who wanders over your skin and leaves a fierce and firey trail of stinging pain.

Diseases from which Europeans suffer are actually few. Malaria, blackwater fever, dysentery and anaemia are the principal, with a rare case of yellow fever and cerebro-spinal meningitis.[22]

Nor did the diet do much to improve one's health. A northern administrative officer has written that 'Colby's soup would have been about average' and added that officers usually returned from leave with a few crates of tinned foods 'from Fortnum and Mason's if you were rich, or Griffith, McAlister if you were less so. When these were finished the local resources were indeed scanty.' The only vegetables readily available were local onions and, occasionally, a few yams from the south. The 'meat was too tough to consider. Chickens not too bad and only 4d each. Eggs literally ten a penny.' The railhead was at Jos over 300 miles away by a road which was frequently – if only for short periods – closed during the rainy season, and extremely dusty in the dry season. 'In Colby's day one might expect a pound or two of butter or bacon from there occasionally and it was difficult to keep that for more than a few days.' Sharwood Smith reckoned that 'only a liberal drenching of Worcester sauce could make the majority of meals palatable', and W. R. Crocker, who headed his account of 'the milieu' of Nigerian administration with the words 'There is death in the air', believed that many officials, especially those living in bush stations, suffered from 'chronic malnutrition'.[23]

From such inhospitable conditions, Colby was glad of a respite, and he arrived, far from well, in England on leave in the autumn of 1930. Again he spent much of his time at Woking with his parents, and towards the end of his leave he was introduced by a long-standing friend, Clive Illingworth, to the latter's cousin, Lilian Florence Illingworth.[24] The Illingworth family at Woking were patients of Dr Frank Colby who had brought Clive, his four brothers and one sister into the world. Lilian, then aged 25, 'a smart, sophisticated girl . . . of sterling character', was a member of the Holden-Illingworth family.[25] By an unusual and interesting coincidence, her great-great-grandfather's brother was Isaac Holden who, we mentioned earlier in tracing Colby's ancestry, had invented the friction match.[26] There had been business dealings between the two families in the 1840s,[27] and the Holden family had become linked with the Illingworth family in the 1860s when Lilian's grandfather, Alfred, married Margaret Holden, Isaac's daughter (1866); his brother, Henry, married Margaret's sister, Mary (1860); and his sister, Margaret, married Margaret Holden's brother, Angus (1860). The two 1860 marriages were celebrated in a double wedding at Westgate Chapel, Bradford, in May. Lilian's father, Dudley Holden-Illingworth, also married (1902) a Holden, Florence, great-grandaughter of Isaac Holden's brother, John. Florence Holden, and her twin sister, Maud – 'both very good looking girls' – had been brought up at the Chateau Marseille, about ten miles from Rheims where they were born.

The Holden–Illingworth family contained many distinguished members. On the Holden side, Isaac Holden (1807–97) made a number of important inventions in wool-processing machinery, and founded the first wool combing mill in France, at St Denis on the outskirts of Paris (1849), and later other large combing businesses at Croix and Rheims (1852) and at the Alston Works in Bradford (1864). He became MP first for Knaresborough (1865–8), then for the north-west division of the West Riding (1882–5), and finally for the Keighley division (1885–96); and was created a baronet in 1893. Sir Isaac's son, Angus (1833–1912) was mayor of Bradford in 1878, 1879, 1880 and 1887; became MP for East Bradford (1885–6) and for the Buckrose division (1892–1900); and was created first Baron Holden of Alston in 1908. On the Illingworth side – which can be traced back to the fifteenth century – Lilian's great-grandfather, Daniel (1792–1854) and his brother, Miles (1789–1869), founded the Prospect Spinning Mill in Bradford (1820) and the Hope Street Mill (1826); Daniel set up business independently at the Providence Mill, Bradford (1837). His eldest son, Alfred (1827–1907), Lilian's grandfather, was elected MP for Knaresborough (1868–74) and for Bradford (1880–95), and became a freeman of Bradford in 1902. Daniel's second son, Henry (1829–95), had a less distinguished career but Henry's son, Albert (born in 1865) became MP for Heywood in 1915, was appointed postmaster-general in 1916, and was created the first Baron Illingworth in 1919. Lilian's father was:

> one of the principal land-owners in Malhamdale and had extensive business connections in Bradford. He [was] a director of the London Assurance Co., Isaac Holden and Fils (France) Limited, the Bradford branch of the National Provincial Bank, the United States Metallic Packing Co. (Bradford) [a family engineering firm founded by Lilian's grandfather in the 1890s] and Holden and Burnley Limited (Bradford).[28]

Such was her father's local standing that the station master would stop the Scottish express at the small local station to let him board for business in London.

Lilian lived with her parents at Hanlith Hall, Bell Busk, Yorkshire, a house 'full of books on shooting and hunting and fishing [with] 3000 acres of marvellous rough shooting, aside from the woods', and – like the other members of her family – was a member of the Craven Harriers hunt. She had two brothers, John Holden-Illingworth (born in 1903), the yacht designer and ocean racer, and Glen Holden-Illingworth (born in 1913); her younger sister, Christine Maud, born in 1908, had died in 1919.

Colby – now confirmed in his appointment as an administrative officer in the Nigerian service and as such permitted to marry, and with an annual salary which had now risen to £600 – announced his engagement to Lilian late in 1930 and, because he had very shortly to return to Africa, they were married soon afterwards.

The marriage[29] took place on Saturday, 17 January 1931 at the fifteenth-century, square-towered, clerestoried, mill-stone grit church of St Michael, Kirkby Malham, where the Illingworth family regularly worshipped at the Sunday morning service. Although there had been a severe and frightening gale on the previous day, which almost persuaded a number of guests to turn back, the wedding day itself was fine and sunny, so that it 'was more like a summer wedding than a winter one'. The bride, on her father's arm, walked through the stone lych-gate, past the old stone stocks nearby, and along the curving path through the old church yard with its large, dark, green yew trees and an ancient oak, to the west door, and entered the packed church with its box pews full of relations and friends. Bright sunshine streamed in through the windows of the ancient church and added a final touch of loveliness to the quietly beautiful scene. On the altar were Madonna lilies; and bunches of silvery honesty, mingled with evergreen, made an unusual and effective decoration in the chancel. The service was fully choral and was conducted by the Rev W. R. N. Baron, a former vicar of Kirkby. As the bride and her father entered the church, both smiling happily, the hymn 'Praise My Soul, the King of Heaven' was sung as a processional.

Lilian wore a graceful empire gown of ivory satin with a low square neck-line, and a train of the same material, over which fell a veil of old Brussels lace held by a head-band of orange blossom, and she carried a small bouquet of lilies of the valley. At her neck was a single strand of pearls. Two small children carried the train: the boy, Henry Tempest, wearing a velvet satin suit; the girl, Christine Illingworth, Lilian's niece, dressed in a long, frilly, white chiffon dress. The two bridesmaids – Isobel Sanders and Annie Illingworth – wore slim-fitting dresses of white chiffon with coatees of crimson velvet lined and edged with white fur. They had crimson bows on their white satin slippers, carried stiff Victorian posies of red and white carnations, and wore wreaths of green leaves. Mrs Illingworth wore a sable coat over a black georgette dress and carried a spray of orchids, whilst Mrs Frank Colby wore a black broadtail coat with a collar of silver fox.

Colby wore a black morning coat, grey pin-striped trousers, wing collar and grey cravat. The best man was his brother, Marcus, and the ushers included his other brother, Reginald, Lilian's brothers John and Glen, and her cousins Clive and Miles. Marcus spent the night before the wedding at Gargrave House, where Lilian over 50 years later was to live for a time whilst convalescing after a major operation.

After the service, the bride and groom, their parents and guests drove from the church and the village of Kirkby Malham with its seventeenth-century cottages the mile and a half along the gently winding, narrow road, bordered by moss-covered stone walls, down to the River Aire.

On the far side of this stood Hanlith Hall, where the reception was held in bright sunshine. More than half a century later, relatives who were present recalled of the wedding: 'It was a large smart affair with lots of relations on both sides and a dance in the evening.'

Later, Geoffrey and Lilian (dressed in a smart blue dress and coat which had a Persian lamb collar and carrying a matching muff) left for a fortnight's honeymoon on the French riviera at Cannes, 'ville des fleurs, des sports elegants', from where he wrote to his mother, 'Having glorious weather and thoroughly enjoying life; it's just like summer here. Both very well.' A week later Geoffrey returned to Nigeria, leaving his bride behind in England. When he had left Africa a few months earlier, he had not yet met his wife-to-be and had, consequently, made no arrangements for her to join him.

Colby was now posted back to Bornu Province, where officers were not allowed to have their wives:

> Living conditions in Bornu at that time were regarded, with a good deal of justification, as amongst the toughest in the whole country, even for the fittest of men and, because of its remoteness, extremely hot climate, difficult conditions for transport especially in the rains, the inadequacy of medical facilities and lack of modern amenities generally, as a far from suitable habitat for a European woman.[30]

Although he immediately applied for a transfer to a post where Lilian could join him, this did not take place for a year. In the meantime he was again posted to Biu – the scene of his illness before going on leave – where he had to undertake very arduous tax-collecting treks in the hills on foot; and then to Dikwa, 'a dreadful swampy spot infested with every type of insect'. This was only 50 miles from Maiduguri yet it was hard of access; in the rains the land was very swampy and 'in the dry season deep sand made travelling a misery'.[31] Dikwa was an unsatisfactory place as a district headquarters and some years later a new headquarters was built at Bama 30 miles up the Yedseram river. He was posted to Dikwa as district officer whilst the substantive holder of that post was on leave, and we are fortunate to have the reminiscences of one of his assistant district officers and his account of their first meeting which highlights both Colby's reputation and his true character:

> As touring Assistant District Officer based on a bush outstation at Gwoza, about 90 miles south of the Divisional headquarters, in an

almost entirely pagan area of the Division, I had Colby as my immediate senior officer. I had served in the same area for most of my previous tour and perhaps for that reason [he] was content to leave me to carry on very largely without intervention from him, but on the understanding that if I needed his help it would be immediately forthcoming – an arrangement which suited me very well. It probably suited him also ... because the road between Dikwa and Gwoza was not ideal for motor transport even in the dry season and was at times impassable during the rains ... and, it being the wet season, it would be reasonable for him to reduce his touring to essential journeys ...

Until I met him and was able to begin to formulate my own opinion of his character and personality, Colby was only a name to me, a name for being the possessor of a first-class brain, but with it a cold and distant manner, particularly towards people he regarded as lacking his own intellectual capacity. It was said that he was over-critical and that he would expose people he was criticising to sarcasm and even contempt greatly out of proportion to the errors of which they were accused. It was therefore with some apprehension that I set out one day to meet him, as had been arranged, at a place called Bama, about half way between Gwoza and Dikwa ... I vividly recall a tremendous sense of relief at finding that most of the unflattering things I had heard about him before we met were not apparent on this occasion ... He greeted me warmly and without a trace of superiority. To my amazement he even displayed a sense of humour. . . . On this our first meeting. . . . he provided dinner for us both in the evening and drinks to precede it. In the circumstances it would have been rather pointedly unfriendly had he not done so: but I remember feeling at the time that his attitude was not that of someone fulfilling a social obligation. He was going out of his way to be friendly ... It is perhaps fair to blame the ungenerous element in human nature for the fact that his critics exaggerated the less attractive traits in his character and failed to high-light the many good features.[32]

Among the very few others who demonstrated 'this ungenerous element in human nature' were those who said of Colby at this time, 'That man is a lead-swinger if ever there was one' and 'He was never very popular in the Service and ... was not a good mixer.'

Colby spent only six months in Dikwa, filling the post on a temporary basis, but the experience was invaluable since he enjoyed a very large measure of autonomy, independence and personal responsibility for administering a large territorial area including some troublesome parts 'whose inhabitants were a wild lot, often violent and largely unsubdued'. In February 1932, his request to be transferred to a more congenial posting was granted – to the Northern Provinces secretariat at Kaduna. Here Lilian quickly joined him, one of the passengers on the Elder Dempster boat on which she travelled recalling many years later that he 'found her a most charming partner at bridge'.[33]

There were not more than about 100 white people altogether in the station. A dozen were in the Secretariat and the same number in the West African Frontier Force, three with the police and half a dozen, including three Sisters, on the medical staff. . . .

All the official houses were in good 'compounds' 100 feet each way, with a variety of trees, some the original bush trees and others flowering ones specially planted; the houses were therefore out of sight of each other. We did not do very well over flowers . . . except for zinnias, marigolds and . . . periwinkles. . . .

The furniture was good and sufficient . . . carpets and curtains were yet to come. However, good floor mats were easily available. Earth closets were unavoidable, and were cleaned by a 'sanitary gang'.

There was a lot of entertaining in a mild way and dinner parties were common and very popular. . . .

Food was easy in Kaduna – plenty of guinea fowl and ducks, and good vegetables and fruit. The canteen was poor but we could get supplies from Lagos by train – frozen butter and bacon and cheese. We still relied largely on our Fortnum and Mason cases.

After dinner people played card games. . . . Of the solemn bridge players some were skilled and indeed some said that they lived off it!

Kaduna had electric light long before anywhere else. . . . The water supply was good and came direct from the river. . . .

Kaduna was very formal. On one's first arrival, 'books' had to be signed and cards left. . . .

There were good hard tennis courts by the club and a rather depressing golf course. The race course contained the polo ground and the cricket pitch: there was a lot of good polo. . . .

In those days there was a little club opposite the Secretariat buildings . . . in this edifice we had dances to gramophone records and sometimes to the WAFF band itself.

Kaduna, then, was a place in which one could lead a far more healthy and a fuller social life than would have been possible elsewhere in northern Nigeria: not a bad place at all for the young Mrs Colby to join her husband.

So far as Colby's professional life was concerned, he was fortunate in being posted to the secretariat and, in particular, to the lands and mines section. The posting suited his career ambitions and was a refreshing and welcome change from the bush:

> With the best climate for white men in the whole country, Kaduna was a Mecca for the ambitious and a plague spot for the true 'bushman'. Here was the Secretariat, where service brought a man into a prominence before his seniors that might do him good – or sometimes ill. The man devoted to his 'bush' division dreaded its office hours, its procedure, its collars and ties. The work was hard and exacting.[34]

Niven, who was also posted to the lands and mines section a few years earlier, has described the work in the section for us:

> I was posted to the Lands and Mines Section, which we who served in it said in our simple way was the training ground of the promising. Many who passed through it did indeed prosper in the Service . . .
>
> The Mines Section . . . dealt with all mining titles and the titles under which land was held by 'non-natives'. . . . Much of this work was legal and in every official action we had to be right: we could not afford to be wrong, dealing with matters involving large private investments. The whole thing was fascinating and developed the mind in the most surprising way. . . . One officer took the statistics for the week and announced that an average of 173 files had been handled by him each day.[35]

Colby found life in Kaduna domestically delightful, socially entertaining and professionally stimulating – recognizing as did others, including Heussler, that 'the road to the top lay through headquarters' – and he sought and was granted an extension of his tour of duty to 12 November

1932. He and his wife spent their first married leave mainly with Lilian's parents at Hanlith Hall. It was a leave of mixed sadness and happiness. On 20 January 1933, his father collapsed and died suddenly, a week before his 68th birthday. Lilian – at the time confined to bed – was unable to attend the funeral. Less than a fortnight later, on 5 February, their first daughter was born at Hanlith: Christine Elizabeth. Three months later still, Lilian and Geoffrey returned to Nigeria, leaving their baby daughter in the care of Lilian's parents in Yorkshire. It became their normal practice after this for Lilian to precede her husband on leave by three months and to follow him back to Nigeria three months after the end of his leave.[36]

Colby's fifth tour of duty was again spent in the Kaduna secretariat from May 1933 to November 1934, at which time he and Lilian returned to England on leave, spending most of their time at Hanlith Hall with their infant daughter – now almost two years old – and Lilian's parents, but also sparing time for a skiing holiday at St Moritz in Switzerland. Here they were accompanied by two Nigerian Service officers, one of whom was James Harford. Harford had served with Colby in Bornu and had recently tragically lost his wife after only two years of marriage. Harford, who long remained a friend of the Colbys, recalled of that holiday Colby's 'promise as a skier and his skill on the hotel dancing floor', and he recalled generally that:

> He was most companionable, generous, highly amusing, eloquent, with an almost perpetual smile: almost a Bertie Wooster type. He had plenty of self-assurance. One gathered that when on leave he moved in 'county' circles, but he was most amusing about this, saying that in this company, rather than talk of his life being spent on 'the coast' with its rough associations, he would say his milieu was 'Central Africa'. He certainly had glamour.[37]

On each of their leaves, they spent some of their time with the now widowed Mrs Elsie Colby in Bournemouth at her flat, 33 Braidley Road, or later at a private hotel there, the Carlton, on the East Cliff.[38] They played a good deal of bridge at the Wessex Club whilst staying at Bournemouth, sometimes with Colby's aunt and his cousin Nancy, entering for the national pairs and narrowly missing getting into the finals which were held at Eastbourne.[39]

In June, Colby returned once more to Nigeria, this time to Niger Province as the district officer at Kontagora, 'a rather remote Division' whose 'prestige was not of the highest', where the 'headquarters was a queer little station, set down in the heart of the bush about a mile from Kontagora native town, and for miles around the country spread and undulated, thickly tree covered, and so sparsely inhabited that an average population of six to the square mile was all that it could produce'.[40]

Sharwood-Smith described Kontagora at this time, saying:

> Our house . . . stood on a low tree-covered ridge. On one side of us was my mud and thatch office. . . . Below us a stretch of open parkland fell away to where the Kontagora stream, winding through dense undergrowth, marked the Station's limits. Beyond the stream the ground, now more thickly wooded, rose gently towards a distant line of hills. . . . So peaceful was the scene around us that even in the daytime antelope would occasionally emerge from the surrounding bush to graze contentedly [and] the rasping cough of a wandering leopard and the sound of a lion roaring mightily night after night [could also be heard].[41]

Two officers who served with Colby in Kontagora, many years later recalled details of those times. The first was the provincial education officer for Niger Province who recalled that 'visits to his station were very pleasant; he was an excellent bridge player and much above my standard and I had much kind hospitality from [Lilian] Colby'. The other officer to whom we have referred was Colby's cadet at Kontagora when he took over that division from Christie Holman. The cadet, many years later, could 'remember the contrast between these two men', a contrast which highlights many of Colby's characteristics and attributes twelve years after he had joined the administration. Holman was an ex-army officer who had joined the service in his mid-thirties, and could speak only just enough Hausa to be understood. He welcomed the new cadet with open arms because he said that he had arrived just in time to write the divisional annual report which 'because he [Holman] was "illiterate" he usually left to his Nigerian Chief Clerk'. Holman found that his administrative job took up more of his time than he liked because he was very keen on shooting and fishing and had made a five hole golf course in front of the district officer's house. 'Geoffrey was the very opposite.'[42]

Cadets often much admired and fell under the influence of their first district officer, especially if the DO was a 'character', and they tended to compare other officers under whom they subsequently served early in their career rather unfavourably. This, to a degree, was the case here, the cadet feeling that Colby may have become rather bored in 'Kontagora where there were no funds for development' and where he may have been 'critical of the Kontagora Native Administration, for beside there being no money to spend, it was most incompetent in what it did do.' The cadet much later recalled that Colby:

> was most efficient and an entertaining conversationalist. We happened to come from the same public school (Charterhouse) which gave us a link.... I knew [he] was ambitious and was looking forward to his promised posting to the Secretariat in Lagos.... To me he had charm and great ability, but was impatient of those who could not keep up with him – a brilliant secretariat man.[43]

Despite the lack of funds and competence in the Native Administration, Colby, by dint of much energetic work, nonetheless brought about a good deal of local development, especially in agriculture and communications. He improved African crop production, particularly by introducing better maize seed and groundnuts and by establishing an experimental farm for these crops near the station. He improved the road system by building a new road between Kontagora and Zungara and by upgrading the road north towards Yelwa, in both cases putting in many culverts for drainage during the wet season. He personally supervised much of the labouring work on these projects, spending many hours day after day in the great heat. He toured at least one week in each month, mainly in those parts of the division which could be reached by motor vehicle. Although his wife usually accompanied him on these tours, she was not always well enough to travel with him on the more arduous journeys, such as a fortnight's trek on horseback in the remoter areas; on such occasions she remained at Kontagora and was visited each day by the emir's representative to ensure that all was well during her husband's absence. Many years later, Lilian recalled of Kontagora that:

> It was a lovely spot – very pretty with good trees and we made such a lovely garden with super dahlias and carnations. It was quite the happiest time of our lives, the two tours we spent there.

More than half a century later, in the last letter she wrote before her death, she still remembered in detail her husband's contribution to the development of the division.[44]

After the first of their two tours in Kontagora, the Colbys went on leave in November 1936, and their second daughter, Carol Susan, was born at the London Clinic a month later, on 16 December. They again spent much of their leave at Hanlith Hall with Lilian's parents who 'looked upon Geoff as a son and he greatly enjoyed trout fishing and rough shooting there'. Hanlith Hall was open house to many friends and relations, including Lilian's brothers and their families. She later recalled that 'In all it was an incomparable paradise where I was greatly spoiled.'[45] Colby – possibly not wishing too soon to leave his daughters and the 'incomparable paradise' of life at Hanlith Hall – sought an extension to this leave, and despite 'a terrific staff crisis in the Province' at the time, was granted the extension to early June 1937, somewhat to the annoyance of the hard-pressed officers remaining in the province.[46]

The Colbys now left both their daughters in Britain; indeed neither of the girls ever accompanied them to Nigeria:

> Up to . . . 1945, the Nigerian Government's attitude to the family life of a married expatriate officer with a child or children had from the beginning been one of total opposition to the idea of allowing him to bring the children into the country to live with their parents. There was no suitable provision for children in Government living quarters, no suitable schools and all too few doctors and hospitals . . .
>
> Government policy in regard to the presence, or rather to the exclusion, of expatriate children received powerful support from the Colonial Office. . . . To allow young children to be brought into this death trap to live would, it was argued, be a crime against humanity.[47]

The two girls continued to live at Hanlith Hall, devotedly cared for by Lilian's parents and their staff, whilst their parents returned to Nigeria, to Niger Province. For a short time during this tour, Colby was senior district officer based at Minna, and one of his earliest tasks was to rebuild the district officer's house which had recently been burnt down. Also during this tour, and for the only occasion, Lilian travelled back to Britain, mid-tour, to see the children.[48]

At the beginning of December 1938 Colby went on leave, never to return to work in the north nor again to be posted to a district bush station, for, on returning to Nigeria in May 1939, he was posted away from the Northern Provinces to the Lagos secretariat, a promised posting to which he had been looking forward for some time.

This last pre-war leave was extremely happy. They took a splendid luxurious and roomy house at Sandbanks – 'Four Winds' – for three months, with the sea on one side and Poole Harbour seen from the other. They were joined by an old family cook from Hanlith Hall, a parlourmaid, and two 'dailies'. There was a French governess for Elizabeth and a nurse for Carol. With plenty of rooms to spare they were able to have many relations and friends to stay with them. Colby played a good deal of golf at Broadstone and Ferndown Club, often with his cousin, Walter Lucas.[49]

The posting to the Lagos secretariat on his return from leave was a crucial step in his career, for 'there were a lot of people in the country who would have given their eyes for a spell in the secretariat':

> It was laid down that all officers as far as possible should have an opportunity of serving in one of the three Secretariats (Lagos, North and South) in their early tours, then going back to their bush jobs and later, if they showed promise, returning to one or other of these offices in a higher Secretariat post.[50]

Colby's first posting in the Lagos secretariat was as assistant secretary in the newly created finance branch.[51] From time to time during the 1930s, the secretary of state for the colonies had addressed governors on the need for sound, specialist financial advice. In a 1932 despatch,[52] he had emphasized the desirability of each colonial government having at its disposal some member of its staff charged with the special duty of advising the government on all financial questions. He added that 'this duty might appropriately be assigned to the Treasurer' and 'definite steps should be taken to stress that officer's functions in this respect'. A number of governments felt that little change was required, since the treasurer's advice was habitually sought on financial matters. Nonetheless, the secretary of state returned to the point with some force in 1937, feeling that experience gained during the depression had 'created the strong impression that the machinery in most Colonies for developing a sound ... policy in the financial and economic sphere is far from being as effective as it should and can be made'. In January 1937, he proposed a reorganization in the colonies, in which a financial secretary should be appointed to form, along with his staff, 'an integral part of

the Headquarters establishment' and 'form part of the central Secretariat'. He also suggested that a separate office of accountant-general
would need to be created to deal with the application, as opposed to the
formation, of policy.

The reorganization took place in Nigeria, as elsewhere, just before
the Second World War and it was to the new financial secretary's office
that Colby was posted on 18 May 1939 on his return from leave. During
this time he was promoted to principal assistant secretary, with two
assistant secretaries under him.

This period gave Colby a close and valuable insight into the financial
and economic aspects of administering a large colony – far and away the
largest British African territory in terms of size, population, civil service
and annual budget. Although the work was extremely arduous, especially
in war time, he extended his tour by some six months to June 1941,
partly because he found the work a challenging, fascinating and rewarding outlet for his many talents as an administrator, and partly also so
that he and Lilian could spend their leave in Britain with their daughters
and other relatives.

It was not at this time, early in the war, easy to travel from West
Africa to Britain. Many passenger ships had been sunk by enemy action,
and those few which remained took a very long time to complete
the protracted and dangerous journey. The principal alternative – one
encouraged by the government – was to take leave in South Africa. Most
of the journey to South Africa was by air, safe from enemy submarine
attack, and there was the additional advantage that if one spent one's
leave in South Africa one's wife was permitted to return with her
husband to Nigeria at the end of the leave. By contrast, if one spent
one's leave in Britain – assuming that passages were available – one's
wife could return to Nigeria only if she were a state registered nurse
prepared to undertake a full-time hospital job from the beginning of the
next tour, or if she were engaged to work in the secretariat on very
special duties, in the Special Branch or – as was Lilian Colby – in the
cypher office.[53]

For a while during the war, a number of officers and their wives were
able to take advantage of an opportunity to travel to the United States in
returning Boeing transport planes after they had delivered vital supplies,
including fighter aircraft, to West Africa for use in the North Africa
campaigns. These aircraft flew from West Africa to Baltimore, and the
colonial service passengers then travelled by rail to New York and thence
by passenger ship troop carrier – often *the Queen Mary* – to Britain.

The Colbys were more fortunate than most because they were able to fly straight from Nigeria in a Sunderland flying boat which was carrying VIPs back to Britain. They spent a much-needed restful holiday at Hanlith Hall with Lilian's parents and with their daughters, now aged eight and four years. A number of family photographs show them in a relaxed and happy mood with their children at Hanlith Hall. Then, on 30 October 1941, Colby began his journey back to Africa in a small cargo boat, a journey which lasted for 43 days instead of the usual 15. The cargo boat criss-crossed the Atlantic to avoid enemy submarines and a number of other boats in the convoy were sunk. He changed ships at Freetown in Sierra Leone and flew on to Lagos from Takoradi in the Gold Coast, arriving in Nigeria on 9 December 1941. Lilian remained with their children at Hanlith Hall.[54]

On his return to Nigeria, he was posted to the newly created supply branch – housed in wooden hutments in the middle of the secretariat lawns – the head of which was initially the financial secretary, but Colby was soon promoted from the post of deputy director to be the director of the branch by Sir Bernard Bourdillon, the governor, who 'thought highly of him'.[55] The work of the supply branch was challenging and one of vital significance to the British war effort:

> The functions of the Branch were wide. They embraced food and price control, coordination of all imports and exports, production of local foodstuffs; in the case of Lagos, the capital, the setting up of markets for the sale of basic native foodstuffs at controlled prices; the encouragement of the production of vital war supplies e.g. rubber, tin, tantalite. It also allocated coal supplies from the Enugu coalfield as between the Nigerian railway, local shipping and power stations. It had a hand in setting up the Cocoa Marketing Board, a Government controlled agency which became the monopoly purchaser of the entire cocoa crop at controlled prices.
>
> The writ of the Supply Branch covered a very wide field, in fact the whole economic field, and it was largely due to Colby's outstanding ability that the machine functioned, with scarcely a hiccup, from its inception until it was wound down in 1948.

Before the war, virtually the whole of the export trade had been in the hands of expatriate firms. This trade included groundnuts, cocoa, palm kernels, palm oil, cotton, benniseed and soya beans, the total value of which represented some 75 per cent of the value of all exports from

Nigeria. With the outbreak of World War II, the established exporters became government-licensed agents for the purchase, storage, transport and shipment of the crops they had handled previously. The British Ministry of Food undertook to buy any surplus quantity that could be made available for export, at prices guaranteed in advance of each buying season. Before the war, there had been a tendency for commodity prices to fluctuate violently, so unpredictably as to create disorderly market conditions and thereby to discourage production of the crops, since it was the Nigerian producers who usually suffered more from these price movements than either the middlemen or the exporting firms.

To ensure that urgently needed supplies would continue to come forward for export, it became a main responsibility of government to bring stability into the market by giving wide publicity to the guaranteed prices to be paid by the licensed buying agents for the whole of that season at specified buying points throughout the areas of production.[56] Purchase for export was confined to these buying agents, each of whom was allotted a quota fixed by reference to his past performance as an exporter. The arrangements then in force for the inspection and grading of all purchases for export were tightened up to ensure that quality standards were maintained and differential prices fixed for each grade. Responsibility for devising and introducing this intricate and important system and for its effective operation was entrusted to Colby as director of supplies. The arrangements proved remarkably effective and were retained in operation throughout the war and long after it was over. When the first produce marketing board – that for cocoa – was set up, followed in the next few years by similar marketing boards for oil palm produce, groundnuts and cotton, Colby's basic organization was retained and, in conformity with constitutional development, continued in existence later still when the regional marketing boards replaced the commodity boards. The whole system was in very large measure Colby's brain-child. That it worked so successfully in practice and withstood the test of critical times must be added to his credit. The branch grew to become, in effect, the Ministry of Economic Warfare, largely divorced from the rest of the secretariat.

As director of supplies, Colby made his own decisions except on matters of major policy when he minuted to the governor through the chief secretary. He also made frequent visits by air to London, Washington and Accra, plus a lengthy trip to South Africa which he described in detail in a letter to his wife, all these journeys being in connection with supplies for the war effort. The South Africa trip in November

1942 was from Lagos to Leopoldville, Coquilhatville and Stanleyville in the Belgian Congo, to Juba on the Nile, Khartoum and Malahal, thence to Omdurman, back to Malahal and Juba, before flying on to Larapi on the upper Nile, thence to Kampala, Kisumu and Nairobi, and onwards to Johannesburg and Pretoria.[57] The tone of his account indicates that he was fascinated by all that he saw, was constantly trying to relate new ideas to how they might be adopted or adapted in Nigeria, and that he enjoyed the social side of the journey as much as the professional side. In many ways it was a relaxation from his arduous life in Lagos.

His journeys to Accra were to visit the headquarters of the resident minister in West Africa, Lord Swinton. Here he met and had high-level policy dealings with a number of outstanding administrators: Lord Swinton himself, Sir Folliott Sandford, Sir Frederick Pedler, Sir Andrew Jones, Sir Roger Makins, Sir Harold Evans, Michael Varvill, and Donald Dunnett. As examples of the kind of matters upon which Pedler, head of the British economic mission in French West Africa, would consult Colby on his visits to Lagos, the former has said:

> In December 1942 and following months there was great argument about the rate of exchange which should be established between sterling and the French colonial franc. The Treasury bombarded me with demands for facts and opinions. It was important to know at what rate the colonial franc was being traded on the North Nigerian border, and Colby would be my main source of information. Nigeria wanted to encourage cattle owners in Niger colony to drive their cattle to markets in Northern Nigeria, to augment the supply of meat for the British armed forces. Colby would ask me to use my influence with the French administration to facilitate this. The transport of groundnuts to rail stations between Kano and Nguru required the attendance of camels and Bussa camel-drivers from French territory. The evacuation of French groundnuts from Maradi took place via Nigeria rail-head at Kaura Namoda, and this required the allocation by the Nigerian authorities of rail capacity, port space and shipping.
>
> Early in 1943, when after initial difficulties I persuaded the French authorities to give full support to the allied war effort, it became vital to give them certain supplies at once and the only source of supply was to draw on shipments already routed to Nigeria. Textiles and trucks were vital items. Swinton made the

decisions and . . . Colby argued as hard as he could against any reduction of supplies destined for Nigeria.[58]

Lord Swinton – whose ancestor S. C. Lister had by a curious coincidence entered into partnership with Lilian Colby's forebear, Isaac Holden in 1848 – seems to have got on well with Colby, since he invited him to visit his estate in Yorkshire during his next leave, in 1943, when Colby and Swinton shot grouse together. Swinton was an influential Conservative minister: he was secretary of state for the colonies from 1933 to 1935, later became secretary of state for Commonwealth affairs, 1952–5, and in him Colby had made an important acquaintance.

This period as director of supplies was one of virtually unmitigated arduous toil and one which taxed Colby's stamina to the maximum. One who 'remembered him best for his great sense of humour' recalled in addition to his very hard work: 'I don't think the climate suited him very well; but however pressed he never lost his philosophical amusement towards his own discomfort.'[59] With his wife no longer in Nigeria with him, he was able to devote all his time and attention to his work. There was a huge and ever-increasing work load. The sheer volume of the work he had to handle, much of it of great urgency, was such that he found it impossible to keep pace without working late into the night, forgoing hours of much-needed sleep. An officer who served with him at this time has recalled that:

he was a fast and accurate worker, decisive, with a clear and logical mind. He expressed himself plainly and succinctly, not wasting words. He would often need to dictate a long and complex minute, covering when typed two or three foolscap pages. When it was ready for him, he would read it through carefully but quickly, and initial it, without having had to alter a word. Nor would the minute contain a single superfluous word.

He applied himself assiduously to the subject in hand and rapidly mastered the essentials. He expected others to work as hard as he did and for them to take considerably longer over a given piece of work than his own quick mind would require – and unless you did he had no time for you. He was swift to detect an inaccuracy and any sign of failure to research a subject thoroughly, any muddled thinking, any conclusions based on shallow or unreliable arguments, any looseness of description. Weaknesses of this kind were liable to call forth a peremptory and probably sarcastic order to do the work again. If there was no early improvement in your performance, he would as likely as not go to great lengths, at a time of continuous staff shortages, to get you replaced. He could be ruthless and often was. If, however, he was satisfied that you had put your back and your brains into your work, even though you might have failed to produce the right answer, he would show that he was willing to trust you and would give you every encouragement. . . .

I doubt if any single officer in the Nigerian service, including the Chief Secretary and the Governor himself, carried a heavier load than Colby.[60]

Another officer who as controller of food and prices worked with Colby has said that he 'was always acutely aware of my difficulties and ever ready to discuss them and offer advice on how they could best be solved'.

The very hard work to which the civil service was subjected at this time was the result of the staff retrenchments of the 1930s – which had not been repaired – and the additional burdens imposed by the war. In order to keep abreast of the never diminishing volume of paperwork, much of it requiring immediate attention and, for the most senior officers, urgent decisions, the idea of being able to finish the day within normal office hours was unthinkable – an impossible dream. Saturdays and Sundays were occupied in the same way as every other day in the week. There was hardly any respite. There were no set hours. Provided the work was finished punctually and provided nothing needing urgent attention was ever put aside until all necessary action had been completed, up to the point when all that remained was to communicate the action that had been taken or the decision that had been reached, it was left to the individual to arrange his day and his night as suited him best.

Officers working in the secretariat, and to some extent in other departments of government, made use of their freedom to come and go as best suited their convenience and the overriding necessity to get their work completed punctually, in a number of different ways. There were those who, having started as most people did by 9.00 a.m., would break off about 1.00 p.m. and go home to eat a hasty lunch and snatch half an hour's rest and a bath before returning to the office for a further three or four hours. After that, some would repeat their morning programme: go home, have a drink, eat some supper and return once more to the office for a further session at their desks, finally leaving for home at perhaps not long before midnight. Others, on leaving their offices in the evening, would take files away and work on them at home. Others again would spend all night in their offices and seize what relaxation was possible during the hours of daylight.[61]

Colby went on leave in 1945, and this time Lilian returned with him. The war was now behind them and they could look forward again to a life together in Africa. Some two years earlier, in 1943, Sir Bernard Bourdillon was replaced as governor of Nigeria, after eight years hard service, by Sir Arthur Richards, to whom Colby's subsequent career was to owe a great deal.

Initially Richards was suspicious of Colby, considering him to be a Bourdillon favourite, and was not particularly kind to him.[62] He was not prepared to let him call the tune and more than once he overruled Colby's anti-inflationary rejection of price rises for cocoa and of increased pay and allowances, and once wrote 'No doubt when Colby dies, the word "inflation" will be found indelibly written on his heart.' There were other clashes also:

> Colby liked responsibility and, as Director of Supplies in Nigeria, more than once sent savingrams to the 'Secretary of State' (when Richards was on tour at the other end of the country) as from 'The Governor' on matters of policy which he had not previously discussed or cleared with Richards; in many cases without even reference to the Chief Secretary. Richards had the feeling . . . that Colby chose his moments carefully. He wrote once 'Colby is very anxious to control all things himself'. . . . Richards again wrote that 'the idea has become ingrained that one does not "bother the Governor" with anything that can be avoided and there is no conception of his being the arbiter of policy. That is "interference". . . . I am having a hard time convincing the Secretariat where about six kings reign that I have no intention of being a "roi faineant" and that the spacious days of my Merovingian predecessor have vanished.' He once described Colby as 'obstinate and self-willed'.[63]

The 'six kings' included F. E. V. Smith, the development secretary; Niven, the public relations officer; Colby; and probably the chief and financial secretaries. Despite this initial unfavourable view which the governor took of Colby, Richards nonetheless gave him very rapid promotion.

The great extension of governmental activities during the war, when government's role had widened from the primary functions of maintaining law and order and collecting revenue, demanded a considerable elaboration of the central machinery of government. Economic and financial matters were the prime responsibility of the financial secretary but inevitably they were also the concern of the chief secretary. Consequently, Richards created the post of administrative secretary responsible to the chief secretary for political and administrative, as opposed to financial and economic, matters, with a staff of assistant, senior assistant and principal assistant secretaries. To this new post, which replaced that of deputy chief secretary, the governor appointed, as the first incumbent, Colby, on 1 April 1945. At the time Colby was ill in hospital and Richards visited him there and told him that he was going to make him the administrative secretary: 'this news', as Lady Colby remarked many years later, 'bucked Geoff up no end'.[64] In being so promoted, he superseded 21 Class II administrative officers; 26 Class I officers, including the residents, the secretary to the Northern Provinces, the commissioner of the colony, and all the principal assistant secretaries; a deputy financial secretary; and all 11 senior residents.[65] This was unprecedentedly accelerated promotion and was, naturally, not well received by all those superseded:

> The Colonial Service worked on the rule of Buggin's Turn – any 'passing over' by special promotion was bitterly resented . . . any suggestion that A was better than B caused upset.
>
> The promotion was alright so long as Colby confined himself to special war measures and all was well as this was considered an emergency, but when he was further promoted to be Administrative Secretary over some 70 or so very able people above him in the [staff] list, this was greeted with horror [and] the fat was in the fire.[66]

Promoting Colby over the heads of so very many of his superiors:

> was a move which was very much in line with Richards' philosophy for it forced Colby to look closely at the work of the other five 'kings' and assess their responsibilities! He did so with great efficiency.[67]

As administrative secretary, Colby acted as chief secretary when the latter was on leave, and as governor's deputy when the governor was away from the seat of government on prolonged tours of the provinces. In a country as large as Nigeria, the duties that fell to his lot would elsewhere have been the principal part of the work of a chief secretary.

Subject to the approval of the chief secretary and of the governor, he was responsible, for example, for the drafting of despatches, as well as for framing submissions on policy and taking decisions, in matters of other than the greatest importance, on political and administrative matters on behalf of the governor. He had a very close insight into the way in which Richards – who by this time had been a colonial governor for 15 years, having been governor of North Borneo, the Gambia, Fiji, and Jamaica before serving in Nigeria – dealt with the legislature and with the Colonial Office. As administrative secretary, he also had a good oversight of the whole central government machine, acting as a filter through which papers from the different branches of the secretariat were submitted to the chief secretary.[68]

There was a kind of mutual liking and respect between Richards and Colby:

They were both realists, both slightly cynical, and particularly during the period when [Colby] was acting as Chief Secretary they hit it off together far more effectively than Sir Arthur did with the substantive Chief Secretary.

The two men were in a sense very much of a kind – both strong characters inclined to be autocratic; both dedicated to work; both determined to get their own way; both intolerant of inefficiency and contemptuous of ill-conceived, half-baked ideas.

They were rather similar in character. Both of them were able, both of them were ambitious, both of them had a streak of dourness about them, both of them had a sharp tongue on occasions. Neither of them, I think, was a good mixer and probably for that reason neither was very popular with his fellow officers.

They had similar brains and a similar somewhat sardonic sense of humour.

They were somewhat similar men; very ambitious, administratively extremely efficient, both inclined to be autocratic, both decisive. . . . Both men were leaders in that they saw their objectives and were not readily diverted from them.[69]

Colby was seen by other officers as one of a small group who had the governor's confidence and regard. Richards fully exercised the powers which he had and entrusted powers to those whom he personally selected in a measure to which the Lagos secretariat had previously been unaccustomed. Colby gained the reputation of making full use of the trust and powers reposed in him by the governor. It was Richards' practice to see the chief secretary every day at noon if at all possible and the latter would then stay on for a drink. Colby, who had never previously consumed alcohol before sunset, greatly enjoyed these meetings when he was acting as chief secretary. It was at one such lunch hour that the governor criticized the substantive chief secretary and said that he was not going to have two dictators in the country; one was enough and that was going to be himself![70]

Over a very short period, Richards and Colby came to admire each other a great deal, and in 1946 the governor strongly recommended the Colonial Office to keep Colby in mind for a chief secretaryship for 'he needs at once the wider experience of another Colony before he becomes a Governor, which I anticipate he will do'. A colleague later said of Colby that 'Anybody in the Secretariat who survived the ordeal of serving successfully under Richards and gained his esteem was certainly an officer of outstanding calibre!!'[71]

In May 1947 the Colbys returned to Britain on leave. They sailed home in the company of an old friend, Thomas Shankland, who had frequently partnered Colby at golf and bridge during their days together in the Lagos secretariat. The golf was a great comfort and amusement to them and was 'light hearted stuff', whilst the bridge was to their 'financial benefit. [Geoffrey] was a thoughtful and intelligent bridge player who was never flustered by the occasional disaster.' On the boat home, Shankland and Colby indulged their bridge-playing propensities to the full and found the journey most enjoyable. Colby 'was, however, a very tired man on the voyage and retreated to his cabin for a long siesta after lunch each day'. He had already been made aware that promotion to another colony was soon to be his and he looked forward to it with enthusiasm.[72]

It is necessary at this stage to examine in broad outline the way in which top colonial civil servants were selected for promotion.

In the Colonial Office in London, the Colonial Service personnel division kept under review two confidential lists of 'flyers': a List A of persons suitable for gubernatorial posts, and a List B of those suitable for posts immediately below the governor.[73] The lists were based primarily on the annual confidential reports submitted by governors on all members of the Colonial Administrative Service, but additions, mainly to List B, were reviewed by the permanent under-secretary with his deputy and assistant under-secretaries. Richards's recommendation in 1946 would have ensured that Colby's name was entered on List B, but he was destined not to become a chief secretary but rather to proceed directly to gubernatorial office. Either on a subsequent recommendation by Richards, or on the initiative of someone in the Colonial Office itself, Colby's name must have been entered on List A. Any recommendation of a man with the experience and reputation of Richards would have carried very great weight in the Colonial Office, and Colby's work as director of supplies and as administrative secretary would have brought his abilities and potential to the attention of several senior officials in the Colonial Office.[74]

Several months before a governorship was due to fall vacant, the personnel division obtained from the geographical department particulars of the appointment – such as the emoluments and any special experience and qualities desirable in the local circumstances – and noted any recommendation submitted by the retiring governor. They then examined the confidential lists and put up a short list for the vacancy, with comments on rival claims and usually with a definite recommendation. In preparing this submission there might be personal consultation with the permanent under-secretary, heads of department in the Colonial Office, and the specialist advisers. The matter was then settled at the official level, either on paper by minuting the file up to the permanent under-secretary, or at a meeting of senior officials presided over by the permanent under-secretary who would finally submit the Office's recommendation to the secretary of state, after discussing it orally with him. The decision, even if it coincided with the official recommendation, lay with the secretary of state personally, although he might sometimes raise points on which he wanted further information and, if the appointment was a strategic or sensitive one, he might consult the prime minister before he made it.[75]

Although this process was largely a 'paper' one, being based on the discovery of talent principally by scrutiny of the annual confidential reports, senior official members of the Colonial Office staff generally had a fairly good personal knowledge of Colonial Service officers in the promotion zone. Finally, in the kingmaking process the role of the serving governor was not to be overlooked; his advice was always important and sometimes decisive.

The actual appointment was the Sovereign's prerogative and the names of all proposed governors had to be submitted to the Palace personally by the secretary of state. To what extent any particular secretary of state would feel bound to accept the permanent under-secretary's recommendation was 'one of the mysteries of administration over which a discreet veil was drawn', but it would depend on the secretary of state's knowledge of the territory in question and the import-ance attached to it politically in the United Kingdom. 'The Secretary of State at the time of Sir Geoffrey's appointment was ... Arthur Creech-Jones who took a deep personal interest in all things colonial.'[76]

In the half decade from 1944 to 1948, all 11 of the British African governorships fell vacant and of these no less than five were to be filled in 1948 – the Gold Coast, Sierra Leone, Somaliland, Northern Rhodesia and Nyasaland. It was of this last, Nyasaland, that Colby – the youngest of the 11 appointees and, save for Reece who became governor of Somaliland, the only one who had not previously been a governor or chief secretary – was selected to be governor.[77]

In filling these African gubernatorial posts, the Colonial Office bore in mind the major problems facing Africa in the post-war years and the qualities to be sought in those who were to handle those problems. The major problems were economic and political in that order: economic, to repair the enforced neglect of the war years and to make fuller use of the economic opportunities of the colonies – to convert the wartime economies into peacetime advance – the chosen instrument being the Colonial Development and Welfare Act; political, to respond to the awak-ening generated by the experiences of war, the chosen instrument in this case initially being through the development of local government. In broad terms, whereas before the war the British saw their economic duty to the colonial territories in terms of grant-in-aid of the budget of any colony with inadequate local resources to keep its administration and economy going, after the war it was considered that assisting eco-nomic and social development was an essential element in preparing colonial territories for eventual self-government. This called for special skills in the control and administration of development funds and their successful application to appropriate projects. In the political sphere, again in broad terms, the problem arose partly from the wartime experi-ences of Africans; partly from the anti-colonial sentiments of some Americans, the Russians and Egyptians; but mainly from the eclipse in British intellectual and political circles of the will for empire and the belief in the imperial mission. This called for a good understanding not only of the Africans, their real feelings and their aspirations, but also of the political scene in the United Kingdom.[78]

These two thrusts, one economic, the other political, demanded for their execution a new breed of top administrator. The qualities required were administrative competence well above the average, wisdom, drive, enthusiasm, personality, political and economic flair, and, because political change was already in the air, tact and forward-looking sympathy with local aspirations combined with firmness to guide constitutional progress. Above all, there was required a belief in the impetus imparted from London by a socialist secretary of state, Arthur Creech-Jones, and a Colonial Office civil servant of the drive and vision of Andrew Cohen.

This was the general African background in which Colby was selected to be promoted governor during his leave in 1947.

The Colbys spent the early part of their leave with Lilian's parents, and their daughters – Elizabeth (now aged 14) and Carol (now 11) – relaxing at Hanlith Hall, for a while relieved of the burdens of a busy official life and of living in the tropics.

In August, Colby received a letter from the Colonial Office asking if he would accept appointment as governor and commander-in-chief of the Nyasaland Protectorate. Excited, naturally, by this opportunity, the Colbys were nonetheless hesitant and cautious.[79]

Of the 11 British African colonies, Nyasaland was sixth in terms of population and eighth in terms of size and administration staff. It was markedly underdeveloped and had a small annual recurrent budget. It was classified at that time as a Class III governorship under the Governors' Pension Act and was ninth in terms of governor's salary (£2500 plus £500 duty allowance). He was privately somewhat disappointed to be offered, as he saw it, such a mediocre governorship at such a low salary. Where, in any case, was Nyasaland? At the beginning of the First World War, Lieutenant-Commander George Dennistoun had been appointed to command the flotilla on Lake Nyasa and he had then been confronted with the question of just where Nyasaland was. He had to 'borrow a shilling atlas from an Admiralty clerk' to answer the question. So also, 33 years later, the Colbys had to look at an atlas to discover where the country was, and like Dennistoun they found it to be 'about an inch long'.[80]

Yet Colby could not really afford to wait, even if he had been so inclined. We have already noted that all 11 African governorships had recently been, or were in the process of being, filled; none was likely to become vacant for several years, since gubernatorial appointments were usually for five years and the average length of service in a governorship was four and a half years. All these posts were likely to become vacant again at a time when Colby would have had time to prove his worth.

He was only 46, and the average age of appointment as governor in African territories was 50 years, whilst that of the five largest (Nigeria, Kenya, Tanganyika, Uganda and Northern Rhodesia) was 51 years – the age Colby would be at the end of his first term of office. There was also the argument that the poorer and less-developed a country, the greater the scope for improvement and success, especially for a person of Colby's abilities and inclinations.

All these factors were pertinent to his consideration of the post offered to him and, although he hesitated for a while, he accepted it before the end of August when the news was then announced in Nyasaland in a gazette extraordinary.

Colby, now rested and refreshed by a few months' leave, was anxious to get to Nyasaland and start his new work, but he was obliged to wait several more months principally, he believed, because the governor, Sir Edmund Richards, wished to return to Nyasaland after his current leave to say goodbye to his friends there. This enforced delay, however, was at a particularly interesting period and as a governor-designate, Colby received many attractive invitations to interesting events in Britain, including the wedding of Princess Elizabeth and Prince Philip at Westminster Abbey on 20 November and the evening party at Buckingham Palace two days previously. They met many interesting and distinguished people and were particularly fascinated by General Smuts – 'a dear, fatherly person' – who entertained them at South Africa House and said that they would love Nyasaland. Colby had been awarded the CMG in the Birthday Honours List and at his investiture at Buckingham Palace he was accompanied by his mother and his daughter Elizabeth; two years later, when he was knighted, his wife and daughter Carol accompanied him. He was appointed Chief Scout of Nyasaland late in 1947. The continued rationing in Britain caused them some difficulties, especially in respect of being able to purchase sufficient and appropriate clothing for the events to which they were invited and for their departure to Nyasaland.[81]

The delay also enabled Colby to prepare himself for the work which lay ahead of him and to take full advantage of the official briefings given to newly appointed governors. There was a series of extensive discussions in the Colonial Office with officers, led by the assistant under-secretary in charge of the geographical department, who provided information and views on the general and political situation and put him in touch with the various specialist, functional departments and advisers dealing with economics, finance, education and agriculture. These discussions were supplemented by documentation but 'the whole process was very informal and ad hoc according to current needs' and there was no question of it being 'a strictly regimented "drill" to comply with some rigid "action sheet" '. Colby also had discussions with the permanent under-secretary and an interview with the colonial secretary.

Finally, before leaving to take up his new appointment, he received an audience with the king 'to kiss hands'. Many governors-designate found the formal part of this ceremony disappointing because, as Colby discovered, 'You no longer literally kiss the King's hands.'[82]

3· Arrival in Nyasaland

'A country overdue for a little attention.'

On 7 January 1948 the Colbys sailed once more for Africa, this time – on the SS *Mantola*[1] – not down the west coast, as on previous occasions, but through the Mediterranean and the Suez Canal down the east coast:

> Geoffrey chose to travel by sea via the East Coast of Africa in order to make useful contacts there. The ill fated groundnut scheme had started and all ports on the east coast were blocked badly. From Mombasa we were able to travel to Nairobi by train and spent a week there staying with Sir George and Lady Sandford. More delay at Dar es Salaam and after a stay of a fortnight with our friends the Leslies (Financial Secretary), we transhipped to a B. I. boat [the Amah] on the Bombay–South Africa route and proceeded to Beira.[2]

And so to Nyasaland. What might have been Colby's expectations on arrival? The general standard set in British colonies was that:

> On leave and on other ceremonial occasions, there was a guard of honour to greet the governor on his departure and on his return. In parts of tropical Africa senior officials . . . were required to turn up at the railway station or airport to bid farewell and welcome.[3]

Indeed, colonial governors were entitled to a 17-gun salute.[4] The standard which he knew best, that set in Nigeria, was impressive, as Niven has written of the arrival of Sir Bernard Bourdillon:

> On the morning of his arrival we all went down to the Customs

wharf, the men in white uniform and the ladies superb in their best; . . . the Commissioner of Police held his drawn sword. The wharf was alive with bunting in a brisk wind. The Regiment mounted one of its immaculate guards of honour and the band played on a flank. . . . The guns . . . fired their slow salute from across the water. The A. D. C. . . . appeared first, setting the standard of the show with his full-dress Lancer uniform. Then the tall figure of Sir Bernard came down the companion way in his blue uniform and plumes, with his dazzling wife. They shook hands with all those entitled and . . . drove off to Government House.[5]

Similarly, the standard set in Nigeria in gubernatorial rail travel was impressive, as both Sir Alexander Grantham and Sir Rex Niven have recorded:[6]

Travelling by rail was the most luxurious, for the Governor had his own train, consisting of six coaches, the Governor's with a lounge and two bedrooms, one for his A. D. C. and Private Secretary, one for the servants, another comprising the dining-saloon and kitchen and a baggage coach for the Governor's car, luggage and supplies. . . . Just before breakfast the train stopped in the middle of nowhere . . . because His Excellency must not be joggled whilst he is eating.

Niven added that in the north, the governor's 'comfortable special train of two white coaches' contained a drawing room and dining room seating a dozen people and that the two bedrooms had 'real beds' and the bath room had 'a long bath'. There was also a flat coach for five cars.

In Tanganyika, Nyasaland's neighbour, the governor's rail coaches contained, in the first, 'two bedrooms with real beds and Dunlopillo mattresses, a bathroom with a long bath, a small drawing room and an observation car', and, in the other, 'a dining room for eight, two bedrooms and bathroom for private secretary and housekeeper, kitchen and pantry' in addition to a van for the band and two trucks for the motor cars.[7]

The final part of the Colbys' journey to Nyasaland was by rail in the railways general manager's coach from Beira northwards to Limbe.

In ideal conditions this journey, a distance of some 350 miles, could be both beautiful and fascinating.[8] The passenger train – owned by the Trans-Zambezi Railway and consequently called 'Tarzan' – left Beira twice weekly and 'for the first hour or so crawled through swamps of blue lotus lilies and past banana and copra plantations' to Dondo, a quiet Portuguese station, the junction of the lines from Rhodesia and Nyasaland. After an hour's wait at Dondo, the train travelled for several hours through the lower Zambezi valley.

In the late 1940s, the train left Beira at 5.00 p.m. and this part of the journey was usually made at night:

> As the train wobbled and swayed cautiously through the dark [the passengers] hung out of the windows, watching for [their] first glimpse of the mighty Zambesi . . . The night was black and illuminated only by the star jewelled sky and the innumerable fire flies whose brilliance was duplicated in the loitering floods.

The train reached the Zambezi river, with its two-mile long rail bridge, at dawn. It then travelled onwards, following the west bank of the Shire river, to Port Herald, the first stop in Nyasaland, where customs and immigration formalities were complied with, and on again to Chiromo, 266 miles from Beira, the junction of the Shire and Ruo rivers where the former was spanned by a rail bridge built in 1908. At Chiromo, the railway line is only 125 feet above sea level but from a few miles beyond Chiromo it rises in 83 miles to 3810 feet, and the country changes remarkably:

> Instead of the wide open flats, the train crawls round curves in steep wooded hillsides, waterfalls appear here and there, while dominating the scene the huge Mlanje range appears at intervals. The line twists and turns in all directions, runs across deeply cut mountain streams, through cuttings and finally emerges, near Luchenza station (2200 feet), on the lower step of the Shire Highlands Plateau. Near Mikalongwe (2622 feet) it starts the climb up the final step on which Limbe stands, 3810 feet.

On this steep stretch, especially in the rainy season, and despite having two locomotives at its head, the train in several places often failed to make the grade and had to run back, get up more steam and have another go at the steep inclines 'with much huffing and puffing and slipping of wheels'.

The journey, then, from Beira to Limbe could be both beautiful and fascinating and, since the governor's aide-de-camp, Robert Tait Bowie, and Misapo, a very old man who had been personal servant to a series of governors, had travelled to Beira to accompany and assist the new governor and his wife on the last stage of their journey to Nyasaland, it ought to have been so for the Colbys in March 1948. But in colonial Nyasaland, as elsewhere, things occasionally fell short of what they ought to be.

Shortly before their arrival at Chiromo, towards the end of the rainy season, a vast island of floating vegetation, which officials and engineers tried in vain to break up with timber saws and explosives, had swept down the swollen Shire river relentlessly carrying all, including the Chiromo railway bridge, before it. This calamity necessitated the passengers leaving their cockroach-infested train on the west bank, crossing the fast flowing river by temporary ferry, and joining another train on the east bank – an irritating, uncomfortable, and in many ways alarming exercise.[9]

Just after the train left the last station before Limbe, the final stop, the Colbys began to prepare themselves for their arrival and the new governor called for Misapo to lay out his clothes, but Misapo did not answer: he had got off the train at the last station to buy himself some bananas with which to fortify his inner self for the important arrival at Limbe, and had been left behind.[10] Since during his St Wilfred, Charterhouse and Clare days, though less frequently during his Nigeria days, Colby had managed without a personal servant, he was easily able to cope with this minor, if unexpected, set-back, but Sward's lawyers and the demons of natural cussedness had not yet retired for the day – even one as important as this.

For reasons then, and now, unknown to others, but possibly connected with the earlier delays at Chiromo, Tait Bowie – who 'kept popping in and out with changed plans' – believed that the train was running late on its final stages up the Shire Highlands escarpment. Being a considerate man well accustomed to the way of life in Nyasaland and not wishing unnecessarily to inconvenience his senior official colleagues, Tait Bowie telegraphed a message to Limbe saying that the train would be late.[11] Recollections vary as to the reported length of delay:

The Colbys arrived in Limbe on a Sunday afternoon. We were all teed up to meet them when we were informed that the train was three hours late (nothing unusual on that wood-fired line especially if there was a 'chip' blowing). So we settled down to a Sunday afternoon zizz.

No sooner were we on our beds when the phone rang and we were told that the train had made up time and was due in Limbe in twenty minutes. Maybe someone had blundered and the train had not lost time. So there was a terrific scramble to get to Limbe before the train – we just made it.[12]

Apart from the chief justice and his wife, the police officer who had phoned them, and the provincial commissioner, who rushed panting onto the platform in the nick of time as the train pulled in, none of the other invited guests were present to greet the Colbys on their first arrival in Nyasaland.[13] The final word on this journey may safely and very appropriately be left to the governor's wife who, reminiscing many years later, said:

It was all rather a contrast after travelling somewhat royally in a special coach with every comfort between Mombasa and Nairobi! In all one was taken down a peg or two.[14]

They must have wondered what sort of country it was in which they had now arrived and in which they were to spend the next few years of their lives. What were the scenery and climate like? Its economy? The officials? Non–officials? What had his predecessors as governor been able to accomplish?

During his leave in Britain, Colby had been able to study many of these questions – at least on paper – and the answers set the broad scene for his administration of the Nyasaland Protectorate over the next eight years.

The country[15] is situated in the south-eastern part of Central Africa, 130 miles from the Indian Ocean at its nearest point, and bordered in its northern half to the west by Zambia (formerly Northern Rhodesia) and to the east by Tanzania (formerly Tanganyika), and in its southern half by Mozambique (formerly Portuguese East Africa) both to the west and to the east. It is a long, narrow country some 560 miles from north to south and between 30 and 100 miles from west to east. It is 46,000 square miles in area, a quarter of which is covered by lakes.

The northern two-thirds of the country are comprised of Lake Malawi (formerly Lake Nyasa) to the east, occupying the southern extremities of the Great Rift Valley, some 11,000 square miles in extent and lying about 1500 feet above sea level (although its deepest parts reach to 700 feet below sea level); and of high plateau country to the west lying generally at about 4000 feet above sea level, but rising to 8000 feet in the Nyika Highlands. The southern one-third is comprised of the Shire river valley, descending from 1500 feet to about 100 feet, and interrupted by cataracts in its middle section, also lying in the Great Rift Valley; with the Shire Highlands plateau to the east, lying generally at about 3000 feet but rising to over 10,000 feet in the Mlanje mountains; and the Kirk Range to the west at about 3500 feet. It is a country of very varied landscapes and one of great natural beauty.

The climate is monsoonal, with a warm to hot main rainy season from November to March followed by a two-month season of late rains (particularly in the north) during April and May, and then a cooler dry season from June to October during which the temperatures first fall and then rise again. Mean temperatures vary with season and altitude. At Fort Hill (4200 feet above sea level) in the extreme north the January mean is 69°F and the July mean is 62°F; whilst at Port Herald (190 feet above sea level) in the extreme south the means are 81°F in January and 68°F in July. Generally over 90 per cent of the annual rainfall occurs during the period November to March, although there are important mists, known as 'chiperones' or 'chips', and light rains during the 'dry' season in certain mountain areas, notably Mlanje and Cholo. Rainfall varies considerably from over 80 inches a year in the far north, the Nkata Bay area, Zomba and Mlanje mountains, to less than 30 inches a year in the Mzimba and Kasungu plains and the Shire valley.

The country's soils closely resemble the parent rock from which they are derived, but the interaction of climate, topography, soil drift and location has given rise to great complexity and variety. The predominant type found in all freely drained areas, are red to yellow latosols, bleached, acidic, friable and freely permeable downwards. The soils of the rift valley floor are alluvial, calcimorphic, grey to grey-brown, weakly acidic and often poorly drained. By African standards, the country is generally regarded as enjoying a relatively high proportion of fertile, intrinsically good soils although their nutrient status shows wide differences, being generally more fertile in the southern than in the northern part of the country. The relatively steep terrain of the Rift Valley, and the intensity of tropical rainstorms render the soils very susceptible to erosion.

Given the marked absence of economically exploitable minerals, the country's economy has always been overwhelmingly based on agriculture, as the history of its annual export trade demonstrates.[16] The period from the founding of the protectorate in 1891 to 1904 was characterized by the rapid rise and then fall, due to disease, of coffee and the similar fate of rubber, and by the decline and termination of ivory as a significant export commodity. During this period, these three items contributed over 90 per cent of the country's export earnings. In 1904, the export trade was valued at £27,500 of which 65 per cent (£18,000) was derived from coffee, as compared with peaks respectively of £78,500 and £62,000 (79 per cent) in 1900. The period 1905 to 1922 set the pattern of exports which to a large extent has persisted ever since; competitors of various types were eliminated until tobacco contributed £316,000 (70 per cent), cotton £73,000 (16 per cent) and tea £20,500 (5 per cent) in a total of £450,000. The next decade, 1923 to 1932, saw tobacco contributing an even greater share to the protectorate's export earnings, and tea increasing as cotton declined: tobacco rose to £550,000 (84 per cent), tea rose to £43,000 (7 per cent) and cotton declined to £35,000 (5 per cent) in a total of £656,120. During the 1930s and 1940s, and especially during the mid-1940s, tea grew further to rival tobacco so that in 1948, the year of Colby's arrival, whilst tobacco contributed £2,250,000 (56 per cent) of the country's export earnings, tea contributed £1,350,000 (34 per cent) and cotton £370,000 (9 per cent), out of a total of £4,000,000.

When Colby became governor of Nyasaland, therefore, the economy, which was overwhelmingly based on agriculture, had an export sector dominated by two major crops: tobacco from the Southern and Central Provinces, which was grown both on European-owned or -leased estates and on African village lands, for sale to the African Tobacco Board (two-thirds by weight and one-third by value was grown by Africans); and tea, which was exclusively grown on European-owned estates in the Southern Province. African village small-holders occupied some 95 per cent of the agricultural land in the country, predominantly producing maize as the main staple food.

In 1948, the African population of the country was about 2,400,000, and there were 4000 Asians, 2500 Europeans and 2000 Euro-Africans or Indo-Africans. The vast majority of the Africans were subsistence farmers; the Asians were overwhelmingly engaged in trading and store-keeping; of the Europeans, about a quarter were engaged each in government service, mission work and agriculture, and the remainder were in commerce or were dependants; the Euro-Africans and Indo-Africans were primarily occupied in trading, transport and agriculture. The country's population density was one of the highest in Africa, being particularly high in the Shire Highlands and growing at a rate which doubled it every 25 years.

European influence in Nyasaland developed after David Livingstone

– 'Her Majesty's Consul at Quelimane for the Eastern Coast of Africa and the independent districts in the interior' – first reached Lake Malawi in August 1859. He was followed by the initially abortive founding of the Universities Mission to Central Africa in the Shire Highlands in 1861, by the Free Church of Scotland Mission on the southern lake shore in October 1875, and by the Church of Scotland Mission also in the Shire Highlands in September 1876. Trading followed the mission work and, in 1876, the Livingstonia Central Africa Company – later the African Lakes Corporation – was set up in Blantyre.

The first British official resident in Nyasaland was Captain Foot who, in October 1883, was appointed 'Consul . . . in the districts adjacent to Lake Nyassa'. Other consuls succeeded him and in September 1889 one of them, Buchanan, declared a protectorate over the Shire Highlands to forestall a Portuguese advance into that area. This protectorate was much extended in 1891 to cover the whole of the area which later became Nyasaland, and the first commissioner and consul-general of the new protectorate was Sir Harry Johnston.

In 1904, the responsibility for the protectorate passed from the Foreign Office to the Colonial Office. Three years later, the name of the country was changed from British Central Africa to Nyasaland, the commissioner was re-styled governor, and the Nyasaland Order in Council created executive and legislative councils. Over the years various minor adjustments to the composition of the councils were made, and at the time of Colby's arrival the executive council had five official and two non-official members, all European, whilst the legislative council had six official and six non-official members, all European.

Colby was the eleventh governor of Nyasaland – although the first had been titled commissioner and consul-general – and a brief review of the contribution made by his predecessors to the protectorate's development and an indication of what sort of men they were will help to set the scene for his own period of office.

In the case of Sir Harry Johnston (1891–7)[17] it is clear that only a person of unusual perception and drive would have undertaken the task of being the first commissioner, and only one of unusual ability and powers of dynamic leadership would have succeeded as Johnston did in creating and developing the nucleus of central government and laying the civil service foundations upon which his successors were able to build. He founded the protectorate, brought it under effective British control, pacified the country, brought an end to the slave trade and also to land speculation, and created the basic system of administrative

stations and the transport framework of essential roads. He was indefati-
gable in surveying and documenting the country's natural resources,
especially its flora and fauna. He displayed much skill in extracting,
albeit inadequate, funding from the British government. During his
period of office, the civil service grew to 478 officers.[18] He displayed
remarkable qualities of leadership, being much admired and loyally
served by most of his officials. He was a man of unflagging energy,
strong personality and considerable charm:

> an enthusiastic and tireless worker himself, . . . he had no use for
> anybody who did not share his unwearying industry. . . . If he
> wanted a thing done, it had to be done immediately. . . .[19]
>
> Johnston's great asset was the power of getting out of his col-
> leagues their very best, and we gave liberally in return, sparing no
> pains to back him up. . . .[20]
>
> Johnston . . . exercised a very real influence not only over his
> subordinates but over almost every person with whom he came into
> contact.[21]
>
> It was sufficient to be in Mr Johnston's company for ten minutes
> to be won over for life by his charming manner.[22]

Moreover, Johnston had youth on his side: he was only 33 when he was
appointed commissioner, and only 39 when he gave up that office.

Sir Alfred Sharpe[23] was commissioner and governor for a period of
14 years (1897–1910), during which time expansion was restricted by
the internal annual budgetary deficit: for the whole period British government grants-in-aid were required and consequently the only changes in
government activity and development other than small scale changes
were those virtually forced upon the government by threats of fatal
disease: small-pox and sleeping sickness. During his period of office, the
civil service grew 6.4 per cent a year, from 478 to 875 officers, and
the internally raised revenue rose from £25,000 a year to £109,000.
Although comparatively young – 44 – when he succeeded Johnston, he
was 59 by the time he left office and lacked the youthful exuberance of
his predecessor. Many observers commented pointedly on the contrast
between Johnston and Sharpe: 'it would have been difficult to imagine
two men more temperamentally dissimilar'; 'Mr Sharpe . . . is a very
different man from the Commissioner.' Although a man with many
other outstanding qualities, he does not appear to have been a particularly
dynamic leader anxious to accelerate the protectorate's development;

rather he was a man who preferred the loneliness, toughness and quiet thrill of the life of a big-game hunter, and it was in this latter profession that many people saw his greatest accomplishments:

If Sharpe was not a great administrator he was at any rate a mighty hunter.[24]

As a Vice Consul he was an excellent elephant hunter.[25]

In a paper read to the African Society at the end of his period of office, entitled 'Recent Progress in Nyasaland', he pointedly and typically devoted the opening section to big-game shooting.[26]

Sharpe was succeeded by Sir William Manning, a military officer who was governor for only two years (1910–12), during both of which the budget failed to balance internally and there was, therefore, little possibility of expansion. During his period of office, nonetheless, the Civil Service expanded 10.2 per cent annually from 875 to 1054 officers, although the internally raised revenue dropped from £109,000 to £97,000 a year. In the financial sphere, he seems to have accepted with a resignation approaching fatalism the early burden of the railway guarantee and the view that this would inevitably lead to severe constraints on development:

We must be prepared to make sacrifices. . . . The community must be prepared for . . . most rigid economy and the postponement of all but the most necessary services.[27]

It is unlikely that even if Manning had stayed longer as governor he would have demonstrated qualities of leadership of the type required to induce and handle anything other than small-scale change.

When Sir George Smith took over as governor from Manning, he was already 55 years of age and fast approaching the expected end of his career. No longer a young man, he had the difficulties of the First World War, the Chilembwe Rising, and the aftermath of both to contend with. Nonetheless, in the immediate post-war period he made fairly detailed and quite progressive plans for development, expansion of the Civil Service, and the raising of revenue internally to pay for these. His opening speech to the legislative council in March 1920 had an expansionist and bold – though by no means profligate – ring about it which had been absent since the days of Johnston:

> Intensive production and the strictest control over extravagance
> and waste must . . . be the guiding principle . . . a considerable
> enlargement of expenditure is contemplated in furtherance of . . .
> many matters of reform and development. . . . Additional expendi-
> ture has to be provided for an increase of personnel in . . . public
> departments to cope with the expansion of work. . . . In mentioning
> all this I do not wish it to be taken as the limit of the developmental
> work the Government has in contemplation, but rather as indicating
> what it is hoped to undertake in the early future.[28]

His plans, then, included expansion in all the major departments of
government, and although he was strongly encouraged[29] to introduce
these changes, not all the pressure was in favour of development, with
some of the non-official members of the legislative council considering
his proposals 'lavish',[30] 'very elaborate', and 'extravagant'.[31] Economic
depression in the early 1920s, and the consequent shortfall in public
revenue, however, obliged Smith to forgo most of his plans for expansion
and deprived him of the opportunity, albeit very late in his career, to
join that very small group of governors who were sufficiently far-sighted,
dynamic, bold and forceful to encourage and supervise anything other
than minimal development. That he was probably capable of such leadership is suggested by the remarkable expansion of rural dispensary
services – the opening of 70 dispensaries in 1922, with a five-fold increase
in the number of outpatients treated – at the end of his period of office,
an accomplishment all the more remarkable in being achieved without
external financial support. During his decade as governor (1913–23), the
Civil Service expanded at an annual average rate of 7.6 per cent, from
1054 to 1932 officers, whilst the annual internal revenue rose from
£97,000 to £281,000.

Sir Charles Bowring succeeded Smith and in doing so returned to
the protectorate – his last assignment before retiring – a quarter of a
century after he had left it as Local Auditor.[32] His period of gubernatorial
office (1923–9) opened with his having to ask the British government
for the first grant-in-aid to balance the budget for over a decade. He
made this request with reluctance and deep regret,[33] possibly because of
his early training in accountancy, and at his first meeting of the legislative
council he set the scene for much of the remainder of his service in
Nyasaland: 'strict economy and cautious anticipation must continue to
be our main aim'.[34] With such a 'main aim' the country was unlikely

to progress significantly. In any event, like Manning, he viewed the railway guarantee as preventing other developments and believed that:

> The services for which provision had been made barely allowed of the administration of the Protectorate without serious risk of breakdown and afforded no possibility . . . of promoting the welfare and development of the native population of Nyasaland.[35]

Although by mid–1927 the protectorate's financial position had much improved, and was considered to be better than at any previous time,[36] Bowring, still the accountant at heart, permitted the treasurer to insist on preserving a balance of £100,000 – a figure almost half as large as the current annual expenditure – against bad years:[37] once bitten, twice shy. A senior civil servant, who knew the governor well, said of him:

> Sir Charles' reputation was that of a rather irascible, prickly man . . . like so many of us, Sir Charles' talents were more in the line of keeping the pot boiling than in innovation.[38]

But 'so many of them' did not occupy the dominant position of governor and the pot was not really boiling at all. Bowring seems to have lacked the ability and inclination to induce and handle anything other than small-scale changes, and he missed a major opportunity to direct the country's future, in 1928, by failing to support Sir Alan Cobham's attempts to route the British intercontinental air service to South Africa through Nyasaland. He appeared also to have been overawed by the difficulties of planning for development during periods of uncertainty:

> The uncertainty of what the position will be from year to year adds greatly to the difficulties of making arrangements for local development.[39]

Consequently, very few arrangements for local development were made during his period of office, although the Civil Service grew at an annual average rate of 6 per cent, from 1932 to 2623 officers, and the annual internal revenue rose from £281,000 to £372,000.

His successor, Thomas Shenton Thomas, was cast in a quite different mould, was by no means a mere 'pot boiler' in the same sense, and was much more of an innovator. He came from the Gold Coast, where he was to return as governor after only three years in Nyasaland. There he had worked with Guggisberg, from whom he learned a great deal about the possibilities of accelerated economic development. His speeches at his first meeting of the legislative council[40] were progressive, forceful and optimistic, and set the tone of expanded development which was to characterize his style and his period of office, and he quickly impressed this style on those he met:

> About two days after he arrived a man who was never afraid of saying what he thought accosted Shenton Thomas, not knowing who he was and by way of making acquaintance asked him 'What are you doing in Nyasaland? Why did you come to this poor country?' and was taken aback by Shenton's forceful reply, 'I am your new Governor and you'll realize that before long because I'm going to knock this country into shape, something that should have been done long ago.' That story exactly describes Shenton Thomas' impact on the country and on the community both official and unofficial . . . Shenton Thomas was with us for a very short time but in that period he certainly made a terrific impact.[41]

Like Sir Harry Johnston he was a man of great drive, forceful personality and charm, one who commanded the admiration and loyalty of most of those who served under him, and who was skilled in extracting money from the British government:

> A well-built, fit-looking man with a brisk manner and keen grey eye. He did not have much time for people who were sloppy or idle – and said so . . . I am convinced that his methods of personal contact would have been useful in getting the best out of his officers.[42]

> On first meeting him one could not fail to be impressed immediately by his drive, initiative and above all, charm. He gave the impression of taking a personal interest in every individual he met particularly in regard to the work they did . . . While Sir Shenton was in the Protectorate CDF grants became available and it is doubtful whether the grants, meagre as they were, would have been made available had it not been for his representations.[43]

Thomas' contribution to development was not so much the level of expansion which took place during his term of office, but rather that expansion took place at all during a severe depression when many other, and normally more wealthy, colonies were forced to retrench staff – a solution which Thomas refused to accept:

> To retrench is in my opinion an unprofitable method of economy unless it can be clearly shown that a post is unnecessary. . . . Retrenchment would be therefore, so far as I personally am concerned, the last resort.[44]

He set a new tone in seeking and securing external development aid and applying it to good advantage. Much of his success stemmed from his determination and optimism: at his first meeting of the legislative council he said, 'I refuse to admit the possibility of failure in a country like this',[45] and at his second:

> the past year has been a period of depression but I confess to a feeling of optimism about the future . . . better days are bound to come . . . and . . . it would be better to prepare for those days now while we have the time, not rashly or extravagantly, but methodically and economically, rather than to adopt an attitude of apathy and despair. It is true that, if we look for it, we can find much to depress us. I prefer to look for that which will encourage us.[46]

He tried also to communicate his enthusiasm to the officials who served with him and to gain the co-operation of all sections of the community, saying, at his third meeting of the legislative council:

> It is the duty of each one of us to make the most of his opportunity . . . For years [the officials] had the bitter experience of seeing their schemes for betterment refused . . . inevitably there was born the feeling that anything will do. And that is a feeling which must be eradicated . . . I know that I can rely on them as a body to give loyal and unstinted support, and I will try to recognize their efforts and base any recommendations on merit, not on seniority . . . for so long as I am here I shall seek – and I expect all officials to seek it also – unofficial advice. . . . No Government can function satisfactorily unless it is stimulated by constructive criticism and reinforced by advice which . . . represents the view of the country as a whole. . . . Much can be done if we only believe

in what we are doing, and I appeal to every one to have faith and to go forward with a brave heart in the work which lies before us.[47]

He was not afraid to badger the British government for financial support for development – making it a principle to ask for a grant 'in every case' rather than a loan – and he argued his case forcefully and persistently, adding 'If the Imperial Treasury considers the arguments which I have put forward to be inadequate, then I shall furnish others: they are here in abundance.'[48] Part of his boldness was based on the additional advantage which he enjoyed of commanding the respect and support of the secretary of state, Lord Passfield.[49] During his three years in Nyasaland (1929–32), he expanded the Civil Service at an average annual rate of 8.3 per cent, from 2623 to 3279 officers, and the annual internal revenue rose from £372,000 to £487,000.

Just as four fallow governorships occupied the years between Johnston and Thomas, so again did four less dynamic governors occupy the years following Thomas' period of office. The first of these was Sir Hubert Young, an officer who had not been a member of the Colonial Service, nor had he previously worked in Africa.[50] He was 47 years of age when appointed. His main task was to introduce the Native Authority system – about which the local officials had been somewhat sceptical and dilatory[51] – and this he did in the short space of less than two years of office in Nyasaland (1932–4); he also indulged his personal interest in aviation, devoting much of his energy and his time to this. He appears to have left little lasting impression on Nyasaland and was much more concerned with what he saw as efficiency and economy than with development and expansion:

> it will not be possible to consider . . . any proposals for new schemes or new appointments unless the proposals themselves are calculated to lead to a reduction in expenditure or are based on a departmental reorganization designed to obtain greater efficiency and economy.[52]

Roy Welensky arrived in Northern Rhodesia as a railway driver at about the time Young moved there as governor and half a century later he remarked of Young, 'We got some very odd exports from Nyasaland.'[53] The Civil Service grew at an average annual rate of only 2.4 per cent, from 3279 to 3437 officers, during his short period as governor, and the annual internal revenue rose from £487,000 to £511,000.

His successor, Sir Harold Kittermaster (1934–9), was remembered mainly for the early, if limited, development of the Native Authority system, for the regulation of emigrant labour, and for the involuntary act of being the only governor of Nyasaland to die in office.[54] Like Sir George Smith, he was 55 years of age when appointed, and his more innovative years were already behind him. After a year in office he told the legislative council that:

> So far as my own policy is concerned I may say that it has been to carry on the policies of my predecessors ... and it seemed to me that the last thing that the Protectorate would require was another new broom.[55]

Which of his very different predecessors, whose policies he proposed to carry on, he had in mind he did not say, but it was unlikely to have been Shenton Thomas who did not believe in automatically following others: 'I must decline to ... participate in a game of follow-my-leader.'[56] Thomas would also have taken a different view of his first full year's budget from that taken by Kittermaster, essentially a pessimist, who went on to say:

> It is an uninspiring work because the prospects ... are not yet sufficiently rosy to justify me in departing from the policy of rigid economy.[57]

He seems to have devoted rather too much of his time and energy to personal and relatively trivial matters: for example, a lengthy and detailed correspondence on whether he should sell his private and virtually unusable car to the government when he retired.[58] He appears to have left little lasting effect on Nyasaland. During his period of office, the Civil Service grew at the slowest rate in the whole of its history, at 0.6 per cent annually, from 3437 to 3534 officers, and the annual internal revenue actually declined, from £511,000 to £506,000.

During his three-year period of gubernatorial office (1939–42), when the Civil Service grew at an annual average rate of 7.4 per cent, from 3534 to 4318 officers, and the annual internal revenue rose from £506,000 to £686,000, Sir Donald Mackenzie Kennedy was much preoccupied with the Second World War. However, it is unlikely that, even if his attention had not been diverted, he would have proved to have been a particularly able governor, responsible for marked accelerated develop-ment, especially since he did not find colonial administrative work particularly exciting but, on the contrary, 'mainly spade work – a hum-drum, pedestrian occupation'.[59] He did not appear to have much of a grasp of what was going on in Nyasaland, although this may have been due, at least in part, to his frequent absences from the protectorate.[60] Nor did he command or enjoy the respect of his officers:

> He is away all the time. He . . . splurges his comments – pithy and very much the great I am – all over documents. . . . Obviously no one has any sense but himself. . . . Whilst most people have some admiration for his keenness and drive there is no startling opinion about his capacity or brains, and a general resentment of his bumptiousness. . . . I doubt if there was ever a Governor who was more cordially detested than DMK. His obvious contempt for his juniors' ability, his constant official sarcasm and his barefaced opportunism are not counterbalanced by his obvious ability.[61]

Nor did his successor, Sir Edmund Richards, who like Bowring had served in Nyasaland a quarter of a century earlier,[62] endear himself to his officers or command their respect. 'He had neither the dignity nor the self-control to command respect – so he didn't get it . . . A common person with a type of hard ability and no imagination on things which did not affect him personally',[63] was the contemporary comment of an officer who worked closely with him at the time of a natural catastrophe – a serious flood – in Zomba in 1946. But a colleague partially explained Richards' moods:

> During his service in Tanganyika he evidently had a serious accident which damaged his back and he periodically had attacks of severe pain which caused him physical and mental pain. When one of these attacks was on him he became morose, unreasonable, rude and sometimes even violent. To . . . disagree with something he said or suggested during one of these attacks infuriated him and more than one . . . official suffered forced retirement. When he was not in pain he was kindly and considerate.[64]

Given this disability, the fact that he assumed office in the middle of the war, and that CDWF grants were very small during his six years of office (1942–8), it is not surprising that Richards did not of his own initiative induce any marked expansion, although the Civil Service did grow from 4318 in 1942 to 4803 officers in 1947, his last full year of office, but at an annual average rate of only 1.9 per cent, and the annual internal revenue grew from £686,000 to £1,310,000. He was said to have 'been affected with that not unknown disease "after-the-war-is-over" [and] left practically no infrastructure behind him'. A very senior professional officer subsequently described him as 'useless', and the wife of a particularly senior official recalled that he was 'just plain stupid'.[65]

This, then, was the background to the country in which Colby had now arrived as governor. It was a relatively small country, somewhat off the beaten track, with scenery, climate and soils varying from the excellent to the indifferent or hostile. Logistically the country was an awkward, elongated shape and this, with its broken terrain and distance from a seaport – in a foreign country – presented severe transport and communication problems. Economically, the country relied overwhelmingly on agriculture: peasant subsistence maize farming with an export economy based almost exclusively on tobacco and tea, much of the value of both being the result of European enterprise on alienated land. The commercial and industrial sector was minuscule. The country was heavily populated – and increasingly so – and the soils upon which the African population lived were susceptible to heavy erosion. Few of Colby's predecessors had been development-minded, the annual revenue and development funding were severely limited, the railway was a depressing financial burden, and the Civil Service was both small and not truly development-orientated: less than a quarter were in the natural resources departments and fewer than one-seventh were in the works and communications departments, whilst more than a third were in the law and order, central administration and finance departments. It was, in short, a country sorely in need of development – as Colby later described it, 'a country which was overdue for a little attention' – and he was determined to develop it. What was to be his strategy for doing so and how successful was the implementation of that strategy?

4· Development Strategy

'So that we may live better and happier lives.'

In the preceding chapter, we gave an outline of Nyasaland's natural resources and production; it was a country whose economy, as Colby said, was 'overdue for attention'. From the outset, rapid development was his major, virtually all-consuming, concern, and he made the objective of this concern clear to all, and particularly to African audiences:

> I am determined that everything possible shall be done to develop our country . . . so that we may live better and happier lives in it.
> I wish to . . . make . . . progress very much quicker and thus bring nearer the day when you can enjoy a prosperity and general standard of living far higher than that which you enjoy at present.[1]

His reference to 'better and happier lives' reflected his feeling – remembered long afterwards – when driving from Limbe to Zomba on the day of his arrival, that the people he saw along the roadside looked drab and not particularly cheerful: 'we were struck by the glum faces . . . no smiling or cheering, quite different from West Africa'.[2]

Although he never articulated his strategy for development as a single coherent concept, he did articulate its component parts which, when brought together, constitute such a concept.

Soon after his arrival, Colby spoke of the development plan, prepared in 1945 – which to modern eyes appears piecemeal and unambitious – and he explained that it would not be possible for the existing 'machinery of Government' to digest the plan and that it would therefore be necessary progressively to improve that machinery:

if the development plans . . . are to be successfully carried out . . .
there must be a considerable increase in Government staff and in
Government services.[3]

In a country with severely limited financial, entrepreneurial and mana-
gerial resources, the state itself was the only realistic medium through
which sufficient development could be generated. Colby's view – given
in respect of trading facilities but applicable to other forms of economic
enterprise – was that:

It is preferable that such facilities should be provided by private
enterprise [but] when faced with the choice between public enterprise and no enterprise, there can be no doubt as to the right
decision.[4]

If development on the scale upon which he was intent was to be achieved,
the machinery of government – an expression which he frequently used
in his early days as governor – would be essential to effect it, although
he clearly recognized the importance of private enterprise.

A year after his arrival he returned to this question. In what he
considered the most important section of his budget speech, he said
that:

lack of funds . . . during the last generation has resulted in the
machinery of Government being seriously deficient, and I firmly
believe that until [it] is put on to an adequate basis . . . we shall
never be able to develop the resources of this country to the full . . .
[The] money must come . . . from increased production, and it
is . . . my intention to do everything within my power to secure a
substantial overall increase in production during the next few years.[5]

Since Nyasaland lacked economic mineral deposits and its manufacturing
was limited to processing agricultural products, increased production
meant increased agricultural production (especially production by Africans since they occupied 95 per cent of the land but contributed only
40 per cent to the value of exports),[6] and Colby emphasized the significance of this:

It will be primarily on the improvement of agricultural practice and in particular the adoption of modern methods of soil conservation that the achievement of higher living standards will depend.

Having said that the main production departments were the natural resources departments, he went on to say that:

> social service departments, such as Medical and Education, also have an important bearing on the problem since fitter and better educated men will be better able to tackle the production problems in the field.[7]

He was also aware that shifting the balance from a subsistence economy to a cash economy, with increased production and exports, required significant incentives, and that increased incomes were unlikely to provide these unless consumption goods were available for purchase. Four months after his arrival, he told the chamber of commerce that he found it paradoxical that so many Nyasalanders left their country to work elsewhere whilst there was a labour shortage internally, and that more people would enter employment locally if the commercial community provided 'consumer goods in adequate variety', since 'harder work is bound up with incentives': he was very clear that increased production could be achieved only by harder work by all.[8] He concluded that trading facilities had not kept pace with increased purchasing power and that they must expand, if necessary by direct gubernatorial intervention in granting trading licences.

Several years later, he outlined the problems he had faced on taking office and explained that his first task had been to examine the needs of 'this country which was at such an early stage of its development', and particularly its public utility needs:

> The first thing we found was that there had never been any loan money spent . . . except on the railway and communications to the outside world. As a result . . . public utilities were . . . almost completely non-existent . . . the telephone system was limited to the south of the territory. It was hopelessly overloaded and completely out of date.
>
> Until we had electricity, water, roads and so forth there obviously could not be any progress. In other words, before we could contemplate any extension of social services we had to create conditions

favourable to the expansion of the revenue which would pay for these services . . .

[Furthermore], investment . . . in public utilities in Africa has the effect of attracting a considerable amount of private enterprise . . .

[I have] concentrated entirely on economic development . . . quite deliberately in order to give emphasis to what I believe is a fact that without it nothing else is possible . . . [It] will do an enormous lot to raise living standards and make further development possible.[9]

Although he rarely made public his views on the need for good race relations and a stable political environment, he was well aware of the need in order that economic development could take place. Soon after his arrival, he said publicly that nothing could be more disastrous to an African country than racial disharmony, which 'makes any developments or progress impossible'.[10] Later he acknowledged the part which friendly race relations had played in his development success:

Without the spirit of tolerance and friendliness which exists between all communities here, the progress which has been made during the past few years in the development and welfare of our country would never have been achieved.[11]

It is also the case, as Colby recognized, that a flourishing economy renders political unrest less likely. In 1950, proposals to exclude Nyasaland from a federation of the Rhodesias were not only welcomed by Africans but were also received with equanimity by Europeans, who felt that with recent economic development and 'with a planned future in sight we are quite happy as we are'.[12]

From Colby's various pronouncements, a clear if inevitably somewhat complex picture of his ultimate objective and his strategic means of attaining it emerges. His objective was to raise living standards so that the people of Nyasaland could live better, more prosperous and happier lives. He proposed to accomplish this through the machinery of government directly by four means: improving social services, raising individual incomes, extending public utilities, and expanding the supply of consumer goods. Social services were to be improved, eventually, by increasing public revenue. Individual incomes were to be raised by increasing agricultural production and stimulating private enterprise. Public utilities and works were to be extended by securing loans and grants. The supply of consumer goods was to be expanded through the mechanism of trading licences and by stimulating private enterprise. Increased public revenue would also be secured through some of these factors: agricultural production, private enterprise, and individual incomes. Private enterprise would be encouraged by improved public utilities. Increased agricultural production, which was at the very heart of his strategy, would be achieved through adopting modern methods brought about by:

a far more effective supervision of farming methods and planting programmes . . . by promulgating and enforcing elementary agricultural laws [and] by setting up marketing boards

and by a healthier and better educated workforce secured by improved social services – and each of these would be accomplished by Civil Service expansion, which would be secured from increased public revenue. The various components – especially agricultural production, private enterprise and the maintenance of public utilities and social services – would be ensured by a peaceful political environment.

The starting point of this multi-faceted strategy was, as Colby said so soon after his arrival, the improvement of the machinery of government both in size and – especially in relation to the senior team – in quality. He not only gave early warning of his general intentions, but also clearly indicated the areas in which Civil Service expansion should primarily occur: the 'production' departments – directly and principally the natural resources departments; indirectly and secondarily the social services departments. He was a little less clear publicly about the impact on the works and communications departments of expanding public utilities – in which term he included water, electricity, telecommunications, roads, and airfields – and he was usually silent about the effect which maintaining a peaceful political environment would have on the law and order departments. We now need to consider each of these groups of departments in turn, and a brief indication of the general expansion of the Civil Service and its major component parts will provide a framework.

During the eight years of Colby's term of office, the Civil Service more than doubled in size from 5112 to 10,693.[13] The largest increase (37.3 per cent of the total) was in the natural resources group, and the second largest (32.9 per cent) was in the works and communications group, whilst the third largest (17 per cent) was in the law and order group. Natural resources, slightly smaller than social services when Colby arrived, rose to become the largest group by the time he left; works and communications rose from third to second place; law and order rose from fourth to third place; whilst social services, which received only 0.14 per cent of the 1948–56 increase, fell from first place to fourth. These changes closely reflected Colby's development priorities. Over half of the increase went to only three, out of 30, departments: public works (25 per cent), police (16 per cent) and agriculture (14 per cent).

Within the natural resources group, Colby saw the agricultural department as the most important since 'the initiative for the development of the Protectorate's economy lay with agriculture . . . and the greatest potential lay . . . in the development of African agriculture'.[14] The basic agricultural policy aims were three-fold – conservation of natural resources, production of ample good food, and increased and more economical production of cash crops – and each was pursued vigorously.[15] Very considerable impetus and determination was given to this vigorous pursuit by the severe drought and food shortage of 1948–50 which 'sharply revealed the vulnerability of the country's livelihood to adverse weather'.[16]

Colby was determined both that increased agricultural production and exports should be at the hub of his development strategy and also that never again would hunger be permitted to divert the country's attention, energies and resources from the prime task of economic development. From the earliest days of his governorship – as we shall see in a later chapter – he had warned of the distinct possibility of famine, but he and the country had not had enough time to ward it off.[17] Now his resolve was strengthened and he insisted on firm action: the basic policy should be implemented with greater vigour and much more coercion. Although aware of the dangers and limitations of dragooning[18] – 'the work is hard and . . . a fruitful ground for agitators' – he used, or permitted his officers to use, extensive compulsion and prosecution to ensure compliance with both the conservation sections of the Natural Resources Ordinance (which he amended and tightened up in 1949) and the Native Authority early planting legislation as the 'surest safeguard against unfavourable weather':

The advantages of [soil conservation] had been advocated for several years . . . but the response was disturbingly small and Government concluded that if it waited for the slow enlightenment of education to change age-old practices the loss of soil in the interim might well prejudice the whole future well-being of the Protectorate. It was felt that a measure of compulsion was necessary for the common good.[19]

The more vigorous and firm approach necessitated a much larger staff, and the number of established posts in the Department of Agriculture rose sharply. The three policy aims required a substantial field staff to encourage and compel soil conservation and crop production, and the general field staff expanded rapidly by 95 per cent. All hierarchical levels of field staff increased, but the greatest growth (137 per cent) was at the lower levels where agricultural instructors were employed. These were the officers most closely in touch with producers and they consequently played a crucial part in Colby's development strategy.

The difficulties of training and supervising this rapid expansion resulted in large numbers of field officers with less than adequate education, training, experience and supervision. This may have contributed to the somewhat over-zealous way in which Colby's agricultural legislation and policy were enforced, but throughout his period of office the vigorous and firm policy remained unabated. In May 1955, the determination, particularly in respect of soil conservation and early preparation of gardens, was reiterated:

> rigid compulsory powers have been given . . . to carry out Government's firm policy . . . This work is . . . unpopular and an easy target for agitation; but it must proceed.[20]

By the end of his term of office, Colby was able to report the 'complete . . . conversion of cultivation methods . . . including the conservation of over three-quarters of a million acres of arable land by means of protective works'. It was a policy which could be implemented only if agricultural practice in the field could be adequately supervised, and this could be accomplished only if the Department of Agriculture staff expanded rapidly, as it did, by 126 per cent (from 628 to 1417) between 1948 and 1956. As late as June 1955, Colby wrote to the director of agriculture who was then on leave in Britain:

> I hope you are getting some promising young men for production work: we are short and could do with twice the numbers we have. If you can put your hands on more than the authorised establishment please let me know because I will see that the necessary authority is forthcoming.[21]

Largely as a result of the expansion, the department's annual recurrent expenditure rose from £17,132 in 1948 to £314,054 in 1956.

If Colby was to shift the balance from a subsistence economy to a cash economy – which was centrally implied in his development strategy – producers needed both the backing of applied research (the recurrent expenditure on which rose from £26,000 in 1948 to £73,000 in 1956, together with £300,000 of capital investment from CDWF sources) and also to be assured of a continuing market for their produce at fair and reasonably steady prices, with an efficient organization to buy it. Here his Nigerian experience as director of supplies was at its most valuable.[22] The Nyasaland government had earlier recognized the importance of African-grown crop marketing but had believed that the solution was to develop co-operative societies. Whilst the co-operative movement did develop, and the number of societies increased from 44 (with a membership of 1903) in 1948 to 81 (with a membership of 6075) in 1956,[23] Colby placed much greater emphasis on larger scale, monopolistic, marketing mechanisms.

The expatriate plantation crops already had an adequate marketing system catering for the relatively small number of producers: tea was auctioned in London, tobacco was sold at local markets, and tung was handled by a statutory marketing board. In contrast, the marketing services for the very large number of small-scale African producers were 'piecemeal, inadequate and too short-term in outlook'.[24] The Native Tobacco Board, created in 1926, was unable to prevent bewildering price fluctuations; cotton was purchased on behalf of the government on an annual price policy; miscellaneous crops were purchased by licensed private buyers; and the Maize Control Board, created in 1946, was in effect a consumers' bulk-purchasing organization rather than a producers' marketing organization. The common weakness was instability, especially in prices. Colby sought to remedy this by creating monopoly marketing boards, for cotton in 1951, for maize, peanuts and pulses in 1952, and then by combining them and the African Tobacco Board in 1956 into a single organization, the Agricultural Produce Marketing Board, of which the director of agriculture was made chairman in order to ensure close co-operation between research, production and marketing.[25] The board established cushioning funds with a proportion of the trading surpluses in profitable years, and withdrew from them for price support in unfavourable years. Marketing became the key of a system based on inducement prices paid to growers and on buying for the export market; surpluses provided reserves against famine and the quantities purchased were not limited by internal demand.[26]

His intention in increasing the agricultural staff, closely supervising agricultural practice, rigorously enforcing agricultural laws, and creating marketing boards was to increase agricultural production and exports as a direct and immediate means of increasing individual incomes and public revenue in order generally to raise living standards. A measure of his success can be obtained, therefore, from the changes in purchases of exportable surpluses from 25,000 short tons worth £4m in 1948 to over 85,000 short tons worth £7m in 1955. The weight of crops exported tripled over the same period. Colby attributed these increases almost entirely to improved farming methods and to the role played by the marketing boards.[27]

Colby's intention in improving the social services – education and health – was less immediate and less direct. In 1946, the Post-War Development Committee had expressed its view that:

> progress in . . . education . . . was an essential foundation to all [their] development plans [and] improvements in . . . general health . . . must, in conjunction with wider education, form the basis of . . . development and progress.[28]

This view was reinforced by the 1947 fiscal survey which emphasized the 'vicious circle of malnutrition, disease, lack of education . . . low standards of living [and] low production'.[29] Colby himself, soon after his arrival, publicly acknowledged that the social services had 'an important bearing on the problem' of production.[30] Yet, whilst he readily saw that improved social services would directly, although neither quickly nor obviously, improve the standard of living and lead to 'better and happier lives', and that indirectly a healthier and better educated population would produce more, he also clearly saw that only through increased production would the funds become available with which significantly to improve them. A degree of social services improvement was therefore important to the production drive upon which revenue earning capacity depended for further improvement of those services. Much beyond this, however, he was not prepared to go: his conviction was that interest should be 'concentrated . . . on economic development [for] without it nothing else is possible';[31] social development should take second place to economic development until the latter could support the former.

Four developments in education were important. First, in order to cater for the increasing number of expatriate officials – with families – upon whose skills a major part of his development strategy depended, Colby opened three expatriate primary schools and staffed them with civil servants.[32] Second, he opened a teacher-training centre, again staffed with civil servants, so that the general education system might expand in order to produce the better-educated workforce at which he aimed.[33] Third, he added to the two non-government secondary schools, which 'only offered arts subjects', a further school, financed and staffed by the government, and insisted on including building, carpentry, mechanics, metalwork and commerce in its curriculum.[34] Fourth, to reinforce this last step, he created a government trade school to conduct three-year courses in carpentry and building.[35] Each of these four innovations contributed to the hub of his development strategy – increased production. The country could not afford a liberal, arts-based education for education's sake.[36] He nonetheless took pleasure in the educational progress which was made:

> In 1948 there were ten primary schools in the country; in 1956 there were 1000. [Senior Primary Schools had increased from 9 to 148.] In 1948 less than 400 pupils reached standard 6; in 1956 . . . 1600. In 1948 there were only four girls in Standard 6; in 1956 there were 280. There was only one secondary school in 1948; now there are five. We have increased the number of teachers in training six times. Our expenditure has correspondingly increased.[37]

His final sentence suggests a certain suppressed resentment. Annual recurrent expenditure by the Department of Education rose from £126,201 in 1948 to £306,466 in 1956 – not a great deal less than what he spent each year on the Department of Agriculture – as the staff rose from 29 to 252.

Although expenditure by the Medical Department rose roughly in line with that of education – from £133,136 in 1948 to £266,000 in 1953 – its staff declined, from 1070 to 1025 (although the contraction was confined to the subordinate class, and the professionally qualified staff – doctors and nurses – increased slightly). Expansion was restrained by three principal factors. First was Colby's view that economic development must precede social development. In a retirement address, he concentrated at length on the economic aspects but, whilst devoting some time also to education, he mentioned medical matters only once: 'I could continue in other directions, such as health', but he said no more.[38] Second, the government medical services were already well developed relative to other government services: at the end of the Second World War, the Medical Department consumed 12 per cent of the government's recurrent expenditure and for over a decade had been the largest spending department; since 1924 it had also been the department with the largest staff.[39] This lessened the persuasive force of any pressures to divert resources into the Medical Department. Third, the missions provided a substantial medical service so that, again, pressures on Colby to expand the government's own services were readily resistible in the short term. There may have been two other factors. If – as became the case in 1953 – the Medical Department was to become a federal government responsibility, Colby may have felt that there was little point in expending as much on it as he would have done if it were to remain a protectorate responsibility. Also, since it is very much more difficult, especially over a short period, to demonstrate output improvements in health than in crop production or even in education, he may have felt that medical services, despite their importance, need not occupy a very high position on his list of priorities.

In respect of infrastructural development, Colby's view was that 'until we [have] electricity, water, roads and so forth there obviously [can] not be any progress'; creating these public utilities was the responsibility of the works and communications group of departments, most importantly the Public Works Department and the Department of Posts and Telecommunications. The developments which Colby achieved in posts and telecommunications are dealt with in a later chapter, as are the steps which he took in respect of the railways which, although vital to the development drive, were privately owned and, as a consequence, largely beyond his control.

The development thrust placed three types of responsibilities upon the Public Works Department. First was the need to construct residential and operational accommodation for the expanding Civil Service; so serious was this need that Colby gave up the use of the governor's lodge in Blantyre as a small contribution to easing the acute lack of residential accommodation.[40] Second was the need to build or improve roads and bridges for transporting the equipment and personnel used in promoting development and the produce resulting from that development. Third was the need to construct buildings for public utilities such as electricity and water supplies, airfields and telecommunications.

In order to cope with the volume of operations, the Public Works Department, under pressure from Colby, broke tradition and recruited relatively large numbers on temporary appointments; contracted public works to private firms (for the first time on anything other than a trivial scale); and increased its staff from 504 in 1948 to 1462 in 1956. An Electrical Services Department was hived off in 1950 and by 1956 had a separate staff of 479.[41] Water supplies continued to be the responsibility of the department and of two statutory municipal bodies. Significantly as a result of the increase in staffing, the annual recurrent expenditure of the Public Works and Electrical Services departments rose from £189,623 in 1948 to £448,006 in 1956.

Simply increasing recurrent expenditure, however, even if largely devoted to personnel, is not sufficient to bring about substantial infrastructural development, which necessarily incurs considerable capital investment. Funds for capital investment are much more appropriately secured through borrowing or from grants than from surpluses on annual revenue; in any case, Nyasaland had little surplus on annual revenue. Colby quickly set about obtaining British government permission to raise loans on the London money market, and badgering them for increased allocations from the Colonial Development and Welfare Fund, especially from an unallocated reserve of the fund which one of his assistant secretaries discovered existed 'to give a boost to the economies of some of the poorer territories'.[42] By the end of 1949, he was able to tell the legislative council:

> Some time ago proposals were submitted . . . for the raising of a loan to finance further development of the Territory. I am glad to say that the Secretary of State has now given his approval to the raising of a loan of three million pounds . . . for financing telegraph and telephone development, electricity and water supplies. [Also] the Secretary of State has approved my request for an additional allocation of half a million pounds from the Colonial Development and Welfare Vote [to] be applied principally to road development and other projects designed to hasten economic development [such as telecommunications and aviation].[43]

Colby was successful in securing CDWF grants totalling £4,383,000 between 1948 and 1956.

In these various ways he expanded his public works staff and secured the loan and grant finance with which to develop the country's public utilities and public works. His success can be measured from the fact that during his period of office the mileage of tarmacadam roads increased from 4 to 217; the mileage of internal trunk telephone lines increased from 364 to 4300; the kilowatt capacity of generating installations increased from 755 to 5742; annual air passengers increased from 4718 to 40,889; and air freight and air mail increased from 135,322 to 315,322 kilos.[44]

Thus did Colby improve the infrastructural public utilities and public works which his development strategy required, both directly to increase living standards and indirectly to attract private investment which, via taxation, would boost the public revenue needed to improve social services as a further means to higher living standards.

Although usually silent about the need for a stable political environment in which development could take place and to which private enterprise would be attracted, Colby was far from uninterested in, or insensitive to, political matters, as later chapters on the African press, Africans on private estates, and federation will show. In July 1948, well over a decade before Macmillan's 'wind of change' speeches in Accra and Cape Town, he said in a public address that it was inevitable that the great development and political awakening that had taken place in West Africa would take place in Nyasaland. He warned that they must be ready to receive the impact that was sweeping Africa and that they could not expect political conditions to remain unchanged.[45]

Ten days later, he devoted the greater part of an address to the chamber of commerce to economic development. However, in his peroration, he pointedly concentrated on politics, saying that elsewhere in Africa great changes had taken place and were taking place and they were sometimes accompanied by 'very uncomfortable manifestations'. He forecast that changes would take place in Nyasaland and added that 'it is only a question of time before we receive their impact. . . . The political awakening of Africa is something irresistible.'[46]

He knew full well that if other development – economic, social or infrastructural – were to proceed apace, he would need racial harmony and internal peace, since conflict and unrest would divert the country's resources, energy and attention; expatriates would be disinclined to work in the country, and as a consequence capital and skills would seep away from it. The maintenance of a peaceful political environment was the responsibility principally of the police force.

Initially, the expansion of the force from 539 at the time of Colby's arrival – partly as a response to expatriate pressures[47] – arose not from civil disorder needs, but from 'the necessity for improved measures for the detection of crime and traffic control'.[48] The establishment was increased to 565 in 1948 but Colby, influenced by recent disturbances in Aden, the Gold Coast and Nigeria, quickly decided that greater increases were required 'to put the general internal security arrangements of the protectorate on a sound footing'.[49] Consequently, the establishment was raised by 30 per cent to 736 in 1949, and again to 788 by 1952, and 'a force of Special Constables' was created 'for the purpose of reinforcing the existing Police Force in the event of a threatened disturbance or an actual outbreak of disturbance in any locality'.[50] He also created the Special Branch, which was to be of very considerable value to him and his successors, and he enacted legislation enabling him to call on the assistance of police forces in neighbouring British territories.[51]

In 1953, the almost unbroken history of internal peace ended as the introduction of the federation met with strong African opposition. The order in council creating the federation, issued on 1 August 1953, was preceded by civil disobedience and the deposing or resigning of a number of Native Authorities; it was followed by riots in which eleven Africans were killed, many were injured, and police reinforcements were brought in from Northern and Southern Rhodesia and Tanganyika to help restore law and order. These disturbances induced Colby to further strengthen the police force considerably and rapidly through three measures so that 'no vacuum should occur resulting in further disturbances'.[52] First, he authorized an immediate increase in staffing. The establishment for 1953 was 863, but supplementary appropriations during the year raised it to 1100. Second, he created a police mobile force, generally known as the 'riot squad', recruited largely from former soldiers, 'for the purpose of dealing with situations which require police action at short notice'. Third, he intensified the recruitment of special constables, whose numbers rose during 1953 from 200 to 922.[53]

Whilst peace was soon restored, Colby and his advisers were aware that they had been unprepared for disorder on the scale experienced, and decided on a 'progressive expansion of the Force towards effective security strength'.[54] The strength rose annually to 1453 in 1956.

Save for a few weeks in 1953, at the time of the introduction of the federation, Colby was able to secure and maintain a political environment sufficiently stable and peaceful for the economic development upon which he was so intent to proceed apace. It is significant that the steps which he took prior to 1953 to expand the police force were sufficient to enable him to cope with the disturbances in that year without resorting to the declaration of a state of emergency, even though he was pressed by his security advisers to make such a declaration.[55]

In addition to expanding the staff of the various Civil Service departments and securing loans and grants, there was a third component of Colby's development strategy: the use of trading licences to stimulate private enterprise and increase the availability of consumption goods, which would directly improve living standards and indirectly improve them by providing incentives to greater production. Two examples of this component are available to us, both concerned with the governor's personal and unorthodox intervention in the granting of trading licences.

In 1950, Colby answered criticism of his granting trading licences to a public body, the Colonial Development Corporation, which recognized that if it were to attract the large labour force which its agricultural projects required, it would have to ensure that trade goods incentives were available. Since private entrepreneurs were not providing these, the corporation applied for licences to trade itself. Colby readily agreed and threatened the private traders with further extensions of this practice:

> the extension of their activities will depend largely on the action of private enterprise. The C.D.C. have no desire to compete . . . where private enterprise provides an adequate service, but if that service is inadequate then they will provide the necessary facilities and in the interest of the development of this territory and particularly of increased production I shall give them every encouragement.[56]

He took a similar view, although more for political than for economic reasons, over the private sector's failure to provide a newspaper for African readers.[57] Both these issues brought enormous criticism from the expatriate business community, which saw Colby's moves as 'the thin end of nationalisation'.[58] In both cases he stuck to his guns; he won the former battle and lost the latter.

The second example of Colby's use of licensing to ensure the availability of consumption goods at a reasonable price is one of even more personal and unorthodox gubernatorial intervention.[59] He became concerned that young government officers in the rural areas drank spirits rather than beer on social occasions and learned that the reason was purely economic: Castle Breweries of Salisbury, Southern Rhodesia, had a complete monopoly on beer, and its price, especially on the outstations, was consequently prohibitive. Colby invited a British brewery director to visit Nyasaland and asked him to establish a brewery locally. The director agreed, provided an exclusive five-year licence was granted to enable the company to recover its initial capital outlay. Colby readily accepted this proviso and when the attorney-general advised that the law as it stood did not provide for such exclusive licences, the governor instructed him to draft amending legislation:

> The bill was published at 9.00 a.m. one day and by noon the same day Castle beer could be purchased throughout Nyasaland at Salisbury prices! The bill was never enacted!

Colby had in mind the effect of high beer prices not only on young government officers, but also on African cultivators who were beginning to earn sufficient income from their produce to spend part of it on alcohol, and he preferred them to consume commercially brewed beer rather than either spirits or traditional beer brewed from maize, which could instead be devoted to a fuller diet or to exports.

A measure of the success achieved in making consumer goods available may be obtained from the fact that the value of imports increased considerably between 1948 and 1953: sugar by 502 per cent, footwear by 96 per cent, vehicles and vehicle parts by 82 per cent, and cotton goods by 10 per cent.

At the same time, there was a substantial increase in the number and type of secondary industries established:

> Prior to 1950 the local consumer market had not grown sufficiently to encourage local investment in the manufacture of consumer goods. . . . The only manufacturing of any significance was confined to the tea and tobacco industries . . .
>
> The early 1950s saw the establishment of a modern factory producing soaps and edible oils (1951), [a plywood factory in 1951], the development of a small clothing industry (1953), a considerable expansion of the bakery industry and the introduction of tyre-retreading and vulcanising (1952).[60]

Whilst it is not easy to attribute increases in private investment to any particular cause – for example, the infrastructural attractions of public utilities or the expansion of consumer demand – from whatever cause, private investment increased, as Colby wished. An indication of this can be gained from the fact that public revenue from general trading licences increased by 57 per cent between 1948 and 1956, and from liquor licences by 26 per cent. Also, the contribution which income from unincorporated enterprise made to the domestic product rose from £3.2m in 1950 to £6.2m in 1956, and the contribution of the net operating profit of incorporated companies rose from £1.7m in 1950 to £2.4m in 1956.

Crucial to Colby's strategy, as we have noted, was the need to increase public revenue. Several of the strategy facets were aimed at this – improving public utilities, expanding private enterprise, increasing agricultural production, and raising individual incomes – and two major facets depended on it: expanding the Civil Service and improving social services. The extent to which he was successful may be gauged from the broad details of the protectorate's ordinary revenue from 1948 to 1956: income tax increased by 511 per cent, African tax increased by 164 per cent, customs duty increased by 129 per cent, post and telegraph services revenue increased by 201 per cent, and overall the protectorate's ordinary revenue increased by 248 per cent from £1.625m to £5.664m.

This chapter has examined the nature and components of Colby's development strategy and outlined the extent to which it was successful. A careful and perceptive observer of events in the post-war decade in Nyasaland has said:

Until after the Second World War no development whatever took place in the country and it had no legs to stand on in the money markets of the world. Sir Geoffrey Colby then came on the scene and by his drive infused new blood into the torpid body.[61]

Some economic and political aspects of the more important parts of the development thrust, such as posts and telecommunications, food supplies, land and federation, will be examined more closely in later chapters, but it is necessary before then to deal with the general way in which Colby operated – his working life – and the way in which he interacted with others, officials and non-officials, both European and African.

5· Working Life

'Nothing happens until a decision is made.'

Colby's typical day started with paperwork in his study at 7.00 a.m., half an hour before his private secretary and his stenographer arrived.[1] He took breakfast at about 8.00 a.m., returned to his study half an hour later and spent the remainder of the morning in meetings with senior officials, principally the chief secretary, the financial secretary, heads of departments and, less frequently, leaders of the non-official community. He broke for lunch from 12.30 to 2.00 p.m. and then returned to the office to carry on with paperwork or further meetings. Following a brief afternoon tea, he worked for a further hour from 5.30 to 6.30 p.m. Drinks parties, from 6.00 to 7.00 p.m., and official dinners from 7.00 to 10.30 p.m., frequently occupied his evening hours. On other evenings, if work pressed, he worked for an hour or so in his study. On Saturdays, he worked from 7.00 a.m. to 12.00 noon, and on Sundays, unless official guests were staying at Government House, from 9.00 a.m. to noon. He rarely went to church because he worked on Sundays, although Lady Colby regularly attended morning service. He often worked 14 hours a day, six or even six and a half days a week. A senior colleague has said that he worked 'twelve hours a day, 350 days a year'.[2]

From the very time of his arrival in Nyasaland, he manifested his enormous capacity for work and his impatience with others who were in the habit of working less hard: 'he was a workaholic and had no time for anyone who wasn't'.[3] He arrived, as we have seen, on Easter Sunday afternoon, in somewhat inauspicious circumstances, after ten months' leave, but at long last had arrived as governor. He was 'raring' to get on with the job. His astonishment and frustration were monumental when he learned that on the following day, Easter Monday, the secretariat and commercial firms were closed for the day![4] Indeed the ceremony of swearing in the new governor at Government House was not to take place until 11.00 a.m. on the Tuesday morning. Before the ceremony, he issued instructions that a memorandum was to be prepared setting out a complete schedule of all public holidays in the protectorate and how this schedule compared with that of neighbouring territories; the outcome eventually was amending legislation to the Public Holidays Ordinance restricting the number of holidays.[5]

Over the following years he was frequently pressed by non-officials, especially the chamber of commerce, who made direct comparisons with neighbouring British territories, to increase the number of public holidays. He never gave in to these pressures, always responding that if businessmen and other employers cared to give their employees a holiday, it was for them to do so.[6] Nonetheless, he did himself declare occasional public holidays, and he was prepared to be humorous about hard work with those who shared his energy: for example to the clerk of the executive council, who appeared at a council meeting disfigured after being hit in the face by a cricket ball during an international match the previous Sunday, he remarked with a twinkle in his eye, 'That will teach you to work instead of playing cricket on a Sunday.'[7]

The governor's study, or office, was in Government House and his staff comprised a private secretary, who was also aide-de-camp – as Colby himself had been when first appointed to Northern Nigeria and the lieutenant-governor's office – and a stenographer. All communications with and from the governor went through the private secretary's office, including telephone calls. Papers were conveyed by a messenger on a bicycle three or four times a day between the secretariat and Government House in wooden despatch boxes sealed with a lock to which the secretariat registry officer and the private secretary each had a key. The private secretary opened the boxes immediately they arrived, checked that the papers were in order and took them through to the governor, later returning them to the boxes and sending them back to the secretariat.

Colby worked fast and normally dealt with papers the same day that they arrived. He dictated in a fluent and concise style to the stenographer, who then typed them using a red ribbon or, if Colby was working out of normal working hours (which was frequently the case in the early mornings, in the evenings, or at weekends), he wrote the replies in longhand in red ink. If matters occurred to him when he did not have the file before him, he wrote notes on pieces of paper a few inches

square which his officials later pasted into the files.[8] He used numerous
abbreviations, some of which were well known and a few others which
he made up himself. Scarcely ever did he correct or alter a minute
which he wrote. He usually wrote short minutes in longhand, but
detailed statements of his views and drafts requiring circulation were
usually dictated and then typed. Most letters to non-officials were drafted by the private secretary, after obtaining Colby's instructions, as
were notes of meetings. He made numerous alterations of wording and
presentation to documents drafted by others for his signature, cutting
down on verbosity and sharpening the clarity of the essential points,
especially if the letters or despatches were addressed to the Colonial
Office; such documents not only went out over his signature but they
also went out in his style.

In his early days, Colby asked to see complete files – for example,
those dealing with Africans on private estates and the Nyasaland railways
– or detailed and careful summaries of them, but soon, having a quick
grasp of essentials and able to handle large volumes of work, he knew
the history of most of the more important matters with which he had
to deal.[9] He normally dealt with issues on paper but if he thought any
points required discussion he asked the private secretary to arrange a
meeting, usually immediately, with the head of department or other
official concerned. On really pressing and important matters he would
speak with the chief secretary by telephone. If any matter lagged he
quickly wrote a minute demanding action or explanation. 'His effect on
the Civil Service was formidable. The Secretariat and heads of departments trembled at the sight of the spate of trenchant red minutes that
passed from Government House, urging them to do this, or asking why
they had not done that. One felt his finger on every pulse.'[10] Once he
was sure that he was adequately informed, he was quick to make up
his mind and reach a decision. Although he thoroughly examined the
background and detail of very important issues and occasionally called
for detailed background papers, he believed that deep research by others
into a matter was often an excuse for delay and he frequently backed
his own hunches in reaching decisions. His view on the complexity of
gubernatorial work was that 'a Governor's task is not difficult provided he
is prepared to make decisions because nothing happens until a decision is
made'.[11] In the case of a few complicated and very important issues,
Colby used a technique which he developed in Nigeria: he would second
an assistant secretary for a period of perhaps three months to thoroughly

research the matter and prepare a report, which he himself would later turn into a full minute or a despatch.[12]

Fixed and important points in Colby's working life were the fort-nightly meetings of the executive council, which comprised the governor as president, the chief secretary, the financial secretary, the attorney-general, the secretary for African affairs, the director of agriculture (a personal, and not *ex officio*, appointment to council made by Colby), and two non-official members, for most of his time M. P. Barrow and G. G. S. J. Hadlow. These meetings were held in the council chamber in the secretariat building, usually in the morning, and rarely lasted longer than two hours.[13] In advance of meetings, the private secretary drafted the agenda on the governor's instructions and circulated notes on each item. These, with a precis paper on each item, prepared by secretariat officers, were circulated a day or two before each meeting; by hand to official members, and by police despatch rider to non-official members.[14]

Colby prepared himself thoroughly before each meeting of the execu-tive council and discussed any controversial item with the non-official members and with the officials principally concerned. In particularly delicate or important cases, he arranged to spend a weekend with the Barrows or Hadlows at their homes, going through the questions, explaining the details and giving the reasons for government's proposals. On these occasions, senior officials might be invited to tea to help in the discussions.[15] The constitution did not leave much room for delegation – for example, to ministers – nor did he exploit this small margin a great deal; but – like Shenton Thomas who declared that he would always seek non-official advice and expect his officials to do likewise – he was at particular pains to carry the non-officials with him, even though with a large official majority the temptation could have existed to steam-roller items through council. Only once was he known to be late in arriving for a council meeting: 'when a test match between England and Australia had reached too critical a stage for him to forsake his wireless!'[16]

He was also keen to streamline the council proceedings, and when the private secretary asked after an early meeting under Colby if he would like a tray of tea to be arranged for members after about an hour and a half, he said that it would only encourage them to settle down and prolong the meeting. Tea was not served! Only two months after his arrival, he prepared a note which members accepted for 'accelerating the business of the executive council'.[17] Thereafter, for relatively routine matters Colby asked for written opinions in advance of meetings so that these could be incorporated into the minutes without being mentioned at the meetings unless any member indicated that he wished to speak on the subject.

Acceleration, however, was never allowed to diminish the thoroughness of consideration by council of agenda items, and Colby was particularly thorough in respect of his exercise of the prerogative of mercy: the confirming or commuting of death sentences.[18] The sentencing judge submitted the records to council and members had before them reports of the Court of Appeal and of the district commissioner of the district in which the offence was committed and of that in which the convicted person lived. Initially, council did not automatically receive reports on the convict's mental condition but when the first case came before Colby in council at the end of April 1948, he directed that a decision should be deferred until a medical report was received – 'at the earliest possible opportunity' – and that thereafter reports on the mental condition of convicts sentenced to death should accompany the papers submitted to council in every case.[19] The exercise of the prerogative of mercy on behalf of the Sovereign was personal to the governor, although he was required to consult executive council. Council's advice was usually unanimous and was accepted by Colby, but on those occasions when it was not unanimous he accepted the majority advice. Confirming decisions were recorded as:

His Excellency accepted the advice of (the majority of) Council and ordered that the law should take its course.[20]

Colby's almost invariable practice in executive council was to introduce each item on the agenda with a cogent outline of its salient points and to indicate fairly clearly his own conclusions. He would then turn to Barrow for his views.[21]

The routine – varied as it was – of life in Zomba was broken by fairly frequent tours of the protectorate's administrative districts. Within his first year Colby visited every provincial and district headquarters at least once, and in the course of these visits took the district commissioners aside and explained to them what he hoped to accomplish, especially in the field of economic development.[22] These were a normal and important part of his work although he made a number of special visits: for example, to the badly threatened areas during the severe drought of 1948–50. Some of the district visits, especially those in the Shire Highlands, were quite short, but others involved a substantial itinerary and these latter may be illustrated by tours which he made to the three provinces between March 1950 and January 1951.

In March 1950, Colby spent 13 days away from Zomba travelling by road to Mbeya in Tanganyika to meet the governor of that country. It took him six days to get there and six days to return – a round trip of 1200 miles – so he spent only one day at Mbeya. On his way to Tanganyika he called at Lilongwe and Fort Hill; and on his way back at Fort Hill, Njakwa and Mzimba. This journey, though brief, took him through the greater part of the length of Nyasaland and gave him a good, relatively early, glimpse of the geography and environmental characteristics of the country.[23]

Two months after this visit to Tanganyika, accompanied by Lady Colby, he undertook an 11-day tour of the Southern Province[24] in which he visited Blantyre and then Chikwawa, where he attended a meeting of the council of chiefs, the Tacoma maize farm, and the Mikolongwe veterinary station where poultry were bred. At Mlanje he had an informal meeting with the council of chiefs and gave a sundowner party at the local expatriate club. He visited the Native Tobacco Board's Palombe station and Chombani, returning via Fort Lister to see the damage caused by a cloudburst on Machezi, Lujeri tea estate, the tea experimental station, and the Ruo tea estates.[25] He then spent two full days, 16 and 17 May, on the plateau of Mlanje mountain, of which more shortly. The following day he inspected the Luchenza plywood and tea-chest company's factory and attended a meeting of the Cholo council of chiefs, spending the night with the Barrows on their estate. He then spent two days visiting the Conforzi tea estates, the Imperial Tobacco Company's Chimweya estate, and Mabonga (where it was planned to resettle African tenants from nearby private estates). Sunday, 21 May was free of all official engagements and the Colbys returned to Zomba the following day.

Four and a half months after these Southern Province visits, Colby toured the Central Province for nine days from 4 to 12 October.[26] On the first day, he travelled to Lilongwe via Ncheu and Dedza district headquarters, and the following day visited the Lilongwe district offices, attended a meeting of the council of chiefs, and met the committee of the Nyasaland Northern Provinces Association – the representatives of the European tobacco growers in the central part of the protectorate. He finished the day by meeting local expatriate residents at the Lilongwe club in the evening. On the second day, he travelled to Dowa where he again inspected the station and met the council of chiefs. Over the weekend, he drove to Kota Kota via Nchisi and visited Lake Chia and the Onze diversion. The next day, he inspected the district headquarters and visited the Kota Kota Produce and Trading Society's rice mill, Chief Msusu's headquarters, the Universities Mission station, and the community school. He then spent two days at Kasungu, where he inspected the district headquarters, the new estates of the Cholo–Kasungu tobacco syndicate, the Colonial Development Corporation's estate, and other tobacco estates. He returned to Zomba on 12 October.

Three months later, he undertook a 13-day tour of the Northern Province, visiting Lilongwe and Kasungu again en route northwards. Once in the Northern Province, he visited: Mzimba; Njakwa; Livingstonia (the headquarters of the Church of Scotland Mission, for long a considerable political force in the land); Nkata Bay; the Vipya Highlands (6000 feet above sea level, uninhabited but with great economic potential for pine plantations and, it was at one time believed, possibly for European agricultural settlement and fruit-growing); Ekwendeni; Mzuzu (the new headquarters of the Northern Province established at the centre of the Colonial Development Corporation's embryo tung plantation); and Paramount Chief Mbelwa's headquarters. He returned to Zomba on 22 January.[27]

During the 11-month period from March 1950 to January 1951, therefore, he spent 46 days travelling on these four tours, in the course of which he visited 13 of the country's 16 district headquarters and travelled through two other districts. The only district which he did not visit on these particular tours was the most southerly, Port Herald, which he had visited a few months previously in examining the food shortages resulting from the recent severe drought. He paid particular attention to inspecting district headquarters and thereby manifesting a special interest in the work of the provincial and district administration; meeting the African chiefs, especially leading figures such as Paramount Chief Mbelwa and Chief Msusa; also meeting expatriate residents, including planters and missionaries; and visiting places of importance to the production and economic development drive, such as tea and tobacco estates, a government maize farm, a poultry farm, a plywood and tea-chest factory, a rice mill, tung and pine areas, experimental stations, and a resettlement block. He was especially interested in those districts which had significant potential for rapid economic development through the medium of increased production of cash crops. In other districts – for example, Ncheu – he spent less time and, at least in his early days:

One very soon became aware that he was really interested in economic development and that whilst he accepted that ordinary day
to day administration must be carried on efficiently, he wasn't
particularly interested in any activities which didn't lead fairly
directly to a positive cash return.[28]

On these and similar tours, Colby was accompanied by his private
secretary and the provincial commissioner. The district comissioner of
each district which they visited or through which they travelled normally
joined them in the car to point out, describe and answer questions on
places of interest, especially those concerned with economic development
projects or potential. Colby always prepared himself well for these visits,
making a habit of reading and mastering the major points in the district
commissioner's annual report of the district he was visiting.[29]

Whilst on tour, he was anxious to take the opportunity to meet as
many non-official members of the community and government officers,
both senior and junior, as possible, and often did so in the course of
sundowner parties at which he insisted upon supplying his own drinks,
cigarettes and cigars, brought from Government House – and upon
which no tax was payable – rather than use the meagre resources of the
district commissioner.[30] In the past it had been the practice for the district
commissioner and his wife to move into a guest room for gubernatorial
visits, taking their clothes and other possessions with them, so that the
governor and his wife could occupy the best bedroom in the house. The
Colbys asked for this practice to be discontinued.[31]

When touring he tried to resolve issues on the spot, and if his response
to a request was negative he was at pains to explain the reasons and to
reassure the person making the request, if necessary by a humorous
remark. When he was pushing so very hard for modernization of the
economy, he was much amused by the retort to one such remark which
he made to the newly arrived wife of a roads supervisor living in the
bush. This lady complained about having a primitive pit-latrine outside
the house and demanded a water closet in the house. Colby patiently
explained the reasons why this was not currently possible and added,
with a smile, that she was lucky to have a furnished house since he,
when he first started, had a tent only, and later a thatched hut. She
promptly snorted and said, 'Really, Sir Geoffrey, you must move with
the times!'[32] Although his general demeanour on such occasions was
considered natural and friendly and it was felt that he did not unduly
stand on ceremony, and although he listened carefully to views, sugges-

tions and complaints expressed to him, he was not disposed to suffer fools gladly and this characteristic may have been interpreted by some as a lack of sympathy.

In the case of issues raised with him which he could not resolve on the spot, he asked the private secretary to make notes for him, and tours resulted in a stream of red hand-written or typed minutes being sent from Government House to the secretariat, raising questions or giving instructions.[33] All issues were dealt with, usually within 48 hours of his return to Zomba, even apparently quite trivial issues, and if the response to a request was negative a memorandum or letter was sent explaining the reasons so that the person making the request would at least know that whatever it was they had raised had not been ignored. A number of district commissioners found that a request made for funds directly concerned with economic development in the districts very rarely failed to secure the necessary finances if Colby was also convinced of their necessity:

As often as not, showing H. E. on the spot some local development project – a road or a bridge needed for better access to markets, for instance – would ensure its inclusion in the next Estimates.[34]

On his return from district tours, he made a practice of seeing heads of department and discussing with them problems which he had identified. Similarly, he insisted on heads of specialist departments discussing with him matters which arose from their own tours, especially development matters, in order to ascertain whether there was any way in which he could influence desirable progress.[35]

His energy and enthusiasm on these district tours were impressive, especially in his early days, and were occasions remembered decades later by district commissioners, and others, as one officer, who was not easily impressed by top brass, recalled with profane admiration:

'Enthusiastic' is the sum-up word for Colby on a District tour. He 'did' Chikwawa when I was D.C there and impressed me no end with his knowledge of the District, although this was his first visit, and his grasp of what was wanted to get its development going . . . He worked long hours on these tours, was prepared to rough it and would indeed accept considerable discomfort in order to see something worthwhile. I remember him exhausting all of his team (and me!) when I took him round Kakoma experimental farm. The moment we arrived, after a [swine] of a journey over dusty rutted tracks, he leapt out of the landrover and disappeared into a field of head-high maize. For the next one and a half hours even I had a job keeping up with the old [man] as he footed it round every inch of that [damned] farm – and you know what Chikwawa temperatures are like![36]

His readiness to tolerate and even enjoy 'roughing it' may be illustrated by brief reference to a day which he spent – relaxed and companionable – with the provincial commissioner of the Central Province in 1949, travelling on an open railway trolley on the northern extension to inspect the progress being made in famine relief work in the lake shore area.[37]

It is likely that the district officer element in his character was able to come to the fore on these tours and that he, consciously or subconsciously, recalled his early days in Nigeria with their opportunities and frustrations. It seemed to many that he was always concerned when travelling the country to meet district staff and support them against the secretariat and other officialdom; he was quick and decisive in responding to complaints on these scores and 'many a General Order was amended to improve allowances, for example, as a result of some comment made to him in the Provinces'.[38] He gained the reputation for travelling much more than his predecessors and doing what he could to produce rapid action to deal with matters affecting the morale of subordinate staff in the field. It was, of course, the case that the field staff played a vital role in economic development and that their morale was an important element in their ability to fulfil that role to Colby's satisfaction.

So anxious was he to support district commissioners and avoid unnecessary bureaucratic procedures that he invited those in districts in which he had a develoment interest, orally and individually in private, to write to him direct about any ideas they had for the advancement of their districts or any defects in administration which they felt were hampering their work, by-passing the provincial commissioner and chief secretary. Most district commissioners believed this to be an unwise invitation and very few ever made use of it, although a senior district officer in charge of land settlement took up the offer, as did a number of agricultural officers to whom the same invitation was extended.[39] In the latter case, Colby may have been motivated by his early experience of the director of agriculture not passing on the warnings received from field staff during the 1948–50 drought and food shortage.[40] Colby expressed the view that the secretariat was a 'machine' and implied that matters of importance, no doubt unintentionally, might be hidden from him or delayed.[41]

An unusual part of one of his major tours was the two full days which he spent on Mlanje mountain.[42] This journey was made at Colby's suggestion and request and he was accompanied by Barrow, Willan (chief conservator of forests), Corrie (private secretary), Barnes (provincial commissioner of the Southern Province), and O'Riordan (district commissioner, Mlanje). Mlanje mountain, at 10,000 feet above sea level the highest mountain in Nyasaland, had well-distributed rainfall which made it the sole site of the valuable Mlanje cedar (*Widringtonia Whyteii*) discovered by and named after Alexander Whyte, government horticulturalist in the 1890s. Its deposits of bauxite and its potential for timber exploitation made it economically important. It was an area of spectacular beauty, but rugged and inaccessible. Colby wanted to see for himself the timber extraction operations for the proposed fuller exploitation of the resources of Mlanje cedar. A large amount of money was required for this development, including funds for making a road from the foot of the mountain as far up the plateau as possible, roads on the plateau itself to the extraction sites, and improved extraction methods including an aerial cableway. About all of this he wanted first-hand information. O'Neill, a businessman from the Mlanje district, was interested in a concession or licence to extract or purchase extracted timber. He had dismantled and transported by carriers a lorry chassis and engine to the plateau, so that travelling to the various sites would be easier, and he had also built a camp for the governor's visit at which he played host. The days were spent in 'walking, talking and listening', but Colby also found time to do a good deal of fishing. At least one of his companions thought that the governor was not particularly fit at the time and must have found the exertion of the steep ascent and descent a very exacting, if not exhausting, experience. He viewed the expedition as a challenge and although he managed the ascent quite well, he did not like coming down. On a particularly narrow portion of the descent he suffered from vertigo and had to be helped by Willan. Nonetheless:

GFTC enjoyed the visit . . . There was no fuss about the expedition and everything was very informal. He was a very pleasant companion.

When they reached the foot of the mountain they rested at the forest

officer's house at Likabula, and when Willan asked His Excellency what
he would like to drink, he received the reply 'Fruit Salts – with gin in
it!', a reply which was reminiscent of the 'gunpowder plot' medicament
upon which he had relied for good health in his early days in Nigeria.

The attack of vertigo was not an isolated incident, since his aide-de-
camp recalled an occasion during Colby's first year in Nyasaland when
they were touring the Northern Province. They were descending the
Livingstonia escarpment, over which the narrow earth road cuts a path
in a huge, almost parallel, series of zig-zag and hairpin bends, with the
next level almost vertically below the one on which they were travelling.
It is said that the labourers constructing the road had to tether themselves to pegs to be able to dig it. The experience was an unnerving
one.

> The GH car was a big black Buick, and at the end of each zig-zag
> the corner was so abrupt as to make it necessary to point the bonnet
> out over the drop below and reverse back. The effect of what looked
> like several feet of black bonnet and chromium sticking out over a
> vertical drop of hundreds of feet was, from the passengers' seat,
> very alarming.
>
> [The aide-de-camp] found it an ordeal, despite parachute train-
> ing, but HE, who had a poor head for heights, must have found it
> even more alarming. Although he turned pale, he said nothing.
> [They] both enjoyed a cigarette at the bottom.[43]

Colby was absent from the seat of government sufficiently long for a
governor's deputy to be appointed on 92 separate occasions during his
eight years of office,[44] and the extensive and relatively frequent district
tours which he made conferred two considerable advantages. First, they
afforded him a measure of relief from the great pressure of routine
administrative work at Government House with its endless paperwork
and meetings with a quite small group of officials and an even smaller
group of non-officials (almost exclusively European). Second, they
enabled him to know, albeit not in great detail, far more of the protectorate than probably anyone else in the country. This second advantage was
of enormous benefit to him in directing the affairs of state, especially
the country's economic development, because it gave him the edge on
most others and enabled him to speak and make decisions with the
authority which personal, first-hand knowledge confers. He both enjoyed

and put to good use the experience which he gained in touring the country so widely and so frequently.

His work, particularly in Zomba, kept him so fully occupied that he had little time for relaxation. In the past he had enjoyed reading history and biographies but he did little leisure reading in Nyasaland. He liked to listen to violin and piano concertos when Lady Colby played them on records but he never put on a record himself. On the radio he regularly listened to the news but, apart from cricket commentaries, rarely tuned in to other programmes. In his early days in Nyasaland he enjoyed fishing and playing tennis, snooker and bridge, but later he had to forgo these pleasures. He was, however, able to continue to relax by fishing occasionally on Zomba plateau.[45]

An interesting form of relaxation which the Colbys enjoyed were the occasional private weekend visits to Mlanje.[46] The governor would himself telephone the district commissioner and ask if he and Lady Colby could stay in the district commissioner's guest house for a night or two. The guest house was well away from the district commissioner's own house, and save for the evenings and at meal times, the Colbys kept themselves to themselves, bringing ample food and drink with them for both themselves and their hosts. Colby made these visits purely for rest and recuperation and to get away from the cares of office. He and Lady Colby enjoyed sitting in the garden or on the guest house verandah, pottering around the garden or by the swimming pool, or taking a gentle walk part way up the mountain path. They particularly liked the sunsets and the views over Portuguese East Africa. Even on these visits, Colby spent a good deal of time reading and writing, and Lady Colby did quite a bit of sewing. Occasionally they would go for a late-afternoon drive with the district commissioner, but save for calling in at a mission station they visited no one else. In the evenings, they enjoyed informally talking with friends of their hosts who called in. Scarcely ever did Colby talk shop on these weekend visits. The extent to which he was able to unwind can be judged from the fact that he was occasionally to be found on the floor of the district commissioner's lounge, on his hands and knees, playing 'tigers' with his hosts' small children.

6· Relationships with Officials

'Little hope for the future of this territory if it is to be administered by second-class men.'

In the course of his daily work in Zomba, Colby came into contact mainly with the heads of government departments, especially the official members of executive council, and with the two non-official members, but in his social engagements and particularly whilst on tour he also came into contact with a large number of government officials, both senior and junior, and with members of the non-official community, both expatriates and Africans (especially – indeed almost exclusively – the chiefs). His relationships with these groups provide further insights into the sort of man and governor Colby was.

First, the officials. The heads of departments, and those of equivalent status, were a vital element in the work of government and in the carrying through of Colby's development strategy, and it took him some time to build the sort of team he needed. He was particularly fortunate in his first chief secretary, F. L. Brown.[1] The chief secretary was head of the Civil Service and 'the channel of communication between the Government on the one hand and heads of department and the general public on the other'. Brown was aged 51 when Colby arrived and had almost three decades of colonial service behind him in Northern Rhodesia and Jamaica, before being promoted to Nyasaland in 1945:

> Frank looked like a mild lay reader, but he had a will of iron – and he did his duty as he saw it . . . and no one who received a rocket from him ever forgot it or was willing to risk another. He was widely trusted by officials and unofficials alike. He was trusted by his subordinates, and shortcomings within the power of the offender to correct were dealt with always in private. He was intrepid, and

thunder from above moved him not . . . His Deputy Chief Secretary had a slight stammer, and on receipt of an unwelcome order from on high (the Colonial Office or the Governor) was used to say 'Y-you c-c-can't [argue] against thunder'. Frank Brown both could and did – generally effectively.

Without exception, officers who knew Brown well spoke warmly of him and with admiration, seeing him as a courageous, honest, competent and dedicated man, a first class adviser to Colby, unafraid to speak his mind and speedy in carrying out executive action. He knew his men, prodded the backward, and encouraged the ambitious. He got on extremely well with Colby, 'acting as a brake on dangerous corners, and as an accelerator on matters to which [Colby] was blind or in which he was uninterested'. It is, however, possible that, loyal and gifted adviser and colleague as he undoubtedly was, he did not fully share Colby's far-sightedness and confidence in the potential for rapid and far-reaching economic development. In his retirement speech to the chamber of commerce in April 1951 – an occasion when many men would have risked a high degree of optimism – he took a surprisingly limited and uncertain view of the future:

Imagining himself gazing into a crystal to see the future he could see a more prosperous and increasingly more prosperous Nyasaland. He could, he thought, see the completion of the Limbe–Cholo road and possibly the Blantyre–Zomba road; he was not sure about other works.[2]

It is possible that Colby recognized that Brown, a man with his feet firmly on the ground, did not lift his eyes sufficiently to the stars, and consequently did not persuade him to stay on as chief secretary beyond his 55th birthday.

Colby did not take kindly to 'yes-men', and respected those who stood up to him[3] – unless he believed they were being simply obstructive – and it was said of him that:

He seemed . . . perhaps given to the odd sharp shot – not exactly acerbic or even sarcastic but indicating rather that he preferred plain speaking.[4]

He did look for men who shared his views on development, his dynamism, hard work, leadership qualities and drive, especially among his heads of department. When men fell significantly short of these standards he replaced them by inducing them to seek transfer, to resign, or to retire. In a very few cases he used the '45 rule', which enabled him to retire an officer upon reaching the age of 45 years in the interests of Civil Service efficiency. It was particularly in those departments which were crucial to the economic development of the country that he needed the 'right' sort of men as leaders. It is not surprising, therefore, that the departments of agriculture and of posts and telecommunications and the provincial and district administration had the spotlight turned on them.

In the case of agriculture, C. B. Garnett was aged 44 when Colby arrived. He had 22 years of colonial service behind him in Tanganyika and Nyasaland, and had been promoted director of agriculture in September 1947.[5] Two months later he went on leave and was quite seriously ill, so he had his leave extended by the Colonial Office medical officer. Consequently, when Colby arrived in Nyasaland in March 1948, his director of agriculture, upon whom so many of his development aspirations crucially depended, was out of the country. Brown visited Garnett on leave and told him that the governor had asked why the director was away and repeatedly enquired when he would be back. He returned to Nyasaland at the very end of September 1948 and for a while relationships were, at least on the surface and so far as Garnett was concerned, excellent: he was regularly invited to drinks parties and dinner parties at Government House and frequently played snooker and tennis with the governor.

Garnett was a capable administrator but his experience and interest were in crop-marketing: he had been appointed to Nyasaland as marketing officer. Marketing, however, was an area in which Colby himself had vast experience and in which he had no great need for outside help. Rather, he wanted advice, help and action in soil-conservation and crop-production – a field in which Garnett, in the view of senior field officers in his department, had little insight, interest or practical experience. Relationships began to deteriorate significantly early in 1949 when Garnett – as we shall see in greater detail in a later chapter – persistently refused to take the same pessimistic view of the seriousness of the food shortage, resulting from severe drought, which the governor took. Colby quickly lost confidence in his director of agriculture's judgement and 'more and more over-ruled [him] in agricultural matters'. It is significant that Garnett never once accompanied Colby on tour or even on local visits to agricultural areas. The final break came over the use of Native Tobacco Board funds derived from marketing African-grown tobacco, which Colby wanted to tap for appropriate production purposes, and the use of Board field staff for general agricultural supervision purposes in tobacco growing areas when they were not involved in marketing. Garnett, as chairman of the Board, was fundamentally opposed to the suggestions and refused to agree to them. The governor 'called a meeting of the Board, gave them a stiff talking to and they caved in'. With the Board behind him, Colby now ordered Garnett to comply with his requests and added, 'if you don't do this then I shall have to get myself a new Director', to which Garnett replied, 'In that case I must get myself a new Governor.' He applied for and was appointed to the newly created post of director of agriculture in the Gambia, and left Nyasaland early in March 1950. Once he had arranged to leave, Colby 'kept ringing up Establishments and asking when Garnett was going to leave and why hadn't they got that chap a passage yet'. By this time, invitations to Government House had long since ceased to be made.

In the case of posts and telecommunications, W. R. H. Morgan was aged 50 when Colby arrived, and he had served with the Nyasaland government since 1926 when he transferred from the African Transcontinental Telegraph Company.[6] He had been promoted postmaster-general in 1946. He was reckoned by his senior colleagues to be 'an easy going sort of person but with a medical problem'; 'he had become [unwell] and took little interest in the running of the department'; 'his earlier abilities which he undoubtedly possessed had faded with middle-age and his indulgences, and he had lost the respect of his staff'. At Colby's request, the attorney-general conducted enquiries of senior postal staff about Morgan's administration, and the chief secretary twice cautioned him about his behaviour and suggested retirement. Morgan initially resisted this suggestion so Colby had the question of his department's administration raised in executive council, upon whose advice the governor ordered that a commission of inquiry – which would have power to summon and examine witnesses in public – be set up to inquire into the administration of the Department of Posts and Telecommunications. The very next day, 11 August 1948, Morgan left Zomba on retirement.

The provincial and district administration was a rather different matter. Here the problem was one of age coupled with an unwillingness or inability to move at the pace and in the direction which Colby demanded. Of the three provincial commissioners at the time of his arrival, H. C. J. Barker was 55 and had served in Nyasaland for 29 years;

J. M. Ellis was 53 and had served for 16 years in the Colonial Service in Cyprus, the Falklands and Grenada, before being transferred to Nyasaland in 1935; and D. W. Saunders–Jones was 49 and had served for six years in the Indian Army and 17 years in Zanzibar before being transferred to Nyasaland in 1939.[7] Saunders–Jones 'saw the writing on the wall' and left the country on retirement in March 1949 on reaching the normal age of retirement. Ellis' was a sad case. He had only one arm and it was he who got off to a bad start by reaching Limbe station in the nick of time to greet the Colbys when they first arrived. He was considered by many of his fellow officers to be 'one of the kindest of men', but as the months passed it became clear that he was wanting in the new style of government:

> In . . . the Spring of 1949, His Excellency arranged a meeting with him in Blantyre, and told him without any warning that he was being retired. As H. E. was lunching with him and his wife Molly afterwards, it must have been very embarrassing for all concerned. By all accounts John Ellis was shattered by the news.

Barker, who stood up to Colby, and was not afraid to say 'no', was, despite his age, a man of drive and initiative who had felt somewhat frustrated previously. Consequently, he lasted rather longer and did not leave Nyasaland on retirement until February 1951. There were two other reasons why Barker's services were not dispensed with earlier: first, the Northern Province was a newly created province and needed a locally experienced administrator at its head; and second, Barker was able to handle and get on with the Colonial Development Corporation officials in the Northern Province, and this ability was important to Colby because of the vital role which the corporation played in the development drive and also because of their original 'total ignorance of local conditions'.[8]

It is possible that a number of other senior officers left because they crossed or could not get on with Colby. A. C. T. Edwards, the deputy chief secretary, had known him in Nigeria and took few steps to conceal from others his dislike of him.[9] 'He had a mildly deprecating attitude towards Colby when discussing him . . . damning by poking gentle fun; a very effective technique although not very gentlemanly perhaps!' In June 1953, he was seconded to the federal Public Service Commission and left Salisbury on retirement in July 1955 without returning to Nyasaland, although in fairness it must be said that his own family's explanation of this was, 'Quite simply he retired in 1956 for purely family reasons, our children having reached the age for boarding school in England.' It may, however, be significant that the CBE which he was then awarded was for services in West Africa and the Central African Federation: Nyasaland was not specifically mentioned. V. Fox–Strangways was appointed secretary for African affairs about six months after Colby's arrival, having previously served, for 25 years, in Nigeria, Nyasaland, the Gilbert and Ellice Islands, and Palestine. In September 1953, at the time of rioting in the Southern Province in opposition to federation, when the governor was being pressed by his military and police advisers and by a number of non-officials to declare a state of emergency, Fox–Strangways firmly advised against it. During a telephone conversation with the governor he said 'Well, Sir, I am fundamentally opposed to it but if you want to declare it, it's your responsibility. I advise most strongly against it,' and he put the phone down, rather hastily. A few minutes later, he was summoned to Government House where, presumably, strong words were spoken.[10] A few months later, in May 1954, he resigned, it being believed by some that he 'was too much of a gentleman and too sensitive by nature' to continue serving under Colby, although again in fairness it has to be pointed out that Fox–Strangways was 56, already past the normal retiring age, when he left Nyasaland, and that all the official members of executive council, and not merely the secretary for African affairs, voted against the declaration of an emergency when the question was formally put to them.

It is important to emphasize that there was another side to the way in which Colby handled the older heads of department reaching the end of their careers, and that it was not merely age, but rather attitudes (which were sometimes coupled with age) which worried him. H. R. Price, the director of public works, aged 57 and with three decades of colonial service behind him when the new governor arrived, was due, if not overdue, to retire shortly after his arrival. He had asked Brown, the acting governor, if he could stay on for a few months for personal reasons but had been refused. When he sought an interview with Colby, however, he received a sympathetic hearing and was allowed to delay his retirement for a few months, much to his and his family's relief and gratitude.[11] The officer whom Colby appointed to replace Ellis as provincial commissioner of the Southern Province was E. C. Barnes who, after some years in the Indian Army, had joined the Nyasaland administration in 1925 and was already past his 50th birthday when promoted in March 1949. That this was a wise choice of officer, despite his long service in the country and his age – and in fact possibly because of them – was soon demonstrated by Barnes' splendid handling of the food shortage in his province during 1949 and early 1950. R. H. Keppel-Compton, who replaced Saunders-Jones as provincial commissioner of the Central Province in March 1949, had been in Nyasaland even longer than Barnes, 26 years, although he was slightly younger: almost 49. He also was a first-rate provincial commissioner, with an unusually deep understanding of rural Africans, and was trusted and respected by all who knew him. He had the great advantage of being on good terms with the Central Province non-officials.[12]

It is important also to point out that in the case of those departments not directly involved in economic development, Colby was far more prepared to tolerate shortcomings in administration and the continued presence of their heads of department in his team. For example, executive council believed, and the governor accepted, that the November 1949 riot in the central prison in Zomba was caused by 'the breakdown over the last two years of discipline and control by the prison staff over the inmates' and that:

> the chief qualification required of the European staff . . . was the ability to handle men . . . and that neither the Commissioner nor the Superintendent appeared to have this essential qualification. Their qualities, while no doubt suitable for employment in other spheres or conditions, were inappropriate to the needs of the Protectorate and Government should consider the possibility of replacing them.

Yet the commissioner, P. H. H. Bayly, remained in office – but then so did the chief justice, Sir Enoch Jenkins, who headed the commission of inquiry into the prison riot and who the governor and executive council were convinced had made a 'thoroughly inadequate' job of it, so much so that many of his recommendations they felt 'should be strongly resisted', 'cannot be entertained', or 'should not be accepted'. They felt that the chief justice had stressed 'matters of relatively minor significance' whilst lightly passing over 'the fundamental cause of the trouble': the breakdown of discipline and control over the last two years – which precisely coincided with Bayly's period as commissioner of prisons.[13]

Once he had secured the sort of men he was looking for as heads of department, Colby placed almost total trust in their judgement and saw to it that resources flowed in the direction of their departments, especially if they were major development departments. H. O. Ellis, who succeeded Morgan as postmaster-general, and R. W. Kettlewell, who eventually succeeded Garnett as director of agriculture, fell into this category. In Ellis' case, Colby made it clear to the Colonial Office the type of man he needed and, although it took them some time to find him, Ellis was recruited from the British postal service via the Allied Control Commission headquarters in Germany, to which he had been seconded as a lieutenant-colonel to help reorganize the postal and telephone services. He was described by his colleagues in Nyasaland as a 'very capable administrator . . . very clever and energetic person who liked to have his own way' and was 'dynamic, confident and articulate and had the ability to lead and inspire others'.[14]

In the case of Kettlewell, whom Colby had already been instrumental in having promoted to be deputy director of agriculture, the appointment was an internal promotion.[15] After Garnett's transfer, E. Lawrence acted as director of agriculture for six months pending retirement, and was followed by G. Roddan, who also stayed for only six months before returning to Kenya to be director there. By this time, three years after arriving in Nyasaland, Colby had had enough of changes at the top of the Department of Agriculture, especially since it was to this department that he principally looked to bring about the increased production which was at the hub of his development strategy. Despite the view of the Colonial Office that Kettlewell should be transferred to another territory to gain wider experience, Colby – using the argument that his transfer would be unwise during the current severe drought and food shortage – insisted that he should be promoted to the directorship in Nyasaland, and the Colonial Office agreed. A factor which appealed to the governor was that Kettlewell had travelled widely in the Northern and Central Provinces, much of it on foot, and knew the country well: 'Sir Geoffrey set great store by his advice.'

Although the former's promotion was internal both to the country and to the Colonial Service, while the latter's appointment was from outside both the country and the Colonial Service, Kettlewell and Ellis shared a number of characteristics. They were both quite young (Kettlewell 43 and Ellis 41); technically highly qualified (Kettlewell with a degree in agriculture from Reading, a diploma in agriculture from Cambridge, and an associateship of the Institute of Colonial Tropical Agriculture in Trinidad, and Ellis with membership of the Institute of Electrical Engineers and the British Institute of Radio Engineers); and they were both very experienced (Kettlewell had entered the Colonial

Service in 1934, and Ellis the British postal service in 1926). They were tough and determined men, in much the same mould as Colby, whom they much admired and respected and whose confidence in them was almost total. They believed in the military maxim long remembered by Kettlewell: 'When you are successful, exploit that success.'[16] Both were welcomed and respected by the non-official community.

We have already noted that when Colby appointed Barnes and Keppel-Compton as provincial commissioners they were not particularly young men. This was wise because it was sound experience and practical wisdom rather than youthful intellectual vigour which was important in field administration, and because men reaching the end of their career can more easily be replaced if their appointments are a mistake – which certainly was not the case with either Barnes or Keppel-Compton. Colby's second set of promotions to the rank of provincial commissioner were rather different in that much younger, although still fairly well experienced, men were selected.[17]

W. H. J. Rangeley was 42 and had served in Nyasaland for 17 years when he became provincial commissioner of the Southern Province in 1952; he had been born in Africa and was deeply knowledgeable about the history and anthropology of Nyasaland. G. C. D. Hodgson was 39 and had served for 12 years in Nyasaland when he became provincial commissioner of the Central Province, also in 1952; he, too, had been born in Africa, and he had caught the eye of both Colby and Barrow, first as clerk to executive council and then as secretary of the African Foodstuffs Commission during the 1949–50 food shortage of which job he made an outstanding success under severe pressure. C. D. P. T. Haskard was only 37, with several years of military service in East Africa, Ceylon and Burma and seven in Nyasaland, when he became provincial commissioner of the Northern Province in 1954. In 1940, he had been appointed to the administrative service in Tanganyika but when he arrived off Dar-es-Salaam he was ill and was taken to Nairobi, Kenya, to hospital. On recovery, he joined the King's African Rifles 1st/2nd Battalion, a Nyasaland battalion; its adjutant was Kettlewell, with whom he became close friends. When Kettlewell returned to Nyasaland in mid-1943, Haskard asked him to try to get him a transfer to Nyasaland from Tanganyika (where in fact he had never served). This Kettlewell was eventually able to do, and Haskard arrived in Nyasaland when he left the army in 1946.[18] In being promoted, Haskard did so over the heads of 21 other officers who were senior to him in the provincial and district administration, much as Colby himself had done in Nigeria nine years earlier when he became administrative secretary. Like Colby also, Haskard went on to become a governor and to be knighted. These three provincial commissioners were all enthusiastic provincial and district administrators, knowledgeable about the country, its people and its rural problems; they were natural and energetic leaders, keen to implement the governor's development plans.

In these various ways, Colby built his team of very senior officials, the heads of department and those of equivalent status. During his final year of office this team numbered 38.[19] Only two of them had been appointed head before Colby's arrival, both in 1947 (co-operative development and prisons), and 24 of them had been appointed in the period 1949–52, including the major development departments (agriculture, public works, and posts and telecommunications), as well as four of the five official members of executive council (chief secretary, financial secretary, attorney-general and director of agriculture), all in 1951 in which year, therefore, Colby had an almost clean sweep of his closest official advisers. Of the 38 senior officials, 20 had been appointed by transfer from other territories, including eight from Nigeria (although this seems to have been by chance rather than at Colby's instigation); the remaining 18 had been promoted within Nyasaland, including seven from the provincial and district administration (three provincial commissioners, a development secretary, an assistant financial secretary, the commissioner for co-operative development, and the director of game, fish and tsetse control). The average age of this team of top officials when appointed was $42\frac{1}{2}$ years; their average length of service at this time was $16\frac{1}{2}$ years. They made a fairly young and well experienced team, with a nice balance of internal and external experience and a good stiffening of those with district administrative experience.

In the preceding paragraph, reference was made to the almost clean sweep of Colby's closest official advisers in 1951. This clean sweep may in part have been the result of representations which he made in a personal letter to Cohen at the Colonial Office in the early part of 1951[20] which he followed up in discussions soon afterwards whilst on leave. In the course of looking back over his three years in Nyasaland and taking stock, he said:

The question that I have never ceased to ask myself since I have been here is this – why is it that Nyasaland is so far less developed than any other territory?

He was puzzled because of what he saw as the general fertility of the country's soils, its abundant water, healthy climate and the quality of its human material, and was inclined to blame the failure of the very large land owners to develop their estates, the private ownership of the railways, treasury control, lack of investment in public utilities, and the quality of the European staff. In respect of this last point he said:

I have studied this particular problem very carefully over three years and I have come to the inescapable conclusion that the standard of staff in this territory, particularly the administrative staff, is considerably below that of other territories.

He added that he had taken a long time to come to this conclusion and found the reason for it obscure:

The explanation [however] may perhaps be that when officers put in their preferences for the various Colonies, Nyasaland comes at the bottom of the list and few, probably, have put in for Nyasaland at all. The consequence may be, therefore, that we get the staff which is not considered suitable for the more important territories. However, whatever may be the reason I am convinced that the general competence of the Government staff in this territory is much below the standards in West Africa for example.

He then turned to the question of heads of department – having recently lost Roddan, director of agriculture, and Bowring, director of public works, both of whom he considered to be first rate officers, on promotion to other colonies – and said:

if we get a good Head of Department here we lose him after a very short interval, and if we get a bad one he stays here until he retires from the Service . . . the more important territories must have the best Heads of Department but the fact remains that there is little hope for the future of this territory if it is to be administered by second-class men.

His comparison with the standard of staff in West Africa was probably little more than the traditional feeling of superiority which some officers from West Africa, and particularly Nigeria, often claimed when considering quality elsewhere in Africa. An officer who served in both Nigeria and Nyasaland has said that 'as regards the quality of the civil servants I should say that, broadly speaking, there was nothing to choose between them', although he felt that – somewhat after Colby's time in Nyasaland – the quality of the top administrative staff in Nigeria was better.[21] Crocker, writing of the 1920s and 1930s, said that 'Nigeria . . . has not always been staffed with first-rate personnel . . . there has undoubtedly been a thread of inferior quality running through the Service larger than was comfortable.'[22] Colby's reference to the standard of 'administrative staff' was in contradistinction to the specialist staff with whom he was fairly well pleased by 1951 – as we shall see shortly in the case of the Posts and Telecommunications Department – and almost certainly meant the senior officers in the secretariat and the provincial administration rather than administrative officers generally because, as we have seen, all three provincial commissioners left between 1948 and 1951 and he permitted at least one, and probably more, of the secretariat officers with whom he did not get on to be seconded to the federal Civil Service, and ensured that they did not return to Nyasaland. Additionally, he promoted a number of district administrators to very senior posts internally, and he attributed his success in agricultural development to 'the close cooperation between the administration and the Agricultural and other development departments'. He was deliberately overstating his views on the standard of staff as a means of gaining Cohen's support for high-quality appointments and the retention of good officers, such as Kettlewell and Phillips, in Nyasaland. Rather than being genuinely critical of the general run of his officers, he was making the point that he did not want his own efforts to build up his team to be jeopardized by the appointment of staff of less than top quality into Nyasaland, by the enforced retention of poor staff, or by the promotion out of the protectorate of his good men.[23]

Colby realized that it was not only at the head of department level that he needed to encourage ambition and to exploit talent. Consequently, he kept his eyes open for promising officials in the departments and saw to it that they were given responsible, challenging tasks where they had the fullest opportunity to make use of their abilities. Into this category fell A. P. S. Forbes, H. E. I. Phillips and W. J. R. Pincott. Forbes, the senior agricultural officer of the Southern Province, then aged 36, was given wide responsibilities during the 1949–50 food shortage, and later became director of agriculture in Tanganyika.[24] Phillips, then aged 35, was taken from being district commissioner in the remote Karonga district into the secretariat, first as assistant secretary in 1948, and three years later as development secretary, in order to forestall a proposed transfer on promotion to another territory; later he became minister of finance – the last European member of the Malawi cabinet – and was knighted.[25] It was Lady Colby's view, expressed many years later, that Phillips and Haskard 'owed everything to Geoff' for their career development.[26] Pincott was the district commissioner of Blantyre district, far and away the most demanding district in the protectorate, when, at the age of 36, he also was taken into the secretariat, as assistant financial secretary. Each of these three transfers to positions of greater responsibility and opportunity was made at the personal instigation of the governor.

Colby's main contacts with junior officials were at social functions and whilst on tour, although his closest continuing contacts with less senior officers were those with his aides-de-camp and private secretaries and with the clerks to executive council. At social functions, such as sundowner parties, and on tour, he would go out of his way to engage quite junior officials in conversation so that he could learn about problems and progress 'at the grass roots'; many such conversations were remembered by officials many years later. Particularly warm memories are retained by the less senior officers with whom he was in closest continuing contact. It may be that the relationships with these men were in fact warmer than with most others, but it is also possible that since these particular observers saw Colby more closely and more frequently than did most others they were able to observe the real Colby and aspects of him which others missed. Two examples may be cited.

H. R. H. Rowland was clerk to the executive council when he became very ill, and many years later recalled:

> During my three months in Zomba Hospital flowers and fruit arrived from Government House, and my wife (with two small children) received tremendous support and encouragement from H. E. and Lady Colby. It was clear that they were extremely concerned for her and gave much practical help. Our flight home by flying-boat was suggested from Government House and H. E. advised my wife that we should store, rather than ship or get rid of our possessions.

Colby then arranged that, assuming Rowland's recovery, he should do a two-year exchange with a principal in the Colonial Office in the hope that by the end of that time he would either be passed fit to return to

Nyasaland or would be in a position to secure another job in Britain. He in fact returned fit to the protectorate in August 1953. 'This sort of thoughtfulness for a pretty junior officer seemed . . . as considerate as one could imagine.'[27]

The first of Colby's aides-de-camp, D. G. Longden, also experienced and long remembered the governor's sympathy and kindness.[28] Longden had served in the army throughout the war and been taken prisoner at Arnhem in September 1944, and after the war decided that it would be difficult to settle down in London as a solicitor. He joined the Colonial Administrative Service and after a year's secondment to the Colonial Office arrived in Nyasaland in August 1946 and spent his first two years in the secretariat and as assistant district commissioner, Zomba. In July 1948, three months after the Colbys' arrival, he became aide-de-camp and private secretary. When he was first unofficially approached about this post, in May, he asked not to be considered because he felt that the job, as it had in the past, would largely consist of social duties 'which would be a poor substitute for district work', and because it had normally been a bachelor post and would be hard on his wife, who was pregnant. Nonetheless, Colby asked to see him.

> H. E. immediately put me at my ease; he was a big man in every sense of the word, with an easy, relaxed, but decisive manner, and a nice sense of humour . . . he said that [my wife] would be welcome at all G. H. functions, as a matter of course. Indeed throughout my time at Government House, H. E. and Lady Colby could not have been kinder to us both, particularly during [my wife's] pregnancy and the birth of our daughter.

A month before their daughter was born, Longden accompanied the governor on a tour of the Northern Province, and Lady Colby insisted that Mrs Longden should stay at Government House. Since they were both keen gardeners, they got on well together.

In these various ways, Colby built the sort of loyal, hardworking team which he needed to work with him and to help him implement his development strategy. Not only did he command the loyalty and admiration of those less senior officers who worked most closely with him, but over a period of time he secured the departure of the senior officers who did not share his views on development and his energy and drive – just as his headmaster at Charterhouse had given unworthy schoolboys 'single tickets for home' or seen to it that they were 'superannuated':

i.e., asked to leave. Colby replaced them with men better equipped by ability and attitude to assist him in rapidly developing the country.

In many ways, what was said of Fletcher at Charterhouse could also be said of Colby:

> He often broke opposition, less often converted it . . . Yet for those who found it, his kindness was as warm as fire.[29]

Looking back during his retirement, he paid public tribute to the role of his officials – to the team as he eventually built it – and to their 'unceasing toil and devotion to duty and tireless energy', adding, 'I am greatly indebted to every one of them.'[30]

7· Relationships with Non-officials

'Daggers drawn most of the time.'

We have already remarked that Colby's principal contacts with the non-official community were with the two non-civil servant members of executive council and that many of his contacts with other members of that community were made whilst on tour,[1] although naturally he had dealings with the non-official members of legislative council and with the chairmen and secretaries of organizations such as the Convention of Associations and the chamber of commerce. His contacts with expatriates were significantly more frequent than were those with Africans, and it is convenient to deal with them separately.

The general view is that his relations with the non-official expatriate community on the whole could not be said to have been cordial and that indeed on occasions and in some individual cases they were distinctly uncordial. He gave one leading non-official the distinct and long remembered feeling that the non-official was 'one of the many things a governor has to put up with!'[2] To the extent that this view that his relations with non-officials were poor is a valid one, it can be accounted for in two ways. First, as a new broom he was a very large and powerful instrument intent upon some drastic clean sweeping: more of a gubernatorial industrial vacuum cleaner than a titular feather duster. He was so very different from his immediate predecessors[3] and so very energetic and determined that it would have been a miracle if he had been entirely accepted by those who for so long had either been left to their own devices or had usually got their own way:

Into this well-ordered, happy, but rather 'Sleepy Hollow', Sir Geoffrey arrived like a whirl-wind.[4]

He was energetic and anxious to wake up this backwater. Since backwaters are usually stirred up rather than woken up, his management technique . . . was essentially that of 'throwing stones into the pond'.[5]

Furthermore, Colby made it quite clear that he saw the rapid development of African agricultural production as being the centrepiece of his development strategy,[6] and since the European planters had always seen themselves as occupying the most important place in Nyasaland's economy, it was almost inevitable that they should resent and distrust Colby's very different way of viewing economic progress. Time and time again, towards the end of his period of office, the expatriate planting community demanded or pleaded for the public recognition of the contribution which they had throughout made to Nyasaland's economic development.[7]

On the other hand, for at least the first two or three years of office, he enjoyed the enthusiastic support of many in the expatriate community and even the (on occasions effusive) praise and respect of the local press. For example, after his budget speech to legislative council at the end of 1949, Colby must have been gratified to read the leading article in the *Nyasaland Times* and may have been somewhat embarrassed by the frequent fond references to 'our Governor':

In our considered opinion the address . . . was quite the most satisfying gubernatorial pronouncement yet made in Nyasaland . . . and we commend it to the careful study of all those interested in the progress of this country. Our Governor indulged in no wishful thinking. We can assure His Excellency that . . . every person with the interests of Nyasaland at heart thanks him for his 'fighting' speech and most sincerely trusts that when he addresses the House this time next year all his plans – whether in hand or now only in embryo – will have matured.[8]

A year later the *Nyasaland Times* again congratulated and supported Colby in commenting on his November 1950 budget speech:

It may sound trite when we say – for we have said it on several occasions before – that when our present Governor makes a public pronouncement he shows both his full grasp of Nyasaland's problems and his high quality of statesmanship, but what is true is never

trite and without question Sir Geoffrey Colby's opening address to
Legislative Council . . . settles this point beyond question.[9]

Even some three years after his arrival, the *Nyasaland Times* was highly
supportive of Colby's leadership and the development successes which
he had achieved and which his stewardship promised. When it was
announced that the governor would be going on leave in May 1951, the
newspaper carried a leader headed 'Au Revoir',[10] in which it revealed its
belief in 'the devil you know' philosophy and its fear that Colby might
not return to Nyasaland: there had been rumours that he would be
appointed governor of Uganda, a post which he would dearly have loved
to fill and which was in fact filled by Cohen in 1952.[11] The governorship
of Kenya fell vacant at the same time. One may speculate that the
Colonial Office, having suffered from his constant badgering for development funds felt that he would be better where he was rather than cause
them greater bother in a new and larger territory. The *Nyasaland Times*
leader said that Colby had arrived in the country 'at an eventful period
in its history', listed a number of important developments, and added:

> We must have an experienced navigator at the helm not only to
> steer the ship in fair weather but also in possible storms and it is
> our considered opinion that Sir Geoffrey is the man. It is more
> essential now than it ever has been that there should be continuity
> in direction . . . Particularly is it desirable that Sir Geoffrey remain
> at the helm at the present time for, without being pessimistic, we
> think we shall see a cloud on the horizon.[12]

The reason why the expatriates and the press were so supportive of
Colby's stewardship and his economic development drive was their belief
that this would put Nyasaland in a much stronger economic position,
thereby making it a more attractive partner to Southern Rhodesia in any
future discussions on federation, and less likely that Nyasaland might
otherwise be 'dropped' by the Rhodesias.[13] Indeed – believing that they
would enjoy better prospects under a federal government led by Southern Rhodesia, rather than under a protectorate government primarily
concerned with African interests – they did not conceal this motivation,
since the chairman of the chamber of commerce, R. Bucquet, said
publicly of the same speech:

> If twenty years ago we had had this understanding of our difficulties

and a similar determination to get things done, we should today be arguing the case for federation from a much stronger position.[14]

He did, of course, overlook the fact that 20 years earlier Nyasaland did have – albeit for a very short time – a governor, Shenton Thomas, who did understand Nyasaland's difficulties and who did have a similar determination to get things done. Nonetheless, his point was valid throughout the whole of the intervening period.

The *Nyasaland Times* published the full text of a letter written by Colby to government officers on the need for greatly increased production in its issue of 2 February 1950[15] and was again fully supportive and full of praise for what it described as his 'masterly document which presents a plan – a real plan and probably the first practical plan that Nyasaland has ever been offered – to bring the country to prosperity'.[16] Once more the paper overlooked Shenton Thomas' 1932 development plan,[17] but again it tied development to the bargaining strength of the protectorate in talks on federation with the Rhodesias, heading its leader 'Nyasaland is not worried', with reference to the prominence being given in the Rhodesian press to moves 'to drop Nyasaland from any future federation plans'.[18]

Of all his relations with expatriate non-officials, none was as close, consistent and important as that which Colby enjoyed with Barrow.[19] They had somewhat similar backgrounds. They were born in the same part of Surrey (Colby at Surbiton and Barrow at Carshalton); they were roughly the same age (Barrow being born in June 1900 and Colby in March 1901); both went to a major British public school (Colby to Charterhouse and Barrow to Malvern); both went to Clare College, Cambridge (although they did not meet there); and both went to Africa in the mid-1920s (Colby in 1925 and Barrow in 1927). Barrow started his life in Nyasaland as a tobacco planter in the Zomba district, but soon moved to tea, building up extensive plantations of tea, tung oil and later tobacco in the Cholo district. He was appointed a member of legislative council in 1940 and of executive council in 1943. He was the longest-serving member of executive council when Colby arrived in 1948, was a major businessman with important connections with businessmen in Britain, was recognized leader of the non-official European community, had over two decades of experience in Nyasaland, and his family was regarded as 'the elite of the settler world'.

Colby and Barrow met for the first time on Tuesday, 30 March 1948 at a drinks party at Government House immediately after the governor's swearing-in, and they immediately took to each other.[20] Thereafter Colby very frequently consulted Barrow both formally and informally, either at Government House or at Barrow's home where the Colbys were frequent guests. In private they argued a great deal and Barrow on occasions went 'almost purple in the face' during the course of these arguments. Barrow's general attitude towards government was understanding and supportive, and Colby responded by using him both as an adviser on the likely reactions of the European community and as a communicator and explainer of government policies and proposals to that community. The governor placed great confidence in him, invariably turned first to him in any significant discussions in executive council, frequently sought his advice on major issues, and entrusted to him the deeply important work of African foodstuffs commissioner during the 1949–50 food shortage. Only over one issue did they eventually significantly differ – the question of Nyasaland's inclusion in the federation – but even this did not seriously affect their basic relationship, although 'the events and attitudes of those days led to a cooling of the previously cordial relationships'. Naturally, once Nyasaland was so included and Barrow joined the federal legislature and cabinet, they saw little of each other and 'Barrow transferred his prime allegiance from the Nyasaland government to the Federal government'. When the results of the elections for the federal parliament were announced, Barrow came fourth out of four Nyasaland Federal Party members. He consulted Colby as to whether he should withdraw – as he himself was inclined – and the governor persuaded him not to back out since 'he was the only one who was any good'.[21] In the event, Barrow became a member of the triumvirate – Huggins, Welensky and Barrow – and of the federal cabinet, and was appointed deputy prime minister of the federation.

Apart from his close relationships with Barrow, and to a significantly lesser extent with the other non-official member of executive council, Hadlow – appointed in 1948 and variously described as Barrow's 'uncritical satellite' and 'rather like the doormouse in Alice: when prodded into wakefulness he would say "Er – what – well – I agree with Malcolm" ' – Colby did not, on the whole, enjoy or indeed seek out particularly close relationships with members of the non-official expatriate community. Two possible exceptions were Bucquet, general manager of the Nyasaland railways when Colby first arrived, and W. D. Lewis, president of the Tobacco Association, a leader of the more moderate elements among non-official expatriates and opposed to federation with Southern

Rhodesia, both of whom, unknown to many, enjoyed the governor's close confidence although they did not always agree.[22]

Whilst he saw them fairly frequently, especially those who lived near Zomba and Blantyre, he did not have close contacts, nor in a number of cases friendly relationships, with the non-official members of legislative council. It has been said that in the case of some non-official members of the legislature 'He didn't like them, but then they were not likable!'[23] Some of them positively detested him. M. H. Blackwood, appointed to legislative council in 1954, decades later admitted that he and Colby were 'daggers drawn most of the time', and considered the governor's opposition to federation a prime cause of its failure.[24] Mrs W. G. Widdas, who was appointed to legislative council in August 1949, was among those who most disliked Colby and years later she still found that recalling the unpleasantness made her feel physically ill.[25] Her dislike – which stemmed from the determined steps which Colby took to ensure that European estate owners did not illegally buy African Trust Land tobacco, thereby depriving the African Tobacco Board of its revenue – was as deep, almost total, and indelible as it was unbalanced and unreasonable:

I went on a short trip to London . . . several letters came to me in London saying H. E. was gunning for me and I'd better return at once and see him . . . I wired for an immediate appointment to H. E. and was given 2.30 p.m. on a certain day. When I arrived at G. H. in the pouring rain there was not a soul about to let me in, no servant, no A de C etc. I could not go in dripping wet by the closed door of G. H. so went along to H. E.'s office and climbed in through his window! Not very elegant. I asked why he was so against me. He replied 'We don't need people like you. Nyasaland can get along quite well without you. The tea people: we need them'. This to the widow of the founder of the African tobacco industry. To be told you were not needed hurt . . . Sir Geoffrey was without doubt the most hated man by every section of the community . . . where Sir Geoffrey failed was the constant change of heads of departments and the inability to get on with any part of the community.

Colby's relationships with the chairman of the Nyasaland railways, Colonel W. M. Codrington, a personal friend of Mrs Widdas, and with A. C. W. Dixon, general manager of the British Central Africa Company, were also poor and the reasons for this will be dealt with in later chapters.[26]

Distant and cool as were his relationships with expatriate non-officials, they were very much closer than those with Africans, but it is important to view these relationships in the general context of the late 1940s and early to mid-1950s in Nyasaland.

Save for a number of occasions in the 1890s, when the country was being 'pacified', and for the important short and limited insurrection of the Chilembwe Rising in 1915, relations between the races had always been good and were the envy of other African countries. Social contact, however, was virtually non-existent and the country was strongly stratified both socially and economically: Europeans at the top, Asians in the middle, and Africans at the bottom; there was also, of course, stratification within these racial groups. The situation was generally accepted by all and was not the source of obvious friction or manifest discontent.

In a number of important ways, the social, political and economic position of the Africans in Nyasaland differed substantially from that to which Colby had been accustomed in Nigeria during his service in the north and in Lagos, and a few examples will suffice to illustrate this.

In Nyasaland there was no equivalent of the six centuries of Islamic culture and the huge empires such as the Fulani with efficient systems of self-administration – for example in tax collection – which were typical of Northern Nigeria.[27] Nor had Nyasaland the long and close contact with Western trade, education and religion which had produced a large indigenous intelligentsia – self-confident, ambitious, and ready to take over national government – which was typical of southern Nigeria. In Lagos there were several African heads of government departments and the secretariat contained a number of senior African officers.[28] In contrast to this, Nyasaland had a senior European Civil Service and a junior African Civil Service, separately regulated and with no overlap. In Nyasaland the African chiefs enjoyed few governmental powers and were in practice subject to the will and directions of the district commissioners who worked through them only to a very limited extent. A senior officer who served in both northern Nigeria and Nyasaland has reported:

The pervading influence of Lugard's principle of indirect rule . . .
I found quite different from anything I saw in Nyasaland. In the
Holy North, the District Officer was technically the adviser to
the Emir who was the de facto ruler . . . Practically it was a case

of the iron fist in the velvet glove. The Emir disregarded the D. O.'s advice at his peril; it was all rather like a stately chess game, conducted with exquisite courtesy on both sides, with the rules well understood. It was an even contest; the Emir was the religious as well as the political head of his people, and he had to step well out of line before Kaduna would consider deposing him – and he knew it! Often it was not an adversary situation. A good Emir and a good Resident or D. O. would form close friendships and virtually rule together in great amity.

In Nyasaland no such close friendships, joint ruling, and political adviser–traditional ruler relationships developed. Important as some chiefs were in their traditional society – and this was not invariably the case – in governmental terms they were in practice often subservient to European officers, especially members of the provincial and district administration.[29] Nyasaland had no equivalent of the large Native Authorities, such as Sokoto, Kano, Katsina and Bornu of northern Nigeria, which administered education up to and including secondary schools and which had their own police forces, and the African heads of which earned very high salaries. Nor did Nyasaland have any equivalent of the growing power of trade unionism or the powerful, sophisticated, politically threatening, European-educated nationalist leaders of Nigeria: Macaulay, Azikiwe and Awolowo. In economic matters, Nyasaland also lacked the skilful and wealthy traders and the thrusting successful businessmen of Nigeria. In social matters, Nyasaland – where there was scarcely any social interaction between the races – differed from Nigeria where, especially in the north, polo played an important integrating role:[30]

> Polo was much more than a game as it performed important social functions. It afforded common ground not only for the expatriate community but also for expatriates and Africans. There was no condescension; the Africans were often better than us and the all-black Katsina team, captained by the Emir, was of world class. In most countries polo has always been a game for the very rich. Not so for us . . . anyone who wanted to play could, and did.
>
> After the game we usually went to some expatriate house and there, regardless of race or colour, had drinks together – non-alcoholic for the Muslims. I am sure that this was very good for race and class relations. Because of tsetse there were very few horses

in the South, and so very few clubs. There was, however, a very big one in Lagos. It was the 'in' thing for the black aristocracy to join as non-playing members. The club was always totally non-racial.

It is against the background of the prevailing conditions in Nyasaland and the differences with Nigeria – from whence Colby had come and where he had spent virtually the whole of his adult and professional life – that his attitude towards and relationships with the Africans of Nyasaland must be viewed.

After his experience of northern Nigeria emirs, Colby was impressed on his arrival in Nyasaland with the apparent weakness of the chiefs and their readiness to do what the government and the district commissioners, and among them particularly the 'strong' district commissioners, told them to do. Such a state of affairs was much to his liking because it enabled him to use the chiefs to induce the African population to join in the massive drive for increased agricultural production which was the hub of his development strategy. It is often said that he used a strongly coercive approach to this question and no doubt there were significant elements of compulsion in the execution of his policies of soil conservation, early garden preparation and economic crop production, but there is strong evidence that in the formulation and personal expression of his policies he himself was not persuaded that coercion was wise or possible and that he was aware of the dangers of compulsion. In a letter to government officers on the need for increased production, especially on African Trust Land, written in January 1950, he said:

The problem of securing increased production is not just a matter of planning and driving: it is a human problem since its solution will depend upon the sum of tens of thousands of individual efforts. Some people may say that the peasants should be dragooned and compelled to produce more. They may be right but we must be realistic and recognize that a handful of Europeans cannot compel hundreds of farmers – it just isn't possible as there is no effective machinery through which orders of such a vast scale can be enforced. In this campaign we must therefore get the people with us – from the Native Authorities through the group councils to the Village Headman . . . right down to the individual.[31]

He looked to the chiefs, with the help of government officers, to ensure
that the African population increased its efforts and expanded agricultural production. He realized that he needed them, but felt also that he
needed to take few positive steps to secure their co-operation since they
were by nature co-operative and generally malleable in the hands of the
district commissioners. Even so, it was very noticeable that an almost
invariable part of each of his district tours was a meeting with the
council of chiefs, and he went out his of way to call on leading chiefly
figures such as Mbelwa and Msusu.[32] Should their co-operation not be
forthcoming, however, he would have little hesitation in depriving them
of their status as Native Authorities, as in the case of Gomani, Malemia,
Kumtamanji and Kapeni in 1953 because of their positive opposition to
federation.

After his experience in Nigeria, with its long-standing African representation in the legislature and its relatively highly developed and
sophisticated African political activity, Colby found the late development
and absence of parallels in Nyasaland a new experience. When he arrived,
there were no African members of legislative council, and the Nyasaland
African Congress, not yet four years old, was exerting little more than
mild gentlemanly pressure on government. By the end of 1948, Colby
was instrumental in securing a change in the constitution which introduced two nominated Africans to membership of legislative council:
K. E. Mposa and E. A. Muwamba, neither of whom was particularly
critical of government.[33] Although the activity and strength of congress
increased markedly, especially from 1952 onwards, it was not until less
than two weeks before he left the protectorate on retirement that Africans
were elected to the legislature – five of them, mainly highly active,
critical, vociferous nationalist politicians – and Colby had already chaired
its last meeting under his presidency. Since the non-European political
activity and pressure were generally so very weak, Colby could afford
largely to ignore them. He made early appeals to the African members
of legislative council to play some sort of leadership role in encouraging
economic development, he appointed them to the advisory board for the
distribution of foodstuffs during the 1949–50 food shortage, and they
were appointed to a number of other government boards and committees,
but not as many as one might have expected (although other Africans
and Asians were increasingly appointed to such boards and committees).

After Nigeria, where Africans had advanced to very senior levels in
the Civil Service, Nyasaland again struck Colby as being very different
in that there was an African Civil Service entirely separate from and

subordinate to the European Civil Service. Although it is commonly recognized that he devoted much energy to the early technical training of Africans – for example in insisting on the vocational elements in the curriculum of Dedza Secondary School, and in creating the School of Agriculture, the Posts and Telecommunications School, and the Trade School[34] – it is equally commonly believed that Colby was not interested in Africanizing the senior Civil Service and advancing African members of the Service generally.

There are three indications that this latter belief is not entirely valid. First, late in 1949, he drew executive council's attention to the practice of employing Europeans in subordinate positions in the Civil Service, and pointed out that 'the continuance of such a state of affairs would inevitably lead to further discontent and criticism'.[35] He added as a matter of policy that unqualified European women should not be employed and that government's aim should be to fill all subordinate posts with African personnel. The arguments which he expressed were principally economic, but he was aware of the political dangers of not beginning to Africanize certain posts. Second, also late in 1949, he had executive council discuss the proposal that a new grade of African official, to be known as African administrative assistant, should be created to relieve district commissioners of routine administrative work. Council advised against this proposal at the time but later, in September 1952, they agreed and African district assistants were appointed, one in 1953 and four others in 1955.[36] This was a small beginning, but it was at least a start upon which others could build later in Africanizing the Service. Third, fearing further influence from South Africa or Southern Rhodesia, in March 1952 he directed that no vacancy should be advertized in these areas without his own specific approval, and that whenever a candidate recommended to fill a particular vacancy was a South African the recommendation for appointment should be subject again to his personal approval.[37] Importation of Southern Rhodesians and South Africans would inevitably delay Africanization and would be a politically sensitive and dangerous issue. In these matters he was several years ahead of his time.

Colby's relationship with non-officials can, then, be summed up by saying that in respect of Europeans they were really close and amicable only with Barrow; that they were neither close nor always amicable with members of legislative council; and that they were particularly bad with the Central Province tobacco planters, the Nyasaland railways, and the British Central Africa Company. In respect of Africans, they were not close and the question of them being amicable did not therefore arise; he did, however, take the first, vitally important, steps towards advancing Africans in the public service.

With non-officials, therefore, as in the case of officials, what was said of Fletcher, headmaster of Charterhouse, could also be said of Colby in that he shared 'that . . . attitude of attack which willingly, and without counting the cost, makes a host of enemies in battling to an appointed end'.[38]

At about this time, Colonel J. G. Bott, a British postal official of long experience, was undertaking an enquiry into the organization of the Posts and Telecommunications Department in Southern Rhodesia. Colby asked him to visit Nyasaland to 'obtain information about the working of the local postal administration'.[22] Bott advised the governor that he needed to recruit a new, high quality postmaster-general from outside the country, since none of the existing staff in Nyasaland was suitable for promotion to the headship of department. With this advice and Morgan's departure, Colby deferred the appointment of the commission of inquiry in order 'to grant the new postmaster-general an opportunity to improve the existing posts and telegraph service'.[23]

It took the Colonial Office some time to find the sort of man with the qualities Colby was looking for – a man with an engineering background rather than a background in postal management – to revitalize the department and enable it to play its full role in the development thrust; but early in September 1949 the secretary of state announced the appointment of Lieutenant-Colonel H. O. Ellis, who had served in the United Kingdom postal service since 1926, and in 1944 had been seconded to the Allied Control Commission headquarters in Germany.[24] He has been described by senior colleagues as 'altogether a different kettle of fish' from his predecessor: a strong-willed, clever telecommunications engineer who liked to have his own way.[25]

> He brooked no interference in the administration of his Department. He would consider a problem from every angle and once a satisfactory solution had been agreed he would see the matter ruthlessly pursued until the result was achieved.[26]

Ellis was, in fact, precisely the sort of man Colby was looking for: a man after his own heart. He was aware that substantial changes were needed and he accepted them as a challenge which he enjoyed. He held Colby in high regard and received much help, encouragement and support from him, although the postmaster-general did not always easily get his own way and they had frequent confrontations over the magnitude and cost of the demands for equipment which Ellis made.[27]

The new postmaster-general's appointment – on secondment from the Home Civil Service – took effect from 25 August and he arrived by air on 3 October.[28] His task was mammoth, and in the interim between Morgan's departure and Ellis' arrival, the department had continued to attract much public criticism – the Convention of Associations in May

1949 recording their 'great concern at the deterioration in all branches
of the posts and telegraph service'.[29] Colby looked to Ellis to get the
convention off his back, to sort out the departments and make it play
its full part in the country's development.

Ellis settled in quickly and spent his first few months consulting with
a wide body of opinion including the chamber of commerce and the
Convention of Associations, whose members had so many complaints to
make, and other 'responsible members of the public as to the services
which they would wish him to provide'. He then moved on to 'concentrating on placing proposals before the financial committee of the legislative assembly and obtaining the financial authority necessary for the
general improvement of facilities within the protectorate'.[30] He spent
much time revising the development programme (to which Colby now
allocated £650,000 over a five-year period for postal and telecommunications improvements, as against the £170,000 over ten years proposed
by the Post-War Development Committee). In addition, in May 1950,
Colby told legislative council that he had secured the British government's authority to raise a loan of £360,000 for posts and telecommunications development.[31]

Two months later, Ellis and his chief engineer, W. J. Silvester, made
a quick trip by air to Europe to recruit technical staff and to negotiate
with British manufacturers for speedy delivery of equipment on favourable terms. This was a most unusual step to take – a corner-cutting
exercise deeply untypical of civil service methods; it was Ellis' idea, but
Colby readily agreed to it and it was a considerable success. They
concluded contracts with manufacturers during their visit and did so at
a lower figure than the cost which seemed probable whilst dealing
with it on paper in Nyasaland before they left. Through his military
connections, Ellis was able to acquire a good deal of ex-war equipment
and have it shipped to Nyasaland.[32] Silvester later wrote:

> With regard to the filling of the posts we had created we did what
> was unheard of. We got a briefcase full of Crown Agent application
> forms and flew off to Germany to the Allied Control Commission
> Headquarters because Mr. Ellis knew just the men and women who
> were about to be released from their Control Commission duties.
> They were all members of the British Post Office and fully trained.
> We managed to find all the personnel we needed and had them in
> the field in record time.[33]

Colby and Ellis were anxious to take quick action in securing staff and equipment because they wanted to repair the damage of the past and allay criticism from the commercial sector, and because in replying to the Convention of Associations' long list of complaints in May 1949, the government, rather than drawing further attention to the quality of administration, had relied on the defence that:

a number of the difficulties are connected with the delay in obtaining the staff and equipment necessary to bring the services up to the desired standard.[34]

Ellis, who found his work stimulating and rewarding,[35] kept Colby fully informed of his actions and continued to correspond at length with such bodies as the chamber of commerce and the Convention of Associations, and from time to time attended their meetings to address them on developments. On one such occasion, in April 1951, he listed the improvements in telecommunications over the preceding 15 months: the number of connecting circuits between Limbe and Blantyre had been increased nearly threefold and an additional circuit provided between Limbe and Cholo; 260 additional subscribers had been given service; the old Limbe telephone exchange had been replaced by a new unit of a size increased by 50 per cent; the Blantyre exchange had been overhauled, modernized and increased in size by 50 per cent; the trunk circuits from Limbe and from Blantyre to Zomba had been increased to two and a half times the previous number; the first automatic exchange in the protectorate, at Zomba, had been opened; two small exchanges at Luchenza and Bvumbwe had been provided and a more modern exchange had taken the place of the old unit at Mlanje; a high-power radio connection with Salisbury had been opened, giving access to all parts of Southern Rhodesia; highly skilled European supervisors from the United Kingdom were introducing a greater degree of training and a closer supervision of junior staff; and one of these supervisors periodically visited subscribers to check on the quality of the service.[36]

Nor did Ellis stop there, for he went on to tell the chamber of commerce about firm future developments:

within the next few months an additional circuit would be run between Limbe and Cholo and two direct circuits between Limbe and Mlanje; a new exchange would be opened at Salima with a facility for connecting with the Lilongwe exchange; tests were being conducted with South Africa and Southern Rhodesia to enable trunk calls to be made to Johannesburg and to Beira; within six months he expected to have telephone communications with Ncheu, Dedza, Lilongwe and Fort Johnston; Mlanje would become automatic and a new automatic exchange would also be installed at Thornwood and at Namadzi; by this time too he anticipated that Makwasa and Palombe would have their own exchange systems; additional circuits would then exist between Cholo/Mlanje and Cholo/Limbe and it was probable that communications to Northern Rhodesia would have been established.[37]

The location of the various developments mentioned by Ellis in this address to the chamber of commerce fell into four groups: the Southern Highlands tea and tobacco plantation and commercial areas; lakeshore holiday resorts; the major administrative centres of the southern half of the protectorate; and Nyasaland's primary trading partners in southern Africa. For production, commercial, tourist and governmental administrative reasons, it was important that these places should have access to a modern and efficient system of communications.

Each of the expectations outlined by Ellis in the second half of his address was fulfilled, and other developments followed. Not only was the internal telephone system extended and modernized, but international communications were greatly expanded. In addition to the radio-telephone link between Zomba and Salisbury – inaugurated on 18 November 1950 by the governors of Nyasaland and Southern Rhodesia talking to each other from their own offices – other services were opened to East Africa and Northern Rhodesia in 1952 and to the United Kingdom (via Southern Rhodesia) in 1953. During the same period many new post offices and postal agencies were also opened and facilities for the public were much improved in the existing offices.[38]

Such, with Colby's backing, was Ellis' success that in 1952 the formerly highly critical members of the standing committee on finance resolved to:

> record their appreciation of . . . the work of developing the Territory's postal, telephonic and telegraphic communications which have taken place during the last two years.[39]

Colby was deeply pleased with the progress. However, the 1953 Constitution of the Federation of Rhodesia and Nyasaland placed 'Posts, telegraphs, telephones . . . and Post Office savings banks' on the federal legislative list,[40] for which the federal government, rather than the territorial governments, took responsibility and, consequently, from September 1954 the whole of the work of the Nyasaland Posts and Telecommunications Department was transferred to the federal government.[41]

Colby much regretted the loss of his departments to the federal government, and particularly the transfer of Posts and Telecommunications after so much impressive development following severe initial worries. He did, however, have the satisfaction of knowing that he handed over a much improved, modern and efficient department run by enthusiastic and highly competent senior officers and well-trained junior officers. He believed that, given time and leadership, Nyasaland could not only survive but could develop on its own without being incorporated in a federation, and his recent experience with the Department of Posts and Telecommunications strongly supported this belief.

Colby was clearly very proud of the developments in posts and telecommunications – indeed a missionary in the country at the time felt that the governor's 'highest ambition for Nyasaland appeared to be the improvement of the telephone service'[42] – and it is instructive to recall the steps which he took to bring them about.

First, he was quick to detect the deficiencies in the administration and leadership of the department and to take steps to secure the resignation of the head of department. Although such deficiencies might be obvious to others, it by no means followed that they would be evident to a very new head of government ensconced in Government House. Second, he did not rush into substantively replacing the postmaster-general by the obvious expedient of promoting another senior officer already in the Nyasaland service, but sought and followed the advice of an experienced postal official from the United Kingdom as to the type of successor needed to head the department. Third, having secured the services of Ellis, he gave him his head and backed his judgement in respect of what was needed for fast development and how it should be acquired. Fourth, he significantly expanded the resources available to the department – both human and financial – although not to the full extent of Ellis' requests which one of his officers has said 'probably exceeded those of all other government departments put together'.[43] The recurrent budget expenditure rose from £83,903 in 1948 to £181,000 in 1953, and the established staff rose over the same period from 386 to 665. In expanding the senior establishment, he revitalized the department by a significant injection of new officials trained and experienced in the United Kingdom postal service: of the 59 senior officers in post in March 1953, a total of 50 had previously served in the UK service and 25 of these were seconded from that service. Furthermore, 39 of the 59 officers had been appointed in 1950 and 1951 as a result of Ellis' recruiting visit to Europe,[44] whereas only one had been appointed to Nyasaland before Colby's arrival.

Colby's purpose, first in ensuring the adequate leadership of the Department of Posts and Telecommunications and then in strongly supporting it with resource provision and personal encouragement, was to reinforce his development strategy at the heart of which lay increased production and exports, particularly of agricultural crops. He was convinced that such increased production and exports could be secured only by an efficient government machine – to stimulate and supervise African agricultural production and marketing – and an efficient commercial sector, especially that part which was located in the expatriate tea and tobacco plantation areas of the Shire Highlands and business centres of Blantyre and Limbe. Each of these needed a rapid and effective communications system both internally and, increasingly, externally. Colby saw that they got it.

9· The Railways

'This most pressing problem.'

In the earlier chapter on Colby's development strategy, the importance which he attached to infrastructural development, including transportation, was made clear. There were two major components of the country's transport system, roads and railways, but only the former were directly under his control because the latter were privately owned. Such was the importance of the railways to the development of the protectorate's economy that his lack of control – or indeed of much influence – over the railways was an early and continuing source of deep concern and frustration to him. The story of how he handled this issue illustrates his quick and clear identification of the fundamental economic importance of the railways to development and his extraordinary persistence in trying to solve the problem.

The railway issue was a complex one and it is necessary first to outline the evolution of the system with which Colby was faced in 1948.[1]

In the two decades straddling the change from the nineteenth to the twentieth century, three factors combined to persuade the British and Nyasaland governments to build a railway as the principal means of transportation into and out of the country to replace the existing means by river between the Lower Shire and the Indian Ocean. First, there was the fluctuating level of the Shire River which made navigation difficult and, beyond certain points, impossible. Second, there were the pressures from expatriate planters whose agricultural labour costs were high when there was also heavy demand for labour to carry goods between the Shire Highlands and the head of navigation on the Lower Shire. Third, there were the persistent representations of the Scottish missionaries that head porterage, especially by children and women, and particularly over the very steep slopes of the escarpment between the highlands and the river, was inhumane.

The early plans, in the second half of the 1890s, proposed two possible routes: one being the relatively short stretch of rail from Quelimane on the coast in Portuguese territory to Blantyre, and the other being a longer route up the Zambezi and Shire rivers and a railway to Blantyre. The second of these, by using an international waterway, would avoid the payment of customs duty in Portuguese East Africa. Both plans at the time came to naught through the failure to secure financial backing, especially since the British government refused to build the railway itself and insisted on private capital being used. Between 1901 and 1903, in a series of agreements, however, the British government contracted with the Shire Highlands Railway Company (SHR), formed by a local businessman, E. C. Sharrer, that the company should build a railway from Chiromo, at the confluence of the Ruo and Shire rivers, to Blantyre, and that the government should grant the company 3200 acres of land for each mile of railway constructed.[2] A further fall in the level of the Shire caused the contract to be extended to Port Herald 42 miles lower down the river but still in Nyasaland territory. The line from Port Herald to Blantyre was opened on New Year's Day, 1908. Yet another fall in the level of the Shire brought about the extension of the railway south of Port Herald to the Zambezi River at Chindio. This railway, 60 miles long and largely in Portuguese territory, was constructed between 1913 and 1915 by the Central African Railway Company (CAR), a subsidiary of SHR. The contracts of 1902, 1908 and 1913 gave the Nyasaland government the option to purchase SHR and CAR in the future under terms specified in the agreements. Uncertainties of navigation, now on the Zambezi, led to the construction by the Trans Zambezi Railway Company (TZR) of a line from Murracca, opposite Chindio, to Dondo, 18 miles from Beira, on the Beira Junction Railway. The railway system was 'completed' in 1935 with the opening of the Zambezi Bridge and the northward extension of the line to Salima on Lake Nyasa; a continuous railway now existed from central Nyasaland to Beira in Portuguese territory on the Indian Ocean.

Nyasaland now had, in physical terms, the railway infrastructure necessary for economic development. In financial terms, however, it was by no means the development blessing which it appeared to be. A series of financial arrangements, imposed by the British government upon the Nyasaland government, prevented or severely hindered the accrual of the full economic development benefits which the railway had promised.

As we saw in an earlier chapter, the financial burden of the railway was viewed with an air of fatality by several of Colby's predecessors, especially Manning and Bowring, neither of whom thought significant development possible with such an incubus standing in their way.

First, the British government recognized that it had been unwise to agree to transfer to the SHR 3200 acres of land for each mile of railway constructed because land, especially in the Shire Highlands, was already, by the end of the first decade of the twentieth century, in short supply and subject to increasingly high population densities. The government was pressed by the Associated Chamber of Agriculture and Commerce in 1908 not to hand over the subsidy lands, because of land shortage, and indeed to take over the railway itself, in effect to nationalize it; the motion to do this was defeated by only a single vote, with the chairman and secretary abstaining. As a result of these pressures, the government agreed to redeem the subsidy lands, totalling 361,600 acres, as part of the 1913 contract to build the CAR line; this was done by paying to the British Central Africa Company (BCA), the SHR's subsidiary, the sum of £180,800 between 1912 and 1915. Britain, however, placed the burden of this payment on the Nyasaland government by providing it with a loan on All Fools' Day, 1916, to be redeemed by 1957 at an annual interest of 3.5 per cent.[3]

A second brake on development, also in the 1913 contract, was that the Nyasaland government had guaranteed to the BCA, for a period of ten years, 4 per cent dividends on £500,000 preference shares.[4]

Third, by the 1919 agreement to build the TZR from the Zambezi to Dondo, the British government, without consulting them, obliged the Nyasaland government to guarantee a public issue of debentures: 6 per cent per annum on £1,200,000 for 25 years. This guarantee was extended in 1923 to cover until 1937 the annual instalments of a £110,000 hire purchase agreement between TZR and the Beit railway trustees to replace the originally intended wooden sleepers with steel sleepers.

Fourth, when in 1923 TZR issued £200,000 of 5.5 per cent ten-year notes to purchase competing river fleets on the Zambezi, additional rolling stock, plant and further steel sleepers, the Nyasaland government's guarantee was extended to cover this issue.

Fifth, during the early negotiations in 1930 for building the Zambezi Bridge, the government agreed to TZR increasing the amount of its first mortgage debentures by up to £300,000, guaranteed by the Nyasaland government, for rolling stock and improvements on the TZR line.

Sixth, when in 1933 the ten-year notes were due for redemption, and the Crown Agents paid TZR the £200,000 involved from the Joint Colonial Fund, the Nyasaland government was obliged to enter into a further guarantee of £200,000 12-year bearer notes.

Also, when the Zambezi Bridge was constructed, its southern end had to be built at Sena rather than at Murracca where the TZR terminus had been originally built. Consequently, a south approach line of 24 miles had to be constructed. The Nyasaland government now advanced to the Nyasaland Railway Company (NR) – a company formed in 1930 to acquire SHR and the share capital of CAR, and to finance the construction of the Zambezi Bridge – the funds necessary to build the south approach.

Finally, there were very complex arrangements made for the construction of the Zambezi Bridge itself but, in this case, the financial burden on the Nyasaland government was removed by the payment of free grants-in-aid by Britain to the Nyasaland government. Although the grants were free, rather than a loan, they seriously reduced the chances of Nyasaland receiving other development assistance from Britain.

Since Nyasaland's own resources were seriously insufficient to service the debt charges incurred by these railway agreements, the British government lent at 5 per cent interest the funds to cover them. During the whole of the 1930s, the Nyasaland government was unable to pay any of the interest on these loans-in-aid, the interest accumulated at a depressing rate, and in 1938 the finance commissioner emphasized that:

> Unless the annual charges can be reduced or Railway earnings very considerably increased, the Trans Zambezi Railway Company's debt to the Nyasaland Government and of that Government to the Imperial Treasury will continue to mount by the same inexorable process which is unsatisfactory to all parties – to the taxpayer in the United Kingdom who is advancing the money with diminishing prospect of its return, to the Nyasaland Government which must come to regard borrowing on the 'never never' system as a matter of course, and to the Railway Company which has insufficient incentive towards showing a profit because it can pay no dividends until all its accumulated and accumulating liabilities to the Nyasaland Government have been liquidated.

In respect of the TZR burden alone, the Nyasaland government paid £2,669,000 between 1920 (the date of the public issue of debentures) and 1948: the equivalent of two years' full ordinary revenue of the government at the latter date.[5]

Given this heavy burden – past, present and future – on the Nyasaland government, given also the vital role which the railway played in the country's transport system and therefore in its economic development, given too Colby's personal experience of the railway's role when he was director of supplies in Nigeria, it is not surprising that the new governor in 1948 very quickly turned his attention to railway matters. He brought Phillips into the secretariat as assistant secretary and gave him a number of special tasks, the main one of which was detailed research into the railways. Phillips spent the last quarter of 1948 doing this work, drafting and finalizing a report which Colby turned into a despatch to the secretary of state by Christmas. Thereafter, he continued to use Phillips in his dealings on railways, both in the secretariat and in the Colonial Office whilst on leave in Britain.[6]

The essential picture which Colby quickly pieced together from Phillips' work and from his own study was that the railway system in Nyasaland was the only one in the British colonies not publicly owned; that private companies – NR, CAR and TZR – all domiciled in London, had been largely financed by the government which had paid for the greater part of the loan capital; that none had discharged its past debts; and that all wished to raise more money in the near future for capital development. The companies' failure to discharge their debts had meant that the cost of servicing the loans fell on the Nyasaland government and was running at about £140,000 a year – a figure which Colby noticed was much greater than that spent annually on either the Education or the Medical Department (c. £107,000 each). The companies were managed on commercial lines from London with two government directors on each board; the NR and the CAR each had two other directors, and the TZR had six other members of the board, four of whom were Portuguese government and Companhia de Mocambique nominees. Although the directors made periodic visits to Nyasaland, there were significant problems of remote control.[7]

Colby's basic, and quite quickly reached, conclusions were: first, that the railway was a public utility, vital to the country's economic development, and that if the railway companies were to play their proper part in the protectorate's development it was essential that the disadvantages of remote control should be removed; and second, that the Nyasaland government was entitled to, and should be put in a position to, exert direct and important influence on the policies of the companies.

He was aware of the recent publicity given to the claims that although the distances were roughly equal, it cost six times as much to rail tobacco from Blantyre to Beira as it did from Salisbury to Beira. He was aware too of the social ramifications of lack of influence over the railways, for the Post-War Development Committee in 1946 had expressed its concern about:

> the effect of high railway rates upon African development and upon the large scale temporary emigration of Nyasaland natives to the South. [There is] urgent need for an improvement in the standard of living and the purchasing power of the African which . . . would be furthered by cheaper rail and other transport rates . . . these would foster production and the development of the country.[8]

It was, however, the economic aspects in which Colby was most interested.

Very soon indeed after his arrival, he secured Colonial Office agreement that the powers of the government directors should be widened and their liaison with the Nyasaland government should be improved, partly as a means of demonstrating to the companies that under Colby's governorship the Nyasaland government intended to associate itself more actively with the policies of the companies than in the past. A little later, he secretly proposed that the government should secure control of voting rights by purchasing the additional 3.8 per cent (58,375) of shares in NR to reach the 75 per cent necessary to force through a change in the articles of association, since he was sure that the majority of the existing board of NR would be opposed to what he saw as a vital element in securing greater influence over policy: the transfer of domicile from London to Nyasaland in order to overcome the disadvantages of remote control. When Colby had broached the question of a transfer of domicile to Codrington, chairman of NR, during a visit to Nyasaland in 1949, Codrington had replied that if the government wished to secure control it should exercise its option to purchase the companies.[9] Since CAR was a private subsidiary wholly owned by NR, acquisition of control of the latter would automatically give control of the former. He recognized that securing control of TZR was out of the question, since the Nyasaland government owned only 25 per cent of the shares, but this was not necessary since the Portuguese would probably agree to a simple change in domicile. Colby pointed out that domicile in the United Kingdom meant that some £27,000 in additional overheads was unnecessarily incurred annually, and that United Kingdom income and profits tax, amounting to £850,000 between 1941 and 1949, had been incurred, whereas no other colonial railway in Africa paid United Kingdom tax on its profits or, indeed, local income tax.[10]

During another visit to Nyasaland made by Codrington, Colby held a meeting on 8 March 1951, chaired by himself and attended by Codrington, Stevens (general manager of NR), Brown (now a government director), Barrow, Hadlow and Phillips, at which Codrington again rejected the idea of change of domicile,[11] and at which the governor made his own views very clear:

> H. E. stated that in his opinion the railways must be an instrument for development and the present attitude of the railway company made this impossible. He was not at all satisfied with the finances of the company and further the Chairman of the Board, Mr Codrington, did not concern himself with Government's views. If he could avoid consulting Government he did so. The remark was endorsed by Mr Barrow.
>
> Mr Codrington replied that it had not been his intention to give that impression which he would like to dispel.[12]

Although these were the words used in the official record of the meeting, one member present recalled later what Colby had actually said: 'they had been duelling most of the day and then eventually Colby pulled off the gloves and launched out and said "I have to tell you Codrington that I don't think you care a tuppenny damn about this country", to which Codrington replied "Oh, really, Governor? You surprise me." '[13] There was a deep and acrimonious difference of opinion and attitude between Colby and Codrington which led to 'rather bitter relations' and to disputes from the summer of 1948 and continued 'with short intervals' thereafter: 'during these years Sir Geoffrey Colby . . . made many complaints both general and specific against the management of the Nyasaland Railways and Mr Codrington personally'. As early as April 1949, the governor told the secretary of state in a meeting at Government House that 'one of the main difficulties with which the Protectorate was faced was the intransigence of the Chairman of the Board of the Railways. If a new Chairman could be found matters might be very different.'[14] Colby saw the railways as essentially a public utility over which the government should have the right of control in the interests of economic development. Codrington saw the railways simply as a private company, with duties primarily if not exclusively to its shareholders, although the Fiscal Survey in 1947 claimed that:

> The development of Nyasaland and its railway is interdependent and both the Government and the railway[s] are cognisant of that fact.[15]

If Codrington was cognisant of the fact it seemed to Colby that the chairman was doing little or nothing about it. Colby tried to use the articles of association to have Codrington removed and replaced as chairman, but the Colonial Office's legal advice was that the articles could not be used in this way.

Colby considered, and favoured, 'orthodox nationalisation' of the railway companies, similar to the extensive nationalization of major industries and utilities in Britain at the time, but concluded that the Nyasaland government could not provide the necessary finances to do this. As an alternative, in a letter written to Cohen five days before going on leave in May 1951, he returned to his proposal to secure voting control of the companies and now sought formal permission to do this and subsequently to transfer their domicile to Nyasaland. His proposal also contained the innovative suggestion that after change of domicile the companies should be exempted from local income tax.[16]

Colby pressed his argument with the Colonial Office whilst on leave in Britain, dealing principally with C. E. Lambert, assistant secretary, whom Colby had met when Lambert was secretary to the West Africa Civil Service Salaries Commission, 1945–6,[17] and who now recommended that the governor's proposals should be supported. Lambert, on Colby's behalf, consulted and secured supportive advice from stockbrokers, counsel and the Treasury.[18] Armed with this support, he then secured the secretary of state's agreement in principle that it would be desirable for the domicile of NR and CAR to be transferred from London to Nyasaland, and his approval to the acquisition of the necessary number of shares to effect this. The secretary of state's approval followed advice from the Treasury that change in the domicile of TZR could not be contemplated and that the suggestion which Colby had made to grant tax exemption 'seemed to raise objections and would require very careful consideration'. Of these two Treasury 'provisos', the first was communicated to the secretary of state and to Colby, but the second was mentioned to neither: an omission which the Colonial Office was later to regret and which Colby was later to exploit.[19]

The day after he returned from leave on 11 November 1951, clearly much gratified by the progress made in London, Colby sent a telegram authorizing the Crown Agents to negotiate up to five shillings each for NR shares 'but of course, unless we can get total number required we naturally do not wish to buy any at all'.[20] In instructing the Crown Agents to acquire the shares, H. Nield of the Colonial Office emphasized that:

> It is of course essential that the purchase of these shares should be raised on a highly confidential basis and that the matter should not come to the notice of the company until the total number of shares required have been bought. It would therefore be appropriate if before instructing your brokers you would confirm that under this procedure there will be no danger of what is proposed becoming known to the company.[21]

The brokers replied, not unnaturally, that whilst they might be able to buy parcels of shares in the name of a nominee over a period of time without the objective becoming known, it would become obvious to the company that someone was interested in their shares, and that consequently they could not ensure that the necessary number of shares could be bought within the price limit specified by Colby. As an alternative, the brokers suggested that they could approach one or more of the existing shareholders and make a direct offer for the required number of shares; this, however, would immediately come to the notice of NR.[22] The Colonial Office favoured the former method despite the risk of rising prices, but Colby first asked for details of one of the major shareholders, Witan Investment, so that he could consider using the latter method, being of the view that it would be unwise to approach the other main shareholder, BCA, because Oury, chairman of TZR, was a BCA director.[23] Witan, however, although not unwilling to sell, insisted on consulting NR first and giving them the name of the prospective buyer. There was in fact an agreement between Witan and the board of NR that the former would not dispose of their shares without the board's knowledge.[24]

Colby now realized that he could not secure the necessary shares without Codrington knowing about the purchase in advance, and consequently, in a telegram of 14 February 1952, he proposed to the Colonial

Office that they should tell Codrington that they planned to approach other shareholders and to negotiate with BCA over the purchase of shares. He pointed out that purchase from BCA would be an advantage since they would re-invest the proceeds in Nyasaland. He added that since they could not now effect the purchase *sub rosa*, it had been suggested to him that he might as well approach Codrington and directly suggest that the company's domicile should be moved to Nyasaland. He did not think this stood much chance of success and, revealing his fuller and longer term objectives, he said that 'control of undertaking by holding necessary number of shares will, I think, be indispensable in future'.[25] It was control through shares rather than control through domicile which he was after, but, by expressing his wishes in the form of share control leading to change of domicile leading to policy control, he encompassed a second best solution – control through domicile – within the best solution, control through shares.

On 19 March, the secretary of state agreed with Colby's proposal – but only after a reminder from Colby on 4 March[26] – and asked for his agreement that Codrington be informed at the Colonial Office, and that thereafter negotiations be resumed with Witan Investment and BCA.[27] Colby telegraphed his agreement the following day,[28] but had to send a reminder two and a half months later asking to be informed of the current position.[29] Codrington, however, already knew that Colby was taking steps to secure control of the railway system, because as early as November 1951 Stevens had reported to him a conversation which he had with the British ambassador to Portugal, in which the ambassador said that Colby had recently told him that 'British ownership of TZR served no useful purpose and it could well be sold to the Portuguese.' Codrington promptly reported this conversation to Cohen.[30] Also, during the first half of 1952, Codrington told Phillips that he knew what Colby was up to and was attempting to buy NR shares,[31] and he made the same point to the minister of state in the course of a conversation with him,[32] although at no stage was the general manager aware of Colby's attempt to nationalize NR.[33]

Until about March 1952, the Colonial Office had manifestly and with some enthusiasm supported Colby's views and proposals, primarily because they were directed towards economic development, which was as much in Britain's interests as in Nyasaland's, but they were now beginning to waver – indicated by the long delay in taking action after the secretary of state's agreement to Colby's proposals for open purchase of shares – not on the matter of principle, but in pragmatic terms. Colby and Codrington were deeply antagonistic towards each other – as Gorell Barnes later said, 'the two men did not get on at all'[34] – and the harder Colby pushed, the more Codrington resisted. At one stage, Codrington felt that Colby's letters were so rude that he ended one of his own letters with the words 'This correspondence must now close',[35] although when Stevens was appointed general manager in February 1950, Codrington 'suggested that one of [his] first jobs was to improve relations with the Governor' and as a mollifying gesture a new locomotive was named 'Sir Geoffrey Colby' – 'which pleased him no end'.[36] Colby was determined to explore any means available to him to secure control of the railways – nationalization;[37] using the articles of association to try to replace the chairman and to enable the secretary of state to direct the board to take the matter of domicile transfer to a meeting of shareholders;[38] direct approach to Codrington to transfer domicile;[39] clandestine or open purchase of a 75 per cent shareholding; a suggestion that an Anglo–Portuguese organization own and run the railways – but the chairman, the law, diplomacy or financial restrictions blocked them all.[40] Furthermore, a general election in 1951 had replaced the British socialist government with a Conservative government significantly less inclined towards state control of private enterprise, and one of the NR directors, C. T. Holland–Martin, was joint treasurer of the Conservative Party.

At the time of this wavering, a solution to the Colonial Office's problem of handling Colby and Codrington presented itself: not a solution to the problem *per se*, but a way out for the Colonial Office. (Or maybe the way out induced the wavering.)

A meeting was held in the Colonial Office on 19 June 1952 between Lambert, Bourdillon and Phillips, during which Nyasaland's finances, railway capital requirements, and the future ownership of the railways were discussed.[41] Phillips pressed a number of suggestions for control of the railways, each of which was mildly countered and then, late in the afternoon (the meeting did not start until 4.30 p.m.) Lambert manoeuvred the discussion round again to the question of buying out the railways. He said that the original objection to nationalization had been that it would mean the end of unified control over the whole railway system down to Beira, but that in agreeing to the transfer of domicile they had in effect agreed to the ending of that unified control; consequently, nationalization could no longer be refused on those grounds. Phillips, heartened by the renewed possibility of nationalization – which he knew Colby much preferred – added that if the Nyasaland government had the money it would be willing to buy out the railway.

Lambert then turned for assistance to the fact that federation had become almost a certainty only a few weeks previously (with the Lancaster House agreement to the draft federal scheme, and the setting up of fiscal, judicial and public service commissions) and he suggested that if federation were finally accepted, the railways would become a federal responsibility. The federal government, he believed, would not tolerate the present set-up and would be in a position to do what the Nyasaland government wished but were financially unable to do: nationalize the railways.

Although members of the meeting cast doubts on this idea – the federal government might have difficulty in raising the required money on the tight market; Rhodesian Railways might take priority; and the current tri-partite control (Nyasaland government, Colonial Office and NR board of directors) might become quadri-partite by the addition of a federal railways department, and under such circumstances Nyasaland might wish to opt out of federal control if this were possible – Lambert 'maintained his view' that:

> if federation were brought about this might well prove the answer to the Nyasaland Railways problem and that it would be unwise to pursue some alternative policy for the future of the railways until the federation issue became clearer at the end of the year.

Following the meeting, Lambert – who knew full well that relations with the federal government would be the responsibility of the Commonwealth Relations Office and not of the Colonial Office – continued to 'maintain his view' and wrote a long letter to Colby on 19 July, pursuing the federal nationalization proposal further by suggesting an investigation into the financial and legal mechanisms of nationalization: 'the time has arrived to give the problem some closer and detailed consideration'.[42] He rejected a proposal made by Footman, the chief secretary, in a letter of 20 June – at Colby's instigation and as a means of countering any further delaying tactics of the Colonial Office – that the British government should purchase the first debentures (in effect, nationalize the railways) 'as a measure of practical assistance of the Federation proposals', and that an immediate decision was essential as being relevant to the deliberations of the fiscal commission. Lambert summed up by saying that the Colonial Office would examine the legal power of the secretary of state to force the directors of NR to take the issue of domicile to a shareholders' meeting, and would also examine the whole question of 'the nationalization of Nyasaland Railways in relation to the question of a hand-over to the federal government'. He concluded by saying:

> We should be glad to have your views on these suggestions and hope that you will agree with our view that we should concentrate on the possibilities which exist under federation. In general we feel that with federation there would be some hope of bringing about the changes we want to see in the running of the railways, but that without it the hopes are slender.

Colby immediately recognized from the tone of Lambert's letter that the only practical hope of broadly getting his way, of defeating Codrington and of bringing the Nyasaland railways under government control, whilst continuing to receive the support and sympathy of the Colonial Office, was to go along with their suggestion, but he was not prepared to accept the delay which he suspected was an important consideration in the Colonial Office's tactics:

> I agree, as I feel I must, to the propositions which you make . . . and hope that you will proceed with them whilst Phillips is available in the United Kingdom . . . I am anxious that the examination should get as far as possible in the next six weeks or so in order that we may be in a position on Phillips' return to assess the position further.

Then, responding to Lambert's statement that 'the time has arrived to give the problem some closer and detailed consideration', which overlooked the scale and depth of Colby's own work on the problem, he added:

> As you know, we have over the past four years or so been engaged in a detailed examination of all matters connected with the railways with a view to getting them on a better basis. I can only say that the position remains unsatisfactory and know you will agree. Despite the powers we are supposed to have through the appointment of Government directors, we seem, in effect, to have little or no control either of the railway programmes or of their policy.[43]

The Colonial Office acted upon Colby's request that the investigations be expeditious and that they involve Phillips. Indeed Colby had made such requests a month earlier in a letter to Gorell Barnes:

> We have particularly asked that H. E. I. Phillips who is now on leave should clear these matters with you now that he is in the United Kingdom and I was disappointed to learn from his most recent letter that no progress had been made.
>
> I should . . . be most grateful if you would be good enough to press on with these matters because I am most anxious that they should be settled and this seems an ideal opportunity for doing so. I shall be very glad to hear from you how matters are going.[44]

It must have seemed to Gorell Barnes that Colby was forever pushing him to get on with the job. Since Lambert had now been transferred to another department of the Colonial Office – a transfer which deprived the governor of the close personal support he had so far received – Gorell Barnes took up the correspondence himself, and on 26 September 1952 he wrote a secret letter to Colby in which he explained that the legal advice was against using the articles of association to compel the board to take the question of domicile transfer to a meeting of shareholders.[45] There was no doubt also, he added, that Codrington's recent correspondence with the minister of state made it abundantly clear that the chairman would not consider taking the question himself to the board and would not co-operate in any way with steps to transfer domicile. This, he believed, left only nationalization as a practical solution.

Gorell Barnes went on to say that because of the complexity of the Nyasaland railway system it would be necessary, before nationalization could be effected, 'for the problem to be investigated by an expert in railway affairs' – a rewording of Lambert's point about the need for 'closer and detailed consideration'. He then turned to compulsory purchase on the lines of recent British nationalization, which would require United Kingdom legislation, and added, 'I think we can assume that Ministers would not be prepared to introduce such legislation, at any rate so long as there is a possibility of finding another solution under federation.' Consequently, he saw the Nyasaland government exercising its option to purchase under the original agreements as the only means of acquiring control over NR, 'but it seems pretty clear to us that there is little prospect of the Nyasaland Government being in a position to buy out the railways in this way. If and when they become the responsibility of a federal government the situation might change in a way which would make nationalisation by purchase possible':

> To sum up then, our conclusion is that the transfer of domicile proposal cannot be further pursued and that the best hope of gaining control of the Railways lies in a federation being created and a Federal Government being willing to purchase such control. If, but only if, that hope were finally eclipsed, we would think it worthwhile asking Ministers whether they were prepared to contemplate nationalisation by United Kingdom legislation on the lines of the recent United Kingdom Nationalisation Acts. I am sorry that this reply seems unhelpful and I can assure you that we are as disappointed as we know you will be that the immediate outlook is not more favourable.

Gorell Barnes had added little or nothing to what Lambert had already said save that he had attempted more firmly to close the door on a number of Colby's suggestions. Colby did indeed find his reply unhelpful and was determined to continue to fight against delay. On 11 November 1952, he wrote back to Gorell Barnes and in a secret letter said that in respect of the 'vital issue of ownership' he was naturally disappointed that it had not been possible to take 'a definite step forward in the right direction'. He noted all the reasons for this, but said that he was not satisfied that the solution of the problem ought to await the outcome of federation. Federation, he argued, was unlikely to be effective for at least eighteen months, which would be a serious initial delay, and even then it would not be reasonable to expect the federal government to take early action because of competing demands for capital expenditure, for new services, and for items affecting the development of the whole of the Central African system rather than items affecting only one territory:

> In fact, if we accept the view that we must delay consideration of this matter until Federation comes about, we run the risk of deferring a solution of this most pressing problem for at least five years.[46]

If the Colonial Office had believed that Colby would give up after the Gorell Barnes letter of 26 September they were mistaken, for the governor, recognizing that there was no hope of changing the domicile other than through the goodwill of the board – however this was to be obtained – and that nationalization by legislation was 'impracticable', pursued the alternative of exercising the option to purchase. He broadly outlined the quite complex financial aspects of purchase and calculated that the whole of NR and the part of CAR in Portuguese territory would cost £6.25m of which, through various means, £4.25m would be recouped, 'so that the net expenditure involved in the transaction would be of the order of £2 million'.

He proposed that this should be made available by raising a further loan, and added:

> It seems to me inescapable that loan monies must be made available to enable the railways to be purchased, and whether we raise them or the Federation raises them is presumably immaterial from the market point of view. From the political point of view, however, I can see no object in waiting for Federation. The Federal authorities will have enough on their plate for many years to come. Let us put our own house in order first and we will then be in a position to hand over a Government-owned railway with all its assets and liabilities, the latter to include of course the liability for the new loan.

This last point was intended to reassure the British government that any financial burden which it or Nyasaland incurred would be short-lived, since it would be transferred to the federal government.

Colby's final paragraph was designed to force the Colonial Office to make an early decision on his proposal by indicating that he proposed to say at the forthcoming federation conference that he fully accepted the principle of the Nyasaland and associated railways being federal, but that, in view of the extremely unsatisfactory nature of the present set-up, he intended during the next year or two to set matters to right, and would suggest that NR should not become federal until the position had been sorted out.

He kept up the pressure and, two weeks after writing this letter, he pushed his case still further by writing to the two government directors of NR asking them to place before the board 'at the next convenient opportunity' the 'straight issue' of whether the board would recommend to shareholders that the domicile of the companies be changed from London to Nyasaland in order to take advantage of a firm offer by the Nyasaland government to introduce legislation to exempt them from Nyasaland income tax.[47] It was in this way that he hoped to secure the goodwill of the board without which he saw that change of domicile could not be secured, rejecting the unqualified conclusion of Gorell

Barnes that 'the transfer of domicile proposal cannot be further pursued'. He had already received executive council's approval to introduce this legislation and the Colonial Office, by not mentioning to him the Treasury's reservations, had failed to cast any doubts upon his proposal to do so when he had made it a year and a half earlier. He provided Brown and Milne with a number of arguments which they could use, including a calculation that by not paying United Kingdom income tax and by not maintaining a full London office, the company would save £100,000 a year: 'This will appeal to the shareholders who, as things are, do not stand a chance of getting a dividend.' At the end of his letter he said, 'I propose to make a passing mention of this proposal in my speech at the opening of Legislative Council on the 1st December' – which was only five days away, with an intervening weekend. He copied this letter to Gorell Barnes with a covering letter, also dated 26 November, in which he said:

> The Board's reaction should be interesting. If they were to turn down the proposal without good cause shown I should seriously consider sending a requisition to the board for the summons of an extraordinary general meeting where the whole matter could be laid before the shareholders. I doubt whether Codrington would in fact risk an exposure such as this.[48]

He went on to argue that change of domicile would be a very useful prelude to outright purchase and that with Codrington 'out of the way' he did not think there would be much haggling over the price. Change of domicile would also be a useful transition from the existing set-up to 'eventual control by this Government'. He concluded, typically, by hoping that Gorell Barnes was pressing on with examining the points made in his letter of 11 November! By re-introducing the issue of domicile transfer and tax exemption, in addition to the main thrust of purchase through exercising the option in the original agreements, Colby was adding a second string – or rather arrow – to his bow, but Gorell Barnes was to claim that 'Sir G. Colby went off, without consultation, at a tangent',[49] and Bourdillon hoped that Colby would 'be able to explain the apparently inexplicable way in which he has been running these two proposals side by side. While his main proposal was under consideration by us, he suddenly came out, quite unexpectedly, with his tax exemption proposal.'[50] These claims were unfair because the tax proposal was not new, and whilst Colby had told Gorell Barnes that he realized that 'any hope of effecting a change of domicile other than through the goodwill of the Board is out of the question',[51] he had certainly not said that there was no means of securing that goodwill. Gorell Barnes had concluded that 'the transfer of domicile proposal can not be further pursued'; Colby had shown that it could.

In the course of his speech at the opening of the 68th session of legislative council on Monday 1 December 1952, Colby, as he had said he would, did make reference, but a good deal more than 'passing reference', to his proposals:

The substantial increase in our exports during the past two or three years has thrown a very great strain on the resources of the Nyasaland Railways and I should like to take this opportunity of thanking the General Manager and his staff for the outstanding efforts they have made in dealing with the much heavier traffic which they are now being called upon to carry.

I know how much hard work and worry this has entailed. I am glad to note that next year we can expect new locomotives and rolling stock which should, I hope, relieve the strain.

I believe however that production in general is very much on the up-grade at the present time and until still further increases in carrying capacity are provided there is likely to be a continuing problem.

Had there been more rail capacity available in the current year we could have exported between 10,000 and 20,000 additional tons of maize. The fact that we have been unable to do this has deprived us of considerable additional purchasing power which, at the present time, would be particularly welcome. This underlines the need for railway capacity to be fully co-ordinated with production.

Honourable Members are aware that the Nyasaland Railways are under private ownership and subject to the direction of a Board in London. While this arrangement may have been satisfactory in the past it is now, in my opinion, out of date and Nyasaland should come into line with every other British territory in Africa and the Headquarters of the Nyasaland Railways should be transferred to Nyasaland; I have accordingly asked our Government Directors to put this proposal before the Board.

It is obvious that with the best will in the world there can never be full co-ordination of the transport requirement of this territory while the control of the Nyasaland Railways remains in London.

Moreover as long as the domicile of the Nyasaland Railways is in the United Kingdom the profits of the Company, unlike other Colonial Railways, are liable to British income tax and I have caused the Board to be informed that if the Company is transferred to Nyasaland the Government will introduce legislation to this Council which will exempt the Railway from income tax.[52]

Colby had now rocked the boat in no uncertain manner and 48 hours later the reverberations hit the Colonial Office. The *Financial Times* carried a report of the domicile transfer and tax exemption passages in his legislative council speech;[53] Douglas Dodds Parker wrote personally the same day to the secretary of state ('My Dear Oliver, I was deeply disturbed by the news in this morning's paper . . .');[54] Codrington, also on the same day, demanded and received an interview in the evening with Gorell Barnes ('He was already receiving enquiries from the market and could expect to receive enquiries both from shareholders as well as from the Portuguese. What was he to say in response to these enquiries?').[55] Also on 3 December, Gorell Barnes, furiously alarmed, particularly over the probable effect on the market price of NR shares, sent a telegram to Colby saying how disturbed he was that the governor had made his legislative council speech without consulting him,[56] and two days later Marnham, assistant secretary in the Colonial Office, wrote to Brown and Milne instructing them – on behalf of the governor who had been asked by Gorell Barnes to give the instruction[57] – to take no action on Colby's letter of 26 November asking that they take the issue to the board.[58] Letters were also received from Sinclair of the Imperial Tobacco Company ('As considerable customers of the Nyasaland Railways . . . we have been somewhat concerned to read in the press . . .')[59] and from Sun Life Assurance, of which Codrington was a director, complaining about the matters raised in the *Financial Times* report.[60]

Gorell Barnes was unfair to complain about Colby not consulting the Colonial Office because when the governor had made his domicile transfer and tax exemption proposals 18 months earlier, the secretary of state had given his approval in principle to the domicile transfer and the Colonial Office officials had neglected to tell either the secretary of state or Colby of the Treasury's reservations about the tax exemption proposal. He was right, however, to be worried about the share prices because whilst on 7 December NR shares stood at three shillings and sixpence, by 9 December they stood at four shillings and sixpence, and by 20 December 'about four to five shillings'.[61]

In the meantime, Colby had first sent a telegram to the Colonial Office saying that he greatly regretted that he should have caused them any embarrassment but that he hoped he could convince them that his proposal was unobjectionable and that he intended to do this in a very early despatch.[62] The despatch followed three days later – exactly a week after the legislative council speech – and must have been in an advanced stage of anticipatory formulation at the time of the speech.[63]

The despatch of 8 December 1952, six foolscap pages long, was addressed to Lyttelton, the secretary of state, rather than to any of the Colonial Office officials as were most of Colby's other communications, and was a masterly, well-argued and clearly expressed document. At the outset he noted with regret that the secretary of state had been disturbed that he should have announced the proposals for transfer of domicile and exemption from tax without first consulting the Colonial Office: at no stage did he say that he had received approval in principle of the former, and he had received no indication of doubts about the latter, nor that he had told them he was going to take this step in his legislative council speech, albeit with very little time for them to object. He then argued that, at first sight, permanent exemption from income tax of one private company appeared to offend against the fundamental principles of taxation, but he suggested, 'with respect', that if it substantially benefited the community and conferred no benefit on individuals, the proposal would be unobjectionable: 'I shall direct my efforts to showing that this is in fact the case.' The fact that the Nyasaland government owned the great majority of NR capital, he argued, rendered his proposal to exempt the company from income tax unobjectionable.

The first part of his despatch was aimed at showing that, as a result of transferring domicile and exempting from tax, the position of the public debenture holders would have remained unaltered; that private shareholders would have received no dividends; that, whilst the Nyasaland government might have lost some revenue in the strict sense, the resulting strengthening of NR would have had an indirect but corresponding benefit on the finances of the government; and that there would have been a further saving to NR and therefore to the government of £100,000 through a reduction of London expenditure and of any income tax payable to the United Kingdom Treasury.

In the middle part of his despatch he took the opportunity of bringing to the secretary of state's personal attention the effect which high freight rates had had and were having on Nyasaland's economic development. By the use of some clear examples, covering both imports and exports, he showed how the general freight rates on the 374-mile Salisbury to Beira line were half what they currently were on the 353-mile Blantyre to Beira line – where the rate was based on the combined rates of NR, CAR, TZR and the Zambezi Bridge[64] – and added:

> I have long taken the view that one of the main reasons for the high rail freights to and from this territory is the fact that the Nyasaland Railways Limited has had to pay Income Tax. So far as I am aware, the Nyasaland Railways is the only railway in British Colonial Africa which is subject to Income Tax and I submit that it is wrong in principle for a Colonial Railway to pay Income Tax since it must tend to result in high rail freights, and these constitute a severe brake on development. Indeed, the fact that the freights on the Nyasaland and Associated Railways have been so high during the past 30 years has, in my view, been a major cause of the lack of development and private investment in this territory during this period.

In the latter part of his despatch, Colby turned to the implications of his proposals on the plans for federation, and countered the suggestion that his income tax exemption proposals might embarrass the federal government, arguing that, on the contrary, the reverse was likely to be the case since it would be 'indefensible' for NR to pay tax whilst the Rhodesia railways were exempt. He was convinced, and said that Lambert agreed with him, that the federal government would not accept the NR domicile being anywhere other than in the federation. It was to take account of this that he had proposed that the Nyasaland government should exercise its option to purchase NR. Furthermore, whilst the right of the Nyasaland government to exercise the option was on 'secure legal ground', the competence of the federal government, as successor to the Nyasaland government, 'might well be challenged' and thus it was advisable to take action now.

Colby concluded his despatch by saying that he had given the problems presented by NR 'the most careful and continuous thought over a period of nearly five years', and that in doing so he had received 'a sympathetic hearing and much valuable assistance' from the Colonial Office whose officers, he believed, supported his view that a change in the organization of NR was necessary:

I hope that you will accept my view that the proposed step is in
the interest of this territory and of any Federal Government which
may be formed. My only regret is that I should have caused you
embarrassment in this matter.

None of this, however, succeeded in abating Gorell Barnes' fury and the
anxiety generally in the Colonial Office where the officials – Nield,
Marnham, Bourdillon, Gorell Barnes and Lloyd – spent long hours
poring over the files, examining Colby's proposals, writing extensively,
and building up to a minute in which the secretary of state could be
advised as to the attitude he should adopt and the action he should take.[65]
The pressure under which Colby forced them to work was extreme. It
was now only a few days before Christmas; Colby was arriving in Britain
on 21 December and, although he would then travel direct to Hanlith
Hall, he would return to London on 29 December;[66] they were dealing
with 'a subject about which Sir Geoffrey Colby feels very strongly
indeed and on which he is sure to demand discussions very soon after
Christmas';[67] and a great deal of their time and attention had to be
devoted to the Carlton House Terrace conference on federation which
was due to start on 1 January, and at which Colby had warned them
that he proposed to emphasize 'the extremely unsatisfactory nature of
the present set up' of NR and that he intended 'to set matters to rights'
in the next year or two.[68] Colby had also split their resources and attention
by having two strands to his argument: nationalization, and change of
domicile with tax exemption. The Colonial Office officials had to work
very hard indeed because they did not feel able to enter into any further
discussions with the governor until they had 'received some guidance
from Ministers'.[69] Colby had forced them into a position in which it
would be very difficult for them to avoid making up their minds quickly
and in which they would have to secure the secretary of state's approval.
He was no longer prepared to let officials dictate the pace, or lack of it,
of progress, nor to stand in his way unless they really were carrying
with them the secretary of state's views and wishes. Yet the Colonial
Office officials were not in a position to advise the secretary of state:

I do not think that we are as yet in a final position to recommend
to the Secretary of State what decision he should take on this
matter ... The matter is ... a very difficult one and I am afraid I
do not see how we can give Sir G. Colby a definite answer, or even
a definite lead, in the immediate future ... I do feel very

strongly . . . that this is not a matter for hasty judgment and that Sir G. Colby can hardly expect anything more positive.[70]

The papers moved up from Nield (who dealt with the various aspects, especially the financial aspects, of exercising the option to purchase, and agreed with Colby's complex calculations made in his letter of 11 November) and Bourdillon ('My provisional feeling is that the Secretary of State should kill the matter and should stop the undesirable speculation [in shares] by telling the Governor quite flatly that he is not prepared to countenance this solution [of purchase by the Nyasaland Government]'), through Gorell Barnes ('I recommend that Sir Geoffrey Colby be told that both his latest and his earlier proposals are unacceptable') to Lloyd, the permanent secretary.

Gorell Barnes, already annoyed by the position into which Colby had forced them, was further irritated by his discovery that no one had told Colby or the secretary of state about the Treasury's reservation on the tax exemption proposal, and still further irritated by the realization that his own recommendation was something of a volte-face which would incur Colby's displeasure because the secretary of state had earlier agreed in principle to change of domicile. On 22 December, Gorell Barnes minuted to Lloyd:

If the policy recommended in this minute is approved, it will, to some extent, represent a reversal of a previous decision of the Secretary of State and will be very upsetting to Sir G. Colby. I am quite happy to break the news to Sir G. Colby myself, provided I can be assured that, after considering the matter fully, Ministers are really satisfied that my advice is right. But it might possibly be better for the Secretary of State to see Sir G. Colby about this himself.[71]

On Christmas Eve, after a very hectic three weeks wrestling with the problems with which Colby had confronted them, Lloyd gave his advice to the secretary of state.[72] He accepted Gorell Barnes' arguments and conclusions, and particularly acknowledged that Colby 'feels very strongly on this issue'. Consequently he advised that the Colonial Office should not confront him with a decision – presumably because they did not wish to antagonize him before the Carlton House Terrace conference on federation – but should offer a meeting at which the secretary of state should preside and that they should 'turn down flat' Colby's 'latest proposal' (which in fact, as Gorell Barnes and Lloyd well knew, was of fairly long standing) to offer local income tax exemption as an inducement to accepting change of domicile, on the grounds argued by Gorell Barnes that:

> Either the private shareholders would get something out of it, in which case the Nyasaland Government would lose revenue, which they cannot afford to lose, or else the private shareholders would not get anything out of it, in which case there is no sense in the proposal.[73]

He added a second reason for refusing the income tax proposal: that it was undesirable in principle that one private company should be permanently exempted from tax. Clearly, Gorell Barnes had either not understood or had ignored the logic of Colby's reasoning.

Lloyd next turned to the governor's proposal that the Nyasaland government should buy out NR and CAR before federation and, accepting Gorell Barnes' views again, recommended that this also be rejected on the grounds that it would mean breaking up the unified direction of the three railways and, 'much more serious', there would be a real danger that the Portuguese government would appropriate TZR and the part of CAR which ran through Portuguese territory, leaving the Nyasaland government, unlike a federal government, in a very weak bargaining position if through-rates and other problems then arose. Again Gorell Barnes had either not understood or had ignored the logic of Colby's arguments. Finally, Lloyd said:

> The conclusion would then be that this must stand over until we know whether there is to be federation. Should that be rejected we could go further with the Treasury into the possibility of Nyasaland being allowed on her own to carry through the purchase. It would be well to make it clear that you are by no means committed to that.

Just before the Carlton House Terrace conference started, Lyttelton accepted Lloyd's advice and a meeting was arranged for 30 January in the secretary of state's room. In the meantime, on 22 January, Nield sent the papers to Gorell Barnes so that he could be as well briefed as possible, and although Colby had been unwell he had recovered sufficiently by 30 January to attend the meeting.[74] He was not, as had been originally planned, accompanied by Barrow, and Lloyd also was not present.

Despite Colby's persistent arguments, Lyttelton rejected the proposal to exempt the railways from local income tax, pointing out that, in his view, even with such an inducement 'there was no real prospect that the Board would ever agree' to change of domicile. He accepted the principle that the railways should be operated for the benefit of Nyasaland's development rather than for the benefit of its shareholders and, to effect this, control should be exercised within Nyasaland, and he would be prepared to consider sympathetically the eventual exercise of the option to purchase subject to two important provisos. First, since he was 'not yet satisfied about the soundness of the financial proposals', he asked for a far more detailed examination of these aspects to be made; and second, since he felt that the proposed local management arrangements had not been sufficiently explained, he wanted them to be clarified. He made it clear, however, that even when he was satisfied on these matters he would wish to leave the exercise of the option to the federal government if it came into existence; if it did not, he would be prepared to consider sympathetically a request that Nyasaland exercise the option itself.

Colby, reiterating his fears that the federal government would have many other demands on its time and money, urged the secretary of state to press the federal government to take early action, and Lyttelton agreed that he would do so. If the Southern Rhodesian referendum went through and the secretary of state believed that federation 'was clearly going to come about', he agreed that Colby, with Colonial Office assistance, should consult the Northern and Southern Rhodesian governments and ask for their agreement to giving 12 months' notice of intention to exercise the option. In successfully urging the secretary of state to press the federal government to give notice of exercising the option, Colby had secured a major advantage, for not only had he made it more difficult for the Colonial Office officials to further delay progress, but also, if he was right in believing that the federal government would take several years to get round to doing anything about NR, the Nyasaland government would now be able to exercise the option itself, albeit on behalf of the federal government to whom they would then hand over the railways: 'Once we have taken over Nyasaland Railways we can hand the undertaking over to the Federal Government.'

The governor had squeezed as much as was practically possible out of the Colonial Office and he pressed forward with working out the details of how NR was to be managed, so as to cover one of the secretary of state's two provisos. In a letter to Gorell Barnes on 12 March 1953,[75] he proposed that at the policy-making level there should be a 'Higher Authority', such as Southern Rhodesia had, comprised of the governors of the three federal territories; or, if federation did not come about, the governor of Nyasaland should exercise these functions in council. Officials in the Colonial Office had no difficulty in accepting these proposals regarding a Higher Authority for policy-making issues.[76] Below the policy-making level, he proposed a board of directors to include the financial secretary, a member of the Rhodesia Railways board, a member of the Mozambique Railways or TZR, someone from within Nyasaland, and the chairman of the Rhodesia Railways as chairman. He proposed that Bucquet – who had worked under Colby during the war[77] – should be the person from within Nyasaland, but in order to overcome to some extent the direct difficulties of appointing the immediately preceding general manager of NR, 'it might help . . . if we were to offer a place on the Board to a nominee of the Chamber of Commerce of which Bucquet is Chairman'. As a further member he was anxious to have Marshall Clarke, former general manager of South Africa Railways, currently in other employment in Northern Rhodesia and a member of the Rhodesia Railways board. Alternatively, he suggested that the East Africa Railways and Harbour Administration should be asked to provide a member in order to secure help in developing the lake service.

Having dealt with his proposals for 'an efficient local Board to replace the present set-up', Colby still niggled away at the income tax issue even if the Nyasaland government was not going to be allowed to grant exemption:

> I hope that consideration will be given to the exemption of the Railways from federal income tax. It seems to me indefensible that the Federal Government should collect income tax from Nyasaland Railways at the expense of our railway users when it will not do so in so far as the Rhodesia Railways are concerned.
>
> In any case I hope that this point is academic and that I shall soon be hearing from you that the Secretary of State is prepared to give approval to the proposal that we buy out Nyasaland Railways.

Once again, he did not miss the opportunity in his correspondence with Gorell Barnes to use his final paragraph to spur him on to early action!

If he treated his own senior officials to such encouragement, why should he not treat senior Colonial Office officials in like manner?

At the same time as Colby was dealing in Nyasaland with one of the secretary of state's reservations – local management – Nield was dealing in London with the other – finance.[78] Nield had been through the governor's calculations before and had agreed with them, and he now went through them again in greater detail and once more agreed with them: 'In my view, therefore, the proposal for purchase of the Nyasaland Railways undertaking is a reasonable proposition from the financial aspect', and he added that the experts in the Crown Agents felt that the Nyasaland government 'would be securing this railway undertaking at a very cheap rate, having regard to present day values'.

Nield then turned to Colby's proposals for managing NR and concurred in every respect save that he did not think it a good idea to appoint Bucquet but suggested instead Barrow, to which Marnham noted 'I doubt if we can dictate personalities to the Governor' and Gorell Barnes agreed: 'No. And Mr Barrow already has enough to do.' Nield's conclusions on both finance and management were strongly supportive of Colby's proposals:

I think that there can be little doubt that the existing set up of the Nyasaland railway system is most unsatisfactory. Remote control from London occasions interminable delays and I feel that recent discussions with the Chairman of Nyasaland Railways about the capital programme of the undertaking have revealed that his primary interest is certainly not the operation of the railway as a major instrument in the development of the Protectorate which I think that the Nyasaland Government has every right to expect it to be. As the purchase price is reasonable and as I think that the Nyasaland Government can demonstrate that a competent organisation could be set up to control and administer the railways I now feel that there is a good case for exercising the option to purchase and I would suggest that this is justified whether Federation comes about or not.

Colby's pressure on progress was relentless. On 18 April he wrote again to Gorell Barnes, saying that as the time was approaching when he was hoping to be able to exercise the option to purchase, Gorell Barnes might care to have his views on what ought to happen to TZR:

> Let me say at the outset that in my view our policy must be to exert every effort to persuade the Portuguese to take over the Trans Zambezi Railways (and incidentally that part of the Central Africa Railways which lies in their territory).[79]

His fundamental reason for holding this view – a view which he had expressed to the ambassador in Lisbon almost two years earlier – was that the Nyasaland government should be relieved of financing a public utility in a foreign territory. An allied but un-voiced reason was that with Codrington on the board of TZR the only way to transfer control from London to Africa was for the Portuguese government to buy the company. He argued his points cogently and clearly, and included arguments for inducing the Portuguese to purchase TZR and part of CAR by negotiating on the basis of a reduced price, from £8.25m to £4.5m, or on the basis of payment over a period of years. He concluded:

> It seems to me, therefore, that the purchase by the Portuguese of TZR and CAR would not only be politically acceptable but would also be a financial proposition.

He did, however, want to know if the Colonial Office and the Foreign Office thought that he had some chance of success in carrying out 'the second part of our considered policy, namely the handing over of the remaining privately owned railways in Portuguese East Africa to the Portuguese Government at a negotiated price', and he also wanted to know what view the Treasury took of his proposal to offer TZR at a lower price or at the full price over a period of years. His final paragraph, as so very often, urged prompt action: 'We do not want to delay, once you have given us the all clear, in serving notice of purchase on Nyasaland Railways.'

Once again Gorell Barnes handed over to Nield the task of finding the answers to Colby's questions. The Treasury's immediate and predictable reaction was that they would be unable to agree to a reduced price, although they might be able to agree to payment of the full price over a period of years; even then they would not commit themselves but would wish to 'consider the position in the conditions at the time'. The Foreign Office's view was that there was no strong political objection to the proposal since it was the Portuguese government's policy to get all public utilities in their overseas territories into their own hands.[80]

Nield advised that the secretary of state's approval to give notice to exercise the option to purchase NR should now be sought. Marnham, Gorell Barnes and Lloyd agreed,[81] although Nield's illness and the coronation slightly delayed progress, and Lyttelton noted the file 'I agree. O.L.' on 5 June 1953; shortly thereafter he also agreed that there was 'a strong case for going ahead with the proposal'.[82] They now authorized Colby to discuss with Huggins and Rennie their joint agreement to giving notice of purchase.[83] In a letter to Gorell Barnes dated 23 September 1953, Colby confirmed that he had secured the support of both Rennie and Huggins,[84] the former as governor of Northern Rhodesia and the latter as prime minister of Southern Rhodesia. The Pre-federal Finance and Economics Working Party, however, proposed that there should be preliminary talks with Codrington before the federal government decided to take over NR.

Colby knew from long experience that talks with Codrington would be fruitless unless the federal government had made a prior firm decision to take over the railways, and he had persuaded the Colonial Office, the Foreign Office and the Commonwealth Relations Office to share this view by December 1953, when he wrote to the federal government to urge them to make an early decision. This urging, however, met with a cool response from the federal government which began to pour cold water on the idea before the end of January 1954.

As Colby had predicted, the federal government found many other matters competing for its time, funds and support:

In the first place, the subject [NR] is not one which looms very large amid the various current problems which confront the [Federal] Cabinet . . .

Secondly, there is the question of where the money is to come from . . . there are so many other more important claims for loan finance that I cannot believe that upward of £2m. can possibly be allocated to the Nyasaland Railways.

Thirdly, Taylor [Secretary for Transport] is himself disposed to doubt whether nationalisation is necessarily the best way of securing Colby's objective over the operation of the Nyasaland Railways.[85]

One can understand the federal Ministry of Transport's dilemma in January 1954. They were being pressed by Colby, with British government support, to reach a firm and early decision to buy out NR. Although Huggins, as prime minister of Southern Rhodesia, had supported the idea, the federal minister of transport, Welensky – a hardy politician with little liking for the views of the British government, and a man whose trade and career had been in railways – had 'not even started to get down to the work of his new department', and was in any case then in hospital. Taylor was new to the job – having formerly been financial secretary of Northern Rhodesia – and, not unnaturally, his ministry had very few files and indeed had no files or documents on NR at all until 18 January 1954 when the Colonial Office sent them copies of two recent letters which had passed between Colby and Gorell Barnes.[86] As I. M. R. Maclennan wrote in reply from Salisbury on 27 January:

We are entirely devoid in this office of any background information about the Nyasaland Railways. The enclosures to your letter under reference constitute the whole of our file on the subject.[87]

With so little knowledge and understanding of the NR problems with which Colby had been wrestling for over half a decade, the federal Ministry of Transport was not going to reach an early decision to invest £2m on nationalizing the railways in Nyasaland.

Once the abysmal inadequacies of the federal administrative machine and the consequent, if understandable, timid reticence of the Ministry of Transport became clear to Colby, he must have decided that further pushing by him was not going to be effective. He had argued his case directly with the Colonial Office over many years and, one way or another, had won them over to his views, but now federal matters were the responsibility of the Commonwealth Relations Office and railway matters were the responsibility of the federal government. He had got on well with Huggins (now Lord Malvern) but Welensky and Taylor were new to him. He must have been astonished at Taylor's apparent naivety when, 'devoid of any background information', he wondered if 'closer control and more efficient operations might not be secured [by] leaving the present management with their existing equity capital . . . as an incentive to run the railways well'.[88] It would have taken longer and more energy than it was worth to try to convince, all over again, the Commonwealth Relations Office and the federal Ministry of Transport – especially Taylor, a man deeply and long opposed to state interference in private enterprise – of the merits of his arguments.[89] Consequently, he was prepared to let matters take their course.

The Colonial Office had earlier told Colby that they shared his hope that it would be possible to avoid delay by going ahead with the take-

over on the basis of the territorial governments' agreement[90] – Huggins',
Rennie's and Colby's – but by mid-1954, given Taylor's views and the
fact that Taylor frequently visited the general manager of NR in Limbe,[91]
they realized that 'as the establishment of federation [has] proceeded so
far, we [have] to agree that this would be very difficult',[92] and since
Colby, untypically, had not for some time prompted them to take action,
J. H. Robertson in the Colonial Office advised Gorell Barnes, 'I don't
think it is worthwhile thinking about this now. B. U. [Bring Up] 3
months'.[93]

Without Colby prompting them and urging them to continued action,
and with negative responses from the federal Ministry of Transport, the
Colonial Office put the NR papers away for three months and were able
to lean back. Codrington sensed this leaning back and the creation of a
vacuum and gradually but firmly moved into it. Early in November
1954, the directors of NR entertained the secretary of state – now
Lennox-Boyd – to luncheon.[94] In addition to Codrington, Brown and
Milne (formerly general manager of the Great Western Railway), the
directors were Holland-Martin and V. L. Oury, a director of TZR and
the British Central Africa Company. Lennox-Boyd's officials advised him
that 'there are no current problems which are likely to merit the Secretary
of State's attention' – which would have astounded the governor of
Nyasaland had he known – and that if the luncheon conversation turned
to business matters he 'might profess ignorance of past history and say
as regards future problems that, as the Directors know, railway affairs
are now a matter for the Federal Government and not for the Colonial
Office'.

At the luncheon, the secretary of state promised to 'look into the
question of the transfer to the federal government of the debenture
stock of the companies at present held by the Nyasaland Government'.
The directors hoped that this transfer could be effected quickly:

> for until this is done officially we are under the Governor of
> Nyasaland as the owner of our securities with the consequent right
> of appointing Government directors etc. On the other hand, the
> railways, we are told, are a federal subject . . . Anything you can do
> to expedite a decision on this point will be much appreciated.[95]

Although Lennox-Boyd did not feel able to press Salisbury, because they
'have a great deal on their plate to absorb already', he told Codrington
in a letter written just before Christmas that he understood the federal

government intended to introduce a bill in February dealing with their assumption of responsibilities for railway matters which 'may well have a bearing on the relations of the Federal Government with the Nyasaland Railways'. He concluded by saying that he was sorry he could not be more helpful, 'but I am sure that you will see that this is almost entirely a Federal Government affair which lies outside my province'. Nonetheless, Codrington found Lennox-Boyd's letter helpful and felt that it was 'extraordinarily kind' of the secretary of state to have enquired into the matter on their behalf.[96] It appears that Lennox-Boyd had in fact contacted Salisbury, had received the helpful information about the bill, had passed it on to Codrington, but then made it clear that he did not wish to be involved further.

Shortly after Christmas, 1954, Codrington and Holland-Martin flew to Central Africa and had detailed discussions with Welensky based on a memorandum prepared by Codrington about the history and problems of NR. It was a meeting to which Codrington had looked forward 'with great interest' so that he could learn 'from Welensky what the Federal Government want to do about us'.[97] The meeting resulted in arrangements for the federal government to take over the financial responsibilities and other rights and obligations of the Nyasaland government in respect of NR.

Even so, Colby did not lose interest in NR. When his government was asked to make suggestions of names of people from Nyasaland who could be considered for appointment to the board, they were unable to find anyone suitable but Colby wrote: 'I feel it would be better to appoint someone from outside . . . While we no longer have responsibility for the railway we have a very great interest in it. It is vital to us'.[98]

Codrington must have persuaded Welensky to support NR rather than Colby, for late in May 1955 Welensky – whom the general manager frequently visited in Salisbury and with whom Stevens deliberately 'established excellent relations'[99] – was entertained to luncheon in Limbe by NR, and in a speech there said:

I want to make it quite clear . . . that the responsibility for running the Nyasaland Railways rests on the Board of the Railways, not on the Federal Government. We do not want to take over the Railways as they are in good hands.[100]

Indeed, the railways remained in these, private, 'good hands' for another 11 years: until the federation had been abolished and the Protectorate of Nyasaland had become the independent Republic of Malawi. In 1966, a decade after Colby retired from Nyasaland, the Malawi government bought out the railway companies, and in the course of introducing a bill to effect this – with a loan from the Farmers' Marketing Board – the life president used words and arguments which would have been very familiar to Colby:

> businessmen . . . have told me many times that the . . . charges on the Railway are far too high by comparison and that they inhibit rather than encourage the . . . development of this country. . . . As at present organised and controlled, the Malawi Railway is a private company and as a private company the Railway has a board of Directors whose main duty and function is to look after the interests of the shareholder . . .
>
> When all this became clear . . . I made up my mind to do something about the problem because I felt that otherwise . . . development in this country would be almost impossible. . . . Therefore, in my view we had to gain control of the railways as a Government . . . by acquiring the controlling block of shares [now held by Lonrho] in the Railway Company. . . . under the Articles of Association of the Railway Company . . . the Government could under certain circumstances gain control of the Railways by means other than buying the controlling block of shares. . . . I did not want to resort to expropriation or confiscation [but] I was ready to use other means than buying the block of shares if free negotiations were impossible or if the directors were unreasonable . . . I am happy to inform the House that the key directors concerned accepted my offer.[101]

The federal government – and the British government by insisting that the federal government, rather than the Nyasaland government, should make the decisions on acquisition – had delayed the gaining of control over the railways by government for over a decade, with consequent continued damage to the development of the country. By this time neither Colby nor Codrington was still alive. Colby would have been saddened by the delay but gratified by the eventual outcome, an outcome based so closely on reasoning which he shared about the effect on development of lack of governmental control over the railways' policy and operations.

10· The Food Crisis

'All the possibilities of a major disaster.'

We have seen how crucial increased agricultural production was to Colby's development strategy, how many other elements depended on this, and how greatly he reinforced the resources of the Department of Agriculture in order to accomplish this. The increased production was needed to keep the population well-fed and healthy and to produce surpluses which would increase both individual incomes and government revenue. Agricultural production, however, depended not only upon any steps which Colby could take or encourage, but also overwhelmingly upon weather conditions, especially rainfall. Inadequate rainfall – or the failure of early rains, since maize succeeds only if it gets established early – could readily bring about a failure of food crops, hunger, falling incomes and revenue, and the diversion of funds, manpower and other resources away from more productive uses.[1]

When Colby arrived in Nyasaland as governor on 28 March 1948, the early general indications of a possible grave shortage of food in the not-too-distant future – although not obvious, and as a consequence easily overlooked – were already in existence. It is true that until then no very widespread serious famine had occurred – unlike the famines in later decades in north-east Africa – principally because Nyasaland was blessed with relatively good soil and rainfall, but from time to time geographically limited, but serious, shortages had occurred. These shortages, common to much of Africa, had caused local hardship over short, seasonal periods, especially in the month or two before new crops were reaped, but there had been nothing to evoke particular and widespread preventative action. For example, at Magomero in the Shire Highlands in late December 1861, Henry Rowley recorded:

At this time our people were suffering from famine. They were literally starving. We did all we could to get food from the surrounding villages . . . but we could not procure sufficient for our wants . . . The earliest crop would not be gathered until the end of January and a month's starvation and sickness . . . soon began to tell upon the weak and sickly, and the young.[2]

A year later, in November 1862, Rowley again reported famine, this time at Chibisas on the Lower Shire, and had to bring in maize and rice from Shupanga.[3] Nor were food shortages confined to the south of the country, since they also occurred from time to time in the northern Angoni areas where Dr Emslie reported:

The question of famine in consequence of drought was agitating the minds of all the tribe. A few showers fell in the November of . . . 1885, and the people had planted their maize. It sprang up for a fortnight, and then, as the rains ceased until the 18th of January, the corn was burned up and the people began [to have] famine staring them in the face.[4]

Again, in 1922 'conditions of drought, followed by a scarcity of native foodstuffs, prevailed throughout the southern part of the Protectorate': 1500 tons of maize had to be imported and 2300 tons of food were distributed.[5] Save possibly for 1922, however, each of the reported instances of hunger was localized and of short duration, and foodstuffs from outside the immediate areas of shortage could be secured to assuage the hunger or, in particularly severe cases, village people resorted to gathering wild fruit, roots, seeds and foliage.

Nevertheless, changes in society and in the economy were beginning to make the country far more vulnerable to poor harvests than in the past. First, the increasing population – which had doubled from 1,200,000 in 1921 to 2,400,000 in 1948, and which increased the demand for maize by 20,000 tons each year – was placing a heavy burden on the country's productive capacity:

Nyasaland's agrarian problem was that of too many people . . . attempting by traditional . . . methods to derive an ever-increasing level of living from a limited amount of land.[6]

Accentuating this difficulty, the war, with its heavy demand for increased crop production, had accelerated the decline in soil fertility. In addition, although Nyasaland's was essentially an agricultural economy and a rural society, its industrial and urban population was expanding rapidly and was placing yet further demands upon the productive capacity of the rural, agricultural areas: the workers and their families in the townships, although retaining their traditional and often distant village gardens, depended more and more on purchasing – as opposed to growing – their food.

During 1948, the government became aware that the country could not rely for much longer on surpluses from subsistence farming to provide adequate supplies of staple foodstuffs, especially maize, for those in paid employment.[7] Colby was quick to see the portents.[8] Only two months after his arrival, and with an uncanny prophetic perspicacity, he expressed his fears to executive council, saying that he 'felt strongly that immediate action was essential to prevent a food crisis in the Protectorate in the near future'[9] and he repeated these views to the Tea Association, the largest non-government employer of paid labour, and to other major private employers:

> There can be no doubt that in this territory, parts of which are already seriously overcrowded, which supports a large and constantly increasing population and in which ... agricultural methods ... result in steady progressive deterioration of the soil, there will inevitably be in a short time a serious food shortage which may well reach famine proportions.[10]

With his West African experience of produce supplies and marketing, he quickly perceived the significance of the small percentage of total maize production which, as a surplus, had been purchased by the Maize Control Board for re-sale in the townships and to estates. Notwithstanding a favourable growing season in 1947–8, when 'the actual production of maize was greater than ever before', the board was able to purchase only 7000 tons of maize, the staple foodstuff – a very small fraction of the estimated total production, and far below the requirements of the industrial and urban consumers.[11]

> At the present time the non-subsistence farming population ... relies on the small so-called surplus of maize produced on Native Trust Land ... [which] amounts to perhaps 3 or 4% of the total crop. It cannot be too strongly emphasised that the surplus of such

small dimensions can be eliminated by a variety of factors in a single season . . . It is therefore vital that all possible steps should be taken now to minimise and if possible avert this dangerous situation before it is too late.[12]

Colby outlined what the government was doing – improving agricultural practice, co-ordinating and stabilizing commodity prices, and planning 'to grow sufficient maize by mechanical means to feed all Government employees' – but hammered home the need for the tea industry to provide enough to feed its own workers, warning its members of the inherent dangers and of 'the hard fact' that they could not rely indefinitely on being provided with maize from Native Trust Land. He added that it was in the industry's own self-interest, and not simply to assist the government or the African population, that it should grow sufficient food for its employees:

> if maize in adequate quantities is not available for the feeding of labour, . . . the point may well be reached when, owing to lack of foodstuffs, labour supplies will drop altogether . . . which would be disastrous to the tea industry in particular and to the Protectorate in general . . . With this grave situation in prospect the tea industry should make arrangements to grow directly the whole of its food requirements.[13]

There can be no doubt that even at this early stage Colby clearly saw the vulnerability of the country to food shortages, and that he feared 'a food crisis . . . in the near future' which could 'reach famine proportions'. He was urging steps to prevent disaster, but each of the steps contemplated was long-term. In respect of the government's attempts to improve agricultural practice, check soil erosion and improve fertility, he said that 'it would be idle to suppose that . . . any substantial results from this policy can be expected for years'; and in respect of finding sufficient land for mechanical production of food crops for industry, although returns could be expected within a year, 'it will not be easy to find a suitable area . . . and it may already be impossible'. 'I realise that the situation cannot be transformed in a few months and it takes time to put large areas under mechanical maize production',[14] he stated. Time to avert disaster was vital but as things turned out such time was not to be available.

An early specific warning of impending danger of grave food shortage came in the first few days of September 1948, when the executive council was asked to approve a loan to the Fort Johnston Native Treasury to meet the cost of hunger relief measures in that district.[15] The council agreed to this request but the warning did not set off general alarm bells in government, although a few field officers were becoming increasingly worried about the possibility of widespread food shortage and Colby himself was deeply concerned about what he had already described as 'this grave situation in prospect'.

By the end of November, the rains in the Southern Province, which normally commenced in the middle of the month – and which were only of four to four and a half months' duration, the rest of the year being dry[16] – had not started, and the field staff of the Agricultural Department and of the district administration, especially in the lower rainfall areas of the Shire River and Lake Nyasa, were very anxious because they were aware from experience that late rains seriously reduced yields.[17] At that time, officers of the Agricultural Department spent three weeks out of every four touring the rural areas and were thus in a strong position to assess the gravity of the situation: by the beginning of December, their reports from the south of the country had become most disturbing. The senior agricultural officer, A. P. S. Forbes, visited all districts in the Southern Province and formed the same view as his field colleagues as to the seriousness of the failure of the rains. Although only one district commissioner – for Port Herald in the Lower River – considered the position critical, the provincial commissioner, Barnes, accepted Forbes' assessment and told the chief secretary, Brown, of his fears. The director of agriculture, Garnett, and his headquarters staff, however, felt that Forbes was over-reacting and were strengthened in this view when the deputy director, E. Lawrence, having visited the Lower River to examine the position, reported that there was no cause for alarm. Lawrence, with two decades of experience in Nyasaland, had spent six years as a field officer in the Lower River and knew the area and its people well, and his views were accepted by Garnett, communicated to the secretariat staff, and accepted by Brown. The result was a significant difference of opinion between the field staff and the headquarters staff of the Agricultural Department and, to a considerably smaller extent, between the provincial commissioner and some of his district commissioners. In any event, it was the director of agriculture's advice which prevailed in the closing weeks of 1948.

Still worried, Forbes had begun to plan an emergency replanting operation when general rains fell and planting began in earnest. Unfortunately, the rain was short-lived and was followed by an even more intensive drought and the new plantings failed. Forbes expanded his plan and Barnes approved it. The district commissioner of Blantyre, Rangeley, was also much concerned about the deteriorating situation and, in an effort to combat the growing black market in maize meal in the urban areas, set up a government store in Blantyre market, distributing a ton of maize a day between 500 buyers.[18] Even so, Colby was still being advised, principally by the director of agriculture, that all was not lost and that there was no cause for general alarm.[19]

At this point, Barnes, now gravely worried, wrote personally to Brown, emphasizing his deep concern about the distinct possibility of extensive shortage, and this letter triggered action in the chief secretary's office and in Government House. It is possible that the governor was already aware of the differing views held about the crop situation and felt that he was being inadequately advised by the secretariat and the director of agriculture, but whether or not this is so, Colby immediately decided to visit Blantyre to have direct discussions with Barnes and Forbes. Three and a half decades later, Forbes recalled:

I showed him the replanting plan [and] . . . confirmed the P.C.'s view that we were in for a severe famine. He questioned me in detail . . . and was most insistent to know [whether] if my plan worked successfully there would still be a famine. I confirmed that in the view of the Southern Province Department of Agriculture there would be. The P. C. confirmed this view. He asked me if I fully appreciated my Director disagreed with my views and I assured him I did. Although he said nothing positive at this time both the P. C. and I had the feeling he accepted our assessment of the situation.

That evening Barnes, apparently without undue worry, expressed the view to Forbes that they had both put their 'heads on the block', and they were much relieved and not a little surprised two days later when Barnes received Colby's instructions that he and Forbes were to accept full responsibility for the province in implementing the replanting programme and preparing to meet a famine. Forbes' plan was to be implemented immediately and they were given responsibility for all means of transport including lake shipping, the railways, government transport and army vehicles. Colby gave clear instructions that, although a supplementary estimate was to be prepared, the work was to be started without waiting for formal financial provision, and that a joint report from Barnes and Forbes was to be sent directly to him weekly. He left them to get on with the job and 'his queries were few and far between'.

Within three days, planting material was being moved from the Central Province to priority areas in the Southern Province; the King's African Rifles sent convoys to move sweet potato and cassava cuttings in the Central Province to the railway where trains were waiting to carry them to Chiromo and Port Herald. District commissioners in the Northern Province were instructed to buy and store cassava roots ready for shipment southwards by tugs and barges,[20] and 'planting material was provided at thousands of collection points'.

In these ways Colby took direct and swift action to deal with the immediate situation. He placed confidence in the provincial commissioner and the senior agricultural officer, allowed them to make on-the-spot decisions, insisted on regular and direct communication between them and himself, gave them wide powers and got things moving quickly. In fact they moved so quickly that Colby, or his secretariat officers, forgot to tell the director of agriculture that Forbes had been given these far-reaching and exceptional responsibilities, and this, together with the realization that the director's advice had been considered faulty by the governor, did little to help personal relations between the Agricultural Department's headquarters and Southern Province field staff. In most of the Northern and Central Provinces, where the drought was less severe, an extensive food-production campaign was energetically pursued which produced a harvest sufficient for local requirements, but in the Southern Province the drought persisted and, despite the actions of the governor, the provincial commissioner, the senior agricultural officer and their staff, 'repeated plantings . . . gave hope of a successful growth, only to wither subsequently as a result of further prolonged dry spells'.

By mid-January 1949, the position in the Southern Province and in the lowlands of the Central Province had deteriorated still further and on 12 January Colby – a man not given to spending excessive amounts of time on meetings – devoted a whole session of his executive council, from 2.00 p.m. to 5.40 p.m., to discussing the worsening foodstuffs situation.[21] He held another executive council meeting the following day to consider a telegram from the district commissioner at Port Herald reporting a critical food shortage following the failure of the bullrush millet crop.[22] Even now, the director of agriculture – who was being regularly summoned to meetings of council although not a member – was not unduly anxious, and:

intimated that it was not unusual for people of the Port Herald
District to experience a food shortage at this time of the year and
that it was caused chiefly by the fact that the people were accustomed to sell their main crop of food in Portuguese territory and
then to rely on purchasing food out of the proceeds of their cotton
crop.[23]

Colby, however, was anxious and determined to visit the Lower River,
including Port Herald, immediately himself.[24] The very next day, he left
Zomba and undertook a tour of the affected areas in the south of the
country. On his return, he contacted the chief secretary by direct telephone from Government House to the secretariat, where a senior officer
was present and recalled the conversation which he heard:

Frank . . . while Geoff was . . . recording his experiences . . . merely
interspersed the odd oh! – I see – yes? – etc. Geoff then . . . turned
to possible solutions or alternatives and Frank said, . . . 'Before I
answer that, I wish to – indeed must – know whether you are just
blowing off steam after a harrowing experience or whether you have
given me a considered assessment of the position and its likely
deterioration.' After a few indistinguishable sparks from the other
end, Frank said, 'Right, I will put all your proposals in hand at
once, save your second which would only result in transferring the
most badly hit area from one place to another. Meanwhile, have
you not left out the most obvious solution – the purchase of say x
tons of Southern Rhodesian emergency reserve' – more sparks –
and finally Frank: 'I will go to Salisbury tomorrow and see the
P.M. and the Minister of Agriculture'. End of conversation.

Within minutes, the chief secretary secured a return air booking to
Salisbury; made appointments to see Godfrey Huggins and the Southern
Rhodesian minister of agriculture; contacted the Central African Council
secretariat to discuss transport and to seek guidance; secured advice
from Garnett on a reasonable price range within which he should try
to negotiate the purchase of maize; and dictated detailed orders to
various assistant secretaries. By the end of the day, also, he had drafted
subordinate legislation, an order to provide powers to the government
immediately to requisition planting material when it was not possible to
obtain possession by voluntary sale – to enforce, if necessary, Forbes'
plan – and to require the submission of returns of all stocks of foodstuffs

in excess of a ton, and by a graduated series of provisions – which included authority to 'freeze' stocks and later requisition them – to cope with a deteriorating situation.

In a general notice[25] published the following day, Brown asked the public to study the provisions of the order carefully, and explained that it provided 'wide powers of direction and control with a view to safeguarding the well-being of the community', and then – echoing the views and possibly the actual words of Colby who remembered the Charterhouse agricultural camps during the First World War – he added:

> The provisions are drastic and are comparable with the emergency powers introduced during the war; the fact is that we are once again at war – this time against hunger.

This account shows how fortunate Colby was in his first chief secretary: a man prepared to speak his mind, to make pointed but fundamental suggestions, and then to act quickly and effectively – all qualities which Colby much admired and needed in his advisers.

Colby, having become increasingly concerned about the quality and consistency of advice being channelled to him, had decided to discover for himself what the true position was. As a result of his 'harrowing experience' in the Lower River – albeit on a very short visit – he had satisfied himself as to the extreme seriousness of the situation and had quickly come to the conclusion that drastic measures needed to be taken, and taken speedily. He deliberately raised the perception of the public and the Civil Service to an emergency level reminiscent of war-time, in order to secure their appreciation of the urgency of the situation and their commitment to coping with it. He determined to involve his executive council closely and fully; he arranged for council to meet weekly instead of fortnightly, and to be summoned to special meetings if necessary; he directed that the non-official members should be given copies of 'all important information reaching government in connection with the present crisis';[26] and decided that Barrow should play a central role.

On 3 February, Colby decided that a non-official African foodstuffs commissioner should be appointed, assisted by a food distribution advisory committee; and that the commissioner's headquarters should be in private business premises in Blantyre and, if necessary, requisitioned.[27] It is of considerable significance that he created this organization outside the Civil Service, placed a non-civil servant at its head, and located it away from the administrative capital, Zomba.

He did this for a number of reasons. First, it enabled decisions to be made quickly and directly by a small group of people without the hindrance of a larger – and longer – hierarchical structure; he was still somewhat distrustful of the advice he was receiving from his headquarters officers, and was anxious not to exacerbate the potential friction between the headquarters and Southern Province field staff of the Department of Agriculture. Second, it enabled him, in appointing the African foodstuffs commissioner, to use the skills and influence of a successful businessman – Barrow – who was the widely accepted leader of the non-official European community. In Nigeria, as director of supplies, Colby had been 'in constant contact with the business community and in fact . . . had a number of non-officials employed in [his] organisation'.[28] He now took advantage of this experience to establish relationships with business leaders much closer than had normally existed in the past and, as we shall see in a later chapter, would ultimately exist in the future. Third, by placing the commissioner's headquarters in Blantyre he located it nearer the affected areas of the Lower River, on the railway line, close to the railway headquarters and offices of the road transport companies, and somewhat distant from the government secretariat. When Johnston had set up his headquarters at Zomba in 1891, it was said that he did so to be two days' march away from the missionaries and business companies in Blantyre; his successor, Colby, saw the advantages of placing a similar distance between his secretariat and the African foodstuffs commissioner's headquarters. That an organization such as this was urgently necessary was clear from the increasing pressures building up on the government at the centre. The district commissioner of Blantyre, for example, was so disturbed by the potential political and security dangers in the townships that on 3 February he wrote to the provincial commissioner, outlining his fears and advocating full-scale rationing or a chit system under which registered essential employees would be able to purchase regulated supplies of foodstuffs.[29]

Whatever system was to be adopted, Nyasaland clearly needed to import large quantities of foodstuffs since there were markedly insufficient supplies internally, and notwithstanding the considerable problems of availability, foreign exchange and transport which imports would involve, Brown's quick visit to Salisbury on 16 January had secured an immediate promise of 2000 tons of grain and had prepared the way for a fuller meeting held in Salisbury on 8 February. Colby wished to attend this second meeting himself so that it 'would be held at the highest possible level' and so that speedy and authoritative decisions could be made, but he accepted the advice of his executive council that:

> His Excellency should not attend the proposed meeting unless the Prime Minister of Southern Rhodesia and the Governor of Northern Rhodesia also attended on the ground that it would not be practicable to make immediate decisions of policy on behalf of the respective governments in [their] absence . . . If [they] . . . were not able to attend the Chief Secretary and Mr Barrow should represent Nyasaland.[30]

Even at this stage, Colby was not prepared to accept an inferior status for Nyasaland in Central Africa. In the event Brown and Barrow were accompanied by Sir Eric Ansorge, the controller of essential supplies and produce, and they had discussions with ten representatives of Southern Rhodesia, including a number of ministers, and two from Northern Rhodesia.[31] The meeting's purpose was 'to discuss the whole question of maize and other bulk food imports [to the] Central African territories including bulk purchases and [the] machinery needed to deal with them at Beira'.

Brown opened the discussions by describing the immediate Nyasaland situation:

> The Northern and Central Province would be able to support themselves but . . . the Southern Province, containing half the population and half the cultivable area of the country, would not . . . in two Districts with a population totalling 230,000 Africans there would be no maize crop. Government held stocks of food were virtually non-existent and the stocks held by planters, storekeepers etc. were not known although a return of these had been called for.

He went on to explain that the Nyasaland government had not yet placed firm orders for foodstuffs because it was aware that Southern and Northern Rhodesia would also need to import food and thought that co-ordination, especially in Beira, would be desirable. Nyasaland's requirements were for 1000 tons of maize almost immediately, with another 5000 tons within the next few months, to bridge the gap until they could be more sure of assessing the success of the root-crop replanting operations. Brown was able to secure agreement that the

Southern Rhodesia government would take care of Nyasaland's maize requirements for the present and would supply 1000 tons to Nyasaland as soon as possible, a further 1000 tons by the end of February, and then 1000 tons a month for a further three months. Brown undertook that Nyasaland would replace the 5000 tons from whatever sources later became available. Thus was the immediate future catered for.

The meeting then turned its attention to somewhat longer-term issues concerning bulk purchases of foodstuffs for the three Central African territories, and finally agreed that the Southern Rhodesia government, on behalf of all three territories, should place a firm order for three shipments of maize from the United States, each of 8000 tons, to arrive at Beira in April, May and June; should make the necessary arrangements about dollar payment when it was seen how much maize was to be received by each territory; should approach the South African government around the middle of March to secure maize supplies; and should take an option on a further 11,000 tons a month from the United States beginning in July which could be taken up if there were then insufficient sterling sources of supply.

In this way, Colby and his senior advisers ensured that Nyasaland would receive sufficient maize to stave off the worst results of the food crisis, but it was clear that a very considerable administrative task existed in seeing that the imported maize was transported quickly and safely to the right areas, was satisfactorily stored and was distributed in an orderly fashion to the right people. Armed with the powers acquired by the order of 15 January, Colby asked Fox-Strangways to work out the detailed organization of the African foodstuffs commissioner's office – created in outline on 3 February – to handle these tasks.[32] The objective and scope of the organization were:

To provide for the distribution of food to Africans where necessary to avert famine and to make sure that the best use is made of any surplus foodstuffs available in the Protectorate [and] arrange for the importation as necessary and the distribution of African foodstuffs from abroad.

In essence, the machinery which was created vested control and direction in the African foodstuffs commissioner, working under the general and special directions of the governor, in close liaison with the Food Distribution Advisory Committee and government departments, and operating directly through district commissioners and special officers.

Even now, the director of agriculture was not convinced that the situation was one of extreme seriousness. At the same meeting of executive council held on 10 February at which the chief secretary reported the results of his visit to Salisbury,[33] Garnett made a statement on the crop situation:

> It would undoubtedly be necessary to feed some of the people, but by no means all, on the Lower River . . . the distribution of any foodstuffs for this purpose should be done very slowly and cautiously [otherwise] there will be certain to be a rush of applications for relief and the conditions of shortage would be exaggerated by the people. He felt that no very large quantity of foodstuffs would be needed.[34]

On 24 February, Colby appointed Barrow as African foodstuffs commissioner.[35] Barrow made it clear to the governor that because of his other commitments he would not himself be able to take an active part in the administration of his office and that it 'would be necessary for [him] to have a first-class executive staff', and he acknowledged later that he 'could not have wished for a more able, efficient, willing, and hard working' team. The staff included H. V. McDonald (an administrative officer well known to Barrow with 20 years' experience in Nyasaland) to liaise between the commissioner's office and the food distribution centres; G. C. D. Hodgson (another administrative officer, with ten years' service in the country) as secretary; Mr and Mrs Kain as clerks; and two stenographers. The Advisory Committee membership was Hadlow, J. Marshall, the two African (E. K. Mposa and E. A. Muwamba) and one Asian (P. Dayaram) members of legislative council, Barnes and Fox-Strangways, but not the director of agriculture or any member of his staff. The African and Asian members had been appointed to legislative council – the first of their races – on 8 February 1949, and Colby was quick to give them an active role to play. It was a very strong team, to which Colby appointed some of his most able officers.

Barrow's task was to keep Colby and his advisers constantly informed of the foodstuffs position so that orders from abroad could be placed and once they had arrived at the port of discharge arrange for their transhipment, receipt, checking, storage, allocation and accounting, and to determine priorities between districts and townships, having received and collated food requisitions directly from district commissioners.[36] The district commissioners were made responsible for monthly estimates of foodstuffs requirements; for drawing up and operating distribution schemes; for indenting for supplies of food and arranging for bulk storage; for allocating staff to food distribution centres for distribution, accounting and control; and for the arrangements to control food purchasers. They were also made responsible for appointing and supervising special officers whose tasks included arrangements for storing and issuing food, local transport, supervising subordinate staff and accounting of stock receipts and issues.

Colby was at considerable pains to make clear his position on priorities and rationing.[37] Apart from priorities between districts, general priority in the issue of foodstuffs was to be, first, the requirements of essential services; second, the relief of distressed areas; and third, relief works designed to maintain African purchasing power. In respect of rationing he adopted a tough line, being anxious to avoid unnecessary dependency on the government:

In the absence of a proper census and since adequate stocks of food are not assured, rationing will not be attempted in rural areas. The issue of any form of ration card or food chit is likely to be interpreted by the [people] as a Government promise to keep [them] fed. Government will not assume any such responsibility and it is important that no suggestion that it will do so be allowed to enter the mind of the [people].

He frequently made this last point publicly: 'Save in cases of infirmity, Government has no intention of distributing foodstuffs free.'[38] What he particularly had in mind was avoiding any tendency in the future for people not to make provision against famine by believing that should food shortages occur, government would provide for their needs. He wished from the outset to disabuse them of this belief.

District commissioners quickly set about drawing up food distribution schemes to cater for those without direct access to village gardens, principally those employed in the townships and on the estates. The scheme for Zomba was typical;[39] it started on Tuesday, 22 March 1949, but before that date employers had registered the number of their essential African employees, government departments had reported on the requirements of their employees and their families, householders had been asked to limit the number of staff wives – and therefore of families – to one in each establishment, employers had been asked to keep the number of food issues to a minimum, and registration cards had been prepared. Maize flour was issued from the court house three days a week, for 3d per pound, one pound a day per adult and half a pound a day per child.

In those rural areas with a marked food shortage, the district commissioners opened distribution centres and, since few people there were in paid employment, they introduced relief works to enable the villagers to pay for the food distributed. Colby's view was that in most of the Southern Province 'ample employment is available and no [one] need have any difficulty in earning money' to pay for food. Once again he was anxious to avoid attitudes of dependency. In some cases communal relief works – which included soil-conservation schemes – were introduced to assist communities better to look after the needs of the aged, infant and infirm members of society.[40]

Thus, in these various ways, by the end of February 1949, Colby made arrangements for importing large quantities of foodstuffs and for the organization with which to handle them. At the sitting of the legislative council[41] on the last day of February, he referred to 'the crisis which faces this territory as a result of the unprecedented drought that we had in December and January [when] we faced a position that held all the possibilities of a major disaster', and added that the replanting, where possible, of grain crops and the planting of large quantities of root crops had been assisted by recent rains and had lessened the difficulties being faced. However, he emphasized that whilst they had done everything possible to 'extricate [themselves] from a position which, at one time, had all the elements of disaster', it was clear that the coming 12 months would be exceedingly difficult and that the emergency campaign to plant root crops, which had 'been prosecuted with the utmost vigour', should not be relaxed.

During the remainder of 1949 and the early part of 1950, Colby imported 25,000 tons of foodstuffs, principally maize, from Southern Rhodesia, Kenya, Tanganyika and the United States of America.[42] Transporting these large quantities presented serious difficulties. Not only was the Nyasaland railways' capacity limited and already strained by the need to import essential development supplies after the war, but the washed-away Chiromo Bridge over the Shire River – a vital link in the rail route from Beira – was not replaced and opened until January 1950, and only then after much pressure by Colby on the Colonial Office.[43] The new bridge consisted of replicas of one of the larger (285 feet) and two of the smaller (161 feet) spans used in constructing the Lower Zambezi Bridge. In the meantime, a ferry service was hastily introduced[44] and successfully so since 'at no time [did] the ferry [prove] to be the limiting factor on the lines of communication to and from the Protectorate'. For three or four months, carriage of freight other than foodstuffs on the railway from Beira was virtually prohibited.[45] Even several months before the need to import large quantities of grain had arisen, Colby had expressed dissatisfaction with the Nyasaland railways: he had threatened to close the line north of Blantyre (in order to release trucks to evacuate tea and tung from the Shire Highlands south to Beira) and to break the railway monopoly on heavy transport over the same route north of Blantyre (in order to move the tobacco and other produce from the Central Province to the South). The general manager of the railways recalled many years later:

> H. E. called me to Zomba to advise or warn me that he would have to give [a certain large scale planter] a road permit to bring his tobacco down to his factory in Cholo because he said the Railways could not handle it. I objected as I saw this as the thin end of the wedge and promised that we would introduce an efficient system. This we did . . . and there was no further mention of closing the Northern Extension.[46]

By October 1949, Beira port had a backlog of 7000 tons of imports for Nyasaland, and very reluctantly Colby had asked the British government to limit supplies from Britain to enable the backlog to be cleared – a painful solution since he was desperately anxious to maintain a high level of imports of equipment, materials and supplies, especially fuel oil, essential to the development plans to which he was so fully committed and which he was so determined speedily to implement. He did 'everything possible to obtain early delivery of new locomotives' and other rolling stock but in the early post-war period they took many months to arrive. Colby secured some relief from congestion at Beira by using the ports of Mozambique and Quelimane, but these were not in direct railway communication with Nyasaland and road transport over indifferent surfaces had to be extensively used.[47]

Colby was concerned about the security of foodstuffs on the railway from Southern Rhodesia and Beira, especially since the line passed through areas with the worst food shortages in Nyasaland.[48] The executive council advised him to seek legislative approval to introduce corporal punishment for the theft of foodstuffs and to create a new criminal offence of carrying foodstuffs after dark, but the secretary of state disapproved of these proposals and Colby dropped them: he had enough battles to fight locally without taking on the colonial secretary in a skirmish which he was unlikely to win.[49]

There were also serious problems of bulk storage. Some of the imported grain was in poor condition when it arrived and bulk storage facilities were rarely available.[50] The situation eased a good deal at the close of the tobacco marketing season when the market buildings in the Central Province and the auction floors in the Southern Province – all dry, airy and permanent premises – were freed to store grain. Although Colby's major focus of relief was on importing and allocating grain through distribution centres, he considered numerous other means of easing the immediate situation or of catering for the future.

The Department of Agriculture and the Medical Department, in particular, played a crucial role, both working in close liaison with the provincial and district administration. The Department of Agriculture's role in encouraging the replanting of maize and the planting of root crops early in 1949 has already been described, and they mounted a vigorous drive to ensure early preparation of gardens in October 1949 and to encourage diversification of crop production.[51] Many officers of the department were appointed special officers to assist at the food distribution centres. The Medical Department[52] staff kept a close watch on the physical condition of the population in the main areas of food shortage by carrying out routine weighing of samples of the community over a period of several months and by being vigilant as to any signs of increased malnutrition. Colby ensured that a medical officer was placed on full-time duty in connection with the establishment of food distribution centres and that, as a precaution, an epidemic disease control unit was formed and equipment assembled so that any major epidemic outbreak could be quickly attacked. The Medical Department also collected stocks of dietary supplement – dehydrated vegetables, food yeast, red palm oil and vitamin concentrates – and distributed them to hospitals in the affected areas, and they co-ordinated the provision of Red Cross dried milk for feeding babies and young children.

Whilst the brunt of the task of coping with the severe food shortage fell upon the Departments of Agriculture and Medicine and on the provincial and district administration, many other individuals and departments were also encouraged to play their part. Colby had the lawns and flower gardens of Government House dug up and planted with sweet potatoes and maize, mainly as a matter of principle and to set an example to others, and he reaped a bumper crop.[53] This example, and Colby's general exhortations 'so impressed one of the biggest tea planters, not an easy man to be influenced or impressed by anyone', that he cleared olive groves on his estate by bulldozer and replaced the olive trees with maize.[54] Colby even called for a day of prayer and was as surprised as he was gratified when rain fell the next day, to the astonishment and admiration of the population.[55] The grounds of the chief justice's house, other private grounds, and the grounds of government premises, such as hospitals, were dug up and planted with food crops.[56]

In an attempt to practise what he had preached to the tea industry a year earlier, and for government to feed its own employees, Colby instituted a scheme whereby 16,000 acres of land were purchased in 1949, and 910 acres planted with maize and other food crops by the Department of Agriculture, the yield producing 'a very useful and increasing addition to the Protectorate's food supplies'. After the food crisis, this land was used for many years as a seed multiplication farm for new varieties of maize, cotton and tobacco seed bulking. He instructed field officers on tour not to buy chickens from villagers so as not to diminish village food supplies even marginally.[57] He tried also to encourage alternative crops including long-term proposals, considering, for example, that 'a large scale coconut industry capable of making an appreciable contribution to foodstuffs in times of shortage, would be invaluable', especially since coconuts grew well in precisely those areas where maize was particularly vulnerable to drought.[58] In reply to this idea – which Barrow supported – the director of agriculture 'warned . . . that the culture of coconuts was not easy and . . . it was extremely difficult to prevent thefts of coconuts which fell when they ripened'. Whether or not the director was correct to pour cold water on the governor's idea, the proposal was unquestionably much more practical and far less bizarre than that of the director of geological survey. This was code-named 'Shower' (Shire offers water ex railways), and proposed that water from the Shire River should be taken in tankers from Chiromo by rail to the drought areas further north along the line of rail. The proposal was not implemented.[59]

One of the main direct consumers of foodstuffs among government departments was the Prisons Department which had to feed an average of 1000 prisoners daily. On 3 February 1949, the commissioner of prisons, Bayly, sought Colby's permission to transfer some 50 recidivists to Southern Rhodesia prisons because, whilst the savings on foodstuffs would be negligible, he was concerned about security. Although:

there were at present no signs of trouble in the Central Prison, as a result of the reduced rations scale ... he had no confidence in his ... staff to deal with any serious trouble which might suddenly arise, and he was consequently anxious to have those prisoners who had bad records ... removed to Southern Rhodesia.[60]

Colby, on executive council's advice, did not grant the commissioner's request, because there was no legislative power to transfer prisoners to Southern Rhodesia, and the commissioner's security fears continued. During a visit which the chief secretary made to the Central Prison in March 1949, a 'mass complaint by the prisoners' was made about the inadequacy of the scale of their food rations 'which had necessarily [and substantially] been reduced by the food situation'.[61] He thought that the daily ration should be increased notwithstanding the general food short-age, and Colby accepted this recommendation. Although not necessarily connected with these facts (because, for example, the prison service at the relevant time was holding stocks of maize surplus to its requirements),[62] on 3 November 1949 there was a 'disturbance' in the Central Prison in which the prisoners mutinied and a police constable, a warder and two prisoners were killed. On the advice of executive council, Colby ruled that the report of the commission of inquiry into the disturbance should not be published.[63]

Private companies, individuals and voluntary organizations such as the Red Cross also played an important role in food distribution. It was an essential and publicly announced part of Colby's strategy that the private sector and all races should co-operate actively with government officers in handling the crisis. He took an early opportunity – at the February 1949 meeting of legislative council – publicly to pay tribute 'to the tremendous efforts [made] by planters, by missionaries, by house-holders, and by the ... community in general', and he repeated this tribute in legislative council a year latter. A few of the larger companies held their own stocks of maize sufficient to last their employees for several months into 1949, and others purchased grain in bulk from the government and either provided hot midday meals or issued grain to their employees at a subsidized rate or as part of their normal free ration.[64] Barrow's appointment as African foodstuffs commissioner was designed by Colby, at least in part, to secure the co-operation of the European business community.

So far as the Asian business community was concerned,[65] Colby appointed the Asian member of legislative council as a member of the Food Distribution Advisory Committee and he, after consultations with the Blantyre district commissioner and the Indian Chamber of Commerce, set up an organization to ensure 'the equitable distribution of rice supplies to the Asiatic Community'. During March 1949, this organization collected details of the families of 'all Asiatic consumers of rice', and the size of the rice stocks which they held. In April the chamber received virtually the whole of the Kota Kota rice stocks for Asian consumption, and in January 1950 a total of 170 tons of imported Tanganyika rice were delivered to the chamber.[66] When, also in January 1950, bowls and cups were needed in a hurry to feed starving villagers, the Indian community in Blantyre and Limbe quickly and freely provided them.

We have already referred to the appointment of E. K. Mposa and E. A. Muwamba, African members of legislative council, to the Food Distribution Advisory Committee, and these two men played a leading role in responding to Colby's wishes by explaining government policy to, and securing the co-operation of, the African population. Village headmen and Native Authority clerks played a major part in assessing individual needs at the distribution centres. Private African entrepreneurs also played an important part: for example, in transporting sweet potato and cassava cuttings from the Northern and Central Provinces to the south as replanting material. When cooking and serving utensils were urgently needed to feed starving villagers early in 1950, the African staff of the Public Works Department in Blantyre voluntarily spent their weekend making the utensils from old petrol cans.[67]

By July 1949, Colby had things well under control and, although a good deal of relief work continued to be needed, the machinery for it was working smoothly in the hands of the district commissioners and other officers working under the directions of the African foodstuffs commissioner, assisted by numerous helpers from all sections of the community. On 6 July, the governor went on leave to Britain.[68]

The director of agriculture's August report to executive council on the crop situation was optimistic:

In the Northern Province . . . there was nothing to suggest that the Province would fail to be self-supporting . . .

In distressed areas of the Central Province the situation was being maintained by foraging from the more fortunate areas but this state of affairs was not expected to last indefinitely. In the meantime no economy in the consumption of food was being practised by the people chiefly concerned who were eating normally from their meagre reserves and supplies . . .

[In] the Southern Province there would not appear to be any major change in the situation. Mr Garnett had visited the Lower River District recently . . . and the District Commissioner expressed the opinion that no further relief foodstuffs would be required anywhere in the District during the remainder of 1949 and that there was a distinct possibility of some areas being self-sufficient until the next harvest.[69]

This report took Barrow by surprise, especially since it was known that in the Lower River in 'June 1949 the population had been living on water lily roots and grass seed'. Barrow complained that he had not been kept informed of the changing position and was unaware that food distribution in the Lower River district would not be required for the remainder of 1949. Executive council, puzzled by the director's report, advised the acting governor that Barnes should be asked immediately to reassess the food requirements and report on them. Again, in September, although he did warn that the worst effects of the drought were now becoming apparent and that distress of increasing severity should be expected in parts of the Southern Province, the director remained generally optimistic and:

> reported that only slight deterioration in the general situation had occurred during the past month and whatever development might take place before the new harvest was gathered it was at least a welcome fact that the September position was far less alarming and less unmanageable than at one time seemed probable[70]

There is no reason to doubt the director's judgement in purely agricultural terms for he was a long-experienced and conscientious official, but the immediate and short-term problems of severe food shortages are medical rather than agricultural, and it was signs of medical deterioration which needed to be very carefully looked for and attended to. Late in August, Barnes reported[71] on a visit he had made, in response to the acting governor's request, to 17 villages in the Linthipe and Mafusi valley areas of the Zomba District where:

> the whole population were existing on very small quantities of food, mainly maize husks and wild yams and in a few cases a little maize.

There were no other food supplies available anywhere in these areas and the Provincial Commissioner was particularly disturbed at the condition of these people, in particular that of the children.

His report was reinforced by one written by the local medical officer who had also visited the area and had found:

signs of early nonspecific malnutrition among a high percentage of the people concerned and specific signs of malnutrition in the case of 11 per cent of the population.

Executive council's response to these worrying reports was simply that food distribution should begin in the 17 villages 'as soon as arrangements could be made at a price of 3d per pound', but that at the same time the maximum possible agricultural supervision should be given 'to ensure that everything possible was done to retrieve the present situation by maximum planting activity in the coming season'.

In Colby's absence, council's alarm threshold was high: they seem scarcely to have twitched in response to the stimuli applied by Barnes and the medical officer. Early in January 1950, however, the situation in parts of the Blantyre district deteriorated distressingly and this time Barnes acted personally and speedily, confident of the support and approval of Colby, now back from leave.[72] He visited the Lirangwe area to see for himself the conditions there:

When I arrived there was a crowd of some 3,000 persons waiting for famine relief to be distributed to them and out of this crowd there were about 200 adults of whom only about half a dozen were males, and 300–400 children who were all in a very advanced state of starvation. Two of the children were actually moribund and I doubt whether they will have lived the night. There were many others approaching the same condition and I was really horrified by the state of these people.[73]

Barnes immediately contacted Dr D. J. M. Mackenzie, the director of medical services, and Dr J. Tillman, a government medical officer, who visited Lirangwe with him and 'confirmed that the deterioration in the physical condition of the people . . . is very great'. Confident of Colby's support and backing, he decided immediately to set up an emergency feeding camp, secured the willing cooperation of Mario Sabbatini, a local tobacco farmer, in lending suitable buildings for conversion into dormitories, and seconded Miss M. M. Smith (an assistant mistress at the Jeanes Training Centre, a welfare officer who had been born in Nyasaland and spent most of her life in its rural areas) to take full-time charge of the camp.[74]

Barnes reported these facts and his decisions to Colby via the chief secretary on 17 January, and immediately the director of public works was instructed to have ready for transporting to Lirangwe the following morning 200 plates and cups, 200 blankets and two dozen sleeping boards, cooking pots, and fencing material.[75] Three days later, Colby gave instructions that Barnes be given, 'concerning the care of cases of malnutrition and destitution in the Lirangwe area in particular and the Southern Province generally . . . full discretion . . . to deal with the situation as it develops.'[76] Colby gave him authority to incur the necessary expenditure for establishing and operating feeding camps – again, as a year earlier in the replanting programme, without waiting for formal financial approval. The provincial commissioners of the Northern and Central Provinces were asked to release three or four administrative officers each for secondment to the Southern Province, and arrangements were made to ensure that adequate equipment was available for opening at least one more feeding camp. This time Barnes, supported by the opinion of the director of medical services rather than relying on the opinion of the director of agriculture, and with Colby back in the chair, had ensured that executive council responded with a jerk to the stimuli he applied.

Really serious food shortages were not confined to the Southern Province but were also experienced in the other two provinces. In January 1950, famine relief maize supplies had to be sent to Karonga[77] in the Northern Province where they sold rapidly in the Mlali and Ulambia areas. By mid-February, the people there were having 'to face possible starvation until the new crops were ready at the end of March', and at least 11 people had died of starvation. The Karonga district commissioner was particularly worried about the possible political repercussions of food shortages since his district had earlier been required to export 600 tons of 'surplus' rice to other districts. In February, in the Central Province Dowa lakeshore area, conditions deteriorated so much that a reception centre had to be opened to care for starving villagers.[78]

In the early weeks of 1950, there was a sudden and alarming deterioration in the physical condition of people in the worst-hit areas, and the African foodstuffs commissioner reported that 'food distribution was . . .

running at a high level. Approximately 350 tons were being distributed per week in rural areas and 250 tons in townships.'[79] By early February, he reported 'that the tempo of distribution had increased very considerably',[80] and the food shortage reached its peak at the end of February, after which new crops gradually became available and the food crisis subsided. The distribution centres were closed down at the end of April.[81]

Without doubt, the worst aspects of the food shortages were experienced in January and February 1950, in the special emergency feeding camps or reception centres, especially in the Blantyre district. 2006 children and 1174 adults – mainly dependants of absent migrant workers – were admitted to these feeding camps, and 14 deaths occurred in them. 1401 very serious cases of malnutrition were admitted to hospitals – 836 children and 565 adults – and 57 of these died. 'It was,' as a local observer recalled over three decades later, 'shocking to see young children looking like the pictures that are shown now of refugees in Somalia.'[82] Government officials at the feeding camps were much assisted by the Red Cross and by many non-official volunteers, and 'they undoubtedly saved many hundreds of lives'. 'You should have seen some of the children who arrived looking like skeletons with that vacant listless look, running around plump and smiling two weeks or so later.' Thirty years later, when a European planter from the Lunzu area died, an African spokesman at his funeral said, 'We have come to pay tribute to the man we shall always remember for feeding us and our women and children during the famine.'[83]

With the gathering of the new season's crops, the feeding camps, like the distribution centres, were closed down in April 1950, and Colby wrote personal letters of thanks to the many people who had helped with famine relief. The 1949–50 grave foodstuffs crisis was over.

Yet Colby was not the sort of man, still less the sort of governor, simply to heave a sigh of relief once a crisis had passed. Rather, he continued to think and to act in an effort to ensure that such a crisis did not recur. His motivation in so doing was only partly directly humanitarian, for he was deeply committed to developing the country economically and with great haste. At its simplest, occurring so soon after his arrival, the food crisis was a considerable nuisance: it diverted his, his officials' and the general population's energies and attention from the major task of economic development; it sapped the country's severely limited resources in terms of funds available for development; it clogged the transport system which he needed for importing develop-

ment materials and equipment; and it was in a sector of the economy
which held the key to development progress and success – agriculture.
As was said by an executive council member, 'The drought . . . came as
a very dirty blow below the belt at a time when we were about to embark
upon our development schemes which were bound to cause a very great
drain upon our resources before we could get any real return for the
expenditure.'[84]

Colby was a man much given to having his major decisions based
upon a thorough and logical analysis of data and other information,
including reports on past events, and he found the food shortage experience disconcerting:

> In this Territory practically no agricultural statistics are available
> in respect of African-grown crops and it has been extremely difficult
> to assess the food position in the drought-stricken areas. Indeed
> the drought has caused some of the most baffling problems with
> which I personally have ever had to deal.
>
> It is no easy matter to deal with a situation in which practically
> all the factors are unknown and calls for judgement of a very high
> order.[85]

At a relatively early stage, therefore – 22 March 1949 – he wrote a
minute[86] to the chief secretary saying that, whilst no one in the protectorate had experience of a similar grave food shortage, in the current year
they themselves would learn a great deal by experience, and that in
fairness to their successors they should record those experiences, and
he directed that the director of agriculture should record them 'in the
greatest possible detail'.

> The report should include . . . detailed figures and distribution of
> rainfall in the various Districts and portions of Districts of the
> Protectorate and the behaviour of all crops and the circumstances
> pertaining in each District . . . the necessary arrangements [should]
> be made to see that all these facts and figures are recorded.

Later, in January 1950, he indicated that the report should cover the
climatic conditions; the measures taken to repair the damage and
the result; the harvest and the resulting food position; and food imports
and distribution. The report was in fact written by Hodgson – since
Garnett had by then left Nyasaland – and was 'a comprehensive and

detailed report on all aspects of the famine, relief measures taken and the lessons learnt'. In this way, Colby ensured that data and other information were collected and recorded, together with details of the steps taken by the government to combat severe food shortages. The report was capable of being of enormous benefit in any future similar situation and filled a gap which was sorely felt and much regretted by the governor and his officials in 1949–50.

Colby also focused his attention on the facts that the country's usual rainy season lasts only four to four and a half months, the rest of the year being totally dry, and – especially in the lower areas – the period of expected rainfall coincides with the highest temperatures with severe effects on young crops in the absence of sufficient moisture; and that any delay in planting beyond the earliest adequate rains to sustain the crop results in reduced yield potential. There was thus generally only one limited opportunity to effect planting which would produce a year's supply of food. 'It was . . . recognised that the earliest possible planting of almost all crops was the surest safeguard against unfavourable weather.'[87] The early seasonal preparation of land was, therefore, the main thrust of Colby's subsequent policy against the risk of famine, and he secured the legislative instruments to be used for this purpose: Native Authority rules which made early cultivation of village gardens compulsory and which later became almost habitual practice. He also paid close attention in the planting season following the shortage to ensuring that sufficient food and seed were available to achieve expeditious planting and to avoid farmers' absences searching for food. Failure to have done this could have resulted in a repetition of shortage in the following season.

Colby was also much concerned that there had been no reserve of grain in the protectorate upon which to draw quickly and cheaply when current supplies ran short. During the latter part of 1949, he arranged with the Nyasaland railways to erect concrete storage silos at Limbe so that any surplus could be carried over from one year to the next. These storage facilities when completed catered for 1600 tons of railways maize and a similar quantity of grain belonging to the Maize Control Board. Additional storage in the Central Province brought the permanent reserve to 6000 tons and Colby aimed at extending the facilities to cater for at least 25,000 tons, the quantity imported during 1949 and 1950. With such a reserve he knew that the government could handle a similar future food crisis effectively, quickly and cheaply, and given Hodgson's report they would know precisely how to do it. Colby's policy was:

to keep our stores full, to turn over our stocks every year, and, in order to encourage production, to buy all that is offered and to export the surplus.[88]

In these ways – the detailed collection and recording of information on the drought and food shortage, the compulsory early preparation of village gardens, and the creation of bulk storage facilities – Colby took swift, systematic and determined steps, so far as he was able, to ensure that any future drought did not cause severe food shortages and hunger which would divert the country's attention, energies, skills and resources away from what he firmly believed was its primary task of economic development.

11· Africans on Private Estates

'The seeds of many forms of trouble.'

In the preceding chapter on the food crisis, reference was made to Colby's early warnings to the tea industry and to expatriate employers generally – especially estate owners – of the dangers inherent in the fast-increasing population and serious overcrowding. His warnings at the time were directed at food production, but there were also serious political dangers, especially where the overcrowding occurred in areas of privately owned estate land.

The history of Africans on private estates was long and complex, and an outline of it, and of the various attempts by his predecessors to solve the problems, is necessary in order to understand the nature and magnitude of those problems at the time of Colby's governorship.[1]

From the early 1880s, a number of expatriate individuals, missionary bodies and companies acquired land from African chiefs, most of which, save that in North Nyasa, was then sparsely inhabited and, it was claimed, not required by the African people for cultivation and expansion.

The proclamations of the Shire Highlands Protectorate in 1889 and of the Nyassa Districts Protectorate in 1891 were followed by what Commissioner Johnston called:

> a wholesale grabbing of land or, where it is not fair to describe the acquisition of land as 'grabbing', at any rate huge tracts had been bought for disproportionate amounts from the natives.[2]

In about September 1892, Johnston began an enquiry into land alienation and every estate or land claim was visited and examined by himself or by his senior officials. In respect of claims to mineral rights, they determined whether each of the chiefs alleged to be the grantors of land had in fact agreed to the concession and whether they had received fair value: if both answers were affirmative, Johnston confirmed the concession. In respect of claims to land, cases of long occupation and improvement in the way of cultivation or building – which were rare – sufficed even in the absence of a properly authenticated document, but in other cases confirmation of the grant depended upon the chief admitting sale, the deed being authentic, and fair value – which varied from half a penny to threepence an acre – having been paid. Where fair value had not been paid, an additional payment or a reduction in acreage was required before Johnston confirmed the grant.[3]

As to the position of Africans residing on the purchased land, Johnston was fully aware that the chiefs by custom had no right to alienate the land,[4] but considered that they had assumed that right and that it was tacitly accepted by their people. It was in order to secure the people from their chiefs' 'heedlessness', and to avoid them becoming 'serfs' of the new white owners of the land,[5] that he made it clear to them that their villages and plantations were not alienated when the surrounding land was alienated, by including in most of the deeds, which he styled 'certificates of claim' when he confirmed the alienation, a non-disturbance clause which read:

> That no native village or plantation existing at the date of this Certificate on the said estate shall be disturbed or removed without the consent in writing of Her Majesty's Commissioner and Consul-General, but when such consent shall have been given the sites of such villages or plantations shall revert to the Proprietor of the said estate. No natives can make other and new villages or plantations on the said estate without the prior consent of the Proprietor.[6]

Johnston was pleased with his land settlement, saying that on the whole it was well accepted by the Europeans and gave distinct satisfaction to the Africans: his proposals were accepted without modification by the British government. Having dealt with the certificates of claim on behalf of the Crown, he entered into treaties with all the chiefs, securing Crown control over the remainder of the land in the protectorate which then became inalienable without his sanction as commissioner; in doing this he took over from the chiefs, and assumed on behalf of the government, the obligation to provide sufficient land for the African people. It was accepted that government thus became the owners in fee simple, and Sharpe later claimed that the chiefs clearly recognized this.[7]

The essential intended results of Johnston's timely intervention in land matters were threefold. First, in the interests of the Europeans and the economic development of the country, he confirmed the alienation of land not heavily populated which had been genuinely agreed by the chiefs and for which fair value had been paid, and he made it clear that the opening of villages and gardens on these alienated areas required the prior consent of the landowners and was no longer at the disposal of the chiefs. Second, in the interests of the Africans, such alienations excluded the areas then devoted to village settlements and gardens and space for their expansion: he confirmed the non-alienated status of these areas, and, in heavily populated areas, he endorsed the alienation only of waste land. Third, by treaty and in the interests of both Europeans and Africans, he reserved to himself and his gubernatorial successors the exclusive right to agree to further alienations; in this way, he imposed strict control over such alienation and thereby nipped a dangerous development in the bud as much as was then possible.

In practice, the non-disturbance clause was never enforced on either side, and little or no hindrance was placed on Africans in moving from one part of an estate to another every few years in accordance with their traditional form of shifting cultivation, and when this happened the estate owner took over the original, now abandoned, sites. In no case was the commissioner asked to consent to the disturbance or removal, and until about 1902 there was no opposition to the movement of Africans on private estates.

From about the middle of 1901, large numbers of Anguru migrated from Mozambique into the southern part of Nyasaland and were welcomed as a substantial source of labour by estate owners, on whose land many of them settled. The relationship between European landowners and African residents now changed from being one simply concerned with residence to one which also concerned labour. The practice grew up of estate owners, led by the Blantyre and East Africa (B&EA) Company, securing from the Africans on their land agreements for the performance of labour or the payment of rent, irrespective of whether they were original inhabitants entitled to security or were immigrants. The company seems to have genuinely attempted to achieve a relationship which was satisfactory to all parties, which spelled out the residence conditions in more detail than had the certificates, and which also dealt with the labour conditions.[8] The Africans did not appear to be aggrieved by this arrangement and none relied on any claim to freehold under the certificates of claim non-disturbance clauses: to have done so might have jeopardized their chances of being given work and consequently their ability to pay tax, and might have run the risk of their being returned to Mozambique.

After Johnston had left Nyasaland, in 1896, there were frequent doubts expressed as to precisely what the intention of the non-disturbance clauses had been. His successor, Sharpe, who, as Johnston's legal adviser and the person who had made most of the enquiries into land claims, ought not to have been in doubt, decided to test the matter in the courts. As a consequence, in 1903, the supervisor for native affairs took the Blantyre and East Africa Company to court and the case was heard by Mr Justice Nunan who gave judgment on 28 April 1903.

Nunan's decisions may be summarized as in effect saying, first, that the company's agreements were unfair and unreasonable because they removed the non-disturbance clause protection from the original occupants. Second, he reaffirmed that the clause rights were vested in the village communities, were freehold rights and extended to eight acres per family, and that the proof that a resident was not an original occupant rested on the landowners. Third, he suggested that the Africans, whether original occupants or newcomers, might find it in their interests to pay a rent, or work, in exchange for a 'fixity of tenure', and that the Europeans might also find it in their interests not to distinguish between original occupants and newcomers. Save for a difference over the amount of work to be performed and its equivalent in rent, and the question of long-term security of tenure for the original occupants, Nunan does not seem to have accomplished any more than the company agreements would have accomplished.

Whilst this case was being heard, F. B. Pearce, who was acting as commissioner during Sharpe's absence on leave, appointed a land commission under Nunan's chairmanship, which began its hearings on the day Nunan delivered his judgment, to consider the best way in which to give effect to the judgement.

As a result of the land commission's recommendations,[9] the Lands Ordinance of 1904[10] was enacted, empowering the commissioner to direct landowners in scheduled districts to set aside locations of up to 10 per cent of undeveloped land in 'favourable situations as regards soil, water and firewood, having regard to the average of good arable land on the entire estate'. The commissioner was empowered to allot this land to African communities or families residing on the estate on the basis of eight acres per family[11], and to permit other families to settle on the locations. Every tenant was required to pay an annual rent of four shillings to the landlord or be liable to eviction. The effect of this ordinance was to extend to all Africans on private estates, whether original occupants or new immigrant tenants, on the one hand the non-disturbance clause benefits of the certificates of claim, and on the other hand the liability to pay rent or be evicted: the original occupants suffered a duty – to pay rent – whilst the new tenants gained a right – to occupy eight acres of land. The ordinance also clarified the status of the areas upon which the original occupants held their villages and gardens: as freehold vesting in the European landholder but leased in perpetuity to the African occupants without power to mortgage, sell or pledge their interest in the land.[12]

Save for setting aside land for African occupation, this ordinance, which was never brought into effect, seems to have done very little but to provide for giving legal effect to a practice already well established: the estate owners wanted labour, not rent, and the practice provided it, whilst the tenants did not publicly object because they wanted to work in order to pay their tax and purchase trade goods. In not bringing the ordinance into effect, Sharpe missed the opportunity to resolve at an early stage a potentially dangerous problem which was to rumble on and worry his successors for the next half-century.

In 1904, a total of 3,618,000 of the protectorate's 26,000,000 acres was alienated: 2,700,000 in North Nyasa, 387,000 in Zomba, 364,000 in Blantyre, 94,000 in Ruo, and 73,000 in Upper Shire. Only 32,809 acres of private land were cultivated and 156,727 were occupied by Africans.[13] Sharrer had developed only 5000 of his BCA Company's 367,000 acres, the B&EA Company only 3000 of its 160,000 acres, and the Bruce Estates only 500 of its 160,000 acres.[14]

The Rev A. Hetherwick of the Blantyre Scottish Mission kept the land question very much in the public eye, and at the May 1910 meeting of legislative council he initiated a debate in which he argued that the government should reacquire land in districts where 'Government land was scarce, by purchase or by treaty with private . . . owners to lease it out to . . . natives'.[15]

The report on the Chilembwe rising,[16] which occurred in 1915 at Magomero in an area of much alienated land on the borders of the Zomba and Blantyre districts, drew attention to cases of discontent resulting from the agreements to pay rent or provide labour in return for residential rights. The report expressed disapproval of the agreements and led to a modification of the 1904 ordinance – which had still not been brought into effect – by the Native Rents Ordinance of 1917.

The bill for this ordinance was discussed by the Blantyre Scottish missionaries, who were particularly worried by the shortage of African land in the Shire Highlands and concluded, in their journal *Life and Work in Nyasaland*: 'We see no way out of the present impasse than that the Government should buy over some of the undeveloped land in European hands.'[17]

The 1917 ordinance[18] forbade the exaction of service, labour in lieu of rent, in order to separate the concept of landlord and tenant from the concept of employer and employee, but authorized the landlord to charge a rent in exchange for residence, and – rather than the eight acres previously specified, because that was now considered 'no doubt too much' – sufficient cultivable land for the subsistence of the tenant and his family. The ordinance provided for six months' notice to quit for rent default and summary eviction by the resident thereafter. The position after 1917 remained that in practice no distinction was made between original occupants and new tenants.

It was very soon recognized that the 1917 ordinance, designed to achieve a system of tenancy based merely on payment of rent, was not going to work successfully, and in 1920 Governor Smith set up a commission to look into the whole question again, chaired by Judge Jackson.[19] The commission in its report[20] accepted that tenancy based simply on rent was 'very desirable':

> This may come in time but not yet . . . for the time being labour is the only return for which the owners of agricultural estates will accept native tenants . . .
>
> Our problem . . . is to define terms which are fair to the native and at the same time such that the European landlord will be prepared to accept and retain native tenants on those terms.

This last point was important because already the Crown lands in the areas of numerous or large estates, such as Blantyre district and the southern part of Zomba district, were insufficient to support the fast-growing African population. Between 1904 and 1920, the population of Blantyre district had risen from 87,000 to 156,000, whilst the density rose from 53.35 per square mile to 95.53; while that of the Zomba district had risen from 46,000 to 102,000, and its density from 24.53 to

51.93. In Zomba, a quarter of the African population was living on private estates, and in Blantyre a half.[21]

Jackson was impressed by what he saw as the way in which the modern extension of a traditional relationship had persisted despite legislative attempts in 1904 and 1917 to abolish it, which showed that it 'has practical convenience for both sides'. Traditionally, villagers worked for certain periods in the gardens of their chiefs who, in return, assumed a responsibility for the villagers, 'which has its parallel in the relations of the best European landlords towards their native tenants today'. This system was known as *thangata* ('help' or 'assistance').

What particularly worried Jackson was that although evictions were currently rare, there were conditions which could well make them frequent, and if they did, the disturbance of large numbers of tenants would 'produce great hardship, discontent and numerous dangers'.[22] The conditions to which Jackson referred were the influx of European settlers after the 1914–18 War, which was splitting up the larger estates, introducing many more landlords than formerly, and removing such security as existed through long relationships with well-known estate owners. The hardship to which he referred was the insecurity of tenure placed upon families who established themselves on private land expecting to remain there for a considerable period. The discontent and numerous dangers to which he referred were potential political and security threats, of which the Chilembwe rising only five years earlier had given heightened appreciation. Even if the problem of Africans on private estates had not been clearly viewed in this light before, it was now seen as having marked and worrying political ramifications: it was not simply a matter of economics and equity but equally a matter of political security.

The 1920 commission recommended that security of tenure should be enhanced by providing four years as the minimum period of tenure of Africans accepted on to private estates, subject to the performance of the terms of the tenancy agreement. To avoid eviction of large numbers for non-performance, which would 'cause serious disturbances', eviction should not exceed ten per thousand acres a year. To avoid exploitation of the tenants, the maximum period of work to which the estate owner could be entitled should be two months a year. Whenever the opportunity arose, government should endeavour by exchange or purchase to regain suitable areas of private estates.[23] In this, Jackson was going a step further than Nunan had in 1903: the latter recommended that government should be empowered to direct estate owners to set aside parts of their land as African reserves; the former now recommended that government should acquire private land by exchange or purchase.

The government did not, however, act on the commission's report, because the acute fears created by the Chilembwe rising subsided and because the economic depression of the early 1920s removed from the landlords – who had difficulty remaining solvent – the need to pressurize tenants to work on their estates.

Governor Bowring, who arrived early in 1924, found that at nearly every meeting of headmen which he attended in the early days of his governorship, feelings of uneasiness among Africans as to the future of their land were expressed. Taking Nunan, Hetherwick, *Life and Work* and Jackson's point about acquisition a stage further, Bowring told the Ormsby-Gore East African Commission which visited Nyasaland in 1924 that in the Shire Highlands:

> the only method of dealing with the problem is to re-acquire from the landowners convenient blocks of sufficient area to accommodate the natives at present resident on the estates for whom accommodation acceptable to them and to Government cannot be provided elsewhere on Crown Land.[24]

When the Ormsby-Gore Report published these views and supported them, there was an outburst of opposition and criticism from the large landowners.[25] The report – which was not primarily or specifically concerned with land tenure matters – and the sharp reaction from European landowners led to the whole question of Africans on private estates being reconsidered.

In 1927 the government became deeply concerned about the number of tenants being evicted from private estates, and Bowring brought a Natives on Private Estates Bill before legislative council 'to solve one of the outstanding problems of vital importance ... with the minimum of delay'.[26] In introducing the bill, the provincial commissioner of the Zomba Province, explained that:

> Difficulties have repeatedly arisen as the development or break up of estates was interfered with by the presence of native settlements, or as the need for labour forced the landowners to try and make work on the estate a condition of remaining. On the other hand, the native found his liberty to choose his own employment limited, and many of his customs ... seriously interfered with. The diffi-

culty was further accentuated by the absence of suitable Crown Land in the neighbourhood on which the ejected natives could settle.[27]

This last point emphasized a worrying change from the position ten years earlier when the governor was able to say that 'it is rarely the case that there is not crown land in the vicinity on which [evictees] could settle'.[28]

Under the 1928 ordinance,[29] resident Africans were liable to pay rent and in return they were entitled to a site and materials for a hut, to cultivable land sufficient to maintain their families, and to compensation for disturbance. Resident Africans could ask for work or facilities for growing economic crops, and the wages for the work or the prices of the crops were to be used in full or partial remission of rent. Eviction was permitted summarily in the event of non-payment of rent or for misconduct, and upon six months' notice without cause in the case of not more than ten per cent of the resident population of each estate on the expiration of a quinquennial period. The ordinance also obliged the government to find land for evicted Africans,[30] but within a few years the district commissioners experienced great difficulty in enforcing legitimate eviction notices because they could not find sufficient land in the vicinity for settling the evictees.[31] The governor was empowered to acquire by compulsion up to 10 per cent of the area of any estate over 10,000 acres in extent for African settlement by exchanging Crown land of equal value. This last provision was another step along the Nunan-Hetherwick-*Life and Work*-Jackson-Bowring road towards acquisition of land for permanent African settlement.

The government had allowed itself to be entrapped by the quinquennial eviction provisions. Landlords had a statutory right to evict 10 per cent of resident Africans every five years. The government had a statutory duty to find land for the evictees. Crown land nearby was not available and, in order to acquire land nearby, exchanged land had to be of equal value; it was extremely unlikely that such land – except by alienating very large areas indeed in remote parts of the country – could be found of value equal to that in the Shire Highlands.

After 1928, therefore, there continued to be a failure in practice to distinguish between those Africans protected by non-disturbance clauses and those who were not. Indeed, the landowners believed, or claimed to believe, that the 1928 ordinance extinguished the non-disturbance clause rights.

In his annual report for 1932,[32] the district commissioner of the Blantyre district criticized the different rates of rent being charged and the level of those rents; and added that there was insufficient firewood and building material available, that large areas of some private estates were still uncultivated, that the Africans were 'losing the habit of working', and that in his view the rent and labour sections of the 1928 ordinance needed changing. The new governor, Young, read this report and quickly:

> concluded that the time had arrived for an attempt to be made to place the whole question of the position of natives on alienated land on a final and satisfactory footing.[33]

In his short time in Nyasaland – 16 months – Young introduced the Native Authority Ordinance and, as he saw it, 'settled the question of unalienated land'; he now looked for a similar quick triumph in respect of alienated land.[34] He awaited the end of the first quinquennial period, 1933, with apprehension, since the eviction of 10 per cent of resident Africans could, on the basis of 1920 figures, result in the removal from private estates of 524 families from the southern part of the Zomba district and 2480 families from the Blantyre district – both areas of insufficient Crown land. He convened a select committee of the whole council to consider what legislation, if any, was required. The deliberations were carefully guided by the governor, who pressed the non-official members to accept legislation which would enable a locally appointed land commissioner, with the Native Authorities and landowners, to calculate the amount of land to which certificates of claim gave security of tenure to village communities, and then negotiate the removal of such 'islands' from the estates and add them to the Native Authorities' land. The non-officials insisted that either the rights no longer existed or that the protected areas could not be calculated, and they picked holes in all possible solutions suggested to them. Young was looking for a way of recompensing the Native Authorities on behalf of the original village communities in exchange for extinguishing the original rights of non-disturbed residence on private estates.

The secretary of state disagreed with Young that the land question should be reopened. In a despatch of 24 October 1934, he argued that the 1928 ordinance was reached only after exhaustive enquiries and prolonged negotiations, and that although the outcome was a compromise it was regarded at the time as the 'final and best possible solution to a long standing difficulty': he did not want Young to 'revive a very difficult problem'.[35] Because of 'public opinion in England' he preferred, if the matter were to be reopened, that an independent land commissioner rather than a local officer should conduct the public enquiry.

In any event, the end of the quinquennial period passed without any difficulties arising from evictions. In 1933, a total of 781 notices to quit were served, covering 3124 people: 299 in Cholo (of which 150 notices were enforced), 208 in Zomba, 207 in Chiradzulu, 42 in Mlanje, and 25 in Blantyre. In Cholo only two of the estates – probably both belonging to the British Central Africa Company – insisted on issuing notices to the full 10 per cent of the number of tenants.[36]

Kittermaster, who succeeded Young in 1934, consulted his district commissioners who advised that if the landlords exercised their right of quinquennial evictions in 1938, 'a serious situation might result' because it would be difficult to find land on which to resettle the evicted Africans.[37]

While Kittermaster was on leave in Britain in 1937, he discussed the question of Africans on private estates at the Colonial Office, admitted that he was frankly unable to put forward any constructive suggestions, but advised that the government should wait and see what the landlords would do at the end of the quinquennium the following year. The secretary of state was most anxious to have information on their intentions as early as possible, and in the meantime he proposed to await the report of Sir Robert Bell on the finances of the protectorate.[38]

If the secretary of state had hoped for positive guidance from Bell, he was disappointed. Bell briefly reviewed the history of the problem and concluded that since, in his view, the original occupants and their direct descendants had their rights abrogated by the 1928 ordinance, there were two possible courses of action: first, to allow the conditions which had become stabilized over ten years to continue, and 'if trouble arises in the future it can be dealt with in the light of the actual circumstances of the time'; or, second, to try to distinguish between original occupants and later tenants, so as to give the former free rights of occupancy and to impose upon the latter the need to enter into individual agreements with the landowner. He concluded, however, that there was 'no certainty that such a result, however fair it might be to all the parties, would be accepted by them as satisfactory'. The choice was a matter of policy and Bell's advice – pragmatic and very short-term – was:

to ascertain the extent to which land owners exercise their right of issuing notices to quit and observe the effects.[39]

Whilst 984 notices to quit were issued (including 359 from BCA Company land, 289 from B&EA Company land and 123 from Bruce Estates land) many tenants reached agreement with their landlords that they should stay on the land under special agreements.[40]

In the event, much to government's relief, no large number of evictions took place in 1938, and consequently no further action was taken on the Africans on private estates problem, especially since the war intervened and occupied the energies and attention of most people in Nyasaland. Lord Hailey, who visited the country early in the war advocated the 'acquisition of certain areas in the private estates in order to provide secured holdings for part of the native population now resident on them'.[41] The concerns of others also existed: the Native Welfare Committee spoke of the growing dissatisfaction and said that 'The purchase of freehold land by government may ... be necessary to relieve congestion.'[42]

Anxiety returned as the end of the next quinquennium approached. In 1942 and 1943, several hundred tenants in the Blantyre district were served with orders to quit the estates on which they were living. They refused to leave, creating 'serious incidents' towards the end of 1943. When members of the administration investigated the troubles, they found that although much of the difficulty stemmed from misunderstanding, there were a number of genuine grievances against the estate owners. Even more disturbingly, they also found that political influences were at work fomenting the discontent. 'This appears to have been the first time that agitators had fished in these troubled waters.' An administrative report of November 1943 stated that agitation among tenants on private estates had increased and was now political in nature. Senior administrative officers and leading non-officials now believed that serious trouble between landlords and tenants would arise if a solution were not found.[43]

Early in 1945 two estate owners in the Cholo District tried to evict 1250 tenants on the grounds of rent default, and the government was faced with the daunting prospect of resettling this large number – totalling, with their families, over 5000 people – on already congested land: 'a very serious problem'. One of these estates was the Mpezo estate owned by the BCA Company who applied for the eviction of more than 500 tenants and their families – over 2000 people. The district commissioner of Cholo, through 'political and tactful handling', succeeded in getting the evictions reduced to about 120 tenants.[44]

As a result of these worrying portents, the secretary of state's 1935 suggestion that an external special commissioner be appointed was revived and the governor, Richards, appointed Sir Sidney Abrahams on 22 July 1946.[45] He spent from 25 July to 4 October collecting evidence and submitted his report on 31 October 1946.[46]

Abrahams believed that the problem was essentially a conflict of ideas – between European concepts of freehold land and African concepts of communally held land – and that the true difficulty was a failure to appreciate this; that reconciliation between the ideas of the landlord and tenant could not be achieved and compromise was 'out of the question':

the only solution is the clear cut one of getting rid of the status of resident native and leaving him free to quit the estate or stay there on terms satisfactory both to himself and the landlord, substituting contractual for statutory rights.[47]

He referred to this process as 'emancipation', and emphasized that it would be possible only if Trust land were available to accommodate Africans who wished not to live on private land.[48] Following, but not acknowledging, the train of thought which had run from Nunan through Hetherwick, *Life and Work*, Jackson, Bowring, Ormsby-Gore, the 1928 ordinance, Young, the 1939 Native Welfare Committee and Hailey, he recommended that private land which was both unoccupied and uncultivated, and land which was occupied and cultivated by resident Africans, should be acquired by government if it would relieve congestion on neighbouring Trust land or provide settlement space for emancipated families from nearby estates. Acquisition of private land should be negotiated, including arbitration and umpiring if needed, but if that failed, then compulsory acquisition would be necessary. He emphasized the political dangers of not settling the problem soon, of failing 'to satisfy the political grievances aggravated by land hunger':

It is obvious that a state of affairs which has poisoned the relations between the estate owners and those who work for them, to say nothing of the relations between European and African in general, must contain the seeds of many forms of trouble.[49]

The government published the Abrahams Report on 15 February 1947,[50] and six weeks later appointed a Land Planning Committee to obtain the factual information required to reach decisions on the report's recommendations.[51]

The committee saw its task as making recommendations to deal with three problems: the economic problem – to which they felt there were no permanent solutions but only palliatives – of relieving congestion on Trust land; the political problem – to the solution of which they felt their recommendations would go a long way – of satisfying the sense of grievance felt by Africans that Europeans were holding large tracts of undeveloped land whilst they themselves suffered acute pangs of land hunger; and the social problem – to which they felt their recommendations would not contribute much – of emancipating Africans resident on private estates.

In considering Abrahams' recommendation that the government should acquire all the estates fully occupied by resident Africans, together with those which were unoccupied and uncultivated if acquisition would relieve congestion on neighbouring Trust land and provide settlement areas for Africans wishing to leave nearby estates, the committee encountered little difficulty, although they pointed out that in the areas where congestion was most severe, most estates were either already developed or earmarked for early development, so that the amount of unoccupied land available for acquisition was negligible. They met considerable difficulty, however, in respect of his recommendation that in the case of estates partially developed and partially occupied by resident Africans, the latter areas should be excised wherever the estate was divisible without being unfair to the estate owner.[52]

The problem which the committee now encountered – one which was unforeseen by Abrahams – was that in the intensely developed areas, where the difficulties were greatest, nearly all the estates were indivisible. This meant that the committee was faced with having to reach a solution without following Abrahams' recommendation of acquiring all the land which the resident Africans then occupied.[53] His recommendation was that in the case of indivisible estates – which he assumed to be few in number and limited in extent – the estate owners should be asked to place all resident Africans on a contractual basis, residing on the estate in exchange for working for an agreed period; if the Africans declined to enter into such a contract, they should leave the estate and reside on Trust land where accommodation would be found as a result of the expected large scale acquisition of undeveloped land sufficiently nearby for them to be agreeable to move to it:

In short, the recommendations in the report for these partially developed and partially occupied estates were founded on two hypotheses, the first being that a large number of such estates would be found to be readily divisible, and the second being that large scale acquisition of suitable undeveloped land in the same neighbourhood would be practicable.

It was the unquestioning acceptance of these hypotheses that secured for Sidney Abrahams the strong support [which] he obtained for his proposals. But . . . the true position is not as it was generally accepted to be, and . . . it does not lend itself to action on the lines proposed in the Abrahams Report.[54]

The committee was nonetheless able to make specific recommendations in respect of acquiring 550,000 acres of private land, of which 500,000 acres were located in the Shire Highlands. They felt it necessary, however, to make a statement about further acquisition, and in their report they said that if their recommendations were adopted, government should make it perfectly clear that 'no further large scale acquisition of freehold land [would] be practicable without seriously prejudicing the European development upon which the prosperity of the [country] so largely depends'.[55]

In summary, the Land Planning Committee recommended that less than half of the protectorate's total of 1,200,000 acres of private land should be acquired by government; that the shortage of land in the Shire Highlands prevented a solution there along the lines suggested by Abrahams; that areas for African settlement should be acquired in the Cholo district totalling 27,558 acres; and that suburban residential areas in the Blantyre district should be similarly acquired. However, they felt that the large blocks of BCA Company land in the Cholo and Blantyre districts should be acquired only by persuading the London directors of the political need to sell them to government; that further large-scale acquisition was impracticable; and that compulsory acquisition was undesirable.

These were the recommendations which awaited Colby when he arrived in March 1948.

For over half a century, the government had vacillated and inconclusively investigated the problem of Africans on private estates. Committee after committee had looked into it and made recommendations; legislation had been changed on numerous occasions. And yet the problem was very little nearer being solved than at any other time since Johnston's original, and in many ways far-sighted, settlement in 1892.

The essence of the problem, and that which made it intractable in the hands of Colby's predecessors, was the conflict of landholding concepts between Europeans and Africans. In practice this focused, on the one hand, on the demands of European landholders to run their estates in accordance with Western ideas of freehold tenure as they wished, unencumbered by resident Africans save those of their own choosing who were prepared to work for them; and, on the other hand, the desire of the African occupants to live on estate land in the manner in which their fellows lived on Trust land in accordance with customary tenure, virtually as of right and without the obligation to work for, or pay rent to, the estate owners.

Successive governors knew where their duty ultimately rested: with the Africans, since Nyasaland was a protectorate and the Royal Instructions given to the governor since 1907 required him:

> especially to take care to protect [the native inhabitants] in their persons and in the full enjoyment of their possessions, and by all lawful means to prevent and restrain all . . . injustices which may in any manner be practised or attempted against them.[56]

Yet the Europeans were politically both far better organized and far more powerful, with a strong voice in London close to the ear of the Colonial Office, and it was they who had played the dominant role, both in economic development upon which depended the country's future and the government's revenue, and in maintaining the status quo in respect of Africans on private estates.

The ultimate solution to the problem – government acquisition of private land on which to resettle families – had been hinted at and developed over a long period, successively by Nunan, Hetherwick, *Life and Work*, Jackson, Bowring, the 1928 ordinance, Young, the 1939 Native Welfare Committee, Hailey and Abrahams. Their message had, it is true, become increasingly clear as the years passed, but even after Abrahams had expressed it so clearly, the Nyasaland government had not initially moved unequivocally forward. They had instead appointed an internal committee to make more detailed proposals, and were of the view that the full scheme proposed was impracticable and that further investigations with a view to acquisition in due course should be made.

Colby, impatient to begin work and with little time at his disposal since he expected to be governor of Nyasaland for only five years at the most, had three important factors at the forefront of his mind. First, the balance of political power between Europeans and Africans was changing. Although the 1915 Chilembwe foretaste of African potential political power had been forgotten or ignored, a reminder had been given in the 'serious incidents' in Cholo in 1942 and 1943, and the Nyasaland African Congress, formed in 1944, had been sufficiently well organized to make a significant impression on Abrahams in 1946. Second, he recognized that the greatly increased economic power which would accompany the marked upswing in African agricultural production which he was determined his development strategy should bring to the Africans would be accompanied by further political power as the economic balance moved in the Africans' favour. Third, he was determined that, so far as he was able, political activity and unrest should not hamper or delay the rapid and substantial increase in agricultural production and economic development which he saw as essential to the protectorate's future.

Aware of the shift in the balance of political and economic power, and in order to avoid the economically disruptive consequences of political unrest inherent in the problem of Africans on private estates, Colby moved quickly towards beginning to solve or rather to remove the problem. Although the balance of power was shifting, government still very much held the scales of power and Colby was not reluctant to hold them firmly and, if necessary, to tilt them.

Bell and Abrahams had both said that the resolution of the difficulty was a matter of policy, a question for the government to decide one way or the other: it was a nettle to be grasped, a nettle the stem of which, as Colby saw it, was held mainly by Europeans but increasingly by Africans, a nettle with a sting which would become very much more severe and disabling the longer it was left ungrasped. The time for dithering was past. One of his earliest tasks was to study the reports and files on land and the problem of Africans on private estates, and only a month after his arrival he addressed a semi-official letter to Andrew Cohen at the Colonial Office setting out his views.[57] He felt that since the question was new to him he could regard it objectively and without prejudice.

His first point was that since Abrahams' investigations were of a general character, and since he had been unable to make detailed examinations of individual estates and areas, his recommendations similarly had been of a general nature, and that he appreciated that more detailed

investigations would be needed. Colby fully accepted the principle of
Abrahams' recommendations about acquisition, but he and his officials
were faced with the difficulty of determining the extent to which they
could be implemented and how far they would go towards relieving
congestion. He accepted the committee's view that 'the true position is
not as it was generally accepted to be and that it does not lend itself to
action on the lines proposed in the Abrahams Report'. He believed that
some of the statements in that report were an over-simplification of the
problem.

He was convinced that there was not and never could be any clear-
cut final solution to the problem: it could only be partially solved and
would remain with them indefinitely. He saw the problem as two-fold:
the political problem of large areas of land in the Southern Province
being held by Europeans; and the economic problem of population
congestion, also in the Southern Province. As to the political problem,
he pointed to the generally welcome acceptance of Europeans actively
working and developing their estates, but added:

> How long this happy position will remain it is impossible to say,
> but judging by events in others parts of Africa, we should not rely
> on it lasting forever.
> So long as Europeans hold large areas of land in certain parts of
> this country so long will a potential political problem remain.

As to the economic problem, he emphasized that as the population
continued to increase, as it undoubtedly would at an accelerated pace, so
would the problem of congestion remain. There was the allied economic
problem that the large estates were simply hanging on to huge areas and
taking few steps to develop them. Given the major contribution of
European agriculture and the great potential of African agriculture,
Colby's development strategy demanded that fuller economic use should
be made of all the protectorate's land, including private estates.

Bearing in mind his conviction that only a partial solution was possible, he felt that the committee's recommendations to acquire 550,000
acres out of a total of 1,200,000 acres of European estate land would be
taking them a considerable way, especially since 53,000 of the 74,400
resident African families on estates in the Cholo, Mlanje, Zomba and
Blantyre districts would be automatically 'emancipated' (a term which
Colby considered to be 'unhappy and possibly misleading'). Although
the owners of the remaining 650,000 acres which had not been recom-

mended for acquisition had given an assurance that they intended to develop them as soon as machinery and materials were available, Colby was uncertain as to how much credence could be placed on these assurances, but pointed out that in the course of implementing the recommendations he would find out the true position on each estate: he was not simply going to take their word for it.

The governor then turned to the way in which he proposed to implement the recommendations of the Land Planning Committee. He emphasized that implementation would necessitate a strong team in charge of acquisition and resettlement, and he indicated quite clearly that he would have important requests to make about staffing since he believed they had not truly realized what a very big job the implementation was going to be.

He was particularly careful about the need to negotiate with estate owners in a pre-arranged order:

> We should aim at first acquiring areas from estate owners who are really ready to meet us, and it seems reasonable to hope that such estate owners will release their land to us at reasonable prices. By approaching the most reasonable owners first we shall thereby have created some precedents in regard to prices to be paid. These precedents should subsequently be of the greatest use to us when we have to negotiate with owners who are not so well disposed and indeed, if it proves impossible to come to an amicable agreement with regard to the value of their land with all the owners, the precedents established at the beginning should be very useful if it comes to a question of compulsory acquisition.

On each estate with which negotiations were commenced, he proposed that his team should establish with the owner how much acreage he held under development, the acreage to remain after early acquisition, and the acreage required for future development, with a view to acquiring any difference between these last two acreages.

He made a particular point of emphasizing the fundamental change needed in securing the disappearance of the part-time agriculturalist:

> I am convinced that the objectives to which we should work are, on the one hand, a definite non-farming permanent labour force living either in the residential blocks recommended by the Committee or on European estates in full-time employment by those estates,

and, on the other hand, a farming community established on Native Trust Land which will supply not only their own needs but the needs of the labourers on the estates.

Colby realized that there was a potential conflict of policies. On the one hand, from a political point of view there were powerful arguments for acquiring as much private land as possible to hand back to the Africans, but on the other hand this would conflict with the British government's economic policy of securing the maximum output of such estate crops as tung, tea, sisal, soya and flue-cured tobacco: 'it seems necessary to effect a compromise between these two conflicting policies'. He pointed out that in paying the estate owners considerable sums for their land he would in effect be providing them with potential capital with which to develop their remaining estates and increase production.

He then turned to the committee's strong advice that government should publicly state that no further large-scale acquisition of freehold land would be practicable, and he made it clear that he could not rule out further acquisitions and that, no matter how unpalatable it might be to the European community, he proposed to make it perfectly plain that the government would investigate land requirements on individual estates and, if they found that lands not scheduled for acquisition were not to be developed, he would consider acquiring them. Furthermore, he would review the position after a reasonable period when development projects had had time to mature, and again consider acquisition of areas not developed in the meantime.

Colby next dealt with the question of finances and, whilst accepting that the £300,000 required for the purchase of lands to be immediately or early acquired should be provided from local sources, he pointed out that this would be a severe drain on protectorate resources and said:

I am wondering whether there would be any chance of seeking your support for obtaining assistance from the general reserve of £12,000,000 under the Colonial Development and Welfare Act.

After this delicate broaching of the question he became more firm and added:

The fact is that unless a great deal more money than is now envisaged is spent on the development of the Protectorate, there will be little chance of our making any real progress. . . . The

problems with which we are confronted . . . arise from past policy
and it seems very hard, at a time when we are striving to set the
Protectorate more firmly on its feet, that we should be faced with
expenditure of this nature . . . in the short time I have been here I
have been profoundly shocked at the almost entire absence . . . in
some cases, and serious deficiency in others, of elementary public
services and I very much fear that, without considerable further
financial assistance, there is little prospect of this territory, potentially so prosperous, being put on a sound footing.

He was, of course, aiming his remarks only partly at the specific question
of private land and was really introducing the thin end of a wedge of
an argument which he was later to pursue repeatedly for general development purposes: in essence, 'The British Government has neglected
Nyasaland far too long. It's now in a mess and if you want me to get
the country out of it, you ought to pay for it.'

Colby was anxious to get on with the job and asked Cohen to seek
the secretary of state's approval for action on the lines which he indicated
'as early as possible'. He proposed then to publish the Land Planning
Committee's report and a statement of government policy along the
same lines. He was not, however, going to let events overtake him, and
concluded his letter to Cohen by saying that it would in any case be
necessary to defer action under the next quinquennial period of eviction
beyond September 1948.

It is quite clear from the drafts of this letter to Cohen that Colby
personally worked very hard and carefully on the letter, altering numerous pieces, writing extensive new paragraphs, adding new sections, and
rewording several passages so that the final version, whilst containing
most of the original points – drafted by secretariat officers – bore very
little resemblance in structure and tone to the original. He took enormous pains over it and his redrafting is one of the very few documents
on which he worked in black pencil rather than in red ink, possibly
because the work was extensive and he was drafting for himself rather
than minuting to others.[58]

In studying the documents on the problem of Africans on private
estates, Colby paid very close attention to a confidential appendix to the
draft (unpublished) Land Planning Committee report which contained
a number of facts and considerations which the committee felt the
government might, for political reasons, not wish to publish. They
recalled that Abrahams had formed the very firm impression that the

Africans expected their grievances to be remedied and their claims satisfied as a result of his report, and that if this did not happen there might be very serious consequences. The committee had no doubt that this impression was correct. They directed their attention to the question of how far the acquisition of land which they recommended in their report would go to satisfy African expectations, and concluded that these expectations could be satisfied only if extensive areas of freehold land in the Cholo and Blantyre districts, in addition to the areas recommended in their report which were not currently actively worked, were acquired by government. Whereas all the areas recommended in their published report would, they believed, be offered voluntarily for sale, these additional lands could only be acquired compulsorily, unless the owners could be persuaded to change their minds. However, they advised against compulsory acquisition on the grounds that it would alienate European support and damage race relations, and that it would deter the investment of European capital in Nyasaland. In addition, the committee felt that even if compulsory acquisition were resorted to, it would be likely to result only in a temporary solution to the problem of congestion in the Cholo and Blantyre districts.

The land the committee had in mind was owned by the BCA Company, 'the largest owner of land and the largest owner of undeveloped land in the Protectorate' and the 'target of considerable criticism'. The company owned large, undeveloped estates in the southern part of Blantyre district and the northern part of Cholo district in the most heavily congested areas of the Shire Highlands. As on adjacent Trust land, where the population density was over 400 to the square mile, these lands were entirely cultivated by Africans on a subsistence basis. In recent years, large numbers of tenants had refused to pay rent and the committee feared, at the least, embarrassment and political discontent at the end of the quinquennium in 1948 if it again applied for mass evictions. Whilst the committee believed that the other major landowners would not have serious trouble from the tenants, the same could not be said of the company because, in addition to the general feeling of grievance against owners of large areas of undeveloped land, the BCA Company was the source of other grievances: compulsory movement of gardens and huts; refusal to permit the growing of cash crops in rebate of rent; poor personal relationships and a lack of active interest in tenant welfare; the unfortunate personality of the European estate superintendents and their attitude towards Africans; and the perpetual fear among tenants of the arbitrary eviction of a tenth of their number at the end of each quinquennial period.

The company was not prepared to sell these additional lands because it wished to keep as much land as possible for the future, not only for itself but also as a foreign-currency earner.[59] Also, it claimed that under a 15-year development plan, the estates were to be worked for extensive cultivation of tung, tobacco and soya beans, and the company would additionally provide for four acres per tenant family, the tenants to be placed on special agreement and restricted to clearly demarcated areas near the development areas, so as to provide labour for the proposed expansion of cultivation. The committee dismissed these plans as being 'quite impracticable'. They were also in grave doubt whether the manager's 'emancipation' proposals would improve relationships between the company and its tenants, and even graver doubt as to whether he appreciated the political significance of past troubles and the danger of future troubles:

He gave the impression that he considered that any unrest among the tenants was entirely the responsibility of Government and that he was unaware of the extent to which the Company's policy in the post war period was the cause of unrest or how such unrest might involve the whole of the Shire Highlands.

The committee could conceive of only one way in which the growing discontent among the company's tenants could be materially arrested: by acquiring those blocks of company land which were thickly populated by tenants and which it was clearly impossible for the company to develop without wholesale disturbance of the tenants. Yet they drew back from advocating compulsory acquisition and instead said that it was 'infinitely preferable [that] the Company should be brought to realise that it was in their own interests and in the interests of the Protectorate as a whole, that such land should be offered to the Government for voluntary sale'.

Having studied this confidential appendix and other documents, Colby quickly realized that he was likely to have the greatest difficulty with the BCA Company because of the size and location of its land holdings, their undeveloped state, the attitude of its management, and its potential as a source of serious political trouble. In order that he should understand the company as fully as possible and be adequately briefed in his dealings with it, he asked H. V. McDonald, a former district commissioner of the Cholo district, a member of the Land Commission and now Native Courts Adviser, to prepare a history of and commentary on the company and its landholding activities.[60]

McDonald's commentary, which he sent to the governor on 12 December 1948, was an extremely well-written, clearly expressed document, as well-researched as the material available permitted, and a devastating indictment of the BCA Company.[61]

In summarizing the company's history to 1924, he quoted from a recent view expressed by Barrow:

> The truth is that the Company's holding of land always was, and still is, too large for them to control. They have always proved incapable of developing any appreciable proportion of their holdings, denied the opportunity to others to develop the land by demanding high prices in the current market, and were quite incapable of looking after the vast area they owned and of preventing its being ravaged by indiscriminate African settlement.

McDonald's own assessment was equally damning, his view being that in consequence of the company's inability to control its land, much of it got into a condition which rendered that land useless for future exploitation and development. One particular aspect he felt would 'always remain unforgivable': BCA knew from the experience of others that tea was the most stable industry in the country; it knew also that the amount of land suitable for tea-growing was strictly limited; and yet BCA itself owned many thousands of acres of that suitable land. In addition, incredibly, from 1920 to 1924:

> they started to allow onto this land uncontrolled immigration of natives from Portuguese East Africa. By doing this they permanently impaired the resources of the Protectorate and at the same time saddled the Government with a grave political problem.

He then turned to deal with the company's history from 1924 to 1947, the period of a reconstituted company, which started with a reduction of its authorized capital. 'But although the Company was reconstructed it was not regenerated':

> Under a joint management with an unenviable reputation for inefficiency it continued to pursue a policy of extravagance, but not in

the direction of useful development. And no check whatever was put onto the continued immigration of natives from Portuguese East Africa onto the Company's natural tea lands. In fact the period between the years 1924 and 1930 were as dark as any in the Company's history.

McDonald then studied in greater detail the previous ten years, 1937 to 1947, which he saw as by far the most interesting part of BCA's history because the company's management was the same as at the time he was writing, it had adequate capital, it had a planned development programme, ahead of it stretched the most prosperous agricultural years the protectorate had ever known, and it had considerably more land available for development than it had later 'owing to the manner in which continued depredations were made by African immigrants in the years immediately before and during the war'.

The world markets during the period 1937 to 1947 enabled the company to make a profit, and it declared a dividend for the first time in 1941. Yet despite this, its assets continued to depreciate steadily, and in 1947 only 6430 of its 329,354 acres were under cultivation whilst 11,000 acres were leased to other planters. About 300,000 acres were not being worked and all the best of this land was in the Blantyre and Cholo districts and in the hands of African tenants. BCA's late attempts to stem the flow of immigration were ineffective and the existing tenants extended their occupation further through the estate lands. McDonald was convinced that:

> The position today is that further extensive development of these areas is now beyond the range of possibility . . . the incalculable disservice the Company has done to the Protectorate in the neglect of its lands is beyond all dispute.

He attributed much of this deplorable state of affairs to the company's parsimony, especially in regard to European staff. The general manager was a generalist in direct charge of all the company's activities, no specialists were employed, the quality of the subordinate supervisory staff was appalling, and the personal behaviour of many of the staff left much to be desired:

> The conduct of these men gives rise to numerous incidents, any one of which might provide the occasion for serious political

trouble. But the Company is not concerned with such dangers which are regarded as the responsibility of Government.

McDonald ended his report by saying that BCA's directors in England had confidence in the current management and did not seem to realize how the company's affairs were actually conducted in Nyasaland, the golden opportunities that had been lost, and the damage that had been caused to its land:

> There seems no hope for improvement until they are brought to realise these things, and to change their entire staff in Africa.

When Colby received and read what McDonald had written, he was reinforced in the view (which he had begun to form from his earliest days in Nyasaland) that the really big nut he had to crack was the BCA Company, and that he should be as ruthless with it as needs be since it had not been, and showed no signs of being, reasonable in its use of land or in its attitudes towards the country's economy and towards the political dangers of land tensions and race relations. It was wasting and destroying the nation's major asset, land, which was allowed to stand idle instead of contributing to Nyasaland's wealth, and in doing so was indifferent to the political and security dangers it was causing.

He studied McDonald's report thoroughly and found himself very much in sympathy with the views expressed, especially the point that there was no hope of improvement until the directors were brought to realize the true position and its dangers. He was determined to have no dealings at a policy level with the local management but to have the Colonial Office negotiate with the company's directorate in London. He made it clear that he was 'not prepared to negotiate prices with Mr. Nicol' locally.[62] So far as price generally, and the price for BCA Company land particularly, was concerned, he introduced the novel, but perfectly serious, argument that although the government was likely to be asked a high price they would in fact be doing the estates a great service in clearing part of their land of tenants and thereby making substantial areas available for further development. 'In other words, the whole operation should be of great financial benefit to the estates who will be relieved of tenants ... the estates will be getting it both ways.' He believed that in view of this argument:

> if we are going to relieve neighbouring estates of a large number

of tenants and thus free land for direct development, we have a very strong bargaining card in our hand, and I should have thought that the estates would be prepared to give a substantial amount of financial assistance to Government in purchasing this and in order to obtain relief from their tenants. We might, for example, reach the point where we said that if the estates are not prepared to give financial assistance, then we will drop the whole scheme.[63]

Clearly, even at this early stage he was prepared to be tough with the BCA Company over price.

Colby discussed his proposals with the secretary of state, Arthur Creech-Jones, during his visit to Nyasaland in April 1949, and Creech-Jones agreed that if private land were not properly used or developed, the government would be justified in 'exerting considerable pressure on landlords to part with it at reasonable prices'; he also agreed that the best plan was to negotiate in London with the boards of directors of the major landowning companies, rather than with local managers in Nyasaland.[64]

In order to exert pressure on the companies, from November 1948 Colby actively pursued the question of imposing a tax on undeveloped land in order to replace the 1912 land tax which had fallen into abeyance;[65] Creech-Jones noted his proposals but did not pass an opinion on them, and now Colby planned to use them in trying to persuade the companies to sell their land at a reasonable price. Whilst Barrow 'viewed with dislike and misgivings' the idea of this tax, he told Colby that, because of the importance of buying considerable areas of land and the danger of failing to do so, if a price could not be negotiated reasonably within government's resources, he would withdraw his opposition and support the imposition.[66]

In July and August 1949, while Colby was on leave, McDonald joined him in London and they began discussions with the BCA and the B&EA companies, and the preliminary arrangements were made by December of that year for purchasing some 200,000 acres of land; over half was in the Zomba district and the remainder in the Blantyre, Cholo and Lower River districts.[67] During 1950, over half the African residents on the acquired estates were resettled by concentrating them into selected sites, so as to provide for the orderly reception of new entrants from congested areas and so as to make good use of the best agricultural land. Government was able to claim:

the response has been excellent and the general rate of progress reflects great credit on the officers responsible.[68]

By the end of 1951, a total of 300,000 acres had been acquired in the Southern Province for resettlement, including 130,000 acres of sparsely populated land at Chingale in the Zomba district from the BCA Company and 72,000 acres of not very fertile land at Magomero from the Bruce Estates in the Zomba, Chiradzulu and Mlanje districts. Following another of Abrahams' recommendations, Colby set aside 21,500 acres in the Kasungu district in the Central Province for private planters and syndicates in exchange for land in the Southern Province. Other, smaller, estates were also purchased during this period from a variety of owners, but none of the important congested and politically dangerous areas in the Cholo district. Some of the transactions were quickly agreed, but more often negotiations took a long time.[69]

The potential for political agitation, conflict and civil unrest inherent in the problem of Africans on private estates had long been recognized and not infrequently expressed, and despite the considerable steps which Colby had taken to reduce the scope of the problem, such agitation, conflict and unrest in fact occurred in 1953, coinciding with the imposition of federation. He was particularly worried and angered by what he saw as BCA's insensitive, provocative and extremely dangerous action in issuing eviction notices to residents on its estates in the first half of 1953, action which had the backing of the Convention of Associations. His view was that:

> The question of land was one on which the African felt most strongly. Indeed it was probable that he felt more strongly on this question than on federation and it was doubly unfortunate that he would inevitably link the two in his mind.[70]

Colby considered mobilizing public opinion against the company and publicly castigating it, but the non-official members of executive council advised against this on the grounds that the steps might in fact rally support for the company.[71] The serious disturbances which then occurred in August and September 1953 were very largely confined to the Blantyre, Chiradzulu and particularly the Cholo districts in the Shire Highlands, where large areas of freehold land were held by European estate owners upon whose land many African families still lived and were liable to pay rent:

Although the Federation issue had created a tension in the political atmosphere, the disturbances were fundamentally the result of land grievances, among them a dislike of the tenant system at present in force.[72]

Colby was acutely aware of the depth of feeling amongst African tenants and clearly saw the need to remove or greatly diminish at a fast pace this potentially explosive source of unrest – or worse. Although he was able, by prompt, firm and decisive action, to bring the 1953 disturbances to a fairly quick end, he emphasized that the underlying causes of the troubles – federation and land – had not been tackled, and that it was of the utmost importance that everyone realized the significance of the disturbances. Unless they took early action to deal with the land problems, trouble could result in a form which would be very hard to handle.[73]

As soon as the disturbances had died down, Colby quickly turned his attention to the land grievances and told the Colonial Office that he intended to see individually 'the comparatively small number of land-owners who own substantial areas of land occupied by tenants' to try to secure a more reasonable attitude and convince them to 'divest themselves' of those areas in the interests of future harmony.[74] He was not optimistic of success, and as a lever he intended to revive his 1949 proposal to impose a penal rate of taxation on undeveloped land. The Colonial Office concluded that 'there is no doubt that [acquiring land] has in one way or another simply got to be done'. They did not, however, agree that penal taxation was appropriate; but rather, if negotiations failed, that compulsory purchase was preferable.[75]

Even without the grievances, including land grievances, erupting in the 1953 disturbances, Colby was aware of the deep and growing African resentment over land issues, and of the political and security dangers in that resentment, because the deliberations of the African Protectorate Council in 1952 and 1953 made the resentment and dangers abundantly clear to him. During the interview which African representatives had in London at the federation conference in April 1952, the secretary of state had suggested that since the land question was complex it would be helpful if they submitted a memorandum giving their representations in more detail.[76] In August, the Protectorate Council appointed a sub-committee consisting of moderate and much respected leading Africans, and they worked hard on preparing the memorandum. In October, Colby studied the draft memorandum and asked Fox-Strangways to tell the council that the governor sympathized with the African point of view in respect of freehold land closely settled with tenants and would like to support their submission to the secretary of state. He added:

> I could not, however, support the memorandum as it now stands and I hope they will alter it to remove all the utter nonsense and political clap trap in it.[77]

Fox–Strangways used more diplomatic language in conveying Colby's wishes to council and asked them to 'carefully examine the draft to see that there was nothing in it which was either untrue or exaggerated'.[78]

At its meeting of 15 December 1953, the African Protectorate Council discussed the draft at length, decided that it should be amended, and then endorsed the re-drafted memorandum which concluded with the warning that in their view 'in all inter-racial relations in this country, the question of land will stand out as the testing standard'.[79] The memorandum was then sent as part of the proceedings of the Protectorate Council meeting to the secretary of state on 14 January 1954. Colby followed this up with his promised comments on 16 March, when he started his despatch[80] by briefly outlining the steps taken by government in recent years and added:

> Since 1948 considerable progress has been made, but despite this the basic problem remains and the African's demand for more agricultural land and for 'emancipation' still persists; in fact since twelve months ago these feelings have become intensified.

He next expressed his view that, although those who subscribed to the memorandum were sincere in all that they had written, they had allowed their views to get out of perspective and had overstated their case, and he tried to put the position into what he considered to be better perspective. Most estate owners, he said, had good relations with their tenants and the grievances were mainly confined to the large estate owners, especially the BCA Company; of the 170,000 Africans resident on private estates, he estimated only half were actively concerned to secure a change in their status as tenants.

He then turned to consider the extent to which acquisition would relieve congestion and pointed out that of the 887,000 acres remaining in private hands, 500,000 were already occupied by African tenants. Of the other 387,000 acres, 100,000 were under direct development by the owners, 200,000 were either under indigenous forest or otherwise for natural resources conservation reasons ought not to be cultivated, so that less than 100,000 acres could be available to relieve congestion.

Colby summarized the early part of his despatch by saying that the land problem was essentially a political one, the Africans directly affected were a relatively small proportion living in a comparatively small and compact area of the Southern Province, the unoccupied land available for acquisition would have little perceptible effect on congestion, and the present African dissatisfaction contained serious political dangers.

He then proceeded to explain his proposed solution to the problem and for the first time clearly introduced a social anthropological basis to the argument:

In my view the solution of the problem lies in the gradual adaptation of the use of land in private ownership so as to conform as closely as possible to African usufructual ideas, which are . . . as strong in the mind of the African today as they ever were, and close examination of the African land grievances will reveal that at the base of them there is always the same factor, i.e. that ownership of land can only go with the direct use of it. For this reason they have never disputed the ownership of land in actual cultivation by estate-owners.

Conversely Africans cannot see that any other person should have any rights to the land which they themselves are cultivating, and it is this belief which is at the bottom of their dislike of the tenant system. Nor can they see that any estate-owner has the right to prevent others from cultivating land which he does not require for his own immediate use, dissatisfaction on this last point being particularly dangerous in closely-populated areas.

With this social anthropological basis to the solution centrally in mind, Colby categorized private land in four groups. First, there was land in direct use by the estate owner; with this he felt there was no political difficulty, since it would not be in accordance with African usufructual principles to claim it, but he advocated that it should be fenced to make it clear that it was in use. Second, there was private land occupied by African tenants; this he believed should be acquired by government for African use, priority being given to the areas where dissatisfaction was greatest, thereby removing tenant status and preventing sale to Asians, which was a growing concern. Third, there was private land

which was under indigenous forest, or incapable of economic development, or which for other conservation reasons should not be developed;
this he felt should be preserved in its virgin state and although this
would not be in accord with African usufructual ideas, since it would
not appear to be used, government should acquire it on the grounds
that 'any resentment about the preservation of natural resources should
be directed against Government'. Fourth, there was land of agricultural
value, unused either by the estate owner or by African tenants; this he
believed presented the most urgent problem:

> Although the extent of this land is not great, feeling about it is
> very high, and if serious political trouble is to be avoided all this
> land should be put fully under development in the course of the
> next five years, or else surrendered for African use: any such land
> which cannot be developed during the next five years should be
> surrendered now.

He went on to tell the secretary of state that he would require the work
of resettlement to be done with the full co-operation and agreement of
the local Africans, their village headmen and Native Authorities, and in
return for the land which they would receive he would require them to
sign a document that the transaction was final so as to strengthen the
hand of future administrations and deter 'profitless pursuit' of the way
in which the original certificates of claim had been issued.

Colby asked for an early response from the secretary of state because
he regarded 'African concern over the whole land question as being of
great political importance'. Lyttelton replied by cable the day he received
Colby's despatch and said that he agreed generally with the governor's
observations but did not wish to reach a final conclusion on land policy
until after his visit to Nyasaland, which was imminent. That he was
strongly disposed to accept Colby's proposals is indicated by the fact
that he asked for a reply along Colby's lines to be drafted to the
Protectorate Council memorandum for finalization when he arrived in
the protectorate.[81] The resultant reply, sent after the secretary of state's
visit, did in fact follow Colby's reasoning, policy and often his words,
very closely.[82]

The signals which the governor received from the disturbances, the
Protectorate Council, and the early 1954 political intelligence reports[83]
persuaded him, or confirmed him in his opinion, that the policy of
acquiring private land and resettling African families from congested

areas now needed urgent acceleration. He publicly and bluntly expressed his opinion that:

> Africans in parts of the Southern Province live in a state of conges-
> tion and that whilst large areas of freehold land, the property of
> European estate owners, remain undeveloped there will exist a
> potential danger to the peace and tranquillity of the country.[84]

He then made direct proposals to owners of several of the larger estates that, except for areas then under cultivation or which would be developed within three to five years, all land should be handed to government for African resettlement.[85] After the indelicate and boat-rocking issuing of notices to quit by the BCA Company earlier in the year, and the serious disturbances in the areas of greatest land alienation, Colby was in no mood to beat about the bush. After decades of gentlemanly negotiation and giving in to the landowners, and after numerous hints that acqui-sition of private land was the only feasible way to handle the question, Colby had made a firm start on settling the problem, and now he was determined to bring it to a swift conclusion. Many of the landowners were aghast when these proposals were made to them and they immedi-ately formed a Land Owners' Association to resist Colby's proposals.[86]

In May 1954, the secretary of state visited Nyasaland for discussions on the land problem and on constitutional reform. He received a long memorandum from the Land Owners' Association and the Convention of Associations, which joined forces to vilify Colby and attack his land proposals.[87] In their eyes these proposals were the culminating iniquity of a governor, appointed by a socialist secretary of state, who had taken systematic steps towards state control and nationalization – the Acquisition of Land for Public Purposes Ordinance, replacing private purchasing of crops with statutory marketing boards, encouraging Col-onial Development Corporation trading stores in competition with pri-vate shops in remote areas, setting up the African Press publishing company, and now land.[88] Their principal contention was that Colby's proposals would not provide a lasting solution because they were con-vinced that to hand over private land to African settlement would in a few years lead to further decimation of forest areas and ruination of the soil. Once this had occurred, the demand for more land would resume and pressure would be brought to bear on the European landowners to give up any remaining undeveloped land, which in turn would also be ruined. The memorandum was sent to Lyttelton by Dixon, general manager of the BCA Company, unofficial member of legislative council, and chairman of the European Land Owners' Association.

During his visit, Lyttelton held a meeting at Government House with landowners nominated by the Convention of Associations, and he opened the meeting by setting out the policy of Her Majesty's Government.[89] He recognized the contribution of estates to the agricultural development of the protectorate and said that it was the 'settled policy' to ensure owners' security in the possession and management of their developed lands, but he emphasized that this security could be assured only if conditions were created which enabled the estate owners to live in amity with the African population. Without these conditions, the growing unrest and political feeling would make it impossible for the estate owners to carry on; it was not possible to use force to implement a land policy:

> Policy would therefore be directed to the progressive abolition of the 'thangata' system which would be implemented by purchasing from estate owners all those areas of land which were occupied by tenants or were otherwise unsuitable for estate development or which could not be developed within a reasonable time.

The secretary of state was anxious to secure the co-operation of landowners and would resort to compulsory acquisition only as a last resort. Whilst small numbers of tenants could be moved to free some estate land for development, it would be 'completely impossible' to evict large numbers. It would be 'impracticable' for landowners to retain unused and unoccupied land in the congested areas for any length of time. If it were to be retained, it would have to be developed within a reasonable time. The ultimate aim was that estate owners would have on their estates no Africans with any rights to land, and the substantial labour force required for tea and other estates would be accommodated either in housing built by the estates for permanent labour or on neighbouring accommodation blocks of land. Since the execution of this policy would be a lengthy process, government would first direct its attention to those holdings in which discontent and political unrest were growing; thus, early action would be needed only on a small number of estates, since he recognized that relationships on the vast majority of estates were cordial.

In this carefully worded, albeit brief, statement of policy, Lyttelton included all the essential points of the proposals which Colby had put to him seven weeks earlier.[90] He ended by saying that the existing settlement and development policy would 'be continued and accelerated', and he asked the estate owners if they were agreeable to it.

All the owners present – save Barrow and Hadlow who had been closely associated with government policy formation as members of executive council – were most deeply opposed to the steps being taken and proposed by government to deal with the land problem, but the main, and most vigorously expressed, opposition came from Brook and Dixon, the chairman and the local general manager, respectively, of the BCA Company. Part way through the meeting, when it was clear to everyone that Lyttelton was strongly backing the governor's views and policy, and was having little truck with the views of the large estate owners, Colby quietly and calculatingly asked why the BCA Company wished to retain large areas of tenant-occupied land. This simple question was designed to embarrass and 'draw out' Dixon, who replied by trying to 'duck' it, saying that it was incorrect to state that his company wished to retain such land since in February they had offered 60,000 acres to government. Colby taunted him a little more by saying that he did not recollect this offer, whereupon Brook came to Dixon's aid and explained that Dixon had mentioned the 60,000 acres to him and that he had felt prepared to discuss it with government, subject to government making it clear what would happen to the land and agreeing to 'undesirables' being kept off the land retained. Colby pushed a little further, saying that it had not been made clear to him by Brook that he had made a firm offer. Brook quickly said that he had not made a firm offer but, in order to get out of what was becoming too detailed and confining a discussion, he suggested that government should now get in touch with Dixon to discuss with him what land it required. This suggestion of Brook's was potentially such a major shift in attitude by the BCA Company that Lyttelton was quick to secure the ground which Colby's simple-sounding question had made available and said:

> that was what was wanted but he had gathered that Mr Dixon found such a solution distasteful. He was very glad to hear that Mr Brook was prepared to discuss the sale of land. . . . He felt that 60,000 acres would be a notable contribution. Mr Dixon had however led him to believe that both he and the meeting were opposed to acquisition of land by Government.

Colby was equally keen to secure the ground presented and possibly to secure even more, and to isolate and expose Dixon, so he said that the impression he had gained from the Land Owners' Association and from Dixon was that Dixon was opposed to handing over tenant-occupied land. He was surprised that Brook now said the company had been prepared to discuss the sale of 60,000 acres, and enquired whether it was prepared to negotiate the disposal of all tenant-occupied land. Brook, however, was not going to yield more in this discussion and said that he was not prepared to negotiate the disposal of all such land as BCA wished to retain some because of the value of tenants as labour. Nonetheless, Colby was well pleased: he had got the chairman of the BCA Company to agree, in front of the secretary of state and many others, that government should suggest to Dixon what areas it required so that it could be discussed and the company could consider the requirements. This was a considerable piercing of Dixon's otherwise implacable opposition to the government's acquisition of tenant-occupied land.

For whatever reason, BCA became considerably more amenable to government's wishes after the May 1954 meeting[91] – agreeing after a while to sell large areas in the peri-urban area of Blantyre for £1 an acre which Colby later knocked down to seventeen shillings and sixpence – although the transformation was not sudden. Rather, Colby, having pierced the company's opposition, was determined to exploit his advantage by isolating the company from the other landowners and pushing it hard. Apart from BCA's recalcitrance, all was going fairly well, and in pursuing Brook and Dixon he did not wish to hinder or retard that other progress. Here he was faced with a further difficulty: the preparation for publication of a document setting out the government's land policy in Nyasaland.

Less than a week after Lyttelton's visit, Colby went on leave to Britain, leaving Footman as acting governor.

In the summer of 1954, Colonial Office officials, after 'months of cogitation' embodied their provisional conclusions in a draft despatch indicating how they intended that the policy of progressive abolition of *thangata* should be implemented: private land occupied by a few Africans but otherwise capable of development should be freed of Africans so that development could take place by moving them on to neighbouring land acquired by government or on to other parts of the estate; private land heavily occupied and undeveloped and not required for early development should be acquired.[92]

Colby, however, was very uncertain of the need for, and wisdom of, publishing the despatch, and there were two influences which made him reluctant to publish it: the changed circumstances in Nyasaland, which he articulated, and what seemed to him, although he did not articulate it, the introduction of almost academic debate at a very late stage into a matter which had deeply worrying practical implications and which he had always, and successfully, treated in a pragmatic way.

During his visit to Nyasaland, Lyttelton had been accompanied by S. R. Simpson, land tenure specialist at the Colonial Office. On his return to London, Simpson wrote a report on the *thangata* system which was sent to Nyasaland three weeks later: it was, therefore, a rather hastily compiled report.[93] In reading the report, one senses a somewhat snide, highly critical, superior, academic attitude in the writer. In his first line, he referred to the 'so-called' *thangata* system – the payment of rent or the performance of labour in exchange for residence – and said that notwithstanding the fact that the secretary of state had recently announced that the system was to be progressively abolished, he wished to draw attention to certain points and to make some suggestions. Pointing out that 'reduction' was not the same as 'extinction', he urged that the rent of Africans resident on private estates should be reduced to a nominal sum, perhaps a shilling a year, and that the provisions as to labour in lieu should be cancelled: 'This very simply finally abolishes thangata.'

When Footman, in Colby's absence, received Simpson's report, he asked executive council to consider it, and this they did on 9 June 1954.[94] The acting governor opened the meeting by outlining what he saw as 'the crux of the problem', agreed with the thrust of Simpson's arguments, and concluded that the rent charged to tenants was excessive and ought to be reduced almost to nothing, as a result of which 'thangata must go automatically because the equivalent amount of work in lieu would be so small as to be useless'.

McDonald, who was invited to the meeting, agreed that *thangata* could not be defended against academic attack, but he was worried by Simpson's proposal that it be abolished immediately, since that would affect the negotiations for acquisition of land; the secretary of state had announced that the course to be taken was progressive abolition by negotiated purchase:

Immediate abolition would render Government's task in removing tenants very difficult since they would have no inducement to move and the negotiations with landowners would be greatly prejudiced.

Whilst he politely believed Footman's arguments to be 'logical' and 'irrefutable', their implementation would not be feasible and would have adverse repercussions. Provincial Commissioner Barnes, who was also invited to the meeting, agreed with Footman that the rent was grossly excessive, but felt that rent reduction 'required very careful timing'.

Council, whilst agreeing that the rent was excessive, found it difficult to reconcile Simpson's proposals with the secretary of state's statement that *thangata* would be progressively abolished, preferably with the landowners' co-operation. Immediate abolition would run counter to this, would lack the landowners' consent, and would prejudice the chances of co-operation and negotiation. They did not agree that Simpson's proposal was simply supplemental to what had been agreed by the secretary of state. To reduce the rent to a shilling would amount to virtual expropriation of estate land by government and would remove any incentive to Africans to move. Footman, faced with this unanimous advice, 'did not feel able to dissent from the advice given and ordered that the whole position be reported to the Secretary of State'.

Footman, in Colby's absence, had been willing, possibly keen, to go along with Simpson's proposals, but his executive council advisers had dissuaded him, countering his arguments of logic and principle with arguments of practicalities, and had steered the ship of policy back to the course on which Colby had set it: progressive abolition of *thangata* by purchasing undeveloped private land, preferably by negotiation, and resettling tenants and others from congested areas on the purchased lands. As a token of government's intentions, however, rent and labour in lieu were to be reduced by two-fifths to 30 shillings a year.

Colby felt that the introduction of Simpson's academic arguments was unhelpful and clouded the issue. His line of advance, though not easy, was clear and simple, and he did not take kindly to arguments – especially arguments from outside – which made it less clear and less simple. On his return from leave in November, Colby found that Footman had already advised the secretary of state that the draft despatch on land policy, when finalized, should be published, and he set about trying to reverse this advice.

He gave the main reasons for his reluctance to have the despatch published to executive council soon after his return from Britain, and later to the Colonial Office, using language very similar to that used by the secretary of state almost exactly 20 years earlier in restraining Young from reopening the Africans on private estates issue:

His Excellency considered that publication would only serve to revive interest in a subject which Government felt could be solved in the very near future by land acquisition and resettlement. He felt that the work on the ground would do far more to convince the public of Government's intention of solving the land problem than the mere publication of documents such as the despatch from the Secretary of State. He also felt that publication of the despatch might stir up trouble unnecessarily with the African Congress and might also upset European opinion both within Nyasaland and in Southern Rhodesia where a wrong interpretation might be placed on the terms of the despatch.[95]

Colby believed that publication could do no good and might well do considerable harm. Things were going quite well; the secretary of state had endorsed his policy and had made this clear to the European landowners; he had weathered the storm of abuse from them and the press; he was gradually forcing open the wound caused by piercing Dixon's opposition and was turning it into a fatal injury; other land-owners were awaiting the outcome of the negotiations with the BCA Company. Also, security threats had diminished since the secretary of state's visit, although Colby would not have wished to emphasize this, in order to keep the Colonial Office somewhat worried. Furthermore – a factor which was not yet widely known – constitutional amendments were soon to be made which would increase African representation in the legislature, and these, when announced, would both indicate to Africans the government's intentions in their favour and help assuage their fears of European domination, and also attract further criticism from Europeans. Why risk publicly raising the land issue again by publishing a major policy document when the policy was already well known?

Unfortunately, the secretary of state was by now much in favour of publication – in fact he had already formally agreed to the draft[96] – presumably because the idea had stemmed from Simpson's report and because Footman, with executive council's approval, had initially advocated publication. He was puzzled by Colby's reluctance and opposition. Numerous telegrams passed back and forth between Colby and Gorell Barnes, on behalf of the secretary of state, throughout March and early April 1955, the secretary of state increasing his pressure to publish, Colby resisting the pressure to publish. Finally, the secretary of state seized on Colby's agreement to a fairly full parliamentary statement and suggested that the despatch should be published in Britain as a Colonial Paper, 'which would not necessarily attract any more attention than a Parliamentary statement'. If this were so, Colby said on 6 April, then he 'could raise no objection to such publication in the United Kingdom'.[97] With this issue out of the way, even if it was not entirely to his satisfaction, he was able to continue his efforts to secure the acquisition of large tracts of BCA Company land.

It is likely that Brook, if not Dixon, realized that Colby had the British government firmly on his side and that the policy of accelerated acquisition could not prudently continue to be resisted. Some time after the secretary of state's visit, in 1954, the company 'voluntarily suggested three areas of land totalling about 21,000 acres which might be purchased' by government, but Brook was still by no means fully won over and he told his shareholders that he did not consider the present policy of the government would result in any orderly or lasting solution of the land problem, and that the whole question of land tenure needed revision.[98]

Pursuing the opportunity which he had opened up at the meeting with the secretary of state, Colby told the company towards the end of 1954 that he wished to take over 50,000 to 60,000 acres of its land, and added that the area would be compulsorily acquired if agreement could not be reached on the compensation to be paid. Brook visited Nyasaland in November but was unable to come to any agreement with Colby on this issue.[99] He visited the country again in April 1955, immediately following discussions which Colby had had with the secretary of state about *thangata* during which the governor asked the secretary of state to say publicly that the company's co-operation was not forthcoming.[100] Colby, deeply concerned that if a settlement were not very soon achieved there would be the 'danger of serious trouble', cabled Footman on 29 April from Britain where he was on leave and turned Simpson's argument to his own advantage:

> In view of the failure to reach agreement with the British Central Africa Company I have suggested that we should now abandon purchase of land as the solution to this problem and instead we should (a) reduce rent to one shilling, and (b) abolish obligation to work. . . . Please urgently consider legislation necessary to give effect to this.[101]

Such a threat helped to clarify Brook's mind and after a great deal of protracted bargaining in which Colby kept up the pressure but was obliged to give some ground on price, he agreed on an average price of £1 an acre.[102] In August 1955, the government announced that the purchase of the area negotiated with BCA had been agreed: almost 50,000 acres.[103] Colby took very swift action to clear the land retained by the company in the Cholo district and to resettle those removed on purchased land. Before the sale on 8 August 1955, BCA owned 74,622 acres with 36,400 residents. Government then purchased 36,470 acres and automatically emancipated 24,600 residents. It then moved 3240 of the remaining 11,800 residents on to acquired land so that by 30 September 1955, it retained 38,143 acres (as compared with 74,622 two months earlier) with 8560 residents (as compared with 36,400 two months earlier).[104]

This agreement was a major step forward and removed a log-jam which had held up other progress in the abolition of *thangata*. By October 1955, Colby believed that there was 'a reasonable prospect of reducing the problem of resident Africans on private estates to very small proportions within the next four or five years . . . and prospects for a permanent and satisfactory solution are now in sight'.[105]

By the end of 1956, all the BCA Company estates in the tea growing areas of the Shire Highlands had been freed of tenants. In all, 3240 families had been resettled from the company's Cholo estates 'without incident of any description'. A further 850 tenants remained to be removed from their Blantyre tobacco estates and agreement had been reached for further purchases to accomplish this.[106]

Whilst this land was being dealt with, work continued on acquiring other estate land. Between 1946 and 1955, government had acquired 296,977 acres and emancipated 20,158 families. In 1956, following Colby's breakthrough with BCA, a further 155,622 acres were purchased, freeing 17,943 families. In 1957, after Colby's departure, the figures were 23,317 acres and 5516 families, and in the following year, 31,157 acres and 3227 families. At the end of 1958, only 20,460 families remained on estate land as tenants. Of these, 6700 were in the Magomero share-cropping tenant tobacco area, and 3500 were in the Mlanje tea estate area; neither of these two cases was a source of grievance or of political concern. Only 3100 remained in Cholo.[107]

In so radically reducing the number of Africans on private estates and resettling them elsewhere, usually nearby, Colby had very considerably reduced a specific cause of deep resentment and of serious political and security danger.

Because of the disturbed general political conditions in the country – connected with Dr Banda's return to Nyasaland and growing opposition to federation – no further purchases were made in 1959, 1960 or 1961. This period, 1959–61, was one of intense political activism and activity, yet in none of it was the question of land in general, or of Africans on private estates in particular, a live grievance or a worrying political issue. That stick with which to beat the colonial government, so potent and readily available only a few years earlier, had been effectively removed by Colby.

One of the earliest pieces of legislation introduced into the legislative council after the Malawi Congress Party's victory in the 1961 elections was a new Africans on Private Estates Bill in June 1962, finally to abolish *thangata* and to release the remaining private land which was not being fully developed.[108] The bill aimed to abolish *thangata* by strongly inducing estate owners to sell their land to government for resettling African families. As Dr Banda said at the close of the debate:

My intention is to abolish thangata altogether but I have drafted this Bill to give [the estate owners] a chance ... to sell their land wherever there are Africans on it, to Government. [It] is giving them a warning.

That the warning was heeded and the chance taken is indicated by the fact that a further 102,272 acres were acquired in 1963 and 12,203 acres in 1964, shortly after which the government announced that no new resettlement acquisitions were to be made. The task was completed.

12· The African Press

'It must work unobtrusively if it is to work at all.'

The problem of Africans on private estates was, as we said in the preceding chapter, one which had deeply worrying political implications in addition to the equally obvious economic aspects. Seldom can the two be strictly separated, and there is the danger, in recognizing that Colby's principal concern was with economic development, that one overlooks his sensitivity to, interest in, and concern about political matters. This sensitivity, interest and concern was present throughout the whole of his period of office. Indeed, a stable political environment in which economic development could be fostered was an essential element in his development strategy.

Two examples in addition to Africans on private estates, one little known and little remembered, the other more widely known and remembered, help to demonstrate his attitude and role in political matters. The first, dealt with in this chapter, concerns his attempts to establish an African newspaper, and the second, dealt with in the next chapter, concerns the inclusion of Nyasaland in the Central African Federation.

The broad political backcloth at the time of Colby's attempts to establish an African newspaper – the early 1950s – can be painted in simple terms. At the central government level, legislative council was comprised of nine European officials, seven non-African and two African non-officials; executive council had five official and two non-official members: there were no Africans on executive council.[1] European political views and representations were expressed through the Convention of Associations, the chamber of commerce and the *Nyasaland Times* whilst African political views and representations were expressed through the Nyasaland African Congress and the provincial and protectorate councils. Of news organs specifically for Africans there was a government weekly, *Msimbi*, and four mission papers – one monthly, the others bi-monthly – all in vernacular languages.[2] At the local level, there were five town councils with predominantly European and Asian membership, and in the rural areas the system of indirect rule through Native Authorities prevailed. The major political developments at the time were: at the national level, mounting European pressure for closer association with the Rhodesias; and at the local level, government moves towards demo-cratizing local authorities by introducing district councils with a signifi-cant non-traditional and in some cases non-African membership.[3]

The really serious *bête noire* of the Africans was the possibility of amalgamation with Southern Rhodesia, principally because of their fears of white domination and land alienation. Nyasaland had long been looked upon as a peaceful country whose inhabitants, particularly the Africans, were remarkably uninterested in politics and especially political agitation; a country in which relations between the racial groups were extremely and enviably good.[4] Developments elsewhere in the world did not seem, on the surface, to have much relevance for Nyasaland, but one needs to take into account the facts that India and Pakistan became independent in the year in which Colby was appointed governor and Palestine became independent in the year in which he assumed that office: in both cases, independence was preceded and accompanied by a good deal of political agitation and violence. But these were countries outside Africa, and although there were various constitutional advances in most British African countries, none became independent during Colby's term of office.

It is undoubtedly true, as we have repeatedly seen, that by far his greatest immediate concerns were with economic development, particu-larly agricultural production, but he by no means ignored political aspirations and developments. For example, in July 1948, only three months after his arrival, he said in words to which Macmillan's 'wind of change' speeches, drafted almost a dozen years later bore a remarkable similarity:

It is inevitable . . . that the very considerable development and awakening that has taken place in . . . West Africa will take place here. We in this country must be ready to receive the impact that is sweeping Africa: . . . It must come and . . . we cannot expect conditions to remain unchanged.[5]

More importantly, ten days later, at a chamber of commerce luncheon, whilst he devoted the greater part of his speech to economic development, his peroration concentrated on politics:

> In conclusion I should like to say something in regard to political development in Africa.
>
> This territory, although there have been big changes since the War, is less affected by the march of events in the last ten years than any I have seen in Africa, and I have seen most of them. In other territories great changes have taken place and are taking place and they have been accompanied with, in some cases, very uncomfortable manifestations. Changes will take place in this country and it is only a question of time before we receive their impact. We should be able to profit from the experience elsewhere and be prepared ourselves to receive them.
>
> I have also heard it said that these changes are the result of government policies and that they can be controlled by government policies but I do not believe it. The political awakening of Africa is something irresistible which arises deep in human nature and no government can arrest it. What we must try to do is guide it and endeavour to direct it into the most useful channels with a view to harnessing its force for good. As these political changes come we must meet them with understanding, patience and tolerance. This will not be easy but it is essential if the cordial relations which exist between European and African are to be preserved.[6]

Colby, then, was deeply aware of political developments elsewhere in the world and in other parts of Africa and was convinced of the inevitability of them spreading through the rest of the continent, including Nyasaland. His earlier career had been confined to Nigeria but he had travelled extensively, particularly during the war, and his work as administrative secretary had brought him into close touch with political affairs at the highest levels.[7] He did not believe that the political awakening could be controlled by government but that it could, and indeed must, be guided and harnessed if good race relations were to be maintained.

He believed that this guiding and harnessing was likely to be very seriously hampered by 'outside political influences', particularly communism. Nor was he alone in these worries. The British government was also deeply apprehensive of the spread of communism, and one of the earliest despatches with which he had to deal, less than a fortnight after assuming office, was one from the secretary of state saying that:

> His Majesty's Government has recently decided that the developing communist threat to the whole future of western civilization makes it necessary to adopt a new publicity policy designed primarily to give a lead . . . in withstanding the inroads of communism.[8]

The Colonial Office sent numerous briefings and despatches at this time to the colonial governors, including much information and publicity material for combating communism. A paper presented to the British cabinet's Colonial Information Policy Committee in the summer of 1949 made it clear that South Africa in particular was considered 'a fertile place for the spread of communism' because of the marked disparity in wealth between the races.[9]

In March 1949, the secretary of state wrote to the British African governors, including Colby, to seek their views on the need for more positive steps to combat the growth of communism.[10] In his reply to specific questions, Colby said that no communist literature circulated in Nyasaland, and although communist influences did not reach the country through returning students since none had yet returned nor would do so for another six months, he pointed to the large number of Nyasalanders working in and returning from South Africa and Southern Rhodesia. He did not add, if indeed he personally knew, that police and customs officers searched the baggage of returning emigrant labourers and removed fairly large quantities of communist literature from them.[11]

A little later, the secretary of state again addressed colonial governors[12] and dealt with the question of 'counter propaganda as distinct from the security and intelligence measures', concluding that 'the general communist situation in Africa has developed sufficiently to demand such action'. He proposed that there should be regional organizations in East, Central and West Africa devoted to anti-communist propaganda and to editing, producing and distributing material which would reach the African communities through the press, radio, bookstalls and reading rooms.

This despatch awaited Colby's return from leave on 7 October 1949, and he immediately asked for the matter to be considered by a small committee which included the secretary for African affairs and the assistant commissioner of police.[13] When they met on 31 October, the assistant commissioner's view was that:

the communist influence is already so close to our borders that it is essential for us to start the counter propaganda before communism has a chance of becoming established.

They all agreed that the secretary of state's suggestion of a regional organization would be insufficient by itself since if it were based in Lusaka, as was most likely, it would be directed primarily at Northern Rhodesia. Rather, what was required was 'a local propaganda office where articles . . . would be written from the Nyasaland angle and would be cast so as to project and maintain before African eyes the British way of life'. They advised that it was most important that its publications – to be 'in all the national languages' – should be produced in Nyasaland and 'recognized by the people as something of their own and particularly for them'.

Colby accepted the bulk of this advice, although he disagreed with the suggestion that articles should be published in the local languages, and on 12 December 1949 he addressed a top secret memorandum to the secretary of state.[14] It was a long and well-reasoned document in which basically he argued that:

Conditions in this territory with its comparatively densely grouped population of two and a quarter million Africans are such that if communism were to take root it would spread rapidly and widely; the difficulty and expense of restoring the problem, once such a state of affairs has been reached needs no emphasis.

Using the known view of the British government that South Africa was 'a fertile place for the spread of communism', he added:

It must be remembered too that the large number of Nyasaland Africans who travel to and from Southern Rhodesia and the Union of South Africa constitute an easy and ever present channel for the introduction of communist doctrine. Though it has not yet been assailed, Nyasaland's position is in fact particularly vulnerable and I feel strongly that it should be strengthened without delay.

He proposed that this strengthening should be secured not by a regional organization alone, 'indispensable and helpful' as it might be, 'but by establishing an organisation within Nyasaland . . . to deliver the propaganda in a form most suitable for local consumption and at a time and in a manner most likely to command attention'. In arguing for an organization separate from that of Northern Rhodesia, he was using the knowledge that the British government already believed that Nyasaland was 'potentially a more likely area for communism than Northern Rhodesia because the [Africans] are more advanced there'.[15] He proposed that the existing Government newspaper, *Msimbi*, should be greatly expanded at a cost in the first year of £15,000 capital and £1500 recurrent.

He was much concerned that the newspaper should 'have some cover if only to the extent that its propaganda activities should as far as possible be unsuspected'. He could not, he felt at the time, risk a free-standing organization, and in a small country like Nyasaland cover was not easy. *Msimbi* would:

> provide the only possible local cover for the organisation which [he] deemed to be essential but it must work unobtrusively if it is to work at all.

He added that he was well aware of the suspicion with which a government newspaper was customarily regarded and of the undesirability of connecting it with propaganda activities, and it was for these reasons that a cover was needed. He concluded his memorandum pointedly by saying that he understood from the secretary of state's despatch that funds would be made available by the British government.

Save on the important issue of finance, the secretary of state welcomed and supported Colby's initiative in proposing an expansion of *Msimbi*, but in his reply of 9 February 1950 he regretted that 'it now appears unlikely that funds will be available from the imperial exchequer' and he made it clear that expenditure would have to be met from local funds.[16]

This was a serious blow to Colby. Having painted a rather bleak picture of Nyasaland's vulnerable political position as a means of persuading Britain to pay for countering the threat, he could hardly now do nothing about it. In any case he believed deeply in the political, economic and social dangers of the spread of communism, he was convinced that steps needed to be taken to combat it, he knew that this could only be undertaken at the government's instigation and with the government's financial support, but he was also aware that if the government were publicly associated with the newspaper – which he saw as the only practical significant means of combat – it would not succeed in its purpose. It would be an expensive initiative and the country was in the throes of a severe drought which had cost the government large sums in famine relief which it could ill afford.

There was, however, one source of financing under Colby's control to which he could turn: the Native Development and Welfare Fund built up from the surplus revenue of the African tobacco, cotton and maize produce boards, a fund held in government trust for the development and welfare benefit of the African people.[17] He noted that his committee of advisers had emphasized that 'It was most important that [the] publication should be . . . recognized by the people as something of their own and particularly for them.' It was important therefore that, in addition to establishing to the satisfaction of executive council the existence and seriousness of the political threat, he should assess the reaction of 'the people' to the need for an African newspaper.

It was natural that in doing this and in considering political developments and the role of the press, Colby should draw upon his experience in Nigeria where in 1943 the governor, Bourdillon, had created a public relations office and a little later set up a government-sponsored newspaper, the *Nigerian Review*, to combat anti-government publicity.[18]

Colby was well aware of these developments; he was a senior secretariat officer when the public relations office was created and he was administrative secretary, and acting chief secretary, when the *Nigerian Review* was set up. One of the people who set it up was Rene Howard, a former Fleet Street journalist and a successful general reporter with the *Sunday Chronicle*.[19] She had travelled out to Nigeria in 1945 on the same boat as Lady Colby, and had been introduced to Colby on the dockside on arrival. A few days later she was invited to lunch by Lady Colby, and thereafter was from time to time a dinner guest of both the Colbys and Sir Arthur Richards, the governor, and she occasionally accompanied Lady Richards and Lady Colby on their official engagements. Mrs Howard worked closely with another colleague of Colby, D. C. Fletcher, the chief public relations officer, and together they were deeply involved in running the government newspaper. Fletcher had joined the Nigerian administration as a cadet in the same year as Colby had, 1925, and they had worked together in the Lands and Mines Department of the Kaduna secretariat.[20]

It was in the direction of this particular Nigerian experience that Colby now turned in Nyasaland. He quickly ruled out the possibility of persuading the existing non-government newspaper, the *Nyasaland Times*, to adopt a pro-government stance, because its whole history, dating back half a century, was one of criticizing the government from a European, 'settler', viewpoint and it was traditionally markedly unsympathetic towards African advancement. Soon after his arrival, he arranged for the appointment of a government public relations officer, M. J. Morris,[21] and was instrumental in having Fletcher transferred from Nigeria to Nyasaland – strangely, as lands adviser.[22] Colby set about establishing to the satisfaction of executive council the existence of a political threat, and then creating the means of combating that threat, and in both these endeavours he used Mrs Howard, with her journalistic skills and Nigerian experience, in what, despite significant differences in detail, he saw as basically similar circumstances.

Mrs Howard had resigned from the Nigerian service in 1949 and had arranged to emigrate to Rhodesia early in 1951. The Colbys sent her a Christmas card which she received just before sailing for Africa, and early in the journey she wrote to thank them, outlined her future plans – in farming – and posted the letter at Genoa. When they received this letter, Colby immediately sent a telegram asking her to go to Nyasaland to 'discuss a government proposition'. The telegram was received at Port Said and she cabled back that for a variety of reasons she could not alter her plans so suddenly, but she did not close the door and gave her address in Rhodesia. Again Colby acted quickly and, by the time Mrs Howard reached Salisbury, a letter was waiting for her, asking if she would visit Nyasaland for a week 'and discuss the political situation which [Colby] felt was going the same way as West Africa', and, if agreeable, would she contact the Nyasaland government representative in Salisbury to make travel arrangements. This she did.[23]

When she arrived in Nyasaland, she dined at Government House where Colby told her that 'in his opinion the agitators for self-government were getting active and following exactly the same routine as that which had been applied in Nigeria and which suggested outside direction'. Since Mrs Howard had played a leading role in combating this agitation in Nigeria, he asked if she would interview all heads of departments and consult them as to the problem in general terms. This she did in the course of the next few days and wrote a brief, four-page report which reached conclusions similar to Colby's. She then returned to Rhodesia.[24]

On 14 March 1951, executive council considered Mrs Howard's report and proposed a further investigation upon which could be based a detailed plan for closer examination. They advised that Mrs Howard should be engaged to undertake this assignment. Colby accepted this advice and a letter was written to her asking if she would conduct 'a six week survey of the whole country, meeting a complete cross-section of the community . . . and make a full report on it'.[25] She agreed and very early in April began her survey, during which she interviewed representatives of all government departments, religious bodies, planters and school teachers, and at the end of which she produced a report which gave details of her interviews, 'which when collated painted rather an alarming picture' and confirmed Colby's assessment of the situation. For Mrs Howard – as for Colby – there were clear 'signs of coming unrest'.[26]

Her report was discussed at considerable length by executive council on 23 May and Barrow said that:

> it was abundantly clear . . . that there was already in Nyasaland a considerable amount of anti-European feeling and many folk who might well be subversive . . . this fact was, of course, well known to Council but either not known or ignored by the vast majority of people in Nyasaland who were thus living in a fool's paradise.[27]

In answer to a question from Barrow, Mrs Howard, who was present, expressed the view that if any newspaper were to be controlled by government many of its objects would be defeated, and when questioned by Hadlow about the language in which the newspaper should be printed she opined that it should be in English to attract the intelligentsia, in whose ranks anti-European feeling was most prevalent. Hadlow's question was a crucial and dangerous one, because upon its answer depended the degree of opposition which could be anticipated from the European community, since the *Nyasaland Times* was already a long-established and influential English language newspaper serving that community, and a similar paper would be in direct competition with it.

Colby's early experience of the *Nyasaland Times* and his relationships with the editor, D. G. Hess, had not been good. During the early and very worrying stages of the 1949 severe food shortage, Hess had voiced highly critical views of government's actions at a meeting of the chamber of commerce and had subsequently published equally critical letters to the editor and an attacking, critical editorial. Fearing not so much the criticism as such but the damaging effects which publication might have on race relations and security, Colby had summoned the directors of the *Nyasaland Times*, including Hess, to Government House to discuss Hess' attitudes and to express his own views on the matter. The other directors disassociated themselves from Hess' statements and assured Colby that during the food crisis they would 'support the Government and avoid adverse criticism likely to encourage undesirable repercussions'.[28]

When Mrs Howard left the executive council meeting, its members continued their discussion, which was very detailed. They accepted that there was an urgent need to counter anti-government influences and to win over African opinion, and that the way to do this was through a newspaper, but this, they recognized, was far from being an easy and straightforward matter.[29]

Colby clearly saw the problems and conflicts. First there was the question of control. The prime intention was that the newspaper should adopt a strong pro-government stance. On the other hand, if it were purely a government newspaper, intelligent potential readers would recognize it as manifestly a propaganda organ, and it would fail to meet its main objective. Consequently, this could probably be achieved only with an element of stealth, by minimizing the extent to which government was known to be in control. There was also the question of whether it was proper and wise to use government money to run a newspaper; such a proposal would be opposed by non-officials in legislative council when dealing with the annual or supplementary estimates. If it were a non-government newspaper, it ran into the difficulty that it would probably not attract sufficient subscribers if a company were floated. Finally, if it were written in English, it ran into the further difficulty that it would be in direct competition with the *Nyasaland Times* and be strongly opposed by those running and supporting that newspaper. Mrs Howard had foreseen these difficulties and, in respect of control and finance, recommended that the newspaper should be quasi-governmental: that is, should be independent of all government departments and staffed by non-civil servants, but have its first directors appointed by government; should at least initially be financed by government loan; and should become commercially viable by selling its issues – unlike *Msimbi*, which was distributed free.[30]

The need was recognized to be urgent, and Colby wished to move quickly, but securing consent to use government funds raised further problems: there was no provision in the government's current estimates which could be used to launch a newspaper, and any attempt to obtain a supplementary appropriation, even for a loan, would encounter considerable opposition in legislative council and would also expose the whole proposal to publicity which would make clear to all its prime purpose – influencing African political opinion through strongly pro-government propaganda – thereby severely limiting its chances of success. The Native Development and Welfare Fund could be relatively quickly tapped and did not require legislative council's approval.[31] This fund was for the purpose of benefiting Africans and was, therefore, less open to criticism by non-African interests. It was to this source that Colby now turned to finance the newspaper, not sharing the doubts expressed by Barrow and the attorney-general as to the wisdom of so using the fund because 'adverse comment upon the fact . . . was inevitable from inside and outside the territory'.[32]

The general lines of advance having thus been established, Colby went on to secure executive council's favourable advice on four, more detailed, steps which he had already rehearsed in his own mind. First, an interim scheme should be prepared under the Native Development and Welfare Fund Ordinance providing for establishing the African Press Company and expenditure of £50,000 for the newspaper. Second, Mrs Howard should be offered the post of editor. Third, immediate steps should be taken to ascertain if two years' supply of newsprint could be purchased; if these enquiries proved unsuccessful, Fletcher – who was appointed chairman of the company – when on leave in Britain from mid-June 1951 onwards, should make similar enquiries and the purchase of machinery should be taken up by him. Fourth, negotiations should be put in hand to purchase the Citrona Soap Company property in Blantyre as premises for producing the newspaper.[33]

Mrs Howard accepted the appointment, some of the senior staff were appointed, at least one other from the Government Information Department was pressed – unsuccessfully – to take up employment, and the premises and some of the equipment were acquired; but the company did not start printing and publishing in 1951, nor – to anticipate – in 1952.[34]

Behind all these preparatory steps to launch the newspaper, significant suspicion and opposition to the enterprise was building up. As early as May 1951, Barrow had expressed the view in executive council that it was most important to explain to the European community the reasons for the newspaper.[35] Such a view was scarcely realistic: the government needed to be less than completely frank about the proposal if it were to succeed. In any event, Mrs Howard's conclusion was that the European community, accustomed to a virtually uninterrupted history of peaceful conditions 'were ignorant of the underground political activities',[36] under no circumstances could believe that the 'polite peaceful people who laboured contentedly for a pound per month and food' would ever rise against them,[37] and just did not believe that African political agitation was a possibility.[38] It was most unlikely that the Europeans, even if they could be told the real reasons for the newspaper, would accept that it was necessary; rather, they would suspect that there were ulterior purposes.[39]

Then, on 4 July, Hadlow told executive council that there was public interest in the venture and thought that it would be prudent to publish a statement about it.[40] So the public already knew! Colby, playing for time, simply directed that a progress report, together with a draft press communiqué, should be prepared and brought before council at its next meeting, but he was, in fact, furious. The danger which he was trying to combat was extremely serious and his proposed solution was extremely delicate. In the early stages, at least, stealth and secrecy were essential. How had the leak occurred? Had an official been indiscreet, or did the fault lie with a non-official member of executive council? Colby initially believed that the leak had come from the office of the secretary for African affairs, where the files on the newspaper were being handled, probably from an assistant secretary or his stenographer. Although the secretary for African affairs himself later made little secret of his view that, at least so far as federation was concerned, there was a positive correlation between government propaganda and political agitation, he stoutly defended his staff, and it is extremely unlikely that the leak occurred in his office (although a senior officer outside the secretariat may have been indiscreet in his conversations with certain non-officials).[41]

At its next meeting, on July 17, council approved the text of a press communiqué based on the progress report which it then had before it,[42] and a fortnight later its members were informed of an enquiry made by E. C. Peterkins about the way in which the newspaper was to be financed. Peterkins was a shareholder in, and a director of, the Blantyre Printing and Publishing Company which owned the *Nyasaland Times*.[43] Colby, relieved that the query concerned finance rather than the purpose of the newspaper, had his answer ready:

initially the Native Development and Welfare Fund would finance the newspaper, since it was intended primarily for the benefit of Africans, but ... it was intended to float a company as soon as possible to take over the newspaper.[44]

In fact, Peterkin's query – brought to executive council by Hadlow – was but the opening shot in the opposition to the newspaper from the European community (or at least parts of it). Colby, Fletcher and Mrs Howard all came in for a good deal of personal criticism, and the whole project was heavily attacked.[45] The criticism came from the *Nyasaland Times*; the London-based *East Africa and Rhodesia*, edited by J. F. Joelson; the expatriate non-official members of legislative council; and the expatriate 'settler' pressure groups, principally the Convention of Associations and the chamber of commerce.

The criticism voiced by the *Nyasaland Times* took two forms. First, there were those correspondents who felt that the government ought to devote its funds to:

> looking after the welfare of the African children rather than waste it on the African newspaper.[46]

Second, there were those who ridiculed the whole idea and suggested that the newspaper be called the 'African Echo', since it would simply be echoing Colby's views,[47] or the 'African White Elephant' in order to emphasize the high probability of failure.[48] The *Nyasaland Times* carried a number of highly critical editorials which generally reflected views expressed by correspondents, the chamber of commerce – of which the editor was a member and at whose meetings he spoke against the African Press – and the Convention of Associations: broadly that it was wrong to provide a newspaper from public funds for 'a handful of intelligentsia' in the African community.[49] A good deal of space was also devoted to reproducing critical editorials from *East Africa and Rhodesia*.

The editor of *East Africa and Rhodesia* published four lengthy leading articles about the African Press during the first half of 1952, claiming that he had received more letters, all indignant, from Nyasaland correspondents than on any other topic, including federation, since pre-war days; none of the letters had suggested 'any justification whatsoever for the extravagance with which the project has been planned and started'.[50] Joelson attacked the scheme on the grounds that Mrs Howard and Fletcher were unable or unwilling to justify the scheme, and on the grounds of government's secrecy, 'imprudent prodigality', and lavish and 'inexcusably extravagant' expenditure.[51]

Expatriate non-official opposition in legislative council was led and voiced – at considerable length – by Dixon, also member of the chamber of commerce and a shareholder in, and a director of, the Blantyre

Printing and Publishing Company, who attacked Colby on three principal grounds.[52] First, he was critical of the way that government, as he saw it, was in a socialist manner trespassing into the commercial field – which was sacrosanct – and in doing so was breaking faith with the business community. Second, he was convinced that the project was not viable, a costly commercial proposition doomed to early failure, designed by officials sadly lacking in elementary business knowledge and skills, and run by people not competent to do so. Finally, he insisted that if there were a need for a newspaper for Africans, which he doubted, then there were existing, expatriate, commercial concerns which could, and were willing to, produce it, and to do so more efficiently and economically than could the African Press.[53]

The chamber of commerce was the most persistent of all the outside bodies criticizing Colby and they pressed him to appoint a committee of investigation into the African Press. Stevens, general manager of the Nyasaland railways, made a particular point at meetings of the chamber that Colby was using government funds to enter the field of private enterprise. Stevens, personally, was a shareholder in, and a director of, the Blantyre Printing and Publishing Company, and the Nyasaland railways were a major shareholder in it. Several other leading members of the chamber were also shareholders in the company including the president, who was also a director. Not unnaturally, Colby refused to appoint a committee of investigation, and he told the chief secretary to convey the decision to the chamber in a confidential letter.[54] The confidential nature of such communications from government placed them within the restrictions imposed by the Official Secrets Ordinance which rendered the further disclosure of their contents an offence.[55] Being to that extent thus muzzled, the chamber wrote again to government, this time listing some two dozen detailed questions, mainly about the financing and the process by which the decision to establish the African Press company was designed and executed. Dixon, ever a leading voice in their deliberations, readily persuaded the chamber to authorize the chairman to call an extraordinary meeting if the government's response was, as he anticipated, unsatisfactory, in order to keep up the pressure.[56]

The government's reply was indeed unsatisfactory from the chamber's point of view, stating that since no 'public' money was involved, it regretted that it could not see its way to providing any of the information requested.[57] The chamber then prepared a memorandum for the non-official members of legislative council and asked them to seek an interview with Colby to ask questions, particularly about financing and competition with existing ventures.

Parallel with these steps, the Convention of Associations, whose chairman also was a director and shareholder in the Blantyre Printing and Publishing Company, was taking similar steps.[58] The Convention also demanded a committee of enquiry and when this was refused they passed a strongly worded resolution deploring the grant of money to the African Press. At the suggestion of L. J. Rumsey, a non-official member of legislative council, they then joined forces with the chamber 'to pursue the matter to conclusion'.

The opposition to his proposals was now so fierce and consolidated that Colby began to wonder if continued battle on this particular issue was worth the cost. Nonetheless, towards the end of July he had a long meeting with the European non-official members of legislative council, and in mentioning this meeting to a joint meeting of the chamber and the Convention on 25 July 1952, Barrow said that:

> as certain matters had still to be discussed he was not in a position to report . . . until such time as these matters were completed.[59]

Three weeks later, the annual conference of the Nyasaland African Congress, meeting at Blantyre, resolved:

> that in order that the views of Congress and African people at large may be clearly understood by the public . . . Congress should establish its own newspaper as early as possible. The newspaper should be called Kwaca. The price should be 2d a copy published twice a month in Chinyanja and English on four pages.[60]

This development, clearly thought out in some detail by congress, and which should have been viewed as of major significance, seems to have passed unnoticed, or at least unheeded, by Colby's opponents, despite being published in the *Nyasaland Times*; but for Colby it was decisive. If congress were to have its own newspaper, including an English-language edition, he had already been forestalled in guiding and directing the political awakening of Nyasaland Africans. If he hoped to harness that awakening, he would have to use means other than setting up the sort of government-controlled newspaper he had in mind. On 9 September, Barrow reported to the chamber that 'certain developments had taken place' since the meeting with the governor, and that before government took a final decision on the matter he, Barrow, would like to discuss it in committee with the chamber, the Convention and the other non-official members of the legislature.[61] Such a meeting was held on 17 September, at which Barrow took the chair:

> He wished to report to them certain developments which had taken place. The proceedings which followed were held in committee and concluded with a hearty vote of thanks to the Chairman.[62]

In this way the affair was brought to an abrupt end. Barrow, who had been such a staunch supporter of Colby's motives and actions in setting up the African Press, clearly changed his mind – as Colby had himself – over the wisdom of continuing with the proposal in practice, although he stuck to the principles involved. Colby used him to mollify the chamber, the Convention, and the expatriate community generally, so as to bring the affair to an end without the necessity of a public climb-down.

We do not know what Barrow said at the joint meeting on 17 September[63] – the communication, being in committee and made by a member of executive council, was thereby brought within the Official Secrets Ordinance – but thereafter the voicing of opposition suddenly ceased. The final flick of the dying, but victorious – if misguided – opposition tail came in the House of Commons seven months later, when John Rankin, the Labour and Co-operative MP for Tradeston, Scotland, asked the secretary of state for the colonies if he was prepared to state in what way the African Press in Nyasaland would be of benefit to the African tobacco and cotton growers, what information would be given in it, and – echoing Hadlow's crucial question in executive council two years earlier – in what language. It was ironic that having been accused of socialist motives by the private commercial sector in Nyasaland, Colby should have faced the final shot from a socialist in Britain. But Rankin was too late – the battle was over:

> Mr Lyttelton: the assets of the African Press Limited have now been taken over by a private company, Kachalola Limited, a subsidiary of the Banthu Press Group which I understand propose to commence publication of a weekly newspaper for Africans in Nyasaland later this year.[64]

Colby agreed to Kachalola being lent £43,000 from the Native Development and Welfare Fund to purchase the assets; a further £1500 from the fund being devoted to covering the outstanding debts; and the sum of £20,693 spent on setting up the African Press Company being written off. Kachalola was owned by the Paver brothers of Southern Rhodesia who over a period of years extended their ownership of newspapers throughout Central Africa, including buying out the *Nyasaland Times*. They began to publish a weekly vernacular newspaper, *Bwalo la Nyasaland*, in 1953 which immediately cut the circulation of *Msimbi* by 10 per cent. They then proposed that it would save the government a good deal of trouble and money if, instead of continuing to publish *Msimbi* it sold the paper to the Pavers who would incorporate government news into their own newspaper, at a cost to the government of £2000 a year.[65] Colby gave this proposal short shrift since:

> Any sale like this would effectively hand over the full control of the European and African press of the country to Hess.
> The disappearance of Msimbi would mean the effective disappearance of all competition. They would then be able to produce any kind of paper they liked.[66]

There were a number of tragedies in the African Press saga. First, although Colby was right about the need for a newspaper to guide and harness the political awakening in Africa which was fast approaching Nyasaland, it is a pity that he did not feel able to persuade the business community, if necessarily through its leaders privately, of the validity of his perceptions and that, as a consequence, he had to be discreet to the point of secretiveness. He relied in this, as in so many issues, upon Barrow to be the link between him and the business community, but Barrow was the sole link in the chain of contact and confidence – Hadlow merely supported Barrow – and the other leaders of the expatriate community were men of much narrower vision, highly suspicious of and antagonistic to government, and with deep financial interests in the Blantyre Printing and Publishing Company with which, they felt, the African Press would be in competition. This difficulty was compounded by the significant degree of overlapping membership of the opposition groups: the chamber of commerce, the Convention of Associations, and the non-official members of legislative council.

Second, there was an insufficiently well-developed system of African political expression to enable Colby to enlist clear-cut support from the African community. It is true that Mrs Howard's survey had been an:

investigation which was a Protectorate-wide investigation from the
north, through the central province, right down to the south of
the territory.[67]

and that the African Provincial Councils and the two African members
of legislative council supported the idea. But the Nyasaland African
Congress was not yet strong enough, nor did the government have
sufficient confidence in it to enlist its support. Indeed, it was precisely
to forestall developments which Colby feared would take place through
congress that he wished to act.

Third, there was tragedy in the attitudes of Colby's opponents. They
were so immovably committed to untrammelled private enterprise; so
entrenched in their views that African political change in Nyasaland was
not only undesirable but also out of the question; so lacking in the
perception and understanding of political developments elsewhere; and
so bound by the narrowness of their own experience, that they were
blind to the signs around them. Had his opponents noticed and heeded
them they might have – indeed they ought to have – recognized that
Colby at least had a point in what he was attempting to do, a point
which was very much more in their own longer term interest than
anyone else's.

Fourth, it was precisely during the period in which the proposal for
an African newspaper was being developed and so vehemently and
implacably opposed that African opposition to federation grew apace
and became increasingly intransigent, vocal, and ultimately violent. In
the same month, March 1951, that Colby took Mrs Howard's report to
executive council, Nyasaland officials were meeting their counterparts
from Northern and Southern Rhodesia to make recommendations on
closer association between the three territories,[68] but Colby's opponents
did not see any connection between these two facts. It was from this
point onwards that steps towards federation were taken quickly and
relentlessly despite a change of government in Britain, and that African
opposition to federation became an increasingly important, worrying
and dangerous factor in Nyasaland politics. When the new Conservative
government in Britain announced its firm support for federation in
November 1951, a leading article in the *Nyasaland Times* said:

With the African intelligentsia what was in the background is now
very much in the foreground which is to say the exaggerated hope
that by resisting partnership they will attain self-government on

the pattern of the Gold Coast and Nigeria. These hopes are unreal and unrealisable . . . for they assume that the same pattern can be followed in . . . Nyasaland where white settlement is permanently established and white enterprise is the foundation of our economy and future progress. For this dangerous development naturally enough Communism is receiving the blame.[69]

Hess and his fellow opponents were beginning to recognize, albeit too late, the influences of outside forces – 'communism', as they saw it – on Nyasaland African politics but they still refused to see, let alone accept, the possibility of Nyasaland receiving the impact of changes taking place elsewhere, of which Colby had warned them over three years earlier.[70]

It has been suggested that Colby, accustomed only to African politicians, was unprepared for, and unable so easily to handle, the European politicians in Nyasaland. Whilst this is far too simplistic an explanation – few colonial governors, least of all one of Colby's robustness, would have found the Nyasaland European politicians more difficult to handle than the Nigerians! – and whilst in any case that view overlooks the very great extent to which he had been in contact with non-Africans, especially businessmen and politicians, as director of supplies and as administrative secretary in Nigeria, it is possible that he was taken somewhat unawares by the lack of vision, the strength, and the persistence of European opposition to his newspaper proposals.

Even more likely to be accurate is the argument that this was an unwinnable battle, since there were too many factors militating against success. First, he could not tell the public the real purpose of his newspaper proposals. Second, the European public, misled by insularity of outlook and a long history of peaceful race relations, were markedly disinclined to believe that a real likelihood of African political agitation existed or indeed was possible. Third, they may have felt that Colby's suspected opposition to the concept of federation would show itself through the newspaper's columns at a time when most Europeans were in favour of federation, and that he would rally African opposition behind him in opposing federation. In this connection it is surprising that they did not accuse Colby of having clandestinely encouraged congress to set up its own newspaper. Fourth, by publicizing and selling newspapers, Colby was entering into the commercial arena, an area hitherto preserved for private enterprise, principally non-African enterprise, and they may have believed that a governor appointed by a socialist secretary of state was bound to have socialist inclinations antagonistic to private enterprise, no matter how long-standing. Finally, there were two other dangerously weak elements in his venture: some would see the use of the Native Development and Welfare Fund as a dubious means of financing a commercial project aimed at the more educated Africans rather than the village farmers whose enterprise financed the fund; and by using personally known colleagues (one of whom, Fletcher, was unworthy of him)[71] from Nigeria – a country which, many felt, was very unlike Nyasaland socially and politically, and experience of which, some also felt, was not entirely relevant to Nyasaland – he ran the risk of being accused of 'old cronyism'.

The failure of the African Press – unwinnable a battle though it may have been – was a great disappointment to Colby. Much as he was convinced of the political need to combat communist influence and to guide African political development, and of the probability of deteriorating relations with the African population, he came to feel that the particular method which he adopted to combat it – the African Press – had been a mistake and a blot on his career, a good deal of money having been invested in it to no avail, money which he desperately needed for other, development, purposes.[72]

13· Federation

'Not by the choice of any of the Protectorate's native population.'

In an earlier chapter[1] we saw how, at least in the African mind, the question of land alienation was closely associated with European domination and federation with the Rhodesias, especially Southern Rhodesia. Whilst on leave before taking up his Nyasaland appointment, Colby was briefly introduced by the Colonial Office to the background to closer association between the Rhodesias and Nyasaland, the most far-reaching and difficult political question with which he had to deal during his period as governor.

The early British Central Africa link between Nyasaland and her neighbour, North-Eastern Rhodesia, was severed in 1907, and the joining of North-Eastern and North-Western Rhodesia four years later was followed by a widely held assumption that a union of Northern and Southern Rhodesia – both the responsibility of the British South Africa Company – would be the logical and inevitable conclusion.[2] Indeed, in 1916, the company prepared a plan for legislation to bring this about. The First World War and the opposition of Southern Rhodesia settlers delayed progress on the plan and, after the war, Southern Rhodesia became more interested in responsible government than in amalgamation, fearing that the latter, and the budgetary deficits of Northern Rhodesia, would seriously postpone the former. In 1923, Southern Rhodesia became virtually independent, whilst Northern Rhodesia thereafter became a protectorate. Throughout all of this, Nyasaland, also a protectorate and heavily dependent financially on Britain, remained apart, not even being included in the customs agreement between the two Rhodesias and South Africa.

In South Africa, the solidarity of the British empire attitudes of Smuts was replaced in 1924 by the extreme Afrikaner and republican attitudes of Hertzog. These attitudes were less in keeping with the views of Southern Rhodesian leaders, heirs to the old Cape liberal tradition, who consequently began to look north, rather than south, for their future political relationships. In any case, Southern Rhodesia had rejected union with South Africa two years earlier.

In 1928, the British government appointed the Hilton Young Commission to enquire into the possibility of closer union between the British East and Central African territories. Among the recommendations of the chairman's minority report were the linking of North-Eastern Rhodesia and Nyasaland with East Africa, and the possibility that the Northern Rhodesia line of rail might be amalgamated with Southern Rhodesia whilst North-Western Rhodesia might become a separate protectorate. The British government took no action on these recommendations, principally because the other three members of the commission disagreed with them.

The world depression of the early 1930s caused doubts in the minds of Southern Rhodesians as to whether their country could survive as a separate economic unit. These doubts coincided with the rise to power of Huggins, pledged to amalgamation of the two Rhodesias and strengthened by the growing economic power which copper was giving to Northern Rhodesia's economy. Southern Rhodesian Europeans wished to widen their economic base and benefit from the rising revenue of Northern Rhodesia, whilst Northern Rhodesian Europeans also wished to widen their economic base and rid themselves of the controls imposed by Whitehall.

In Nyasaland, too, there was an expressed desire on the part of Europeans for amalgamation to include Nyasaland. Very shortly after Hubert Young was appointed governor in 1932, the leader of the non-officials in legislative council asked him if he would support such a development. The governor's reply then was that it was unkind to suggest that he commit official *felo de se* so soon after his appointment.[3] Nonetheless, the non-officials hoped that Young would be instrumental in securing amalgamation when, after a short period in Nyasaland, he was transferred to be governor of Northern Rhodesia.

Pressure to persuade Britain to agree to amalgamation of the Rhodesias continued throughout the 1930s. In April 1935 the governors of Southern and Northern Rhodesia and Nyasaland, and the prime minister of Southern Rhodesia, held a formal conference to discuss closer union in research, customs, communications, education, defence, trade and currency. In 1936, these discussions were continued at a meeting of white parliamentarians and officials at the Victoria Falls. Huggins of Southern Rhodesia and Moore of Northern Rhodesia advocated amalgamation under a single government, but others pointed to the British government's responsibilities which excluded amalgamation without the consent of the African peoples of the protectorates.

In 1938, Britain appointed the Bledisloe Commission to consider further the promotion of closer association between the Rhodesias and Nyasaland, 'with due regard to the interests of the native inhabitants'. The Bledisloe Report, published early in 1939, concluded that amalgamation could not be achieved immediately, principally because of differing native policies between which it was yet too soon to choose, the limited European populations, the different constitutional status of the three territories, and – most importantly – the general opposition of Africans in Northern Rhodesia and Nyasaland to amalgamation: 'a factor that cannot be ignored'. Bledisloe, however, did recommend that Northern Rhodesia and Nyasaland could be combined under a single government immediately and that an inter-territorial advisory council should co-ordinate economic and financial development in the three territories.

So far as Nyasaland was concerned, Bledisloe turned its probable future away from East Africa, the direction to which Hilton Young had turned it, towards the Rhodesias, resulting, in the short term, in the association with those latter territories being effected through an inter-territorial secretariat, later to become the Central African Council.

The Second World War delayed further progress, and the 1945 British general election brought to power the Labour Party, pledged to prevent amalgamation until and unless the Africans desired it. There were no signs then or at any other time that the Africans did or would desire it. The Europeans of Northern and Southern Rhodesia, however, continued to press for closer association and their hand was strengthened by the growing power of the Nationalist Party in South Africa, which was committed to carrying out the policy of apartheid against which a more liberal state in Central Africa began to be seen as a bulwark, just as it was beginning to be seen as a bulwark against the spread of communism.

Early in 1948, the question briefly surfaced again when Welensky and the other non-official members of the Northern Rhodesia legislature unanimously asked for responsible government in that country: it was felt that this might be a first step towards him demanding amalgamation with Southern Rhodesia. In response to a suggestion from the Colonial

Office that Nyasaland African opinion be sounded on amalgamation with Northern Rhodesia, the Nyasaland government advised that they were 'not in favour of reviving this controversial subject at the present juncture' and added that the constitutional position in Northern Rhodesia would need to be clarified before Nyasaland should be invited to consider amalgamation with that protectorate.[4] The colonial secretary agreed with this view in a telegram dated 19 March 1948.[5]

It was this political scene which Colby entered as governor of Nyasaland at the end of March 1948.

Although he did not immediately study the question of federation very deeply, his initial views, after two or three months and having had some discussions with non-officials, was that:

> Although there is a body of European opinion in this territory which is in favour of amalgamation, my impression is that there is a greater body against it. Moreover, I should think that African opinion, if . . . canvassed, would be solidly against it.[6]

During a visit to Northern Rhodesia in October 1948, Colby accepted an invitation to Stewart Gore Browne's house to meet 'prominent Nyasalanders working in Northern Rhodesia' and the idea of amalgamation of Nyasaland and Northern Rhodesia was discussed. In his letter thanking Colby for sparing time to visit him, Gore Browne said:

> For myself I can see nothing but good in the amalgamation of the two protectorates. . . . Both territories would, I think, have a lot to gain from each other. Our own people here dread amalgamation with Southern Rhodesia as I fancy do most Nyasalanders but the amalgamation of the two protectorates would surely strengthen the hands of Africans in resisting political fusion with the South.[7]

This visit, and the belief that federation was 'liable to become a live issue in the near future', persuaded Colby to give the matter much more close attention, and his views were recounted to Lord Milverton – formerly Sir Arthur Richards – a few days before Christmas 1948.[8] Colby still felt that the Europeans in Nyasaland were not particularly interested and that the pressure came from Northern Rhodesia Copperbelt politicians – in order to secure European responsible government and avoid the Colonial Office policy of self-government – and from Southern Rhodesians – in order to control migrant labour from Nyasaland on which both industry and agriculture in Southern Rhodesia very largely depended:

> Southern Rhodesia fears, with considerable justification, that as the tempo of development in Nyasaland increases, as it will, and as wages and conditions of life improve, so will the number of labourers going to Southern Rhodesia be reduced, with very serious results on their economy.

In dealing with Nyasaland African opinion – which he had quickly judged with great accuracy – he said that 'there can not be the slightest doubt that African opinion would be solid against either amalgamation or federation with Southern Rhodesia' because they would assume that federation would 'bring all the evils of the south to a country where they are free to live their own lives'.

In February 1949, on Welensky's initiative, Huggins called a two-day unofficial conference at the Victoria Falls to which no Africans or officials were invited. Leading European politicians from Southern Rhodesia and Northern Rhodesia attended, as did Barrow, Hadlow and Marshall from Nyasaland.[9] At this meeting, the plan for outright amalgamation was abandoned and replaced by a unanimously accepted proposal to form a federation of the three Central African countries. Barrow expressed the view that:

> With a population of two and a quarter million Africans against two and a half thousand Europeans and the same number of Asiatics, it will be essential to have African opinion on our side. I do not think, however, that there will be difficulty in carrying African opinion along with us.

The three Nyasaland delegates said the conference could only be exploratory and that all decisions would have to be confirmed by the people of Nyasaland, and reiterated that 'in particular it would be essential to sound the opinion of the Africans through the Provincial and Protectorate Councils'. As a consequence of these views, the conference unanimously resolved:

> It is agreed that all the existing rights now enjoyed by Africans in Northern Rhodesia and Nyasaland shall be guaranteed by the Fed-

eral Government and that any change affecting such rights can be effected only with the consent of the local legislative council.

On their return, Colby discussed federation with Barrow, Hadlow and Marshall and found them 'very uncertain as to what line to take'. He formed the view that they were not keen on federation and he decided to be very cautious about the issue in dealing with the secretary of state because he thought:

it would be so much better if unofficials in this country throw cold water on the proposal, and I rather think they will do so.[10]

In this latter view, upon which he initially relied, he was eventually and unfortunately mistaken.

Two months later, when the secretary of state, Creech-Jones, arrived in Nyasaland, his visit was not particularly connected with federation. Rather, the *Nyasaland Times* saw the visit as an opportunity for him to see the drought and severe food shortage which were then assailing the country and for him to appreciate the need for development aid.[11] Certainly Colby wished to see the visit in this light. Indeed, so absorbed was Colby in looking at development work at the edge of the airfield when he went to meet Creech-Jones at Chileka airport, that he was alarmed by the arrival of an aircraft 20 minutes before the secretary of state was due to arrive and had to scurry back to the airport building in great haste. In fact it was a false alarm and Creech-Jones' aircraft arrived some minutes later.[12] The Convention of Associations and the chamber of commerce, in their memoranda[13] to the secretary of state, did include passages urging federation but they did so only as one item among many concerned with economic development. The Nyasaland Christian Council, however, made clear its grave concern with reports of the Victoria Falls conference and particularly the absence of Africans there; it considered the three Europeans – who in fact represented the Convention of Associations and the chamber of commerce – to be 'self-appointed representatives':

They expressed the fear that if Federation occurred on the lines proposed at the Victoria Falls Conference, Southern Rhodesia would dominate the Federation in no uncertain manner and the Federation would, therefore, merely be a first step towards complete amalgamation, against which the Christian Council were deter-

mined to fight. They hoped that before any decision was taken by
the Imperial Government . . . full weight would be given to the
opinion of the Africans and to the judgement of those who had
long and continual contact with them.[14]

The secretary of state's reply[15] stressed that the British government had
had no definite proposals put before them for consideration by the
Victoria Falls conference, that it was an unofficial conference, and that
the British government would give very serious thought to the matter
before coming to any decision. He assured the Christian Council that
the interests of the African community were paramount, that Britain
was compelled by treaty to protect the interests of the Africans of
Nyasaland and Northern Rhodesia, and that the British parliament
would never consent to any proposals which were against the material
interest of the African communities, but that any proposal which was
considered to be to the direct benefit of the African would receive
serious consideration. No decision would be arrived at until the Africans
had been given every opportunity of expressing their opinions; they
would be consulted before any decision was reached.

Although the chamber of commerce had raised the question as only
one among many dealing with economic development, the secretary of
state took the opportunity to speak much more clearly and forcefully to
them than he did to others during this visit. He asked members if they
realized the full implications of the Victoria Falls proposals and added
that under these proposals Nyasaland interests would be completely
swamped:

> Any financial measures would naturally always be framed to benefit
> Southern Rhodesia, and the other two territories, if they accepted
> these proposals, would more or less sign away their own indepen-
> dence and chances of economic development.[16]

During the secretary of state's visit, Colby both met him in Nyasaland
and travelled to Northern Rhodesia in order to discuss with him and
the governor there 'matters of common interest to the two territories'.[17]
Creech-Jones agreed that the British government would study any proposals on federation submitted to it, but later he declared that the
Labour government was inflexibly opposed to federation and emphasized
that he believed the Central African Council to be all that was currently
needed in the way of closer association.

Huggins shortly began to take serious steps to have the council abolished.[18] His ostensible reasons were that it derogated from ministerial and parliamentary responsibility, but, as Benson, chief secretary of the Central African Council secretariat, and others saw it:

> The real reason why the Central African Council is politically objectionable is that while it exists and if it is supported, it provides machinery for the settlement of common problems, so that no new organization more in accord with aspirations can logically be demanded.[19]

Following a meeting with Southern Rhodesia representatives on 29 November 1949,[20] the secretary of state, in a secret letter of 20 December,[21] asked Colby for his views on the Central African Council, and particularly on three points. First, with regard to the council's limitations and defects, Colby pointed to what he saw as the considerable progress which it had made. He thought that these very successes tended towards its undoing, since the Southern Rhodesia government used the council's accomplishments as a basis for attacking it by suggesting that it had to some extent usurped the functions of the legislature, a criticism Colby believed to be misconceived.[22] The real fault, he felt, was the administrative incompetence of Southern Rhodesia, which he accused of muddled thinking for not evolving a system which did not derogate from the powers of their parliament:

> I consider that the retention of some such body as the Central African Council is not only necessary but that it is capable of considerable accomplishments in the administrative and economic fields, but an essential pre-requisite is the goodwill, now lacking in Southern Rhodesia, on the part of the three Governments to enable such a body to work properly.

Second, Colby dealt with the question of political integration short of amalgamation. He believed that the handling of the whole position since the original proposals of the Victoria Falls conference had been inept, and that Welensky, together with Huggins and other Southern Rhodesia ministers, had:

> created such an attitude of suspicion among the African community and, indeed, a lack of confidence on the part of the European

community, that . . . the possibility of federation offering a successful solution of the problem of political integration must be ruled
out in the foreseeable future.

He thought that a solution along the lines of the East Africa high
commission might have worked, but Huggins had publicly ruled this
out as being unacceptable to Southern Rhodesia. Colby confessed to
having no other suggestions to offer and concluded that it was currently
impossible to find any measure of agreement on any form of political
integration.

Third, he considered how far it would be possible to proceed in
constituting a body which would be effective in the economic field. He
prefaced his remarks by saying that, since Huggins was virtually committed to abolition of the Central African Council, they must assume that
it would disappear, but he felt that Huggins realized that some machinery
would be necessary for dealing with common problems. He then considered three possibilities and dismissed the first – that the Southern
Rhodesia cabinet secretariat should do the work now done by the Central
African Council secretariat – as being not acceptable to the Nyasaland
government. Next, he concluded that although *ad hoc* inter-territorial
committees would be practicable, it was 'eminently desirable' to have
some co-ordinating machinery to arrange meetings, circulate papers, and
prepare minutes. He then turned to continuing the Central African
Council secretariat under a different name and at a 'lower level', with a
joint body on a ministerial level meeting once or twice a year to deal
with any matters arising from the joint secretariat.

Colby's letter, addressed to Cohen, finally contained two deeply perceptive and telling remarks of considerable political significance. First,
he told Cohen that the Nyasaland African Congress in January had
asked government for an assurance that it was aware that the African
population of Nyasaland was unanimously against federation, and
additionally that there was a growing European disenchantment:

The developments which have taken place since the Victoria Falls
Conference have done great disservice to the cause of federation in
Central Africa and I have seen a good deal of evidence to show
that opinion among European unofficials in this territory is hardening against Southern Rhodesia and whereas the idea of federation
might have been acceptable to the European community twelve
months ago, I am doubtful whether it is today.

His other concluding remark was that so long as federation and amalgamation were synonymous in Southern Rhodesian eyes, since amalgamation was impossible, federation was 'equally impracticable'; but there could be a change of heart in Southern Rhodesia in its attitude towards federation. He noted the increasing Afrikaner immigration into Southern and Northern Rhodesia and thought that, if this immigration into Southern Rhodesia continued and if the Afrikaner influence there increased, there would be the likelihood of incorporating Southern Rhodesia into the Union of South Africa. He believed that a very large number of Southern Rhodesians would 'view this with considerable alarm' and might be prepared to consider more reasonable proposals for political integration 'designed to form a British bloc in Central Africa'.

This letter, which Colby drafted at the very end of 1949, is remarkable in showing his very clear grasp of political realities and his keen perception of political possibilities and probabilities in Central Africa.

At the meeting of the Central African Council on 25 January 1950, Huggins had the future of the council discussed.[23] Much work had been done behind the scenes, Benson playing a stimulating and co-ordinating role in respect of all three heads of government and being a particularly close and confidential adviser to the governor of Northern Rhodesia and to Colby.[24] The Southern Rhodesia government had discussed a draft memorandum, which unbeknown to them Benson had produced for Huggins, but they could not agree on it or on any other memorandum to submit to the council: there had been three cabinet meetings on the subject and 'several drafts of a memorandum [had] been prepared and mangled and torn up since then'. At the meeting, Huggins said that his government had never been enthusiastic about the council and had only agreed to support it in deference to the wishes of the British, Northern Rhodesia and Nyasaland governments, but it was now 'intensely unpopular' in Southern Rhodesia. He believed that the council should be abolished and some other organization should be set up to take its place at a lower level; he added that the council's secretariat had done very useful work and he had no criticism of it.

Colby, supported by the governor of Northern Rhodesia, said that he thought there was nothing seriously wrong with the existing arrangements and regretted that there were misconceptions prevalent in Southern Rhodesia regarding the council's powers and functions; there was no such misconception in the northern countries. The council was purely advisory and non-executive, and consequently there could be no substance in the belief that the council derogated from the responsibilities of the individual governments or legislatures. He believed that inter-territorial co-operation could not succeed unless it was fully supported by the individual governments and unless there was a 'real desire and will to cooperate'. He continued, 'Given that will, practically any organisation that could be established would work.' The Southern Rhodesia government representatives said they were not prepared to continue membership of the council as presently constituted for more than another year. All agreed that in the meantime they should continue to give full support to the council while examining the existing machinery and alternatives to it.

In this way, with Rennie's help from Northern Rhodesia and Benson's assistance, Colby prevented the immediate abolition of the Central African Council.

In the meantime, Nyasaland African opposition to federation continued and the Southern Provincial Council was unanimous in opposing the Victoria Falls conference proposals:

> All speakers pointed out the fundamental difference in the constitutions of Southern Rhodesia and the two protectorates of Northern Rhodesia and Nyasaland, and none of them could see any difference between the proposals put forward at the Victoria Falls conference and those that had been discussed in 1938 with the Royal Commission on the question of outright amalgamation between the three territories[25].

Faced with these clear messages from the Africans and the changing attitude of Nyasaland Europeans – which Colby had pointed out to Cohen – the federationists in Rhodesia began to frame 'new forms of federation . . . behind the political scenes' which were designed to exclude Nyasaland and simply link the two Rhodesias.[26] This news was greeted in Nyasaland with a mixture of indifference and equanimity, and the editor of *The Nyasaland Times* illustrated this from the European viewpoint in a leading article in mid-February 1950:[27]

> Several years ago, Nyasaland . . . became an ardent advocate of amalgation with Southern Rhodesia and Northern Rhodesia into a Central African dominion.
> However, that was before the war . . . at a time when Nyasaland – with a negligibly small European population and starved of capital – was ignored, neglected and dubbed 'the Cinderella of Empire'.

Then, in a paragraph which paid tribute to the wisdom of Colby's basic development strategy – including the view that not only does a stable political environment contribute to economic development, but also, conversely, economic development contributes to political stability – the editor added:

> Since then, and particularly rapidly during the past two years, the scene has changed. The European population has doubled, roads and aerodromes are being put down to tarmac, and the Colonial Development Corporation has already launched several agricultural schemes and has others in contemplation.
>
> So it will be appreciated that the news . . . that there is a move . . . to drop Nyasaland from any future federation plans [is] being received, naturally, with satisfaction by our African and Indian communities and . . . with complete equanimity by our European population. The all round opinion seems to be that 'With a planned future in sight we are quite happy as we are'.

The British government was collecting views on amalgamation, and late in October 1950 Colby received a copy of a 'Confidential Note by Lord Hailey on the Bearing of Native Policy on the Proposed Amalgamation of the Rhodesias and Nyasaland'.[28] Hailey had hoped his study would have presented no obstacle in the way of amalgamation, but he was forced to advise that the divergencies in African policies needed to be seriously considered. He believed that there would be no problem on these grounds in amalgamation between Northern Rhodesia and Nyasaland, but since the proposed amalgamation of the two Rhodesias called for an early decision he thought it better to defer the question of linking Nyasaland. He pointed out that European opinion in Nyasaland did 'not show any great concern in the matter' and that there was even some division of European opinion as to the material advantage of amalgamation for Nyasaland. Colby was gratified that Hailey was not advancing the cause of Nyasaland's closer association with the Rhodesias and he was comforted by the absence of great concern, the division of opinion, and the equanimity of the Europeans of Nyasaland.

A general election in Britain in November 1950 returned the Labour Party in power but with a greatly reduced majority, and Creech-Jones, who lost his seat, was replaced by James Griffiths as secretary of state for the colonies. External factors, however, were having a marked bearing on attitudes towards colonial affairs in British politics. The British public noted the bloodshed which had accompanied independence in India and Pakistan in 1947 and Britain's withdrawal from Palestine in 1948. In South Africa, Malan was demanding that the three high commission territories should be incorporated into the Union; he was threatening to take steps to attain republican status, and he passed the Group Areas Act as a clear step in the implementation of his party's policy of apartheid.[29] As we have seen,[30] there were fears, also, that communist influences were penetrating Central Africa, including Nyasaland. Public opinion in Britain, and opinion in parliament, including the Labour government, was now more inclined to the creation of a strong British bloc in Central Africa as a buffer between, and a bulwark against, apartheid and communism. Smuts' death on 11 September 1950[31] seemed to symbolize the end of a relatively liberal tradition in South Africa. Welensky particularly pressed the point of the developments in South Africa:

> If it was the wish of the majority of the people in South Africa to become a republic they were entitled to do so but if that was so, the creation of a British dominion in Central Africa was now a matter of urgency.[32]

Despite the urgency, Griffiths, realizing that Labour's slender majority indicated that he was unlikely to remain long in office, and not disposed to move fundamentally from his predecessor's stance, played for time by setting up a conference of officials in London, by subsequently visiting Central Africa himself, and by ending that visit with the third Victoria Falls conference. He gave an instruction that Nyasaland officials were neither to advocate nor to criticize federal proposals – a step which served only to increase African suspicions. Griffiths' decision to convene the conference of officials was made – following a suggestion by Huggins – at the behest, and with the encouragement, of Cohen, who privately favoured a federal solution and who now persuaded the secretary of state to permit a committee of impartial civil servants to consider whether the Central African territories could feasibly and profitably federate. Cohen did not then appreciate the depth of African opposition to any scheme of closer association, no matter how benevolently conceived and executed.[33]

Griffiths' announcement of the conference of officials took Nyasaland by surprise since, as the editor of *The Nyasaland Times* confessed:

much of the settler population of Nyasaland had resigned [them]-selves to the fact that the much discussed and much desired amalgamation, federation or closer union . . . was not for this generation.[34]

The announcement shook Nyasaland's expatriates out of their indifference, and *The Nyasaland Times* now urged that the settlers could not afford to sit back and watch developments but rather that a vigorous settler case should be prepared and led by the non-official members of legislative council.

Colby's attitude towards the forthcoming London conference of officials was one of not wishing to rock the boat by saying too much about it in advance. He got the chief secretary to emphasize to legislative council the exploratory nature of the talks and the assurance of full consultation with African opinion, so that the opponents of federation would feel that decisions had not already been made and that opportunities for dissuading the British government still existed.[35] It was only later, when the Africans realized that their opposition was to be ignored, that they resorted to violence, and Colby, appreciating that this was a likely outcome, wished to delay it as long as possible, partly in the hope that it could be avoided and partly to give himself time to prepare to meet the violence if it could not be avoided. There was still time for the British government to reject closer association. In any case, since the London conference was to be of officials and not politicians, there was a distinct possibility that they would advise against federation or at least hedge recommendations with so many fundamental safeguards of African interests that any resultant federation would be of very limited significance. In the meantime he was anxious that peaceful conditions should prevail.

On 21 February 1951 executive council discussed the forthcoming conference.[36] In the course of discussion, Barrow and Hadlow accepted Colby's contention that European non-officials who in the past had favoured closer association with the Rhodesias had done so largely in order to get closer control over the Africans. Members agreed with Colby that, if at any future time a constitution were framed to effect closer association, it would be very difficult to ensure that Nyasaland had a sufficient share in the control of affairs and that 'it was unlikely that the Southern Rhodesian tax payer would be willing for his money to be spent on the development of Nyasaland'. Colby remarked that the conference had not been sought by Nyasaland and that Nyasaland officials should participate in it 'with an objective frame of mind particu-

larly as to what benefits would accrue to her from closer association'.
Colby's view, shared by council, was that whilst the Nyasaland officials
should not show themselves unsympathetic to proposals for closer association, they should take great care not to compromise the essential
interests of Nyasaland and her people.

The London conference began on 4 March 1951 and was attended
by four officials from Nyasaland: Footman, Fox-Strangways, Pincott,
and Corrie, Colby's private secretary and aide-de-camp. They met
officials from the United Kingdom, Northern Rhodesia, Southern
Rhodesia and the Central African Council: a total of 27 officials.[37]

It appears that the members of the Nyasaland delegation received no
briefing from Colby or any of his senior advisers before the conference.
One of them many years later recalled:

All the Nyasaland Administration were dedicated principally to the
welfare and advancement of the African population and no one
more so than Sir Geoffrey Colby. To that extent the Nyasaland
delegation did not need any briefing from the Governor on that
score. He knew it and we knew it. He certainly did not brief me
in any way whatever ... Whether or not the Governor briefed the
leader of our, Nyasaland, delegation I do not know. Certainly
Charles Footman gave me no indication of this during the Conference or even to the rest of the delegation outside the Conference
to my knowledge.

The Nyasaland delegation operated exclusively through its leader, Footman, who acted as their spokesman. His colleagues supplied him with
facts and opinions as he required them and he was mainly concerned
with addressing and countering issues raised by the other delegations
rather than operating to a brief. They 'did not get much of a say in any
of the fundamental arguments, except to stick steadfastly to the view
that African interests had to be safeguarded if [they] were to carry
African opinion in any subsequently agreed closer association structure.'
Fox-Strangways supported Footman on African affairs issues, and Pincott supported him on geographical, historical and economic affairs.
Corrie's support was of a more general nature and his major role was
probably discreetly to 'keep an eye open' on behalf of Colby. It does not
appear that the Nyasaland delegation at any time took the initiative in
proposing or suggesting closer association than that which already existed
in the form of the Central African Council.

On the other hand, [they] did not demur when the Conference was clearly headed in that direction, presumably . . . because it was virtually impossible to argue convincingly against the preponderance of facts and opinions displayed in favour of a much closer, positive, association. Moreover, there was no hint that the Colonial Office would encourage any contrary view . . . not . . . that the Nyasaland delegation had, in fact, a contrary view. If any of them did have such, it was not voiced even among the delegation itself [but there is] no doubt at all that they were, at the outset of the Conference, no more than lukewarm about *any* form of closer association. There was always an underlying suspicion concerning Southern Rhodesia, a territory felt to be 'contaminated' by the South African influence. As the Conference developed [they] began to be convinced of the economic and politically defensible advantage of an *effective* closer association. Towards the end of the Conference there was a distinct feeling in the delegation about the inevitability of federation.

The Southern Rhodesian delegation – the largest – was led by Andrew Strachan, secretary to the Treasury, and included the secretary to the cabinet, the secretary for external affairs and the director of census and statistics. Their quality impressed the Nyasaland delegation, who found them competent professionals, aloof from politics and friendly and co-operative as individuals; they also found that the Southern Rhodesian team in no way attempted to dominate the proceedings but, on the contrary, were especially sympathetic to Nyasaland's problems. On the other hand, they found the Northern Rhodesian team 'in virtually all respects quite different', and persistent in arguing most of the issues that came up for discussion; they seemed over-ridingly concerned with Northern Rhodesia's own interests rather than the interests of the whole of Central Africa. Their leader, R. C. S. Stanley, chief secretary, seemed 'Victorian or Edwardian in manner, humorless and apparently not much enjoying participation in the Conference. He appeared to have complete control of his team [which] needed a lot of encouragement to agree to the eventual recommendations . . . They did not appear to have any enthusiasm for any form of closer association.'

On the United Kingdom side, G. H. Baxter, assistant under-secretary of state in the Commonwealth Relations Office, chaired the conference and did so in:

an entirely unbiased fashion. He did not 'condition' the Conference either by personal views or by directing its discussions to areas of his own manufacture. [Nyasaland delegates] did not detect any hint whatever that [he] was aiming for any particular outcome to the Conference. In contrast, however, the Colonial Office, via Andrew Cohen, did far more to steer the Conference to its conclusions than did the Commonwealth Relations Office. While the latter [chaired the conference] it was very evident that the whole conduct of the exercise was weighted in favour of the colonies, not Southern Rhodesia . . . The direction and tempo of the Conference was clearly masterminded by Andrew Cohen. At times he was petulant when things were not going according to his wishes – indeed [on] at least one occasion . . . he stalked out of the Conference in apparent high dudgeon.

There was also a good deal of vested interest lobbying of the participants at the conference, including that by the British South Africa Company which 'wined and dined' the delegates generously, including 'a sumptuous dinner at Claridges Hotel'.

The public had to wait three months to learn the outcome of the conference: that is, until the report – which was ready by the end of March – was published in mid-June.

The report[38] pointed out the economic interdependence of the three territories and the importance, therefore, of integrating economic policy. Although currently relatively prosperous – thanks it might have been added, in Nyasaland's case, to Colby's efforts – they were individually vulnerable economically and would be stronger as a single unit with a more broadly based economy. A generally accelerated expansion of the economy would benefit all the inhabitants and help more rapid social development of the African population. A number of officials in Nyasaland took the view that 'looking at it from a purely economic point of view . . . the concept of federation was of great importance to us', and this view was shared by their colleagues from the other territories: 'the economic enticement was something that you couldn't just brush aside, whatever the politics of the case and . . . many of us were torn in half by this'.[39] The report concluded that the need for action was urgent, and its main recommendations were that closer association between the three territories should be brought about by a federation rather than amalgamation, and that substantial safeguards for African interests should be included.

As soon as the report was published in Nyasaland, Colby announced his plans for consulting the African population: meetings were immediately held at district headquarters, at which the district commissioners read the summary of the report but at this point encouraged no discussion.[40] This in itself must have appeared suspicious to those who opposed federation. A month later each district council of chiefs met to express its views – all meeting on the same day – and very soon thereafter the three African provincial councils discussed the issue. No one challenged the statement made later by Chief Chikowi that although the district commissioners had discussed federation in every village there was not a single African in favour of it.[41] *The Nyasaland Times* published the report in full but did not immediately comment because it had not yet been accepted even in principle by the three governments.[42] Having long been an ardent advocate of amalgamation or federation, *The Nyasaland Times* did, however, search for an explanation of the *volte-face* by the imperial government and its sudden sense of urgency. They found it – and presumably the main selling point to Africans – in the spectre of apartheid:

> Thinking Africans as well as Europeans of the three territories are becoming increasingly anxious about the course of native policy south of the Limpopo.[43]

In essence, this argument was: you might not like what you see south of the Zambezi, but it's a good deal better than what you see south of the Limpopo. It ignored the point that neither was necessary, a point of which Colby was privately convinced.

In July 1951, four British members of the Commonwealth Parliamentary Association visited Central Africa to provide the House of Commons with more evidence of local attitudes to federation.[44] Members of the Nyasaland Chamber of Commerce who met them made a particular point of stressing that the final decision on federation should be made by the United Kingdom government and not by the three Central African countries.[45] Since they clearly knew the views of the Southern Rhodesia government and the likely balance of views in the Northern Rhodesia government, with its large and strong non-official European membership, it may well have been that they feared Colby's opposition and the possibility that he would make it public, thereby delaying or avoiding the reaching of a conclusive decision.

The chamber, and the Convention, alerted Griffiths to the totality of

African opposition to federation and also pressed their own views on the secretary of state when he visited Nyasaland a month later.[46] The memorandum the Convention presented to Griffiths – unlike that presented to Creech-Jones two and a half years earlier – was exclusively concerned with pressing the cause of federation. This change reflected the fact that very great economic progress had been achieved in the interim and consequently economic development was less of a worrying issue for them, but more powerfully it reflected the view that federation was very much more a possibility, indeed a high probability, than ever before, and they were increasing the pressure. It may also have reflected a defensive European reaction to the growing and threatening activities of Congress, a reaction which saw the security benefits of being linked to stronger, richer, more 'Europeanized' territories.[47]

Griffiths also met the African Protectorate Council, the three African provincial councils, and the Nyasaland African Congress, and at each of these meetings the Africans' strong opposition to federation was made abundantly clear, an opposition based on fear of the absorption of Nyasaland into Southern Rhodesia, of more European immigration, and consequently the loss of African land to immigrants.[48] He strove, unsuccessfully, to allay their fears. Chief Chikowi, ever a loyal, clear-thinking and outspoken man, summed up the causes of opposition by looking only beyond the Zambezi, not, as did the Convention of Associations, beyond the Limpopo: 'The reason for refusing federation is that we do not like Southern Rhodesia.'[49]

An interesting light is shed upon Griffiths' motivation in entertaining the idea of federation by Kathy Smith, who interpreted for him – as she did for many other visitors – during his tour of Nyasaland.[50] When Miss Smith was first introduced, Griffiths said he understood that she was opposed to federation, and she replied that this was the case, but that she had never made her views public. When asked, she gave the reasons for her opposition, whereupon Griffiths said that Southern Rhodesia – presumably Huggins – was insisting on Nyasaland being in the federation and that, if this did not happen, Southern Rhodesia would 'go in with South Africa' and that he did not want to have it on his conscience that he had 'sold' two million Nyasalanders. Few people then or later believed that there was a real possibility of Southern Rhodesia joining South Africa, but it was a powerful fear which could be played on by those who wished to see a federation come about.[51]

Griffiths' visit concluded with another conference at the Victoria Falls. This time the conference was attended by three representatives of the

Nyasaland African Protectorate Council,[52] who made it clear that they firmly and uncompromisingly opposed federation and were not prepared to accept any argument in its favour; they also objected to the absence of any Africans from the Southern Rhodesia delegation and to the fact that the proceedings were *in camera*. Colby flew back from leave in Britain to attend the conference,[53] which was also attended by Barrow. They both gave others present the impression that they were 'not much in favour' of federation and Colby indicated that he did not think it would succeed.[54]

The conference came to an unexpectedly sudden ending because Attlee, the British prime minister, was about to resign and seek the prorogation of parliament so that an early general election would ensue. On the night of Friday, 21 September, the conference issued its final communiqué[55] in which it stated, despite strong refusal by African members to assent,[56] that it favoured federation in principle, but that differences existed on the principle of federation as well as on the proposals made by the conference of officials, and that further discussions within each territory and exchanges of views between the four governments would be necessary. Barrow was careful to say on behalf of the Nyasaland European non-officials:

> We and others have agreed on federation but we shall not agree if we cannot go together with the people with whom we live.[57]

The conference agreed that any form of closer association should enshrine the exclusion of amalgamation unless a majority of the inhabitants of all three territories desired it; that the protectorate status of Northern Rhodesia and Nyasaland should be preserved; and that land and settlement matters and African political advancement at both local and central levels, subject to the ultimate authority of the United Kingdom government, should be reserved to the territorial legislatures and not to the federal government.[58]

Griffiths had been placed in a difficult position, an impasse from which only very firm, virtually autocratic, action could secure a way out. Huggins and Welensky were uncompromising, European opinion was in the process of becoming firmly in favour of urgent federation, and African opinion was virtually unanimously opposed to it. Perhaps for the first time, despite the many powerful indications over a very long period, Griffiths and Cohen now appreciated the real depth of African antagonism and began to feel that they had been unwise to tread the

federal path, certainly to have allowed the conference of officials to open
the gate to the federal path and to have gone so far down it. Griffiths
must have been relieved to learn of the impending general election as a
means of drawing the conference to an abrupt, and inconclusive,
end. As *The Nyasaland Times* saw it, federation was in cold
storage.[59]

There can be little doubt that had the Labour Party been returned
to power the federal proposals would have undergone major revision,
especially in strengthening safeguards to meet the more severe of the
African objections, or, indeed, might have been abandoned totally. In
the event, however, the Conservative Party assumed government after the
November 1951 elections and Oliver Lyttelton – less susceptible to
the persuasive charm of Cohen, or perhaps Cohen had changed his own
mind – became secretary of state and concluded that indecision over
whether to federate had gone on long enough.

On 21 November, exactly two months after the final communiqué
from the Victoria Falls, federation was taken out of its brief period of
cold storage, and the new secretary of state announced that the British
government was convinced of the urgent need to secure closer association
between the three Central African territories and that it believed this
would best be achieved by federation.[60] The new government fully
endorsed the final communiqué and in 'the light of economic and other
aspects' hoped the Africans would accept the assurances contained in
the report of the conference of officials. Like Griffiths, who everywhere
he went 'found concern at the growth of Afrikaner propaganda in the
three territories',[61] Lyttelton feared the spread of apartheid views in
Central Africa and the ultimate conflict which such views would bring
between the races. What he seems to have discounted was that similar,
albeit less extreme, views already existed in Southern Rhodesia, and it
was this which the Nyasaland Africans feared. More than three decades
later, Welensky said:

> Even today I often wonder whether the British Government – in
> the light of the knowledge which they had particularly behind the
> scenes – should have gone on with including Nyasaland in the
> bringing together of the two Rhodesias, because they knew of
> the opposition as well as we knew it; and yet they proceeded with
> it on the basis that they knew better than the . . . African as to
> what was good for him.[62]

There was a view in the Colonial Office, held, for example, by Sir Peter Smithers that:

> While there was no chance that black politicians and white settlers could be brought to trust one another, it might be possible for the Colonial Office to retain the confidence of both.[63]

Possibly some of this type of thinking induced the British government to continue to move towards federation.

Notwithstanding the British government's announcement of its support for federation as an urgent necessity, and indeed only nine days after the announcement, Colby sent a secret and personal telegram to the secretary of state, for Cohen's attention, in which he boldly and bluntly expressed his personal views:[64]

> It is now my considered opinion that there is no possibility in next 12 months of getting Africans to change their attitude towards federation and consequently that there is nothing to be gained and much to be lost by endeavouring to make them change their minds. I am concerned that political situation has deteriorated considerably in recent months and I attribute this entirely to federation talks. If such talks are now continued deterioration will grow . . . I believe that informed European opinion would come down in favour of postponing further discussion of federation . . . I feel very strongly that we should take the initiative and pull out.

Colby and most others had not expected the British policy announcement in favour of federation and his telegram 'frankly . . . came as a shock' to Cohen and his London colleagues.[65] In an urgent reply on 3 December 1951, Cohen very much doubted if it was politically practicable, after the secretary of state's announcement, 'to abandon [the] campaign of persuasion now and in our judgement it would have disastrous consequences if Nyasaland were to pull out at this stage'. He hoped that the governor would soon 'take a less gloomy view'. Colby believed that he could still gain European support for postponement, but through no fault of his own his warning had come too late; he had missed the boat – and only by nine days.

When Colby presided over legislative council a week before Christmas 1951, the African members urged the British government not to default on its historical promise not to transfer power in Nyasaland to other than the African people. They feared that the federal government would control Nyasaland 'and in this way the development of the country will be at the mercy of Southern Rhodesia', and again said that 'the African people unanimously and strongly adhere to their opposing federation entirely'.[66]

On 16 January 1952, Colby travelled to London[67] to advise Lyttelton during informal discussions with Huggins, at the conclusion of which the British government reaffirmed its opposition to amalgamation since this would lead to the merging of the northern protectorates with Southern Rhodesia into a new self-governing state, losing their identity, which would not be the case with a federation.[68]

Whilst the Colonial Office discussions were going on, *The Nyasaland Times* published a long leading article on African opposition to federation:[69] 'They are one hundred per cent against it, and that fact is well known to the imperial Government and all the people of Southern Africa.'

Nyasaland may have federation imposed upon it but it will not be by the choice of any of the Protectorate's native population.

At this stage, then, not only the leading members of the Labour Party in Britain,[70] but also the press in Nyasaland, were convinced of the Nyasaland African population's total opposition to federation. Nonetheless, at the close of the discussions with Huggins, the British government announced on 4 February 1952 that it was reconvening the Victoria Falls conference in London in April.[71] In the meantime, despite the extremely short notice, they wished to ascertain specific African views on the June 1951 white paper, by 1 March. Colby asked for special meetings of the provincial councils to obtain these views, but the provincial commissioners were unable to get their councils to debate the proposals.

Having been taken by surprise three months earlier and not having been able to give his advice and warnings to the British government before it announced a decision, Colby was not going to risk being caught out again. A month before the Lancaster House conference, he addressed a long and detailed memorandum to the secretary of state, in which he said that since discussions on closer association were approaching a stage when decisions would have to be made, he felt that he should inform the British government of the views which he had formed 'after four years' close study and almost continuous discussion of the problem'.[72] He emphasized that he did not write the memorandum to decry feder-

ation, but rather to show that the recommendations of the conference
of officials were appropriate to the two Rhodesias rather than to Nyasaland, where they were outweighed by considerations which he proceeded
to deal with in detail.

Since Southern Rhodesia was separated from Nyasaland by 200 to
300 miles of Portuguese territory, Colby disputed the geographical
grounds for closer association and pointed out that developments in a
transport network could take place without including Nyasaland in
a federation. Similarly he argued that the Central African Council could
have been developed to secure all the economic advantages which federation was claimed to secure. In respect of the political advantages,
Nyasaland's presence or absence in a federation would not affect the
Rhodesias' potential for merging with the Union of South Africa. His
main argument, however, was Southern Rhodesia's lack of goodwill, a
point to which he returned repeatedly over the years:

> The case for the proposals in the white paper and the successful
> achievement of Federation presuppose goodwill and a spirit of
> compromise on the part of all concerned; without goodwill those
> proposals cannot succeed. After meeting and conversing with
> Southern Rhodesian Ministers over a period of four years I have
> grave doubts as to whether in fact they would be able or prepared
> to extend and maintain the necessary goodwill towards
> Nyasaland. . . . To the Southern Rhodesians the Federal Govern-
> ment and the Southern Rhodesia Government are synonymous. . . .
> I find it difficult to visualize a situation in which Southern Rhodesia
> will sponsor capital development in Nyasaland when this can only
> result in greater opportunities for employment in the Protectorate
> and thus a reduction in the flow of African labour to Southern
> Rhodesia.

Colby then turned to European reaction. He considered that if the
British government decided not to include Nyasaland in the federation,
the decision would probably be accepted by the Europeans in Nyasaland
without much comment and many would be relieved that the matter
had been disposed of without their having to take any responsibility for
the decision. In respect of a vote in the legislature he believed that if –
as he recommended – the officials did not vote, the two African members,
the Asian member and one of the Europeans, Doig, would vote against
federation. Of the remaining five Europeans, he was certain that three

would vote for inclusion and assumed that Barrow and Hadlow would also vote this way, notwithstanding the fact that this would involve turning 'a complete somersault' since they had both told the Victoria Falls conference that they were prepared to proceed with federation only 'subject to the agreement of the Africans of Nyasaland'. Having discussed federation with Barrow and Hadlow on many occasions and in considerable depth, he concluded that they had grave doubts about federation but lacked the courage to come out into the open and say so since they feared the criticism of the more conservative members of the European community. This analysis indicated that the majority in favour of federation would almost certainly be only five to four, 'which on an issue of this importance seems insufficient'.

Turning to Nyasaland African reaction, he reiterated that 'opposition to all ideas of federation with Southern Rhodesia remains obdurate and indeed is hardening', since they were convinced that:

> federation with Southern Rhodesia would not only open the door to vastly increased [European] immigration, with further alienation of African Trust Land but would also in the nature of things (since Nyasaland would be the weaker member of the federation) result in the gradual but inexorable imposition by Southern Rhodesia of her native policy and of what may be termed the Southern Rhodesia attitude to Africans.

So strong and growing was African opposition that Colby felt that a situation might develop which was beyond the capacity of the police to deal with, 'and which would necessitate military aid with all that that implies'. Such a situation did, indeed, develop some seventeen months later.

The British government was, therefore, left in no doubt about Colby's views on including Nyasaland in the federation, but it felt that the warnings were either too late or too inconvenient, and Colby's pleas to exclude the protectorate did not dissuade it. By going along with the idea of a federation but one which did not include Nyasaland – a view which Welensky shared[73] – he was showing the British government a way out of its dilemma of having publicly accepted the federal concept and yet having received consistent and strong advice from the governor against Nyasaland's inclusion. Furthermore, he had shown it the mechanics of operating the way out: oblige the official members of legislative council to abstain from voting, and then decide that the resulting majority of one was insufficient to include Nyasaland in the federation.

Three groups travelled to London for the Lancaster House conference.[74] Colby led the official party comprised of Fox-Strangways, Barrow, Hadlow, Marshall and K.O. Shelford, president of the Convention of Associations. The two African members of legislative council, Mposa and Muwamba, accompanied by C. Kumbikano, were invited by Lyttelton to go to London before the conference to discuss the African point of view, but they boycotted the official proceedings. Finally, there were the representatives of the Nyasaland African Congress, now with Creech-Jones as their adviser, who had no official standing: Chief Msamala, O. E. C. Chirwa, E. Mtepuka and J. R. N. Chinyama. The African delegates were invited to attend the conference as observers; they at first accepted, but later changed their minds when they realized that the press would not be present. Colby and his colleagues were away from Nyasaland from 19 April to 10 May, during which period the conference compiled a draft federal scheme and appointed three commissions to recommend solutions to outstanding judicial, fiscal and staffing problems.[75]

In Nyasaland the draft scheme was reprinted in full by *The Nyasaland Times*, whose editor concluded a leading article by saying that in his opinion, an opinion long held, the only satisfactory future for Nyasaland was within a Central African federation.[76] The Nyasaland African Congress rejected the scheme outright, and its president-general, Chinyama, was heavily abused by the editor for doing so:

> If this is African leadership, then the Africans must not be surprised if, for decades to come, their views are looked upon as valueless as those of unweaned babies.[77]

This and other objectionable statements by the editor of *The Nyasaland Times* can have done nothing to improve relations and to win over the Africans.

The press – *East Africa and Rhodesia*, as well as *The Nyasaland Times*[78] – also fiercely attacked Colby for not debating or even mentioning federation during the July 1952 meeting of legislative council, accusing him of nonchalance, of either culpable apathy or intentional obstruction, of deliberately disregarding the legislature, and of flagrant mismanagement 'or something worse', dubbing him 'the Duke of Plaza Toro' who 'led his regiment from behind – he found it less exciting'.[79]

The policy of His Majesty's Government is to explain the advantages of the White Paper proposals and recommend them to the communities primarily concerned. Yet in Nyasaland, the best platform, the legislature, has been deliberately disregarded. To what must be attributed this refusal to fall into line with the action taken by the imperial government and the governments of Southern and Northern Rhodesia? If to apathy it was culpable and demands an explanation. If to intentional obstruction, sharp censure is surely warranted. The Governor knows that African opinion has been grievously misled by biased and dangerous propaganda organized both within and without the territory. That circumstance laid upon him a special obligation. . . . It is no exaggeration to say that at this moment no responsibility upon the Governor can be greater than that of enlightening African opinion. . . . That in these circumstances the legislature should have met and adjourned sine die without any statement on the subject of federation is incredible; but it is nevertheless true. Mismanagement – or something worse – could not have been more flagrant.[80]

This article must have been designed by Joelson, the editor of *East Africa and Rhodesia*, and Hess, the editor of *The Nyasaland Times*, which carried a full reprint, to undermine confidence in Colby's loyal administration of British policy and to force him to avoid all actions which could possibly, even remotely, be construed not simply as negative or hostile but also as neutral, and to take every possible step publicly to demonstrate positive support for federation. It was a cunning attempt to force Colby's advocacy of federation.

For the settlers, federation was now very much more close and attainable than ever before; Joelson, Hess, the Convention and the chamber realized that they had only to keep up the relentless pressure and federation, of a type to their liking, would be achieved. In the short term, they were right. In the long term – as Colby so clearly foresaw – they were tragically wrong.

In Britain also there was criticism, faintly veiled, of Colby: C. J. M. Alport, a Conservative member of parliament and later British high commissioner to the federation, told the House of Commons that opposition to federation was not exclusively the result of outside agitation, but probably the result of the reaction of the:

small isolated administration of Nyasaland which felt that being drawn into the orbit of a bigger federation would diminish its influence.[81]

This was an unworthy comment, and Alport must have known that it could do little to assist the relationships between the three territories, or between the government and non-government communities in Nyasaland. His motivation may have been to weaken Colby's suspected opposition.

Following the publication of the draft scheme, Hopkinson, minister of state, visited Nyasaland where he met representatives of the African provincial councils and of the Nyasaland African Congress.[82] The great opposition of the African population was impressed upon him, although in return he claimed – as did Colby who was in a better position to know – that there was evidence of intimidation being used to suppress pro-federal views. He was repeatedly asked if federation would be imposed and he consistently ducked the question by saying that it could not be answered 'until a final examination of all aspects had been considered'. The clear implication of the word 'imposed' was not 'introduced' but 'forced against the wishes of the African population', but Hopkinson chose to interpret it as the former. He also met the African Civil Servants' Association and listened to a number of restrained and well-expressed views, all in opposition to federation, in which Britain's protectorate reponsibilities were emphasized, as was the fear of Southern Rhodesian and European domination. Again he was asked if the British government would impose federation and again he gave his now standard answer.[83] He appeared to treat their views no differently from other African views. Colby told him mildly that 'the people of Nyasaland were not favourably impressed with the benefits of federation'.[84]

Three decades later, Sir John Marnham who, as head of the Central Africa department at the Colonial Office, accompanied the minister of state on this visit, recalled that the Nyasaland officials' fears were based on:

the suspicion that Federation was regarded by the Southern Rhodesian Europeans as a means (failing outright amalgamation which they would have preferred) of increasing and perpetuating their own supremacy and that however ingenious the safeguards in the constitution, that was what was likely to happen: the Europeans ... would constantly try to erode the safeguards and it was optimistic to suppose that the [British Government] would

have the political will to resist. [Colby] also thought that we under-
estimated the power of Dr. Banda and his adherents to fan opposition to the proposals and that there was far more likely to be
trouble than Whitehall claimed to think . . .

In at least one place and I am pretty sure most of them, we
conducted an amateur sort of Gallup poll by walking round the
market place with an interpreter, picking individuals at random and
asking them what they thought about Federation (explaining the
idea as simply as we could) . . . The Gallup poll victims . . . either
had not the faintest idea what we were talking about or said 'we
will do as the chief says.' It seemed reasonable to conclude, as
we did, that the alleged African opposition need not be given much
weight, and that when Federation did arrive the ordinary African
would hardly notice; but I suppose there must have been a strong
element of wishful thinking on our part.[85]

On his return to Britain late in August, Hopkinson said that 90 per cent
of the Africans in Nyasaland did not understand what federation meant,[86]
but he did not say what attention he paid to the other ten per cent, nor
whether the 90 per cent included such people as the African Civil
Servants' Association.

One can only conclude that Hopkinson was well aware of the breadth
and strength of African opposition to federation – indeed it had been
consistently, widely and firmly expressed over a very long period – but
that, genuinely or not, he believed it to be misplaced,[87] based on ignorance, and unimportant. Perhaps the British government had already
gone too far to permit him to take any other view. The turning point
had been the officials' conference in March 1951, and the point of no
return had been Lyttelton's announcement of support for federation in
November 1951.

It is a puzzling question as to why the British government should
have insisted on federation – knowing the long-standing and almost
universal deep dislike and fear of closer association on the part of the
Africans, the former uncertainty of the Europeans, and the strong advice
of the Nyasaland governor against it. There are a number of probable
reasons.

The economic reason appeared to be strong. If the wealth of Northern
Rhodesia could be shared with the other two territories, this would be
to the general economic benefit of them all, and particularly Nyasaland.
Allied to this was the grave difficulty in which Britain found itself over

the balance of payments and the wish not to have to support Nyasaland financially more than was absolutely necessary. We have already noted how the British government used federation to avoid paying to take over the Nyasaland Railways and providing money for purchasing private estates once federal monies became available to Nyasaland.[88] There were also the strong commercial vested interests of British companies based in the city of London, which believed that with Southern Rhodesia in control of a federation, pro-African priorities would be submerged and expatriate commercial interests supported and reinforced.

On the political side, providing a general bulwark against both apartheid and communism was an argument frequently advanced in favour of creating a federation in Central Africa. More important, the increasing likelihood of widespread, costly and embarrassing agitation and violence in Africa was a major factor. Sir Peter Smithers, who accompanied Hopkinson as his private secretary in Nyasaland, has said:

At the time Governor Mitchell in Kenya was telling the Colonial Office on his retirement that his territory was calm and happy with no major problems in sight. I went to Kenya [from Nyasaland] and could not imagine that any man could seriously think as he did. On returning to London I put in a report saying that I thought the position in East Africa explosive, and that I feared that what were then isolated problems within individual territories, would become related to one another. Then we would feel a pan-African political problem instead of a series of local ones. This would be almost impossible to deal with. The progress towards independence should therefore go forward as fast as possible. Since the Central African territories then seemed quite unprepared for self-government (except for Southern Rhodesia) this meant that the federation had a part to play in the rapid evolution of independence which I considered necessary.[89]

Although apparently greeted with 'jocular disbelief' by the secretary of state and the permanent secretary, it is possible that Smithers' views contributed to Britain's insistence on federation. In short, several years before Macmillan's 'wind of change' speeches, the British government wished to shed its colonial responsibilities and to evolve a convenient and politically acceptable procedure for doing so. They believed that a Central African federation would help them to take a step in this direction, although it took them some time to finally make up their minds about imposing such a federation.

On the day of Hopkinson's arrival in Blantyre, the Nyasaland African Congress at its ninth annual conference, also in Blantyre, resolved that Congress 'after hearing reports from all the Congress branches [and] affiliated bodies within and outside Nyasaland, does once again reaffirm the total opposition of the African people of Nyasaland against federation'. Congress went on to state that any move to bring about federation 'in the face of the Africans' solid opposition' would be regarded as a 'formal breach of trust and of friendly relationships'. They called for a day of national prayer against federation.[90]

Colby was deeply concerned about Congress's opposition to federation and particularly about its influence on the chiefs who had traditionally been extremely loyal to government. Late in October 1952, two months after Hopkinson's departure, he summoned Chinyama and Chinula, the president-general and vice-president of Congress, to Government House, where he spoke very bluntly to them.[91] He warned them, in Fox-Strangway's presence, that 'Congress was playing with fire, with things that they did not understand, and things which were likely to get out of their control.' When self-government came, he continued, it would take account of the rights of all races and Congress should understand that 'once and for all'. Furthermore, when and if the Nyasaland government decided that federation was not in the interests of Africans, it would say so. Colby gave the Congress leaders little opportunity to reply or to object to what he was saying. He gave them, as it were, 'a flea in their ear'.

He was also worried about the British government's unclear attitude towards imposing federation. He advised the secretary of state that if federation went ahead it would have to be imposed in the face of African opposition, and that it was highly desirable that the British government should make up its mind before the forthcoming conference whether it was indeed prepared to impose federation. Colby believed that it was 'of vital importance' for the British government to make a decision on this point:

> Supposing that the Conference reached agreement and the sub-
> sequent referendum in Southern Rhodesia was favourable to feder-
> ation then it would be nothing short of disastrous if Her Majesty's
> Government then failed to impose the implied decision on the
> Central African territories. Such a failure would make it quite plain

that the decision to abandon the idea of federation was taken in view of African opposition which would be extremely dangerous politically. If in fact it was the case that, in the circumstances stated, Her Majesty's Government would be unwilling to impose federation, then it would be advisable to oppose unreasonable Southern Rhodesia demands and to insist as far as possible on African safeguards written into the White Paper being maintained.[92]

Colby was urging the secretary of state to decide whether he was prepared to impose federation against intense African opposition. The decision had to be made – if not necessarily announced – because, in Colby's opinion, the electorate of Southern Rhodesia would soon agree on federation. At that time, the British government would either have to impose federation (and lose the chance to oppose unreasonable Southern Rhodesian demands and insist on strong safeguards), or alternatively have to decline to impose federation, which all would recognize had resulted from African opposition. To do the latter would be politically extremely dangerous, because the dangers of deteriorating race relations were more likely to be long-lasting and irreparable if the Europeans were thwarted than if the Africans were thwarted, as a result of the relative degrees of organization, unity, and strength of political power at the command of the two races. By insisting on a decision on imposition, Colby may also have been making it clear that *he* was not going to decide: the British government had both to decide and to take full responsibility for its decision.

At the 17 December meeting of executive council,[93] which was attended by Bucquet, chairman of the chamber of commerce, and Marshall, chairman of the Convention of Associations, Colby told council of the advice he had given the British government and said that it was necessary to establish whether the Nyasaland government was in favour of federation being imposed. The non-official members, Barrow and Hadlow, were in favour, the former being 'definitely in favour of imposition', adding that they had gone too far to turn back. Fox-Strangways and Kettlewell agreed with imposition, as did Footman, who said: 'indeed this Government had no option'. The opinions of Bucquet and Marshall, neither of them a member of executive council, were also sought. Both believed that federation should be imposed. Marshall thought that there would be trouble on only a small scale and that there would be just as much trouble if the proposals were dropped on account of African opposition. Bucquet held that the recent Mau Mau events in Kenya were an argument for proceeding rather than the reverse. Colby did not express his personal opinion; he simply wished his advisers to state their opinions and the British government to make up its mind.

At the December 1952 meeting of legislative council,[94] Colby spoke of the Nyasaland African Congress's reaction to the federal proposals, and publicly clarified his attitude towards Congress:

> The original aims and reasons for the formation of the Congress were unexceptionable. There is no reason why any racial group should not form an organization to look after its interests and to further its legitimate aspirations, and so long as such a body concerns itself with such activities there can be no criticism of it. I have, however, been concerned to note in the last year or two that the activities of Congress members have gone beyond these laudable objects. There have been instances in every province of the Protectorate in which Congress members have sought to undermine confidence in the administration and in the central Government and have incited both chiefs and civil servants to displays of irresponsibility and disloyalty. To what extent this policy is being directed by the heads of Congress or is being carried out by individual members on their own initiative I cannot say, but the fact remains that the heads of Congress cannot divest themselves of the responsibility for these acts of their members since I have seen no indication that they have been discouraged from headquarters. The activities which I have mentioned, if continued, will do untold harm to the future of this country and I shall not hesitate to use the full resources of the Government to check them. . . . The future of this territory will depend on racial harmony and understanding, and anybody of whatever race who directs his activities to stirring up racial hatred is an enemy of Nyasaland. I can only express the hope that all the leaders of African thought will take note of my remarks and make sure that the activities of all their sympathisers are not only within the law but are directed towards the progress of this country. In particular, I would suggest to the Native Authorities, who hold their position from Government and are bound both in law and in the general interests of their people to assist the administration in the maintenance of good government in their areas, that they should pause and consider carefully the situation which I have outlined and where the future happiness and welfare of the people lie.

Notwithstanding Colby's warnings, the conference of chiefs held in the same month was attended by Congress leaders, nominally as advisers but actually dominating the proceedings.[95] This event set the seal upon the development which was taking place in which the vast majority of chiefs adhered to the line taken by Congress over federation.

Just before Christmas 1952, Colby travelled to Britain ready for the opening of the Carlton House Terrace conference on 1 January 1953,[96] and in particular to urge the colonial secretary to make up his mind on Britain's preparedness to impose federation. The purpose of the conference was to consider further the draft scheme in the light of the three preparatory commission reports and to reach agreement on a revised scheme which could be submitted to the electorate of Southern Rhodesia and the legislatures of Northern Rhodesia and Nyasaland. The conference was chaired jointly by Lyttelton and Lord Swinton, secretary of state for Commonwealth relations.[97]

The representations Colby made, and the general stance he adopted, at the Carlton House Terrace conference were based upon a brief he had presented to executive council on 17 December 1952[98] immediately before he left for Britain, and were in accordance with the view he had formed – resulting from an assessment of the existing relative strengths of the European and African political organizations – that a thwarted European opposition would present a longer-lasting and less reparable threat to race relations than would a thwarted African opposition. It was typical of Colby that he should view politics and race relations from the perspective of their impact on economic development:

> The line taken throughout is that the Nyasaland delegation should do all in its power to achieve a Federal Scheme which has the best chance of acceptance by all administrations and interests concerned. Not only has prolonged examination proved beyond doubt that Federation will be of the greatest economic value to this territory but it is all-important to bear in mind the consequences of a failure to federate, after all that has gone before. It is probable that the internal political situation, in the event of a rejection or an indefinite postponement of the Federal proposals, would deteriorate to a point where race relations would seriously affect the country's economy.

It followed from this, Colby said, that every caution should be exercised in opposing Southern Rhodesian suggestions to modify the draft scheme and where possible their views should be accepted, given four important provisos. First, the Nyasaland government's responsibility for the welfare of its African population should not be weakened or impinged upon: he was taking his obligations as governor of a protectorate very seriously. Second, the scheme should be acceptable to the British government, whichever political party was in power – although he must have been convinced that a Labour government would accept federation only, if at all, with the most rigorous safeguards of African interests. He knew, of course, that the possibilities of securing acceptance by a Labour government were remote, but he did not want a federation once imposed to be subsequently quickly abandoned. Third, the suggested amendments should not be in a form so obvious and so reactionary as to 'give a handle even to uninformed African opposition'. Finally, the future of colonial civil servants in Nyasaland should not be prejudiced. In particular, and most important, Colby felt that the draft scheme's proposals were financially so favourable to Nyasaland that it would be worth a number of concessions to preserve the basic framework of the proposals. All of this, however, was subject to the important consideration that it was 'highly desirable' that the British government should indicate now whether it was prepared to impose federation:

> If Her Majesty's Government indicate that they would not be prepared to impose federation, then the implementation of the scheme would be impossible, and there would be nothing to be gained by acceding to Southern Rhodesian demands for modification of the draft scheme and, tactically, much to be lost.

This was the general position Colby took at the Carlton House Terrace conference. During the conference, an African delegation, including a number of chiefs, flew to London to mount a public campaign against federation. They asked to see the Queen as their 'Mother and Protector', they emphasized their mistrust of European settlers, and they received a much-publicized telegram of support from Chief Mwase, who also denounced federation and placed reliance on the impartiality of the Crown.[99] The London *Times* pointed out the seriousness of the chiefs' support for Congress's anti-federation views and the consequent threat of breaking the link of loyalty to government: 'Nobody cares to contemplate what would happen if this link was broken.'[100]

The chamber of commerce bridled at the 'mistrust of settlers' remarks of the African delegation and, ignoring the contribution of African agriculture under Colby's development strategy in the past half-decade,

demanded – in offensive terms that could scarcely have helped race
relations – that the Nyasaland government should give the fullest possible
publicity to the 'actual position' by preparing and issuing a 'factual'
statement on the way in which the settlers were:

> mainly if not entirely responsible for what economic progress the
> country had made during the past seventy years: i.e. from the time
> when the African inhabitants were completely uncivilized human
> beings scratching a bare living from the soil.[101]

The Carlton House Terrace conference concluded its deliberations in
public agreement and produced a constitution for the federal state,
shortly to be embodied in a White Paper:

> We are convinced that a federation ... is the only practical means
> by which the three Central African territories can achieve security
> for the future and ensure the well-being and contentment of all
> their peoples. We believe that this Federal Scheme is a sound and
> fair scheme which will promote the essential interests of all the
> inhabitants of the three territories, and that it should be carried
> through.[102]

The Nyasaland African leaders were now desperate.[103] Dr Banda and
the representatives who had gone to London to see the Queen predicted
bloodshed. Paramount Chief Mbelwa made known his view that Britain
could impose federation only with bombs and guns, and Chief Maganga
said of the British, 'They are a powerful country ... They can come
here and kill every child, man and woman, and then they can federate
our country.'

Dr Banda addressed a public meeting at Church House, Westminster,
and claimed the protection of the Atlantic Charter which guaranteed all
people the right to choose the form of government under which they
wished to live. On Sunday 5 April, an emergency general meeting of
the Nyasaland African Congress was held in Blantyre and addressed
by the Rev Michael Scott, a Briton with an international reputation as
a vociferous opponent of the South African government, who had arrived
to advise Congress with instructions from Dr Banda to initiate a campaign of civil disobedience.[104] The meeting considered what it should
do if federation were imposed as a result of the referendum in Southern
Rhodesia the following Thursday. They agreed to set up a council of

action consisting of chiefs, Congress members and the African members of legislative council – potentially a very powerful group capable of commanding the following of virtually the whole African population – to 'consider and direct the resistance movement' which would include widespread stoppages of work (including that in the Civil Service), withdrawal of labour from farms and estates, stoppage of labour recruitment for Southern Rhodesia, non-payment of all types of taxes, non-collaboration in district, provincial and legislative councils, boycotting of European markets and stores, and appeals to the United Nations Organization and the International Court of Justice.

On 9 April, the electorate of Southern Rhodesia overwhelmingly accepted the federal proposals in a referendum. The following Sunday another meeting – lasting six hours – was held in Blantyre attended by Scott, Congress members and many chiefs, and chaired by Chief Mwase, who explained to those assembled the points which the chiefs had raised in London with the colonial secretary, including demands to replace the governor, the chief secretary, the secretary for African affairs and the provincial commissioners, and expressing their bitter disappointment at being refused permission to see the Queen. Chief Mwase and two dozen other traditional leaders asked to be heard at the Bar of the House of Commons or, alternatively, for the Commons to appoint a select committee to determine the true feelings of the Africans of Nyasaland.[105]

Executive council discussed the question of internal security on Thursday 16 April, and Barrow asked if government was satisfied that it had all the legislative powers necessary to deal with any possible action taken against the federal proposals. In particular he expressed his view that the majority of estate and industrial workers would not wish to stay away from work or to strike in political sympathy with Congress agitation, but that they could easily be frightened into doing so.[106]

The following Monday, legislative council in its sixty-eighth session[107] opened with the chief secretary moving, ' . . . that this Council is in favour of the federation of Southern Rhodesia, Northern Rhodesia and Nyasaland in terms of the proposals contained in Parliamentary White Paper, Command 8754.'

Every member of legislative council then spoke and the chief secretary replied to their speeches. Finally, Colby reread the motion and asked, 'Would those in favour of the motion, rise?'. Mposa and Muwamba walked out,[108] all nine officials and Barrow, Hadlow, Dixon, Hunt and Mrs Sharpe rose, whilst Dayaram and Doig remained seated in dissent. Colby cast his deliberative vote in favour of the motion and declared:

'The motion is carried by 15 votes to two'. The governor's forecast of how the non-officials would vote, made over a year earlier, proved correct.

Two principal concerns occupied the thoughts and energies of Colby and his officials in the following six months: finance and security.

The financial secretary had been a member of the fiscal commission, and the Nyasaland government accepted that the fiscal report was very favourable to the protectorate. In responding to the reports of the three commissions, the final papers prepared in the secretariat covered one sheet in respect of the judicial report, two sheets in respect of the Civil Service report, and eight in the case of the fiscal report.[109] It was finance in which Colby was most interested. He was convinced that Nyasaland could survive and develop on its own, but if it were obliged to join a federation he was going to get the best financial deal out of it that he could. In briefing his officials prior to the March 1951 conference, he had told them to keep in the forefront of their minds 'what benefits would accrue to Nyasaland from closer association,'[110] and it was to this that he henceforth devoted his thoughts and energies.

Much of the documentation now prepared for him by the financial secretary was very detailed and was designed to secure advantage on numerous points. The general advice which he received was:

> The Fiscal Commission's Report will, if adopted, be advantageous to Nyasaland and will hold out a prospect of the Protectorate being able to function on an even financial keel and with reasonable prospects of finance for development expenditure being available on a scale commensurate with the country's need and in accordance with the capacity of the country to absorb development monies.[111]

Colby accepted this advice – which concerned a matter most dear to his heart – and informed the other governments that all three commission reports were, save for minor points, acceptable to Nyasaland.[112] If anything was going to persuade him to go along with federation, it was the prospect of more adequate finance for the protectorate's development. It was the good financial deal which he stood to get which made him prepared to make other concessions at the Carlton House Terrace conference which led up to the legislative council vote in April.

Colby also turned his attention to securing adequate capital funds for the continued development of Nyasaland.[113] He had exhausted the £3 million loan agreed to in 1949, and nearly all the Colonial Development and Welfare Fund allocation, and yet half of what he hoped to accomplish under the post-war development plan remained to be tackled. He had pressed the British government to agree to a further £3 million loan being raised and to additional sums being granted from the CDWF, but it was reluctant to agree since the projects for which Colby wished to secure finance were all likely soon to become federal responsibilities: reconstruction of the main Lilongwe-Salima road; building an all-weather aerodrome at Salima; continuing the main road reconstruction between Mlanje and the Mozambique border; erecting a group hospital and a European boarding school in Blantyre; and building a permanent terminal at Chileka airport.

Colby was anxious not to fall between two stools: the British government, which was in the process of somewhat bowing out of the scene, and the federal government, which had not yet entered the stage. He exploited his position between the two with great ingenuity. Publicly he argued that he needed an early favourable decision because two major construction contractors were getting near the end of their contracts, and unless further work was forthcoming they would withdraw from the protectorate. This would be very unfortunate since they had taken a good deal of time to adjust to Nyasaland conditions but had now done so; if they left it would be very difficult to get others, and those others would also take time to adjust, which would be unnecessarily costly.[114] Less publicly he used the argument that both the British and the federal governments would wish to be seen in a favourable light in respect of federation, and it would help them to be so seen if it could be announced that significant development finance for Nyasaland had been agreed.[115]

He then set about getting all the parties concerned on his side, and in doing so he used not only the arguments outlined in the preceding paragraph but also his own connections with Rennie, governor of Northern Rhodesia, and with Lloyd at the Colonial Office, Barrow's connections with Huggins and Welensky, and Phillips' connections with Sir Andrew Strachan, until recently secretary to the Southern Rhodesia Treasury and now chairman of the Federal Joint Preparatory Commission.

He began to put together his proposals for further development financing in February and very early March, after the Carlton House Terrace conference but well over a month before the Southern Rhodesia referendum and the Nyasaland legislative council vote on federation, believing that his request had 'a reasonable chance of being approved since the Secretary of State will be anxious to sugar the pill of federation'.[116] He asked his officials to examine his draft proposals very carefully, and if other federal projects occurred to them to mention them for inclusion in the list of projects for which he was seeking finance. Colby appeared optimistic of success and his minutes on the draft request were confident, courteous, friendly and encouraging: they had the air of a man enjoying his work.

On 11 March, he took the proposals to executive council and explained that they would cost about £3 million, but the projects should be put in hand only if the referendum in Southern Rhodesia was favourable to federation:

> The point was that there were heavy capital programmes in Southern and Northern Rhodesia but that there was no such programme in Nyasaland owing to the lack of funding.[117]

It is deducible from this, from the fact that all the projects proposed were in the area of intended federal responsibility, and from his invitation to his officials to mention other 'federal projects' which occurred to them, that Colby had deliberately so selected the projects in order to take the fullest advantage of the larger loan raising and servicing capacity of the federal government. If federation did not come about, he would wish to seek a smaller loan for Nyasaland and one more within its ability to service, and to give priority to projects other than those which he was now putting forward, projects which fell within the proposed territorial, rather than federal, area of responsibility.

Colby sent a personal telegram to Lloyd at the Colonial Office on 7 March[118] dealing with federation and Nyasaland's capital programme, giving him his proposals and asking that the secretary of state should be requested to approve them and that they should be in addition to and independent of other negotiations – on CDWF financing – then in progress. Gorell Barnes answered this telegram;[119] Colby was irritated that Lloyd himself had not replied (although it later transpired that he had approved the draft reply), that the proposals had not been placed before the secretary of state, and that they had not received independent consideration. He consequently wrote a demi-official letter to Lloyd, in effect appealing to him as a senior colleague:

> In recent years we have had many discussions on a wide range of subjects and I have always been left with the impression – a very agreeable impression – that if I wished to give emphasis to a matter which I considered to be of particular importance you were content

that I should address you personally and I should thereby enlist your interest. I have acted in this way on a number of occasions with very helpful results: I only hope I have not overdone it and become a burden.[120]

The Colonial Office response, conveyed again by Gorell Barnes, was that they had put to the Treasury a proposal that Colby should be authorized 'to seek the concurrence of Rennie and Huggins in a minimum programme sufficient to keep the contractors in the territory'.[121] Once again Colby wrote to Lloyd,[122] indicating this time that he found the Colonial Office attitude unhelpful and hinting that he thought they were questioning the motives underlying his proposals and were treating them light-heartedly. He was impatient of talk of minimum requirements. Lloyd, in replying himself to Colby's letter, denied all of these implied criticisms, saying that he shared the feeling of impatience, that he was sympathetic to Colby's requests, and that he was being as helpful as he could be:

So do not take this as a set back to that 'very agreeable impression' which you mentioned at the beginning of your letter. I shall be as ready in the future as I have been in the past to do my best whenever you write to me direct on important topics.[123]

In the meantime, Colby and Barrow had seen Huggins and secured his support for Nyasaland's loan expenditure proposals, and Colby now asked Barrow to write to Welensky to enlist his support.[124] In his letter of 21 May, Barrow told Welensky – whose dislike of the Colonial Office and all its doings Barrow well knew – that they were 'having trouble with the Colonial Office, trying to persuade them to let [Nyasaland] go further ahead with [its] development plans', and added that the Colonial Office would look on the proposals with a more favourable eye if they first secured the backing not only of Huggins, which they already had, but also of Rennie, to whom Colby had just written. Since it was most probable that Rennie would discuss the matter with Welensky, Barrow hoped that Welensky would 'support our modest request':

I need hardly add in conclusion that the early initiation of the next phase of our development programme will be a good advertisement for federation.

Please do all you can to help us in this. We reckon here that with your support added to that of Huggins the Colonial Office opposition will crumble.

Welensky, with some relish, agreed with Colby's proposals and he sought and secured Rennie's support.[125]

Colby's letters to Lloyd were beginning to take effect and he was making some headway in respect of the CDWF application, since the secretary of state arranged to be asked a parliamentary question in the Commons on 17 June:

> Whether notwithstanding financial benefits which will accrue to Nyasaland under federation, Her Majesty's Government with its continued responsibility for that territory are continuing to assist as far as possible its economic and social development.[126]

The secretary of state's reply was affirmative, and added that recently a further £500,000 of CDWF money had been allocated to assist the expanded programme of capital development in economic and social projects, which would bring the total allocation to Nyasaland to £3,872,000. The secretary of state was anxious that this announcement should be made then and not await the final outcome of negotiations over the loan financing.[127]

In respect of the loan proposals, Colby already had the agreement of Huggins and Welensky and the provisional agreement of Rennie, whose support depended upon the Federal Joint Preparatory Commission in Salisbury agreeing to include in the federal development plan the £3 million asked for by Nyasaland. Colby now asked Phillips to approach the chairman to enlist his support. In writing to Strachan on 22 July,[128] Phillips explained that it was necessary to have an early decision because of the imminent departure of the contractors: 'Meantime we are going on stalling with the contractors but we can't do this for much longer!' Phillips' plea was successful and Strachan agreed to allocate £2,225,000 of federal loan money to Nyasaland for the capital projects proposed. On 25 August, the secretary of state authorized Colby to enter into commitment on these projects totalling £2.5m in anticipation of the allocation of the federal loan funds.[129]

Several months of hard and careful work had secured for Colby a satisfactory set of financial arrangements: the federal scheme was financially very favourable to the protectorate; he had secured further allocations from the CDWF; and he had achieved a significant share of the federal loan expenditure.

Colby's thoughts and energies and those of his officials during this period in 1953 were devoted not only to financial matters but also to questions of security. Almost a year earlier, when a visiting journalist told him that most of his officials and the leading figures in Southern Rhodesia did not think that there would be security trouble because there was 'no power to Congress threats', he had replied, 'Do they now? Well I will not go as far as that. I think we will avoid trouble. But then, I have been a long time in the continent – and one never knows in Africa.'[130]

During the April 1953 debate, a procession had formed outside the legislative chamber and chanted anti-federation slogans, at the instigation of a senior African clerk from the Medical Department, and Colby became concerned about the loyalty of African civil servants and their political activities.[131] Eighteen months earlier, his view had been that 'it was not undesirable that African civil servants should at this time be members of Congress'.[132] He had hoped that they would add a moderate element to Congress's deliberations and make Congress's views more acceptable to the British government and to Nyasaland expatriates. Recently he had agreed to the dismissal of an African school teacher for anti-government activities and this had had a quietening effect on other government servants.[133] The activities of the Medical Department clerk, however, were much more blatant and challenging, and Colby sought executive council's advice on what he should do about it.[134] The director of agriculture said the clerk should be dismissed, since decisive action would 'show other Government servants exactly where they stood'; he thought there were a number who believed government was bluffing. The acting attorney-general agreed with dismissal, provided that the person concerned had been previously warned. Fox-Strangways, Barrow and Hadlow agreed, but also believed that there had already been a proper warning and that 'he and others like him fully understood their position'. The acting chief secretary agreed with dismissal, even if there had been no previous warning, because 'the present circumstances alone fully justified dismissal'. For once Colby did not indicate immediately to his advisers exactly what he would do; he directed that the papers on the clerk should be put up to him for his orders.

The security situation – as he had frequently warned in the past – now clearly became one which could deteriorate dangerously and Colby was anxious not to rock the boat more than necessary. He was, therefore,

particularly concerned when the British Central Africa Company, supported by the Convention of Associations, issued large numbers of
eviction notices to rent defaulters on their estates.[135] It was a very
sensitive issue, as he told executive council on 22 April:

> It was most unfortunate that the BCA Company . . . should have
> precipitated this question at the present time. The question of land
> was one on which the African felt most strongly. Indeed it was
> probable that he felt more strongly on this question than on feder-
> ation and it was doubly unfortunate that he would inevitably link
> the two in his mind. It was desirable that all possible steps should
> be taken to see that the present situation should not recur.

Colby asked if it would be desirable to mobilize public opinion against
the company's attitude. Barrow advised against this on the grounds that
public castigation might have the effect of rallying public opinion round
the company's general manager, Dixon.

Another potential boat-rocking issue also arose at this time but was
more easily dealt with. Huggins wanted to broadcast a message, relayed
in Chinyanja to Nyasaland Africans, publicizing federation. Colby's reply
was that such a broadcast would be 'politically unfortunate' and would
cause an adverse reaction among Nyasaland Africans.[136]

Anticipating that any positive steps by Africans to demonstrate their
opposition to federation would include strike action and absenteeism
induced by intimidation, Colby discussed this probability in executive
council, particularly since he had information that 1 May, Labour Day,
might be used for demonstrations by strike action.[137] Council advised
that a notice should be published 'to reassure Africans who wished to
work that Government would do all in its power to protect them from
intimidation or violence', and advising them that those who attempted
to intimidate them into staying away from work were committing an
offence. Colby asked for a draft to be given to him to this effect that
afternoon. He accepted and issued the notice and backed it up a little
later by a letter to employers asking them:

> to assist in inculcating a spirit of confidence in their employees by
> explaining to them that the vague threats of intimidation which had
> recently been spread about by members of the African Congress
> were in fact empty threats, and that Government would give every
> protection to people who ignored them.[138]

On 6 May, a directive was circulated throughout Nyasaland, signed by the 'Clerk of the Nyasaland African Supreme Council' and cited as 'Order No. Cl/5/53', which ordered Africans not to attend a list of 11 specified governmental bodies, ordered chiefs not to issue exit permits to prospective emigrant workers, ordered Africans to boycott the imminent coronation celebrations and ended:

> All you Africans must know that we are at a sad event crying for our country, and there must be no one to create dances, or happiness, which does not help us to fight against federation that it may cease.[139]

Colby saw in this and related indications of imminent disruption the hand of Scott, and the question of refusing an extension to his visitor's pass was considered by executive council the following day.[140] Colby's own view was that in such cases government had to choose the lesser of two evils. He accepted the dangers which were pressed upon him if Scott were to remain, but it was also necessary to look at the other side of the question. He thought that Scott 'was an agitator rather than a criminal and his primary characteristic was a desire to remain in the limelight'. Colby felt that if Scott remained in Nyasaland for a further month he would not necessarily have the continued success which he had achieved so far: he 'doubted whether it was possible successfully to go on repeating the same opinions and complaints at public meetings'. If Scott stayed it was doubtful if anything further would happen, and even if there were disturbances Scott would lose credit with the Fabians, who opposed violence. Colby believed Scott to be 'the worst kind of nuisance', but possibly also something of a restraining influence on the more aggressive Congress leaders and members. If, on the other hand, Scott were deported, he would make great political capital out of it and it would provide Congress with 'a new focus for allegations against Government'. He would also in practice have a few days in which to leave during which he could publicize his expulsion and advise African leaders on the lines of propaganda they should follow. This was a restrained, unruffled, balanced, objective assessment of the position by Colby, who weighed the arguments and then, despite advice to the contrary from Fox-Strangways, Barrow and Hadlow,[141] extended Scott's visitor's pass for three weeks.[142]

Six days later, Chief Gomani of the Ncheu district circulated a directive ordering his people to disregard agricultural, forestry, veterinary and tax laws. He refused the government's request to withdraw these orders and Colby thereupon suspended him from the office of Native Authority with effect from 19 May.[143] On 24 May, Gomani was given 24 hours by Colby to remove himself from the Ncheu district. The chief refused, the police were called in to arrest him, a riot ensued, and Gomani escaped into Mozambique with Scott.[144] Colby attributed the Ncheu and other troubles to the activities of Congress 'encouraged by troublemakers from outside' Nyasaland and 'reinforced by widespread intimidation'. He revoked Scott's visitor's pass and issued a deportation order against him.[145] He also called Chinyama to see him in Zomba and personally warned him and other Congress leaders 'where this foolishness could lead'.[146]

Things seemed to quieten down for a while after this and Colby and his wife were able to travel to Bulawayo with the governor of Northern Rhodesia and Lady Rennie to attend the official opening of the Rhodes centenary exhibition by the Queen Mother. They were the guests of the governor of Southern Rhodesia and Lady Kennedy.[147]

Chief Mwase wrote to *The Nyasaland Times* on 13 July and lamented:

> We are not protesting blindly. We are protesting for our future centuries. We cannot sell our freedom. I am sorry that many officials and some of the Lords feel that it is an easy thing to oppress us in this way . . .
>
> Even today we trust . . . Queen Elizabeth II will . . . not hand us over to a Government which . . . aims to use Africans [as] labourers and not as partners.[148]

Mwase's hope was in vain, however, since the Commons had already agreed to the passage of the Federation Bill, the Lords followed shortly after and the Queen then assented to it. The affirmative resolution on the Order in Council bringing the federation into force passed both houses of parliament on 28 July.[149] The federation became a legal entity on 1 August 1953.

A fortnight after his return from Bulawayo, Colby was given a sharp warning of events shortly to come.[150] During the morning of Thursday 16 July, a large number of African villagers entered the Mkhani estate in the Cholo district and began to chop down trees and open up new gardens without the owner's permission. This was a deliberate, open and provocative act in an area of much alienated land and high settler population, two months before the normal garden preparation season.

An administrative officer from Blantyre, a detachment of African police and 30 European special constables went to Mkhani, and the 500 people there – who were polite and friendly – dispersed peacefully and left the estate. The incident was designed partly as a warning and partly to test the reaction of the government and its security forces. A year earlier, almost exactly to the day, Colby had taken a proposal to executive council 'that a striking force of thirty European Constables should be formed at Cholo ready for use in any disturbance that might occur anywhere in the Protectorate'.[151] Consequently, the security forces were virtually ready and waiting for the Mkhani testing of their strength. Even so, Colby had an amendment made to the Police Ordinance which enabled him to request reinforcements from neighbouring British colonial police forces if he needed to do so.[152]

A far more serious incident occurred a month later, also in the Cholo district.[153] On 18 August, at Mangunde estate, the owner caught two Africans in the act of stealing oranges. Immediately a large crowd assembled and forced the release of the two men before dispersing. The following morning, the district commissioner, with a small party of police, went to Mangunde only to be faced with a large crowd which dragged him from the verandah from which he addressed them. Reinforcements of police, including European special constables, arrived from Blantyre and baton-charged the crowd to disperse them. One African was killed and a number of others, including police, were injured before the crowd broke up and moved off.

Colby – who had repeatedly and over a long period warned the British government of the security dangers of including Nyasaland in the federation – immediately placed the country's security forces on alert and set up a commission of enquiry under the chairmanship of the chief justice to enquire into the disturbances and their causes and to make recommendations.[154]

The disturbances spread, however, as labourers on the Cholo tea estates and the railways went on strike, telephone lines were cut down, stones were thrown at vehicles, and roadblocks were erected. Intimidation and looting occurred. The police and King's African Rifles, assisted – at Colby's request – by reinforcements of 100 Northern Rhodesia and 50 Tanganyika police, carried out frequent and widespread patrols to disperse crowds and to clear roadblocks.[155] Barrow made the point to his fellow executive councillors that the disturbances showed 'the importance and need for a large federal police force which could be moved from territory to territory as desired'.[156] The worst affected area was the Cholo district, from which many Indian traders and about 40 European women and children moved temporarily into Blantyre.[157]

The prosecution of a village headman, Mgamwane, for being implicated in the rioting brought about a serious situation as 3000 Africans crowded around the Cholo magistrate's courtroom on Wednesday 26 August.[158] The prosecution was withdrawn at the last moment but the crowd refused to disperse. The police used tear gas and batons on the crowd, which they then pursued for two miles in order finally to disperse them. Police patrols intensified and Colby asked for, and received, three reconnaissance aircraft from the Southern Rhodesia Air Force to obtain information on crowd concentrations and roadblocks.[159]

At noon on Friday 28 August, Colby broadcast a message on Blue Band Radio, the police broadcasting channel.[160] His general tone was one of confident firmness, as his opening words indicated: 'In the last few days we have been getting organized to deal with the bother at Cholo.' He assured his listeners that there were now sufficient security forces to deal with the situation, and emphasized the need to get back to normal as soon as possible. He urged everyone to get on with their ordinary jobs and he particularly urged employers to stay in close, reassuring touch with their employees and provide them with leadership and support. 'In other words, business as usual.' He encouraged expatriates to set up their own intelligence organization and to feed information to the police. They should exercise their rights of self-defence, but not otherwise take the law into their own hands. In tones worthy of an Old Carthusian – especially one who as a schoolboy had helped to extinguish a major fire in the morning and had returned to normal school-work in the afternoon – he concluded with the words:

> From time to time every country has its trouble and this is our testing time. The British people would not be the greatest force for good in Africa today if they could not come through a test like this with flying colours. It is up to all of us. Good luck, and remember 'Business as usual'.

The disturbances – as the government called them for many years to come, and which *The Nyasaland Times* referred to as 'our present little domestic squabbles'[161] – continued for a while longer. Chief Kadewere and his wife were tied up by rioters in Chiradzulu, and crowds attempted to 'depose' a number of chiefs loyal to government. Roadblocks, unlawful assemblies, patrols, tear gas, baton charges, village searches, arrests, seizure of arms and weapons, prosecutions – including a number for sedition – and widespread disruption continued, especially in the Southern Province, and the Nyasaland, Northern Rhodesia and Tanganyika police were reinforced, again at Colby's request, by a force of 30 European and 40 African members of the British South Africa Police from Southern Rhodesia.[162]

Colby's actions – his broadcast message, the frequent use of Blue Band Radio as an information medium, his 'business as usual' style, the prompt bringing in of police reinforcements from neighbouring territories, the prosecutions, and the creation of an African special constabulary[163] – soon began to have an effect and the country gradually returned to its normal peaceful condition. Colby was not, however, able – or possibly not disposed – to travel to Salisbury for the formal arrival of the governor-general of the federation on 1 September.[164]

Colby called Chinyama to see him at the end of August, and addressed him in the most direct and severe tones, reminding him that his father had been summarily executed in 1915 for his part in leading the Ncheu supplementary rising during the Chilembwe rising.[165] Following this sharp, blunt warning from the governor, Chinyama was much chastened. Colby suggested – virtually instructed – that Chinyama should visit the disturbed areas in the Cholo district, denounce violence on the spot, and encourage people to quieten down; he made the point that no matter how provoked Congress members might feel, no degree of provocation justified violence and that the cause of Congress was being harmed by the rioting, intimidation and damage in the Cholo district.[166]

Colby's blunt and direct tactics worked: Chinyama took the point, decided that discretion was the better part of valour, and visited Cholo during the week 13–20 September, along with Chief Mwase, and addressed a number of African audiences, saying that as leader of Congress he had always been and still was totally opposed to violence 'because I believe that it will help neither the African nor the European cause':

No matter how genuine the grievances may be of the tenants and other land-hungry people in Cholo, no responsible African leader can approve of these incidents . . . I believe that our cause will only be harmed by the use of violence or even the threat of violence. Those who follow Congress must be prepared to turn their face against violence. That is the path we wish to walk.[167]

The voice was Chinyama's but the words were Colby's. Other Congress leaders followed suit and the secretary-general, Mtalika Banda, announced to the press that:

> the passive resistance and non-cooperation policy which . . . Congress [pursued] against federation has been abandoned. [Africans] in Nyasaland have been urged to cooperate with the Government.[168]

No doubt Chinyama and his colleagues were influenced by the fact that the Nyasaland Council of Chiefs had recently denounced violence and non-co-operation, and were also conscious of the growing strength of a newly formed African political party, the Nyasaland African Progressive Association, which was led by a number of well-respected African civil servants. The Progressive Association was very much more likely to command the respect and ear of the government and the expatriate communities than was Congress. At a meeting on 6 September,[169] the chairman, Matinga, said that:

> since federation [has] now become an accomplished fact it is the duty of all right thinking Africans to look forward to the future and help in the building up of a strong, happy and prosperous Central Africa, and consider the place of Nyasaland Africans in the Federation.

He concluded by saying that the Association would be pleased to welcome 'all Africans who have the welfare of our country at heart and want to . . . help build good racial relations by subscribing to a policy of cooperation'.

Just as Chinyama's words at this time sounded like Colby, so Matinga's words sounded like Hess, who encouraged Africans to join the Progressive Association: 'It is to the Nyasaland African Progressive Party that all sensible Africans will look for guidance in the years to come.'[170]

Clearly, Colby's dressing-down and the support being given to the Progressive Association deeply influenced Chinyama, who could see that a rival or alternative African political party could readily sound Congress's death knell. It may well have been the view of the governor and his senior officials that once the federation came into existence and its benefits became more obvious, the influence of Congress would fade.[171]

Successful as Colby was in bringing a relatively swift end to the disturbances, and in weakening Congress by straight talk to Chinyama and by encouraging more moderate African opinion, and much as he was admired by Europeans in Nyasaland for these actions, others saw him differently, especially Joelson. In an editorial of 10 September, he attacked Colby viciously, blaming the growth of Congress from a 'small coterie of disgruntled politically inclined Africans . . . in such junior official jobs as clerks . . . and teachers' on the fact that 'the Government of Nyasaland [had] ceased long ago to give recognizable leadership'. He compared Colby unfavourably with Rennie, whom he praised for having travelled widely, meeting Africans of all types, telling them the 'blunt truth' and counselling them to loyal obedience:

> Because there has been no comparable display of initiative, energy and firmness in Nyasaland it is there that violence has now to be suppressed. . . . Disregarding the warning of settlers that bloodshed would follow, the Government adopted an attitude of appeasement to the African trouble makers. Is it surprising that they continued their machinations? Northern Rhodesia had already clapped a number of the worst offenders in gaol, dismissed others who were on the official payroll and restored a sense of realism. If Nyasaland had done the same, lives would have been saved and great damage to race relations averted.[172]

Joelson chose to ignore the facts that Colby had travelled widely – much more so than any of his predecessors, except possibly Johnston and Sharpe in the very earliest days of the protectorate; was in touch with all shades of African opinion through his district commissioners, the system of protectorate, provincial and district councils, and the normal government intelligence network; had deposed some Native Authorities and ensured that the others 'toed the line'; had brought in police from neighbouring countries; had set up European and African special constabularies and had expanded the regular force; had taken an extremely firm line with Chinyama; and, virtually alone, had for years warned of the political and security dangers of not carrying African opinion along with federation. It is true that Colby was reluctant to clap political opponents in goal or strike them off the official payroll – which Joelson somehow thought would improve race relations. He was also reluctant to exacerbate matters by taking extreme action even when advised to do so by 'the warnings of settlers', whom he told that to do what they suggested might very well result in them getting their own throats cut.[173]

It may, however, be the case that Joelson knew, by some means or other, that at the very time he published his attack, the Nyasaland executive council was carefully pondering the question of whether a state of emergency should be declared, and he may also have known that, notwithstanding the advice of his security advisers, Colby was not convinced that such a declaration was either necessary or prudent. Indeed, Barrow, who raised the question in executive council on 1 September – only nine days before the appearance of Joelson's editorial – said that 'in certain quarters there might be criticism that the disturbances were not being handled with sufficient force'.[174] If Joelson knew of these discussions, his article might well have been designed to put pressure on Colby to declare a state of emergency.

Hess, who reprinted Joelson's attack in full in *The Nyasaland Times*,[175] for once did not share Joelson's views, but pointed out that although Colby had the means and could have quashed the disturbances in a few days, he had to handle the situation with one eye on the disturbances and the other on 'a vociferous opposition Labour Party and its Fabian hangers-on'. Hess believed that Colby handled 'what might have been an extremely dangerous situation in an entirely adequate manner' by treating the disturbances purely and simply as a police matter, with the result, although perhaps fortuitously, entirely justifying his approach:

Finally, we think that in so far as the Nyasaland Government's handling of the disturbances is concerned, the proof of the pudding is in the eating. The disturbance is at an end; probably there will never be a recurrence . . . No damage of any consequence – physically, materially, or to morale – has resulted and both communities are friends once again as they have been for so many years.[176]

Colby was glad of Hess's support on this occasion, although he recognized that by reprinting Joelson's article Hess had spread the malicious and unfavourable attack.

By the middle of September, when Colby visited all the operational centres in the Southern Province with General Alexander Cameron,[177] the security situation was under control but he was very conscious of two things: first, the cost of having secured and of maintaining peaceful conditions; and second, the underlying causes of the disturbances remained and had not been tackled – federation and land. He told executive council that it was of the utmost importance to realize the significance of the disturbances and was strongly supported by Fox-

Strangways, who said that, unless government and others understood the omens and took early action, trouble would recur in a form which would be very hard to deal with.[178]

Although the security situation was under control, it was holding the government machine in what was virtually a continual state of alert and was costing a good deal of money – money which Colby would have preferred to devote to further economic development. It was typical that he saw even the declaration of a state of emergency from the point of view of its effect on economic development. Consequently, he sought the advice of executive council on the need for, and wisdom of, declaring a formal state of emergency.[179] Colby and Fox-Strangways emphasized the political disadvantage of doing so, whilst Barrow again pointed to the possibility of outside criticism if the disturbances were not handled with sufficient firmness. Hadlow, clearly worried and nervous, felt that there might be a danger of a general uprising if police or military operations became widespread, he believed that 'the disturbances could not end until the gang leaders themselves had been exterminated'. Cameron asked, and answered, two questions. First: is it a matter of vital importance to end the present emergency and to take the consequences which might result in the application of any additional power that was taken to end the emergency? He answered this question in the affirmative on the grounds that although the activities of the 'insurgents' – as he repeatedly called them – had been confined without any large loss of life, this state of affairs might not continue. Second: could the present disorders soon be ended with the existing means at government's disposal? He answered this question in the negative and concluded that a state of emergency should be declared.

Colby listened very carefully to this advice and concluded that it was necessary to declare a state of emergency but that this need not necessarily be done immediately:

> He suggested that all the preparations should be made but that the actual signing of the proclamation could be deferred until these were complete. If at that time it was apparent that there was no need for him as Governor to sign the proclamation the decision could be revoked.[180]

As a result, it was provisionally decided to declare a state of emergency in approximately ten days' time – about 26 September – and that preparations for this should be made immediately.

On 24 September, however, Colby asked each member of executive council and others present individually whether the draft declaration of a state of emergency should be implemented.[181] Cameron and Apthorpe, commissioner of police, said that a declaration should be made; the secretary for African affairs, attorney-general, director of agriculture, chief secretary and acting financial secretary said that a state of emergency ought not to be declared. Hadlow was not present and Barrow seemed to be of the opinion that a state of emergency should be declared. Colby then told executive council that he proposed to inform the secretary of state that he did not intend to declare a state of emergency and that, although the situation had improved, it was essential to emphasize the fact that the danger of further unrest remained and consequently it was necessary to introduce legislation enabling government to detain persons as proposed in the draft emergency regulations. Cameron felt that the acquisition of such powers by government was essential.

No further outbreaks of violence occurred and things had so quietened down by early November that the last of the Northern Rhodesia mobile police units returned to their home country.[182]

In the meantime, federation had become a legal *fait accompli*. Colby had originally advised the British government against Nyasaland's inclusion, not because he objected so much to the idea of federation but rather because he was convinced that there was no goodwill towards the protectorate or understanding of its problems in Salisbury. Having had that advice rejected – and having decided not to resign over the issue as he had contemplated[183] – and having seen some of the political and security trouble which the federal proposals had already caused, but having nonetheless faithfully, indeed skillfully, guided the country into the federation, he now had two and a half years ahead of him in which to guide – or at least govern – it through the early stages of its life within the federation.

A number of formal and inevitable steps were taken in setting up the federal political and legal structure. The Nyasaland representatives in the federal legislature were elected or appointed in December 1953. Colby appointed the Rev Andrew Doig, W. M. Chirwa and C. R. Kumbikano.[184] When he had originally asked Doig to accept nomination to represent African interests, Doig had, after a while, declined, whereupon Colby – presumably not wishing to be accused of delay – asked an experienced and much-respected education officer, who readily accepted. Shortly after this, Doig, under some pressure from friends, changed his mind, and Colby had the unpleasant task of telling the education officer whose wife, in her excitement, had already told some of her friends of her husband's 'appointment'. In the event Colby handled the difficulty with great tact and kindness, being instrumental in securing a British university appointment for the officer after his retirement, which soon followed.[185]

The European voters elected to the federal legislature Bucquet, president of the chamber of commerce, with 903 votes; J. Foot, leader of the Northern Provinces Association, with 879 votes; F. P. Brereton, founder of the Nyasaland Association and a leading figure in the tobacco industry, with 822 votes; and Barrow, with 808 votes – all members of the Federal Party.[186] Barrow was paying the price of having been too closely associated with the Nyasaland government as senior non-official member of both legislative and executive councils and a known close confidant of Colby. He asked Colby if, in view of his low rating in the election, he should stand down from the federal assembly, but Colby strongly advised against this since he was, in Colby's view, the only man worthy of the position.[187] The governor may also have hoped that, after years of closely working with the Nyasaland government, Barrow would be able to exercise significant pro-Nyasaland influence in the federal assembly and cabinet, 'armed with Colby's arguments'.[188]

In consequence of the federal constitution provisions, a number of government departments became the responsibility of the federal government. This change took place formally on 1 September 1954, although much of the operational, practical transfer took place during the preceding 12 months.[189] All the officers in these departments were then seconded to the federal Civil Service: Posts and Telecommunications, Civil Aviation, Health, Prisons, Customs and Immigration, Income Tax, Audit, and non-African Education – a total of eight departments with 2640 of Nyasaland's 8758 civil servants.[190] These, now-federal, departments included all the major revenue-collecting departments – Income and Profits Tax, Customs and Excise – but only one major revenue-earning department – Posts and Telecommunications. Only Health directly affected the lives of the majority of the African population.

Other early changes, mainly a formality from Nyasaland's point of view, included the creation of a federal supreme court, the issue of federal postage stamps and currency, and the appointment of the governor-general, Lord Llewellyn. In mid-August, when it was anticipated that the governor-general might wish to make an early visit to the protectorate, Colby took the view that 'such a visit would be inadvisable at the present juncture' because of the security position in Nyasaland.[191] When the governor-general arrived in the federation – in a special South African Railways coach – on 1 September 1953, Colby, Sinclair (the chief justice) and Barrow were prevented by the continuing security problems from being present.[192] The governor-general, however, accompanied by Huggins and Barrow, made a special one-day visit by air to Nyasaland on 1 October, had 'informal conversations' with Colby, lunched at Government House, and returned during the afternoon to Salisbury.[193] Colby's first meeting with the federation's governor-general and with Huggins as federal prime minister was therefore on Nyasaland ground and lasted a very short time.

Colby also took early steps to attempt to have a Government House for the governor-general built in Nyasaland.[194] He mentioned the idea to Barrow and the governor-general, both of whom favoured the idea.[195] Colby then wrote to Huggins saying that from time to time the question of building a Government House in Blantyre had been considered, partly as a means of lessening the division between the Blantyre commercial and the Zomba official communities, but he felt that to occupy it himself for a few weeks each year would be insufficient justification:

> I feel however that the federation brings this proposal nearer and I wondered what you would think of the idea of building a house in Blantyre which would be used by the Governor-General, myself and by visiting federal ministers.[196]

In this way, Colby hoped to make the federal presence in Nyasaland at the highest level a reality, to secure federal expenditure on a building which he himself could use, and to try to heal the rift which many saw between himself and his senior officials on the one hand and leading members of the non-official community on the other. For a while Huggins and his ministers not only welcomed Colby's proposals but wanted a somewhat larger residence than Colby, who did not feel that 'a large barrack' was needed. He was aware that many of the contacts, certainly the political contacts, of federal ministers would be with Europeans in the Blantyre area, and he would have found it convenient on a variety of grounds to have them accommodated in an official residence which he himself could also use. Colby showed Huggins and Barrow three possible sites in April 1954, but in the event the Blantyre Government House was not built.

Once he was sure that the disturbances in the Southern Province had indeed died down and no longer presented a security problem, Colby went on leave to Britain; he was away from 13 May to 11 November 1954.[197] Whilst on leave, he reflected on recent events and was able to 'see rather more of the wood and less of the trees' than would have been possible had he not been able to stand back from those events, and he concluded in respect of federation that he – and Benson, now governor of Northern Rhodesia – had 'a heavy responsibility . . . vis-à-vis HMG'. He was particularly worried about Southern Rhodesia's attitude towards Africans, the hardening of anti-African opinion, and the growth of racial intolerance fuelled by unwise and provocative public statements by federal MPs, especially Brereton and Bucquet.[198]

Only two weeks after his return from leave, he visited Huggins, now prime minister of the federation, with whom he had a number of talks during which Huggins agreed to his request that Colby should write to him, on a purely personal basis, giving his thoughts on a number of pressing problems in Central Africa.[199] He also had a long talk with Barrow whom he found to be 'very depressed', and who said that Southern Rhodesia 'already has apartheid in all but name', a remark which Colby found 'illuminating'. As a result he began to doubt – incorrectly as it turned out – whether Barrow would 'stay the course'.[200]

During September, Colby drafted a letter to Huggins, a letter which he clearly believed to be one of great importance: it was lengthy and detailed – over a dozen pages of typed foolscap – and he sent copies of the draft to Footman (who suggested 12 amendments, ten of which Colby ignored or rejected),[201] to Gorell Barnes and to Benson.[202] It dealt with African advancement in the Civil Service and other employment, the immigration of a potential 'poor whites' class, the growth of African nationalism, and the increase in racial intolerance. Colby worked hard on the document and made many adjustments of wording, together with several minor deletions and additions. He was acutely aware of the problems involved in writing this letter. First, there was the probable reaction of the Colonial Office:

> The attitude of the C.O. is in my view something like this – federation is a good thing, it is working, Nyasaland is getting benefits, thank God we can put away the papers and let us hope that . . . Colby won't write any letters to us about it.[203]

Second, there was the question of whether Huggins could have any real influence. Colby had very early on formed the opinion that he was 'an outstanding personality but his assistants . . . are pygmies', but much more recently he had gained the impression that 'Huggins is ageing fast and losing grip and that he will retire at the end of the present Parliament.'[204] He was faced with an intractable dilemma:

If on the one hand Huggins is honestly progressive in these matters – and to be candid I am very doubtful if he is – and were to make a move in the direction of a more tolerant policy he might easily be thrown out, and we should get a Confederate Government. If on the other hand he does nothing things will go from bad to worse.[205]

Colby did not pretend to know the answer; he believed that, on the face of it, a considerable extension of African franchise would help in a more tolerant policy, but how, he wondered, could this be achieved without endangering Huggins' government?

Gorell Barnes used Colby's draft in a background brief which he prepared for Lennox-Boyd[206] to use in discussion with Huggins, by this time elevated to the peerage as Lord Malvern, and then two months later, having confessedly overlooked the draft in the meantime, he wrote to Colby saying how much he agreed with the views expressed in the draft:

the issues you discussed in it are important and . . . failure to deal with them adequately in time was part of the cause of the Mau Mau in Kenya. I am sure therefore that you cannot be wrong to make these points to Lord Malvern.[207]

In the event, Colby decided that Malvern's influence was so much on the wane that it would be better to send his letter to Welensky, whom he visited early in June 1955. Following this visit, he slightly modified the wording of the letter, marked it secret and personal, and sent it to Welensky on 27 June.[208]

Welensky was minister of transport and deputy prime minister, and was acting prime minister during the latter months of Colby's term of office. Colby's relationship with him – powerful in Northern Rhodesia and now in the federation – was important. They had known each other from meetings of the Central African Council, and many years later Welensky recorded of Colby:

I thought he was affable and, frankly, I took a liking to him – from his attitude generally. He wasn't at all difficult. He was always very reasonable in his discussions in the Central African Council. I found him very helpful in those days . . . I got to respect Colby more and more as time went on.[209]

In the opening paragraph of his letter of 27 June, Colby first set the tone by saying:

I write in no spirit of destructive criticism or arrogance; it is rather a feeling of anxiety which actuates me – we must make this federation a success and we shall only succeed in doing so by progressive and constructive policies.

Some three years later, and within a month of his death, he was still urging Nyasaland officials to make sure that federation worked smoothly and well.[210]

He explained to Welensky that during the pre-federation talks and conferences, he advised against the inclusion of Nyasaland because he took the view that the gulf between Southern Rhodesia and Nyasaland was too wide to be bridged by federation. Once the British government had decided to include Nyasaland, however, he had done, and would continue to do, all in his power to ensure that federation worked, a claim which Welensky fully accepted and about which he had 'never had any doubts'.[211]

He turned next to what he saw as 'without doubt the greatest single political problem which faces the Federal Government': African advancement, particularly in the Civil Service. If the growing body of educated Africans were given decent jobs they would become not only a contented middle class, but also a valuable stabilizing influence, an insurance against revolution, and an effective opposition to communism. He argued that Southern Rhodesia's policy of employing Europeans in jobs which Africans could readily do was having a deeply damaging effect on the economy and was preventing the advancement of Africans. He asked if immigration standards could not be raised:

Is it prudent to continue to encourage the immigration of the more lowly type of European who will be in direct competition with the African for employment? If this is done is not a racial clash inevitable?

His argument about African advancement 'as the greatest single political problem' became more forceful as he proceeded, saying it would be idle to ignore the possibility of Nyasaland becoming a black state, and highly unwise not to have this possibility constantly in mind. Believing that a 'black state' was one in which Europeans played little or no part, he felt it could only be avoided by 'conciliating African opinion and by building up a contented and influential African middle class whose interests are our interests'. Using arguments similar to those he had used in pointing out the ultimate futility of coercion in securing better agricultural standards after the 1948–50 food crisis,[212] he rejected the view of some that African advancement could be avoided by force: 'Can two hundred odd thousand Europeans deal by force with seven million Africans?' He drove home this point by pointing out, first, that 'the population ratio will inexorably move in favour of the Africans', and second, that there would be an increasing number of far better-educated and mature Africans to deal with:

> We must therefore expect an intensification of African nationalism and the emergence of African leaders of real calibre. I can speak with some experience of dangerous African agitators: there has never been one yet in Central Africa but we shall inevitably get our Azikiwes, Nkrumahs and Jomo Kenyattas in due course. My concern is that when one does arise he should not have the fertile field for agitation that exists at present and I do urge that we reduce the fertility of this field by giving the African reasonable opportunities, by progressively removing the colour bar and eliminating some of the grosser forms of exploitation which exist, particularly in this territory. We must also I suggest give the African a greater say in the Government of the country. To say, as many do, that the African is not ready for it is to my mind irrelevant. If by agitation and rebellion he can make the position of the European intolerable unless concessions are made, this is surely a sufficient reason to make them.

He concluded his letter by itemizing the causes of his anxiety: the growth of racial intolerance, the opposition within the Federal Party to a progressive racial policy, and the continued flow of immigrants from South Africa.

Welensky's reply, of 14 July,[213] was courteous and detailed and he agreed with Colby on many points. They did not in practice, however, see eye to eye on the essential point of African advancement. Welensky expressed his belief in African advancement, the building up of a contented middle class, and the creation of more posts and better opportunities for the African, but with the provisos that the advancement should be 'as far as his natural ability will permit' and 'that he makes himself a better individual and one who is capable of filling these posts on his ability':

> a man or woman, irrespective of colour or creed, is only worth what he can earn . . . [The African's] earning capacity is very limited and his skill even more so. His stability and his continuity in industry is still very much of a question. For a long time the white man will have to provide all these characteristics . . .

Welensky used this argument as justification not only for rejecting what he called a 'hot house' approach to African advancement – as opposed to his own 'let it happen naturally in the course of time, if it happens at all' approach – but also for not altering the federal government's immigration policy.

Colby had one more go at making his essential points to Welensky and did so in a letter dated 15 August 1955.[214] He agreed that the 'hot house' approach to African advancement must be avoided, but argued that the reverse – the reservation of certain jobs for people because they were European – was also abhorrent. He did not believe that the Africans of Southern Rhodesia were allowed to advance in accordance with their ability, which was damaging both politically and economically: high wages were paid to Europeans when lower wages could be paid to Africans for the same work. He added that only federation had saved Southern Rhodesia from the bankruptcy which would inevitably have followed from the failure to employ Africans in posts for which they were suitable and from living on imported capital. This bankruptcy would, he believed, have rendered absorption by South Africa highly probable. He refused to accept Welensky's view that race relations in Southern Rhodesia were better than in the two northern territories simply on the evidence that there had not been shootings in Southern Rhodesia such as had occurred in the other two countries:

> Moreover, it would I think be wrong to infer that because there has not been trouble in Southern Rhodesia for all these years that there might not be trouble in the future.

He followed this prophetic warning with one of equal perspicacity in concluding his letter:

> I may be interpreting your views wrongly but as I understand them they are that it is we, the Federal Government or the Europeans, who will be the arbiters on whether Nyasaland, for example, becomes a black state or not. I believe that is fallacious: I believe that looking five or ten years ahead it will be the Africans who will be the arbiters and they will be the deciding factor . . .
>
> We must I think also realize that at the conference in seven years time . . . the African will have a far greater say in things than he had in 1952 and 1953. It will not be possible to ride over him roughshod as we did last time. We must therefore do everything we can in the meantime to get him on our side and in favour of federation. I feel bound to say that we have not made much progress in that direction so far.

Federation was now an accomplished legal fact; the federal machinery had been created – the departments, the courts, the legislature – and had been set in motion. In respect of the extent to which he could influence the running of that machinery and the general direction and speed it should take, Colby had two aims: one which he did not publicize or indeed admit to, save possibly to a few trusted officials;[215] the other which he stated publicly.

The first aim was to try to hold the line where it had been drawn in 1953, and whilst doing nothing to hinder progress[216] in what had already become the federal sphere, to do nothing which would extend it; but rather to squeeze every ounce of benefit to Nyasaland he could in the federal sphere, and to push ahead independently with Nyasaland developments outside that sphere of responsibilities. In a rare moment of indiscretion he told Stevens that he 'would not lift a finger to help Federation',[217] and an American doctor who called on the governor remarked of his 1954 visit, 'To say the least, enthusiasm with respect to entering the Federation seemed to be questionable or absent.'[218] Other prominent businessmen and visitors found him very discreet about federation: 'I never heard him express a view on Federation . . . unlike Benson, the Governor of Northern Rhodesia who was quite outspoken on the subject.'[219]

With this 'holding the line' view in mind, he seconded some of his most able finance and development administrators to work with the federal ministries in Salisbury: people like Phillips and H. S. Norman-Walker. While he may well also have got rid of a few officers for whose abilities and attitudes he had less than the highest regard, he seconded Phillips and Norman-Walker undoubtedly because he had the greatest respect for their abilities and the benefits which they could exact for Nyasaland whilst working in Salisbury. It did not escape Welensky's notice that these two officers, whom he recognized to be 'a cut above the average':

> were on the financial side. I think that basically – and I think I can see the sense of it – he probably wanted to make certain there were men that would see that Nyasaland got a fair share of . . . what was going.[220]

Three attempts, of varying strength, were launched by the federalists – not only the federal government but its European supporters – to extend the federal sphere of responsibilities: into police, public works and agriculture.

The federal constitution placed on the federal legislative list:

> The establishment, training, maintenance and administration of a Federal police force for service in the employment of, or use in, any territory at the request and under the operational control of the Governor of that territory in addition to or in substitution for the police force of that territory.[221]

During the disturbances in 1953, Barrow had advocated quite strongly the 'importance and need for a large federal police force which could be moved from territory to territory as desired'.[222] This point was made from time to time, but Colby was able to resist it and to retain a purely Nyasaland police force. Given the forestalling powers which he already had secured just prior to federation, and had used in 1953, to call on the assistance of neighbouring police forces, including those in Southern and Northern Rhodesia, he did not need a federal police force, nor did the federalists – whose case was weakened by the powers to call on neighbouring forces – want to push too strongly on a question which was clearly so delicate a matter politically.

Rather greater pressure was applied, however, to public works, where the federal list gave the federal legislature power to make laws in respect of constructing, altering and maintaining inter-territorial roads, but neither federal nor concurrent list referred directly to other public works. Consequently, public works other than inter-territorial roads remained a territorial responsibility. In mid-1954, however, proposals emanated from the federal government to federalize the Public Works Departments of the northern territories.[223] Colby's reaction was quick and predictable:

> I should certainly not agree to federalizing territorial P.W.D. I regard the present position as satisfactory and we should try to hold it.[224]
>
> Our line is quite clear. If the Federal Government wish to set up their own operation to deal with either buildings or roads, we can't stop them. We shall, however, retain our territorial organization for both.[225]
>
> Of course we can't stop them doing this if they want to – what we will not have is federal P.W.D. doing territorial works.[226]

He was not going to give up a department which he had so carefully built up over the previous five to seven years and upon which he depended so much for continued development in Nyasaland. Nor was he best pleased to learn that his former development secretary, 'was the person most in favour of federalization [and] that the federal Director of Public Works was merely following the lead given by ... Bell'.[227] Fortunately, Barrow 'did not appear to be very strongly in favour of federalization' of public works, although he did emphasize the need for the federal government to have effective control of the expenditure of federal funds and full knowledge of what was happening with federal building projects in the northern territories.[228]

With Barrow's relative indifference, and with the support of the chief secretary of Northern Rhodesia and of N. F. Richards, the Nyasaland director of public works,[229] Colby was able to resist the pressures of the federal government to extend its sphere of responsibilities into public works.

Much more powerful pressures were placed upon Colby in respect of federalizing non-African agriculture. The federal constitution included Southern Rhodesia's non-African agriculture on the federal legislative list, but that list did not mention agriculture in the two northern territories where, consequently, agriculture, whether African or non-African, remained a territorial responsibility. There was provision, however, for the northern legislatures – with the consent of the respective governors – to place on the concurrent list non-African agriculture, including animal husbandry, animal health, and plant pests and diseases. For a while, few serious steps were taken to use these provisions and to expand the federal sphere of responsibility into agriculture.

On 28 January 1954 J. Caldicott, federal minister of agriculture, had discussions in Zomba with Colby, and their conversations covered four main aspects.[230] First, in regard to the marketing of African Trust Land produce – a matter dear to Colby's heart – Caldicott seemed fully to accept that, at least for the present and probably for some time to come, marketing boards would have to remain territorial. He was, however, interested in marketing generally, especially with regard to the disposal of surplus crops, and he reminded Colby that a working party of which Kettlewell and Simmonds had been members had recommended that there should be a standing committee on marketing and prices. Second, he recognized in respect of European agriculture that:

this matter was not divisible in [Nyasaland's] agricultural set up and that little advantage would accrue from an attempt to divide it.

After a few remarks in which he expressed his favour of a federal land bank, Caldicott turned to animal health services and asked Colby if he was 'in a position to consider making them federal'. Colby recorded:

I replied that I thought it would be injudicious to seek to do so at the present time. The point was made that it was not possible to make any division between Europeans and Africans and that if anything went over it would all go over because animal health was itself indivisible. As at present constituted our Veterinary Department deals not only with animal health but with animal husbandry to a certain extent which further complicates the issue.[231]

Finally, Caldicott turned to research and experimentation and it was agreed that Nyasaland 'had really no research' and that all their work was experimentation. On the question of basic research, however, Colby agreed that there did not appear to be any specific difficulties in federalizing it. At the end of this early meeting, then, Colby had successfully resisted overtures to federalize African produce marketing, European agriculture, and animal health services, but had conceded the case for federalizing basic research, an area in which he stood to gain from federal investment.

About a year later, in the early part of 1955, the scene changed as

Europeans in Nyasaland began to press strongly for the federalization of non-African agriculture. The pressure built up as Colby's accelerated policy of land acquisition and African resettlement from congested areas began to take hold, as changes in the protectorate's constitution, designed to give non-Europeans parity with Europeans in legislative council, were announced, and as European agriculture in Northern Rhodesia was federalized.[232]

In March 1955, the expatriate Nyasaland Farmers' Union, in a circular letter, called upon political associations and representatives in both the territorial and federal legislatures to support its declared aim of federalizing non-African agriculture. The editor of *The Nyasaland Times* recognized that whilst the letter might be 'criticised in places for emotional tones rising almost to hysteria', it did bring forcefully to the public's attention an important debate which had serious political implications:

> In a few years time the federal constitution will be reviewed. By then the European farmers in the Rhodesias will be under federal control for the common good. The Union wisely points out that if Nyasaland's non-African agriculture is not by then federalized, it might well be forgotten in the overall planning – and many benefits will be lost.[233]

The editor called for support from members of the legislature and from the various political associations, since 'the assistance which they give might well be considered elsewhere as their measure of support for the principle of federation'.

The non-official expatriate pressure to federalize non-African agriculture was widespread but not total, for the Nyasaland Tea Association opted to take over from the Nyasaland government responsibility for tea research. It did so fearing that control of its research interests, in the event of federation, would be removed from it and dominated by Southern Rhodesia, which had far less knowledge and experience of tea research and production than it had itself. The Association retained the staff and asked Kettlewell to remain as chairman of the Tea Research Council.[234]

The Nyasaland African Congress was alarmed by the moves of the Farmers' Union, and, at its annual conference in April 1955, cabled Colby and reiterated its total opposition to federalizing non-African agriculture 'as the land on which such agriculture is practised is land belonging to Africans'.[235] As Colby had so often said, the Africans linked the question of federation closely with that of land.

Blackwood, 'the most fiery speaker in Legislative Council',[236] pushed the Nyasaland Farmers' Union case in the legislature and was told by the financial secretary that 'no steps have been taken by the Nyasaland Government to place non-African agriculture under federal control.' The union attacked steadily and more and more strongly, whilst at the same time the federal government pressed to take over the marketing of maize in Nyasaland. Writing to Kettlewell – who was on leave – on 20 June 1955, Colby said:

> You will probably have heard . . . that I have kept the federal boys out of our maize marketing. I told Huggins that it was worth £100,000 a year to us to keep [them] out of our affairs. I think he took the point having regard to the mess they have made in Southern Rhodesia![237]

Late in 1955 or early in 1956, Colby visited Welensky, now acting prime minister of the federation, in Salisbury and made clear his views on further federalization, especially of non-African agriculture. The meeting was between Colby and Welensky with no officials or others present. Some 30 years later, Welensky recalled:[238]

> We took over agriculture in . . . Southern Rhodesia with the federation, but we began to take over other things. Now, Colby came down and made a special trip to come and see me . . . and he said he wanted to discuss this [agricultural] question with me. And he pleaded with me, and I accepted his plea, that it was unwise to take over more things in Nyasaland, because it would only lead to more trouble. He said he would do his best, and I believe he did, to try and make things tick over; but he said if we insisted on taking things over – which we could according to the constitution – it would make the position much worse. . . . He came and I agreed with him . . . he was quite frank about it and he said, 'You know my view. It's been consistent all the way through', and it had been – he never changed it.

On another occasion Welensky said, 'I found him to be a man of integrity. He never believed that the Federation could succeed, and he never made any bones about it.'[239] Colby's rearguard action in respect of federalizing non–African agriculture was also evident in his attitude towards the federal Standing Committee on Agricultural Production, whose membership was comprised of representatives of the agricultural departments of the three territories, but which was well attended only by the Southern Rhodesia representatives. He considered this committee to be 'a staggering waste of the federal taxpayers' money' and insisted that meetings should not exceed two a year; the chief secretary was prepared to agree with Northern Rhodesia on three a year, but Colby dug in his heels and said, 'Let us stick to our draft. Two meetings are quite enough.' He ordered that, after October 1955, no Nyasaland representatives should attend without his personal approval.[240]

As a minor, and jocular, example of his stubbornness in giving away no more than was absolutely necessary to the federal government, Colby, as the last commander-in-chief of the Nyasaland Protectorate, said, 'They tried to make me give up the title of Commander-in-Chief but I refused unless they gave me abolition of office terms. The conversation then ceased.'[241]

His publicly stated view – which he reinforced privately in, for example, his letters to Welensky in June and August 1955, and in correspondence with Lennox-Boyd and with his successor, Sir Robert Armitage, early in 1956[242] – was that it was imperative that African fears of federation and of Southern Rhodesia in particular should be removed. Indeed the two views were closely linked. In his speech at the July 1955 opening of legislative council he said:

> The object of removing fears of federation among Africans will not be achieved if persons and public bodies in this country continue to make statements that this or that activity should be federalized or that everything should be federalized. . . . Such statements are calculated to keep alive all the old fears. . . . Surely it is self evident that the Federal Government must be allowed time to consolidate before further moves are considered . . . our primary object in the next few years must be by our actions to remove these fears and to convince the African population that federation is in the best interests of all.[243]

His plea and warning went largely unheeded, for some five months later when he saw the election manifesto of the Nyasaland Association, which had the largest number of registered voters for the forthcoming non-

African elections, he must have been both distressed and alarmed –
although not surprised – to read:

> [The Association plans] to protect and foster the interests of Euro-
> peans in Nyasaland [as its main plank]. It will also urge that
> Nyasaland's new constitution should not be revised until at least
> one year after the [revised] federal constitution is made known. It
> will work for the complete take over by the Federal Government
> of all federal departments and responsibilities and campaign for
> federalization of European agriculture and the police.[244]

Towards the end of January 1956, only two months before he left
Nyasaland, Colby addressed a long, detailed and well-argued top secret
and personal letter to Lennox-Boyd.[245] It was almost a *Nunc dimittis*:

> As I shall shortly leave this Protectorate on retirement I feel that I
> should not have discharged my duty to you if I did not invite your
> attention to tendencies and developments in the federation which
> seem both to me and to my advisers to threaten the continued
> existence of the Federal state and if I did not place on record my
> views as to the action which is needed to check these tendencies
> and developments.

He dealt first with the question of European immigration, the steady
building up of a potential poor white population in Southern Rhodesia,
and the disastrous financial effects of failing to employ Africans in the
post office, Civil Service, railways, commerce and industry. He had
already refused to allow the federal government to set up local advisory
committees on immigration. Next he dealt with federal finance – which
he saw as 'irresponsibility amounting to something near dishonesty' –
and particularly the failure to allocate to Nyasaland a fair proportion of
development finance whilst Southern Rhodesia was outrageously over-
favoured:

> the main justification for the inclusion of Nyasaland in the feder-
> ation was the prospect of economic development: if such develop-
> ment does not materialize the justification for including Nyasaland
> in the federation falls away.

He added that unless every opportunity was taken to broaden and strengthen the economy of Nyasaland, the great majority of its rapid growing population would be condemned to subsistence peasantry an would 'become a political and security liability to the Federal Govern ment'. Colby then turned to the federal Civil Service, much of whic he considered 'second rate', and which as a machine was 'creaking badl and kept functioning only by the efforts and loyalty of the office seconded from the northern territories. Whilst at the time of federation a proportion of Nyasaland civil servants were in favour of federation an the majority were at least ready to judge it on its merits, 'today it probably true that close on 100 per cent are against it' – and this aft less than two and a half years of existence! His last major point concerne the moves towards amalgamation implicit in the steps to federaliz further territorial functions. He concluded with a clear and tellin warning:

> The introduction of federation was attended in the Southern Prov-
> ince of Nyasaland with serious disturbances amounting to incipient
> revolt. These were very firmly handled and the effect was salutary;
> the effect is now wearing off as disillusionment over federation
> grows: political agitation is gaining momentum again and unless it
> can be countered with some tangible act of goodwill towards Afri-
> cans on the part of the Federal Government, it will undoubtedly
> continue to grow and again culminate in a dangerous security
> situation; this would clearly prejudice the whole future of the
> Federation.

In an accompanying private and personal note to Lennox-Boyd, tinged with a trace of sadness, Colby apologized for inflicting his letter on the secretary of state at a very busy time, but felt that he would be 'com-pletely failing in his duty' if he did not indicate his 'profound disquiet with the way things are going in the Federation'. It had, he said, been his 'unhappy lot during the past four years' to have had to give 'unpalat-able advice' to the Colonial Office, but no honest man in his position could have acted otherwise: 'Please give me credit for sincerity and loyalty to yourself and H.M.G.':

> I am utterly convinced that unless H.M.G. takes very strong mea-
> sures with the Federal Government at an early date, federation will
> fail . . . I know that it means a first class row with the Federal
> Government but this must be faced.[246]

In a private note which he wrote to his successor, Armitage, only a week before he left the protectorate at the end of March 1956,[247] he referred to his initial feeling that there was no goodwill towards Nyasaland in Salisbury and said that this feeling had been borne out in practice during the first two and a half years of the federation. More than five years earlier he had told executive council that he felt it unlikely that the Southern Rhodesia taxpayer would spend much on Nyasaland's development. In numerous of his public addresses, from his first months to his last months in Nyasaland, he stressed the importance of good race relations, and it was the importation of European race attitudes from Southern Rhodesia to Nyasaland which he – and the Nyasaland African Congress – feared most. In his note to Armitage, Colby said:

> I do not believe that federation can succeed unless there is a complete change of heart in Salisbury – at present I see no sign of this. The fundamental fact to my mind is this – in a country where there are 550 Africans to every one European, what the Africans say will go: it is just a question of time and I don't think there is very much left and in that interval the Federal Government must get the Africans on their side by making substantial gestures – if they don't this country will inevitably become an African dominated state and break away from the federation.[248]

Colby's general approach to, and attitude towards, federation have been well summed up by Welensky:

> I began to realize fairly early in the day that Colby never believed that it was possible to bring the three Central African territories together under any type of Government that would have been acceptable to the whites ... Well, the reasons, I think, Colby felt that it would never work in practice [were] because [of] the political aspirations of the Nyasalanders – because by then we were beginning to feel the effects of the rising tide of nationalism. He felt that the whites would not go along fast enough with the changes that would satisfy the Africans. ... My own feeling ... was that he felt from the word go – and I go back to the conference – that it couldn't work. He thought – when I talked privately – he didn't see that the day would ever dawn when the Africans would accept the kind of constitution that men like Huggins and I wanted for the Federation.[249]

Events proved Colby right. He was correct about an 'intensification of African nationalism' and about 'the emergence of African leaders of real calibre' who would find a 'fertile field for agitation'. He was right too – even as to timing – that 'looking five or ten years ahead it will be the Africans who will be the arbiters and they will be the deciding factor', and also that at the 1960 conference 'the African will have a far greater say in things than he had in 1952 and 1953. It will not be possible to ride over him roughshod as we did last time.'[250] Despite his pleas and warnings, the federal government did little or nothing about immigration, African advancement, race relations, and uneven and unfair allocation of federal finances (particularly development finances): little or nothing in fact to get the Africans on the side of federation. There was no 'tangible act of goodwill towards the Africans on the part of the Federal Government',[251] and consequently, as Colby had warned so very clearly and repeatedly, political agitation 'continue[d] to grow and again culminate[d] in a dangerous security situation [which] clearly prejudice[d] the whole future of the Federation'. Had the British government accepted Colby's 1952 advice and not included Nyasaland in the federation, the Central African Federation might have accomplished all, or most, of what Britain sought to achieve and might have continued in existence. In the meantime, the chances are that Nyasaland would have continued the rapid economic development which Colby had set in train and have reached independent status more smoothly and more quickly than turned out to be the case, speedily as it was in fact reached.

The Africans of Nyasaland never did accept federation, and less than three years after Colby's departure, his successor had to declare a state of emergency – a disastrous step which Colby himself had avoided – to handle the severe political unrest in which their resentment and opposition to federation manifested itself. There was no change of heart in Salisbury and the federal government did not make the gestures which Colby warned were essential to winning over the African people. As a consequence – as Colby predicted – Nyasaland broke away from the federation and became an African state. It was, as he said, just a question of time: seven years after his departure the federation was abolished.

14· Changing Relationships

'Dawned fresh and fair but later became unsettled and turned snowy.'

The last five chapters have been concerned with a number of major problems which Colby had to handle: the railways, the food crisis, Africans on private estates, the African press, and federation. In each of these problems his relationships with the non-official community were important: as Shenton Thomas had said much earlier, 'No Government can function satisfactorily unless it is stimulated by constructive criticism and reinforced by advice which ... represents the view of the country as a whole.'[1] Colby's job would have been very much easier and more sure of success if he could have counted on the support of the non-officials. Yet, as we have remarked earlier, the general view is that his relationships with them, on the whole, could not be said to have been cordial.[2]

These relationships, never close, did not, however, seem to worry Colby or inhibit him in any significant practical way during his first few years as governor, but thereafter, and especially after 1952, they began to deteriorate in ways which impinged on his freedom to act as he wished. The influences which brought about the deterioration were political, economic and social.

In the political sphere, the change in Britain from a Labour to a Conservative government in 1951 did not markedly change Britain's policies towards Nyasaland, and clear examples of this were the continuation and bringing into fruition by the Conservatives of Labour's steps towards introducing federation[3] and the basic continuity in policy regarding Africans on private estates.[4] Nonetheless, the mainly conservative European non-official community believed that they would get a more sympathetic hearing from a Conservative government in Britain, and

this belief emboldened them and sharpened their opposition to an
aspects of Colby's policies which displeased them.

This can best be seen in their deep suspicion of, and vocal antagonism
to, any government encroachment, real or imagined, great or small, into
the commercial, private business sphere.[5] They niggled away at Colby
granting of trading licences to the Colonial Development Corporatio
and his creation of monopoly marketing boards for African-produce
crops, and lost both battles, discovering, as de Putron had discovered in
Nigeria, that Colby 'was not prone to give way' on many issues; the
hammered away at his creation of the African Press, and won; the
worried about the African Book Centre taking business away from privat
booksellers; they objected to the construction of the Group Hospital no
being put out to private tender; they believed his export taxes on te
and tobacco to be 'a grave mistake' over which they 'had to fight [him
for their very existence';[6] and they doubted the *bona fides* of the Norther
Provinces African Co-operative Union being allowed to set up its ow
bulk retail trading store at Rumpi. They saw any government moves, n
matter how slight or indirect, to enter commerce as the thin end of th
wedge of nationalization; it was fortunate for Colby that his attempts t
bring the Nyasaland railways into public ownership did not becom
public knowledge.[7]

In these skirmishes and battles Colby's opponents used the Conven
tion of Associations and the chamber of commerce to bring pressure o
the government, and used the *The Nyasaland Times, East Africa an
Rhodesia*, and journals such as that produced by the British Empir
Producers' Organization. By June 1952, the first of these publication
was already giving editorial prominence to the second's published vie
that 'The Governor is widely regarded as dictatorial and unduly opinion
ated.'[8] They also used the non-official European members of the legisla
tive council to push questions and seek interviews with the governo
and exploited their contacts with British businessmen and MPs to rais
questions with the British government: we have seen how immediat
and great was the pressure on the Colonial Office when Colby announce
his proposals to transfer the Nyasaland railways' domicile to Nyasalan
and to grant it tax exemption.[9] This growing political activity and powe
of the Convention, the chamber and the press, especially *East Afric
and Rhodesia*, was a major factor in the changing relationships betwee
the governor and the non-official European community. After Octobe
1952 – almost six months before his term of office was due to expire
when the British government made public its decision to reappoint hir

for a further three years, it was clear to his expatriate opponents that the simple passage of time would not get rid of Colby. Consequently, their most effective means of influencing him was to increase the pressure on him through political groups and the media.

One could almost pinpoint the change of attitude of the local press by reference to the leading article in *The Nyasaland Times* of 7 January 1952, in which a recent meeting of legislative council was reviewed.[10] In such reviews in the preceding three years, the editor had been fulsome in his praise of Colby, but on this occasion whilst he said that 'His Excellency's opening address was a remarkably good one [which] closed on a note of high hope and confidence in what could be achieved through a little determination and cooperation', he ended by giving prominence to Dixon's attack on Colby's proposal for establishing the African Press and added threateningly that 'the question of this "intelligentsia" newspaper may be the subject of another editorial at some future date'.

An important change in the political sphere occurred in 1953 with the departure of Barrow, and (to a lesser extent) Hadlow a year later, from executive council. Barrow, of similar social background to Colby, played the part of conciliator between factions, of advocate and explainer of Colby's policies; he was a man with a large personal stake in Nyasaland since he headed companies which were Nyasaland-based and which he owned; and he was a man who, when he criticized government and the governor, did so to their faces but in private. He was replaced after a brief period by Dixon, a stirrer rather than a smoother, and head of a London-based company with large interests in Nyasaland – the British Central Africa Company – which was also a shareholder in the Nyasaland railways, both of which companies had been attacked by Colby for their failure to assist in the protectorate's economic development. Dixon, whose criticism of government and of Colby was openly and publicly expressed – often in strong words and at length – believed himself to be infinitely more knowledgeable about business than any official, even the governor, could possibly be.[11]

Dixon's influence was strengthened by support from *The Nyasaland Times* whose editor, in a leading article late in 1952, said of a recent legislative council meeting: 'Plain speaking was employed by the Hon. A. C. W. Dixon . . . and plain speaking is what we like.'[12] The change was noted at the time by a correspondent to the paper:

In marked contrast to the atmosphere we have been accustomed to in the past of complacent approval and mental eulogy between officials and non-officials at [Legislative Council] sessions, the one that has just been started appears from the speeches delivered by some officials to have ended on a note of acerbity and disapproval mainly directed against Mr Dixon who had the audacity to question certain utterances on the part of Government and the policies followed by departments of the Government.[13]

Barrow's departure from, and Dixon's appointment to, executive council highlighted a fundamental inadequacy in the protectorate's constitution. Given the extremely small number of expatriate non-officials and the even smaller number of gifted non-officials from whom the governor could select two to become members of executive council, there was no certainty that those he did select would feel obliged to owe him genuine personal loyalty, share his essential views, and fully accept his decisions once made. In Britain, the prime minister, drawing on an incomparably larger and more gifted pool, is able and expects to appoint to the cabinet only those who are at least broadly like-minded and whose loyalty, at least in public, can be depended on; in colonial Nyasaland this was not necessarily the case. Dixon had publicly revealed himself as a vociferous opponent of government, yet was appointed to the executive council. So long as government and the expatriate community acted broadly in unison, so long as they were 'on the same side', and so long as the latter felt that the former was acting in their interest, the inadequacy in the constitution did not matter, but as soon as this state of affairs changed – as it did around 1952–3 – the weakness revealed itself.

There were changes not only in executive council, but also in the legislature. The 'flavour' of legislative council after 1952–3 changed considerably as the planters (Barrow, Hadlow, Mrs Sharpe, Mrs Widdas and Rumsey) who had lived in the country for many years, gave way to commercial men and lawyers (Dixon, Blackwood, Collins and Sacranie) who were – with the exception of Sacranie – relatively recent, post-war arrivals. A few days after Sir Robert Armitage, Colby's successor, took office he granted an interview with Dixon who told him that:

a month or so before Sir Geoffrey Colby retired there was a determined attempt on the part of several . . . Members of Council to put down a Motion of No Confidence and to debate the Motion during the last sitting of Council.[14]

Dixon believed that although the motion was to be put down in the names of the three African members, he was of the 'confirmed opinion that the whole unpleasant affair was engineered by [one of the other members] who was led to use the three Africans . . . through personal animosity towards Sir Geoffrey. Undoubtedly, all Un-Officials felt a considerable sense of frustration', but in the event a protracted private meeting of members led to the withdrawal of the proposal and no debate took place. Dixon concluded a letter to Armitage shortly thereafter by claiming that:

> there has been almost no opportunity, in the past, for Un-Officials to have a frank discussion [with the Governor] on matters that have given us cause for worry and on which we have felt very strongly.[15]

The most potent political factor in Colby's changing relationships with the non-official community was undoubtedly federation. Almost exclusively, the Europeans from the planting and commercial sector were or became strongly in favour of federation, and the Africans were even more strongly opposed to it. The former, fed on stories in *East Africa and Rhodesia* of the Nyasaland representatives' obstructive and damaging attitudes in the Central African Council[16] – which Welensky later said were untrue[17] – believed that Colby was personally opposed to federation and feared that he would influence the British government against it, while it appeared to Africans that he was in favour of it and was in any case subject to the directions of the imperial government. The missionary and church elements and the Asian community generally shared the African view. Colby could scarcely expect to come out of such a nutcracker situation unscathed. The nature of the ultimate clash, but little, if any, appreciation of its virtual inevitability, was contained in a leading article in *The Nyasaland Times* as early as November 1951:

> with the African intelligentsia what was in the background is now very much in the foreground which is to say the exaggerated hope that by resisting partnership they will attain self-government on the pattern of the Gold Coast and Nigeria. These hopes are unreal and unrealisable . . . for they assume that the same pattern can be followed in . . . Nyasaland where white settlement is permanently established and white expertise is the foundation of our economy and future progress.[18]

The European non-officials' opinion was that through federation their interests – political, economic and social – would be made and remain paramount. This is precisely how the Africans also saw it: the European non-officials, through federation, would seek to halt and reverse the economic trends which Colby had set in motion – the rising significance and therefore strength of African producers, their increasing incomes and standards of living. Colby abandoned the paternalistic approach to the African population in economic matters and saw them as instruments of production – individual and personal instruments, since African agriculture was individual smallholder agriculture. The European non-officials knew, or at least sensed, that the abandonment of paternalism in economic matters would inevitably lead to its abandonment in political and social matters, and consequently they wished to reverse the trend. In answer to a question from Colby in executive council, Barrow and Hadlow:

> agreed that the European non-officials who had in the past been in favour of closer association [with the Rhodesias] were largely those who thought they might get closer control over Africans thereby.[19]

The Africans, however, naturally wished to pursue and accelerate progress along the course on which Colby had set the country, yet in their eyes the governor himself appeared to accept federation: indeed in October 1952 he told Chinyama that when and if the government decided that federation was not in the Africans' interests they would say so, and six months later he cast his deliberative vote in favour of it and was extremely firm in handling the disturbances that followed its creation. It is not surprising, therefore, that African nationalist politics, opposed to government policy, grew apace, especially after October 1952 when it was formally announced that Colby's term of office was to be extended by a further three years and it became clear that any hopes his opponents might have of his early departure were dashed. By the end of 1952 Colby publicly warned the Nyasaland African Congress of his concern about their activities:

> There have been instances in every Province . . . in which Congress members have sought to undermine confidence in the administration and in the central Government and have incited both Chiefs and civil servants to displays of irresponsibility and disloyalty . . . [These] activities, if continued, will do untold harm to the future

of this country and I shall not hesitate to use the full resources of Government to check them.[20]

It was not only political matters, however, but also important economic issues which contributed significantly to the change in Colby's relationships with the non-official European community.

In his first four or five years, Colby had brought about unprecedented economic progress, based on a development strategy which had at its heart increased production and exports, and in which improved communications played a crucial part.[21] A number of critics argued that the pace of development was too fast, but the large majority of European non-officials stood to benefit financially from the progress and, in political terms, believed that the more developed Nyasaland became economically, the more likely it was that Southern Rhodesia would see the protectorate as a desirable, or at least acceptable, partner in a federation. Colby was able to exploit to the full the freer-flowing supply of post-war development aid from Britain, the imperial government's willingness to raise development loans, the high prices received on the world markets for primary products, including Nyasaland's exports, and the European planters' initial acquiescence, albeit reluctant, in his imposition of export taxes on tobacco and tea, an acquiescence induced by relatively high profits.

By 1952, however, the steep climb in the graph of development progress began to ease off.[22] Very considerable development continued, but not at the spectacular breakneck pace of the first four or five years, and a number of major government projects had to be postponed: the Blantyre Group Hospital, the Lilongwe–Salima road, and the Chileka airport terminal building. Proposals for private development projects, such as a sugar estate and factory in the Lower River area, also came to a halt. Even Colby could not go on working miracles indefinitely. In no way was it that he was beginning to run out of steam, but simply that the really major thrust had already taken place and the time had come 'to draw breath and to consolidate before deciding what the next step should be'.[23] This easing off coincided with a change in the world economy from a sellers' market to a buyers' market, as a result of which prices received by Nyasaland exporters declined at precisely the same time as the British government 'made it abundantly clear' to Colby that if they were to continue to support him with substantial grants and with loans, he would have to put his own house in financial order to their liking: that is, raise more revenue internally and economize in government expenditure. Indeed, the secretary of state agreed to the raising of further loans only:

> provided that you take earliest opportunity to introduce measures designed to fill gaps between recurrent revenue and expenditure [and to] ensure servicing charges can be met.[24]

This attitude of the British government was entirely acceptable to Colby, who understood very well the beneficial effect on increased production which a measure of increased taxation could bring about. The increases in taxation which Colby then introduced fell mainly on expatriate producers who were already feeling a significant reduction in profits. One is unlikely to be favourably received when one asks people who are already feeling their shoes pinching to tighten their belts!

For economic as well as for political reasons, then, Colby's relationships with the non-official expatriate community began to deteriorate from about 1952. Since he also increased duties on items purchased by Africans at the same time as their returns on production were declining, even although the burden fell much more heavily on expatriates than on Africans, it is likely that a degree of economic resentment was also present in the African community, and combined with their political resentment of what they believed to be Colby's pro-federation attitudes. The expression of any such resentment, however, was muted, since the Africans did not possess direct access to the media – Colby's attempts to establish an African newspaper having been thwarted – and their political organizations, principally the Nyasaland African Congress, lacked the sophistication, experience, funds, close links with British businessmen, and clout of the chamber of commerce and the Convention of Associations.

Colby was also concerned about certain social aspects of life, which were connected with a difference in the sort of European then becoming more common in Nyasaland, and which may have contributed to the change in his relationships with the non-official communities.

There was, first, a growing number of Europeans from Southern Africa who, it was thought, tended to bring with them the social and racial attitudes of the south. We have already noted Colby's personal intervention to keep control of the advertising of civil service posts in South Africa and Southern Rhodesia and the filling of vacancies by South Africans, and many people saw federation as an attempt to create a bulwark against growing apartheid influences in Central Africa.

Second, there was an influx of Europeans, other than those from the south, who brought social attitudes and behaviour which were untypical of Nyasaland. The construction firms who secured contracts as part of Colby's development drive brought in fairly large numbers of expatriates unused to the social mores of the protectorate's expatriate community. In a significant number of cases before the magistrates' courts, in prosecutions for such matters as affray, assault and dishonesty, the accused person was a newly arrived employee of one or other of the construction firms. Further, *The Nyasaland Times* took these newcomers to task for behaving impolitely to 'our Africans'.[25]

It is unlikely that these new elements in the non-official expatriate community would have had much patience with what they must have seen as the elitism, old-fashionedness and remoteness of a colonial government which was increasingly being seen, by expatriates, as pro-African. It is difficult to be sympathetically impressed by gold braid and white plumes when one is dressed in dust-laden khaki shorts and a sweaty, open-necked bush-shirt, or if one has been brought up in countries which for a quarter to half a century have been free of imperial control.

After his retirement, Colby privately expressed to a very few particularly close and trusted former colleagues a view, a regret as it were, which is pertinent to his relationships with non-officials. This view, humorously expressed but demonstrating a shrewd understanding both of his own social stance and of the nature of much of the politically active expatriate community, and also a recognition of his failure to have got on better with that community, was that he felt it to have been an error not to have poured more gin down the throats of the non-officials!

Finally, his relationships with the Colonial Office were also important. Colby had little respect for the Colonial Office, although he was normally careful to conceal the full extent of his views from them. We have seen how he constantly urged them to take action on his letters, and he found their dilatoriness deeply frustrating. In private correspondence with Sir Philip Mitchell, he referred to 'the mists of make-believe and unreality which at present enshroud so many of the activities of the Colonial Office':

> The spate of paper flowing from the Colonial Office continues to grow; the mail arrives two or three times a week and one flicks through in the hope of finding replies to important despatches. One is generally disappointed ... the basic machinery of the Colonial

Office ... is clogged and cluttered up with boards, with advisory committees, with panels and councils, many, indeed most, of the members of which have little idea of the local implications of the matters they discuss ... The primary function of the Colonial Office, I suggest, is to be at the service of Colonial territories and to provide a body of experienced and other officers whose main purpose should be to assist in the solution of the problems submitted to them by Colonial Governments and to be far less concerned with the initiation of correspondence in London. It would be of the greatest benefit if the Colonial Office left Colonial Governments alone for two years and sent them nothing other than answers to their own letters.[26]

Even in a letter to Cohen which he asked should be shown to the secretary of state, he was prepared to say that, whilst Cohen himself had been helpful on every occasion that Colby had enlisted his help, he was bound to quarrel with 'the soul-less machine of the Colonial Office'. 'A Colonial Governor has many frustrations and not the least of them is the Colonial Office machine.'[27]

On the whole, the Office was very supportive of Colby, acceding to his many requests in the early days for more funds with which to develop Nyasaland and generally giving him a free hand to implement his development strategy. In these relationships, however, there is again the possibility of a hint of a change around 1952. By about this time, Colby's somewhat antipathetic views on federation had become clear to the Colonial Office, although this does not appear to have been held against him. Sir John Martin, head of the Central Africa Department of the Colonial Office, recalled:

from March 1952 ... until it became an accomplished fact Sir Geoffrey Colby thought that from Nyasaland's point of view Federation was a mistake ... I certainly recall gaining the impression during my visit in August/September 1952 ... that Sir Geoffrey and most of his officials disliked the prospect.[28]

In mid-1952, two officers who had been strongly supportive of Colby were moved to new posts where they were unable to play a direct personal part in Nyasaland affairs: Lambert was moved to a different department within the Office, and Cohen became governor of Uganda. Correspondence from the Office to Colby thereafter was conducted by

Gorell Barnes and Lloyd, and in the documents one senses a somewhat cooler, less helpful, less positive attitude, for example in respect of Colby's attempts to bring the railways under direct Nyasaland government control, and in respect of the requirement that Colby should raise more revenue internally and economize in government expenditure as a condition of receiving further substantial grants and loans. If indeed there was a change in attitude from about 1952, it was a selective one, for in many respects Colonial Office support continued, as was clearly the case, for example, in 1954 when the Office and the secretary of state personally fully endorsed and supported Colby's recommendations as to policy concerning Africans on private estates.

Colby himself felt that a change in relationships occurred around 1952, because a month or so before he left Nyasaland in 1956 he wrote a private and personal letter to the secretary of state, tinged with a rare – possibly unique – note of combined sadness and near desperation, in which he said:

> It has been my unhappy lot during the past four years to have been put in the position of having to give unpalatable advice to the Colonial Office: I do not believe that any honest man in my position could have acted otherwise.
>
> Please give me credit for sincerity and loyalty to yourself and HMG.[29]

Colby's relationships with the non-official community in Nyasaland and with the Colonial Office in London, like the weather at Surbiton on the day he was born, 'dawned fresh and fair but later became unsettled and turned snowy'.

15· Departure

'Looking forward to better weather.'

Colby celebrated his fifty-fifth birthday on 25 March 1956, and two days later he left Nyasaland for England and retirement. With Lady Colby and their daughter Carol, he left Government House in Zomba at about eight o'clock in the morning and travelled the 40 miles to Limbe, where they reached the railway station at nine o'clock.[1] No doubt their minds went back to the first time they saw the station, only one day short of eight years previously, when they arrived on a quiet Sunday afternoon and were met by such a small and unprepared group of officials hastily awakened from post-prandial slumber. Now all was changed. Officials no longer slumbered and there was a large crowd of Europeans – the women in smart dresses, the men in suits – and a number of Asians and Africans to bid them farewell and a long and happy retirement.

As Colby stepped from the large black Buick, the police band struck up the royal salute, the national anthem, and the well-drilled guard of honour presented arms. For the last time he was accorded the formal respect due to the Queen's personal representative in the protectorate. He briefly inspected the police contingent and then, almost as briefly, said goodbye to as many of those present as he reasonably could. Lady Colby did the same and had time for a kindly word with even the most junior assistant district commissioner present:

> Colby, tall and erect, took it all smartly and naturally. Lady Colby, when she spoke . . . seemed tired and rather upset at leaving. Carol Colby looked relieved that the whole affair was nearly over.

They climbed aboard the waiting train and occupied the general manager's private coach, waving goodbye from the observation platform at the rear of the train as it puffed gently and pulled slowly away from the station. On the platform people lingered for a while and quietly chatted; the acting chief justice anguished publicly over whether it was proper for him to administer the oath to the acting governor before the governor himself had actually crossed the protectorate's frontier with Mozambique; and then they left for their day's work, calling briefly at their homes to change into everyday wear. Colby would have been pleased that his departure was sufficiently early for his officials to put in almost a full day's work after bidding him farewell!

On the train, as it reached the edge of the Shire Highlands and wove its way down the escarpment and across the Lower Shire plain towards the Zambezi, the Colbys were able to begin to relax and to allow the mixed feelings of departure gradually to surface in minds which had been much too full of official duties and goodbyes to entertain such sentiments in recent weeks. They travelled south out of Nyasaland and through Mozambique to Beira, where they boarded the ship for England.

After 31 years – much more than half of his life – in Africa, 23 in Nigeria and eight in Nyasaland, during which he had risen from being the most junior of district officer cadets to become the governor and commander-in-chief of a protectorate, Colby left the 'dark continent'. Like the first of his gubernatorial predecessors in the country, he had worked right up to the last moment, and like Johnston[2] when he left almost exactly 60 years earlier, he was tired and very unwell. During his last tour, Colby had had a number of blackouts, having on one occasion collapsed in the bathroom and hit his head badly on the wash-basin, and on another been forced to leave the table during a dinner party to sit on the stairs outside until he felt better. He had not told Lady Colby of these incidents for fear of worrying her, but by chance she had overheard reference to them when he was talking to one of his doctors. He was so ill with bronchitis on his way to England that he gave up his very long-standing habit of cigarette-smoking, 'there and then', never to return to it, and Lady Colby believed that he 'could easily have died on the ship'.[3]

He was not best pleased when he reached Britain to receive a bill from the general manager of the Nyasaland railways, Stevens – who claimed to have 'made his departure as pleasant as possible, with the use of the General Manager's coach, food and drinks for the journey'[4] – charging him for the use of the special coach in which he had made his exit from Nyasaland, as if to remind him that the railways were still in private, commercial, hands! Colby spoke with the chairman of the railways, with whom he had so often and for so long quarrelled, but who now gave a luncheon in honour of the Colbys, and the bill was withdrawn. They were able to smile at this pettiness, but decades later Lady Colby remembered it and coupled it with the occasion upon which she officially launched the Nyasaland Railways' steamer '*Ilala*' and was graciously rewarded for her trouble by the general manager presenting her with a box of chocolates of modest dimensions!

Kirkby Malham, where the Colbys now set up home, is a beautiful area to which to retire. It lies in the North Yorkshire moors where the fast-flowing, tumbling, Kirkby Beck joins the River Aire which passes close by Hanlith Hall. The fifteenth-century millstone grit church of St Michael the Archangel is stone-walled and ferns grow from the crevices in the wall. Numerous blue and great tits, pied wagtails and green finches flit among the yew trees and into the church porch. Snowdrops in early spring add much to the churchyard's quiet beauty. The large stained-glass east window shows – although it did not do so then, since it was not installed until several years later – the risen and glorified Lord, with seven stars beneath his feet, flanked by Mary, St Joseph, St Michael and King David. It was installed by members of Lady Colby's family in memory of her mother, Florence Holden Illingworth, to replace the plain window installed after the Roundheads had destroyed the original 'very beautiful east window' in Cromwell's time.[5] Half a mile away stands Hanlith Hall, light-grey stoned – like the cluster of other buildings nearby – dignified and overlooking expanses of parkland pastures with scattered trees. The nearby Aire – holding 'some of the finest and gamest trout in Yorkshire'[6] – moves swiftly beneath the stone bridge by which the Hall is reached, flows through the pastures and 'rather lovely woods', and marks the line of the Pennine Way. To the west lies Scotsdrop Moor, to the east Carlton Moor, and to the north Craven Park.

For Lady Colby this was a return to the home in which she had been brought up, where her family had lived since the turn of the century, from where she had been married 25 years earlier, and where she and her husband had spent most of their home leaves. Here, too, her daughters had been brought up by their grandparents whilst their parents were in Africa. She loved and cared for it deeply, describing it as 'an incomparable paradise'. For Sir Geoffrey – who had no family ties with other parts of Britain[7] – Hanlith Hall offered much that he could have desired: beautiful rural surroundings, an estate to manage, the life of an energetic country gentleman, fishing and shooting nearby, and within convenient distance of the main railway line to London which he could visit easily if business required his attention there. His cousin Nancy remarked 'he loved the beauty of Lilian's old home in Malhamdale',[8] and other visitors recalled that 'Their life style was that of wealthy landowners though they lived very simply.'[9] It was a place in which to combine the rural attractions reminiscent of his early district officer life with an estate management and public figure role reminiscent of his later secretariat and gubernatorial life, albeit in very different surroundings, scope and circumstances. Their retirement, however, contained more than its fair measure of sadness. In 1957, Lady Colby's mother died and the following year her father also died. Both were buried in the churchyard of St Michael the Archangel close to their home.

Soon after he arrived back in Britain Colby addressed a joint meeting of the Royal Africa and Royal Empire Societies in London – on 7 June 1956 – taking as his subject 'Recent Developments in Nyasaland'.[10] It was a masterly and typically concise account of the way in which the country had progressed over the preceding eight years. Typically also, he concentrated on his old favourites:

In thinking of the particular aspects which I should stress today I decided to concentrate on the subject of economic and agricultural development because these two aspects are absolutely crucial in that particular country.

Even so he also dealt – albeit less fully – with forestry, transport, education, political development at the central and local level, and with federation; and he concluded by paying tribute to those who had helped him in his work:

any progress we made in Nyasaland during my term of office was due in very large measure to the unceasing toil and devotion to duty and tireless energy of the members of Her Majesty's Overseas Civil Service with whom I had the good fortune to serve. I am greatly indebted to every one of them.

He had hoped very much to secure appointment to the boards of various companies in Britain so that he could continue for a number of years to find an outlet for his financial and administrative talents, but in this he was disappointed.[11] His knowledge, judgement and administrative ability would have made him an invaluable director of companies with Nyasaland interests, but those companies suspected his opposition to federation – which they believed would improve business opportunities – and they also suspected that he had fallen out of favour with the Colonial Office and consequently would exercise little influence with the British government. He had, in any case, alienated two of the largest companies: the British Central Africa Company and the Nyasaland Railways. Although no directorships came his way, he did take over the administration of the Hanlith Hall estate,[12] with its 3000 acres, which until then had been losing a good deal of money, and 'put it on its feet'. His old characteristic of what some saw as ruthlessness, and others saw as sensible management, persisted, and he dispensed with the services of several of the old staff. His principal leisure pursuit in retirement was fishing and he fished locally with friends from nearby, but particularly enjoyed fishing in Scotland and on the Eden.[13] He also did a certain amount of shooting and played a good deal of golf.[14] He became a member of the Kirkby Malham Parochial Church Council and went to church, where he frequently read the lesson at Matins on Sundays. He was also appointed a governor – with significantly less onerous responsibilities than those to which he was accustomed – of the Kirkby Malham village school, and was the chief guest of honour at the annual speech day at Ermysted's Grammar School in 1957.[15]

In presenting the prizes on this occasion, Colby congratulated the prize winners and attributed their success to 'ability, industry, memory and luck', qualities which he was sure would be of great value to them in life after school. He then turned to those who had not won prizes and – no doubt thinking of a number of colonial governors – assured them that they need not despair for there were many examples of people who had achieved fame after undistinguished academic records at school. Scholastic ability, he added, was only one ingredient of success; there were others 'of equal or greater importance' which he would shortly describe. He said that the boys would realize what the school had done for them when they left and believed that they could repay their debt by providing the leadership which was so much needed.

In this short speech at Ermysted's, the 'Ancient Free Grammar School of Skipton', Colby was able to look back to his own schooldays 40 years earlier at Charterhouse, and to distil into the speech the essence of his experience and beliefs about what counts in life: ability, industry and memory contribute to academic success, but they must be accompanied by luck, and fuller success requires them to be accompanied by courage, integrity, humanity and generosity. He believed that those who were fortunate enough to be educated at the great schools had an obligation to provide wise and sympathetic leadership in their careers in order to overcome the ignorance which he saw as lying at the root of many ills in the world.

Exactly five months short of a hundred years earlier, David Livingstone, also recently returned from many years in Africa, delivered his famous Cambridge Senate House lecture, the peroration of which contained the words: 'I beg to direct your attention to Africa. I know that in a few years time I shall be cut off in that country, which is now open; do not let it be shut again . . . do you carry on the work which I have begun. I leave it with you!'[16]

Now, Colby, a century later, having worked for eight years in the area to which Livingstone had been appointed the first British consul, reached the close of his address to an audience of scholars, admittedly less distinguished. He had pushed the door of development – originally opened by Livingstone – very much more open than ever it had been before, and he did not want to see it begin to close again. He had already spoken of the need for leadership to combat ignorance in the world and he now, finally, turned to Africa. He spoke of the many opportunities there available to young men and, reflecting Livingstone's 'do you carry on the work which I have begun', added the hope that some of those listening to him would 'go out to help in the development of that continent'. His final words were: 'Life can still be an adventure.'

Colby's health, far from robust when he arrived, seems for a while to have improved; doctor friends – one of whom had been his and Lady Colby's personal physician in Nyasaland – who visited him in September 1956 noticed nothing of concern,[17] but in the winter of 1957–8 he became very ill indeed and was later taken to Leeds hospital where he was visited by a number of relatives, including his cousin Nancy Tallents.[18] When his brother Marcus went to visit him there and told the nurse who he was and whom he wished to see, she said, 'Oh, yes; he's dying. You know he's dying?' He had not, in fact, had any reason to suppose that his brother was so seriously unwell and was consequently somewhat alarmed by the nurse's Yorkshire bluntness.[19] Colby left the Leeds hospital and became the patient of a doctor in Manchester who specialized in leukaemia and was trying a new form of treatment with which, he said, his patient would live for another five years. Thus reassured and comforted, he was able to leave hospital and return to

Hanlith Hall, and although still very weak and able to do little, he looked forward to recovery and considered his weakness and his inability to write very much to be temporary and the result of his fingers being affected 'by my disease'; he had not been told what it was.[20] He had fallen behind with his correspondence and in writing to Kettlewell asked him to thank Apthorpe, commissioner of police, Matthews, district commissioner, and Haskard for their letters and to convey his and Lady Colby's love to the Hadlows. He sent his regards 'to all the Agricultural chaps'. He asked Kettlewell to buy and send to him a hundred pounds of coffee – unless it was a bore, in which case not to bother. He showed a keen interest in what was happening in Nyasaland and he looked forward to the Kettlewells and Apthorpes visiting Hanlith Hall when on leave: 'I shall look forward to hearing more details, when you get back in the late summer.' In March 1958 he wrote:

> I am gradually getting better but it is very slow and I can't do much yet. I am looking forward to the better weather and to being more in the open air – we have had a bellyful of cold and snow in the last two months and it is not until the last day or two that we have seen the sun.[21]

He still wrote with the firm, bold, quick handwriting with which he had penned so very many documents over the years. When he was visited by his cousin Nancy Tallents and her husband and son on 16–18 April at Hanlith Hall, they found him 'cheerful . . . but frail though able to walk and fish gently'.[22] The Apthorpes visited him in the summer of 1958 and Colby took them out in a Land-Rover to see some of the farms belonging to the estate. He was at the time 'having blood transfusions fairly frequently'.[23] The Kettlewells visited him at Hanlith Hall in November 1958 and found him, in appearance, in normal health. He enjoyed long walks by the streams with Kettlewell, talking endlessly about his time in Nyasaland with his mind as acute as ever and still demonstrating his remarkable grip on the country's affairs, but when Mrs Kettlewell asked Lady Colby how Sir Geoffrey was keeping, she received the reply, 'Oh, please don't ask.'[24] After this visit, he gradually lost ground until the end of November, when the disease started to advance rapidly. He was taken to Manchester hospital from where he made one of his periodic telephone calls to Marcus. The conversation seemed to be nothing out of the usual and Marcus recalled that Geoffrey then 'seemed one hundred per cent' and gave no cause for anxiety.[25] He was, however, putting on a very brave face and concealing from his brother how desperately ill he in fact was. It was his last telephone call. Lilian was with him in Manchester on a mild, showery day when he died on Monday, 22 December 1958, the forty-sixth anniversary of his grand-father's death: 'The last days were very very terrible for him because he had always looked forward to recovery.'[26]

His life's work was done, work which had culminated in an outstand-ing contribution to the development of Nyasaland, utilizing to the very full the last period in which economic development was possible, before massive preoccupation with political and security activity effectively frustrated it in the closing decade of colonial government in Nyasaland.[27] Hopefully, he was able to gain comfort from recalling the sentiments which he made clear to his audience at the meeting of the Royal African and Royal Empire Societies 18 months earlier when, even though no longer a governor, he was still at the height of his powers:

> The years I spent in Nyasaland were of great personal enjoyment and satisfaction to me. It was a great privilege and a fascinating experience to play a part in the development of a country which was overdue for a little attention.[28]

Far away in Nyasaland, where the day was warm and cloudy, with a few thundery showers,[29] a Viscount aircraft landed at Chileka airport, and from it stepped Dr Banda, returning from the All-African People's conference in Accra, Ghana. Barbed-wire barriers and lines of police mobile force officers greeted him while his followers – prevented by the police from entering the airport – waited 200 yards down the road. Banda defiantly announced to the waiting crowd and to reporters that 'civil disobedience, passive resistance and non-violence is the policy of the Nyasaland African Congress' and added:

> In Nyasaland we are the masters and . . . it is no use Welensky . . . whining now about the rising tide of African nationalism. It is simply the reaction to years of European domination.[30]

Colby, although he would have been saddened, would not have been surprised by this turn of events. He had recognized that in shifting the balance of economic power – by his development strategy which emphasized increased production for the fuller well-being of the African people – the political power was bound to shift also in their direction;

and he had given a few other nudges to the political balance of power, by introducing and then increasing the number of Africans in the legislative council, by creating non-racial district councils, and by taking the first, albeit small, steps in advancing Africans in the Civil Service. In his very earliest days in the country, he had warned that 'the political awakening of Africa is something irresistible'; he had tried to create a newspaper to guide African political thought; he had created the police mobile force to handle civil unrest; he had removed the tinder from the political powder keg of Africans on private estates; and he had advised against the imposition of federation.

Whilst Colby's life slipped swiftly away from him in Manchester, at the airport building at Chileka – itself a monument to his development drive – Dr Banda was taking an early step on the road along which he was to be rapidly propelled to the presidency of independent Malawi. That propulsion would not have been so smooth had not the British government had cause to believe that fast economic development was possible and that the country could manage on its own. It was Colby's contribution – his clarity of vision, his accuracy of perception, his steadfastness of purpose and his unceasing labours – between 1948 and 1956 which proved that such development could indeed be accomplished, and which later made it possible successfully to argue that Nyasaland could survive and even flourish independently of the federation – which Colby had disliked and thought unnecessary – and, within a reasonable period, independently of Britain, whose interests in Africa he had so long and so faithfully served.

In a blue bound volume in the nave of St Michael the Archangel, dedicated 'In memory of those who lived in Malhamdale and were cremated', is the entry, formal, modest and brief:

Colby, Geoffrey Francis Taylor

of Hanlith Hall, b. 1901 d. 1958

In many ways the essence of an epitaph had long existed in his Charter-house reputation: 'He was a brave player, a fast bowler and a hard hitter, being caught more often than bowled.' The *Times* obituary said of him:

> [His] appointment was much to the advantage of Nyasaland, a small inland territory which had always found it difficult to make ends meet . . . his special contribution, for which he will long be grate-

fully remembered, was the energy and efficiency with which he threw himself into the prosecution of a programme of economic development including notable improvement of agricultural production and marketing facilities. He was a good administrator and his work in Nyasaland may fairly be said to have set the protectorate on a new and more hopeful road.[31]

The most fitting epitaph, however, is provided anonymously by one who worked closely with him in Nyasaland:

He was a big man in all respects, physically, intellectually and with great moral courage. He had acute economic perception, ability to distil the essence of any problem, and exceptional drive and determination in promoting its solution. He seemed to thrive on difficulties and to enjoy challenge. His commanding influence pervaded the entire Service which, under his direction, worked as never before. All respected him, many were in awe of him, but most of those close to him revered him. His personal government of the country was undisputed: he was certainly the greatest development governor the country ever had.

Notes

Chapter 1

1. *The Times*, London, 25 March 1901, p.11.
2. *The Times*, London, 27 March 1901, p.1.
3. Information on Colby's family background is from correspondence and interviews with Lady Colby, Marcus Colby and Mrs Nancy Tallents.
4. *Medical Directory*, 1876, p.388; 1877, p.1250; *Medical Register*, 1859, p.61.
5. *Medical Directory*, 1876, p.388; *British Medical Journal*, 25 January 1913, p.202; *Medical Register*, 1859, p.61; 1884, p.232; St Thomas's Index to Pupils Entry Book, 1827–1930, IV.XNA; J. Auld, Archivist, University Library, Dundee to C.A.B., 24 February 1984.
6. *Medical Register*, 1884, p.232; St Thomas's Index to Pupils Entry Book, 1827–1930.
7. *Medical Directory*, March 1913, p.558; *British Medical Journal*, 22 March 1913, p.643; D'A. Power and W. R. Le Sanu, *Lives of the Fellows of the Royal College of Surgeons of England, 1930–1951*, London, Royal College of Surgeons of England, 1953 p.256; A. J. Flavell to C.A.B., 29 September 1983.
8. The following details are from D'A. Power and W. R. Le Sanu, *op. cit.*, p.154; J. V. Mitchell, St Peter's School, York, to C.A.B., 20 March 1987; St Peter's School, York, Entry Book, 1844–1915, p.203; Venn's Cambridge University Alumni; D. Owen, Keeper of the Archives, Cambridge University, to C.A.B., 23 July 1983; J. Foster, District Archivist, St Bartholemew's Hospital, to C.A.B., 18 July 1983, 14 September 1983, 5 January 1984, 21 May 1984; Marcus Colby, interview with C.A.B. 26 June 1984.
9. Surrey County Directories, 1909–34; A. McCormack, Surrey County Archivist, to C.A.B., 13 October 1983; N. Tallents to C.A.B., 19 August 1983; D'A. Power and W. R. Le Sanu, *op.cit.* pp.154–5; Marcus Colby, interview with C.A.B., 26 June 1984; *The Times*, London, 13 November 1954.
10. The following details are from P. Beavor to C.A.B., 21 October 1983, enclosing Beavor's draft history of Bryant and May; *Brymay Magazine*,

Autumn 1964, vol.31, no.1, pp.20–21; Bryant and May, *Making Matches, 1861–1961* (London: Newman Neame, 1961), pp.2–3, 6, 9, 10, 20.

11. *Dictionary of Business Biography* (London: Butterworths, 1983), vol.1, pp.488–91.

12. N. Tallents to C.A.B., 19 August 1983.

13. *Sugar in the Everglades* (n.p., US Sugar Corporation, 1941), p.5; *Sugar County: The Cane Sugar Industry in the South, 1753–1950* (Lexington: University of Kentucky Press, 1953), p.367; *Lure of the Sun: A Story of Palm Beach County* (n.a., n.d., n.p.), p.37, copy supplied by D. Coles, Florida State Archives, to C.A.B., 1 December 1983.

14. N. Tallents to C.A.B., 6 July 1983; *Charterhouse Register*, 1900–1925, pp.207, 243; A. J. Flavell to C.A.B., 29 September 1983; *The Times*, London, 15 August 1969; R. E. Colby, 'Mayfair, a Town within London', *Country Life*, 1966; *No.44 Grosvenor Square, London* (London: Country Life, 1962); *The Waterloo Despatch*, V & A Museum, Monograph 24, 1961.

15. Marcus Colby to C.A.B., 4 March 1982, and interview with C.A.B., 26 June 1984; N. Tallents to C.A.B., 6 July 1983.

16. L. J. Bartley, *The Story of Bexhill* (Bexhill on Sea: Parsons, 1971), pp.46, 89, 144, 162.

17. Information generally on Charterhouse is from *The Carthusian* (school magazine); *The Charterhouse Lists* (Blue Books); *Charterhouse Register*, 1900–1925; *Robinites Journal* (house magazine) supplied by Dr Ian Blake, Robinites housemaster, 1983; R. L. Arrowsmith, *Charterhouse Miscellany* (London: Gentry Books, 1982); A. L. Irvine, *Sixty Years at School* (Winchester: Wells, 1958); R. C. Robertson-Glasgow, *46 Not Out* (London: Hollis and Carter, 1948); F. Fletcher, *After Many Days* (London: Robert Hale, 1937).

18. *The Carthusian*, October 1914, p.359.

19. Arrowsmith, *op. cit.*, p.154.

20. Robertson-Glasgow, *op. cit.*, p.60.

21. *Robinites Journal*.

22. F. H. D. Pritchard, *Sixty Years Ago: A record of life at Charterhouse School, 1919–24* (mimeographed copy, privately held), p.10.

23. Ibid, p.4.

24. Ibid, pp.10–11.

25. Marcus Colby, interview with C.A.B., 26 June 1984.

26. R. L. Arrowsmith to C.A.B., 7 October 1983.

27. C. H. Burgess, Surrey County Cricket Club, to C.A.B., 17 March 1982, 22 March 1982, 2 April 1982.

28. Arrowsmith, *op. cit.*, p.149.

29. *Ibid*.

30. *The Carthusian*, vol.XI, 1914, to vol.XII, 1919, *passim*.

31. *The Carthusian*, vol.XII, no.400, October 1917, p.138; vol.XII, no.401, December 1917, p.153; vol.XII, no.404, October 1918.

32. Robertson-Glasgow, *op. cit.*, pp.69–71.

33. Fletcher, *op. cit.*, pp.201–4.

34. Lord Pearce to C.A.B., 9 October 1983.

35. Information generally on Cambridge, Clare College, and Colby's time there

is from A. C. Coulson to C.A.B., 21 May 1984 and 25 June 1984; N. T. Glynn to C.A.B., 1 May 1984, 22 May 1984, 28 May 1984 and 23 June 1984; J. G. Bond to C.A.B., 6 June 1984; W. Nightingale to C.A.B., 18 May 1984; C. Pickering to C.A.B., 22 May 1984; J. C. B. Wakeford to C.A.B., 20 May 1984; Lord Baker to C.A.B. 28 May 1984; R. Paul to C.A.B., 28 May 1984; C. Foster to C.A.B., 22 May 1984; J. Wardale to C.A.B., 21 May 1984; V. J. Marshall to C.A.B., 17 May 1984; D. Lysons to C.A.B., 21 May 1984; C. A. M. Thornton to C.A.B., 21 May 1984; R. Aird to C.A.B., 19 May 1984; H. de G. Gaudin to C.A.B., 20 May 1984; Marcus Colby, interview with C.A.B., 26 June 1984; University of Cambridge, *Historical Register*; D. Owen, Keeper of the Archives, Cambridge University, to C.A.B., 20 July 1983; M. D. Forbes, *Clare College, 1326–1926*, (Cambridge University Press, 1928).

36. W. A. Nightingale to C.A.B., 18 May 1984.
37. Lady Colby to C.A.B., 8 May 1984.
38. P. Collymore to C.A.B., 18 May 1984.
39. N. T. Glynn to C.A.B., 23 June 1984.
40. A. Coulson to C.A.B., 21 May 1984 and 25 June 1984.
41. C. A. M. Thornton to C.A.B., 21 May 1984.
42. Marcus Colby, interview with C.A.B., 26 June 1984.
43. D. Owen to C.A.B., 20 July 1983; Marcus Colby, interview with C.A.B., 26 June 1984.
44. N. T. Glynn to C.A.B., 22 May 1984.
45. Lord Baker to C.A.B., 28 May 1984.
46. D. Lysons to C.A.B., 21 May 1984.
47. Marcus Colby, interview with C.A.B., 26 June 1984.
48. J. Wardale to C.A.B., 21 May 1984.
49. Sir Harry Godwin to C.A.B., 8 May 1984.
50. Marcus Colby, interview with C.A.B., 26 June 1984.
51. Ibid.
52. Ibid.
53. A. Coulson to C.A.B., 25 June 1984.
54. N. T. Glynn to C.A.B., 1 and 22 May 1984.
55. V. J. Marshall to C.A.B., 17 May 1984.
56. V. J. Marshall to C.A.B., 22 May 1984.
57. J. C. B. Wakeford to C.A.B., 20 May 1984.
58. Lady Colby to C.A.B., 28 April 1981; Lady Colby, interview with C.A.B., 19 June 1983.
59. E. Parker, *The History of Cricket* (London, Seeley Services, n.d. [c.1950]), p.644.
60. R. Alston to C.A.B., 3 May 1984.
61. Lady Colby to C.A.B., 28 April 1981; Marcus Colby, interview with C.A.B., 26 June 1984.
62. H. McMorran to C.A.B., 12 February 1984.
63. I. Blake and H. W. Foot to C.A.B., 5 February 1984.
64. A. J. Flavell, Bodleian Library, Oxford, to C.A.B., 30 January 1984 and 6 February 1984; *The Isis*, 25 January 1922, p.14.

65. Lady Colby, interview with C.A.B., 19 June 1983; Marcus Colby, interview with C.A.B., 26 June 1984.
66. R. Furse, *Aucuparius* (London: Oxford University Press, 1962), Appendix 1.
67. Marcus Colby, interview with C.A.B., 26 June 1984.
68. Furse, *op. cit.*, p.230.
69. Furse, *op. cit.*, p.151; *Geographical Journal*, vol.LXXII, 1933, p.89; C. Kelly, Archivist, Royal Geographical Society to C.A.B., 16 May 1982; Sir Bryan Sharwood-Smith, *Recollections of British Administration in the Cameroons and Northern Nigeria, 1921–1957: But Always as Friends* (Durham, N. C.: Duke University Press, 1969), p.xvii.
70. Sir Rex Niven to C.A.B., 8 August 1983.
71. Nigeria Government Staff List, 1925, FCO Library Ref. no. JF 1521.

Chapter 2

1. A. C. G. Hastings, *Nigerian Days* (London: The Bodley Head, 1925), pp.222–3. See also Sharwood-Smith, *op.cit.*, pp.3–4.
2. Sir Rex Niven, *Nigerian Kaleidoscope* (London: Hurst, 1982), p.60.
3. Sharwood-Smith, *op.cit.*, p.4.
4. Hastings, *op.cit.*, pp.224–5; See also Sharwood-Smith, *op.cit.*, pp.48–9.
5. Lady Colby to C.A.B., 28 April 1981. Dates of tours in Nigeria are from this source. Information on Palmer is taken from Sir Richmond Palmer, *The Bornu Sahara and Sudan* (London: John Murray, 1936), p.vii; R. Heussler, *The British in Northern Nigeria* (London: Oxford University Press, 1968), p.62; and Niven, *op.cit.*, p.73.
6. Sir Alan Burns, *Colonial Civil Servant* (London: George Allen and Unwin, 1949), p.57.
7. Niven, *op.cit.*, pp.153–6.
8. Touring is well described in Niven, *op.cit.*, pp.64ff.
9. M. J. Bennion to C.A.B., 18 April 1982.
10. J. E. B. Hall to C.A.B., 25 September 1983.
11. Niven to C.A.B., 8 August 1983.
12. Niven, *op.cit.*, p.158.
13. Niven to C.A.B., 8 August 1983.
14. Bennion to C.A.B., 18 April 1982.
15. A. A. Shillingford to C.A.B., 15 March 1982.
16. Sir James Harford to C.A.B., March 1982.
17. J. E. B. Hall to C.A.B., 25 September 1983.
18. Harford to Lady Colby, 5 November 1980; Bennion to C.A.B., 8 April 1982.
19. Sir Donald Cameron, *My Tanganyika Service and Some Nigerian* (London, George Allen and Unwin, 1939), p.269.
20. Harford to C.A.B., March 1982.
21. Lady Colby, interview with C.A.B., 19 June 1983; Niven to C.A.B., 8 August 1983; Hall to C.A.B., 25 September 1983; Marcus Colby, interview with C.A.B., 26 June 1984.
22. Hastings, *op.cit.*, pp.246–8.

23. Bennion to C.A.B., 18 April 1982; W. R. Crocker, *Nigeria: a critique of British colonial administration*, (London: George Allen and Unwin, 1936), p.193; Sharwood-Smith, *op. cit.*, p.17.

24. Lady Colby to C.A.B., 28 April 1981; Marcus Colby, interview with CAB, 26 June 1984.

25. N. Tallents to C.A.B., 19 August 1983.

26. Lady Colby, interview with C.A.B., 19 June 1983.

27. Details of the Holden-Illingworth family are from *The Holden-Illingworth Letters* (Bradford: Percy Lund, Humphries and Co., The Country Press, 1927); John H. Illingworth, *The Malham Story* (London: Harrap, 1972); Lady Colby, interview with C.A.B., 19 June 1983; N. Tallents to C.A.B., 19 August 1983.

28. Illingworth, *op.cit.*, p.13.

29. Details of the wedding are from *The Yorkshire Observer*, 19 January 1931; Rev C. Trevor to C.A.B., 12 March 1982; N. Tallents to C.A.B., 19 August 1983; Marcus Colby, interview with C.A.B., 26 June 1984.

30. Hall to C.A.B., 25 September 1983.

31. Lady Colby to C.A.B., 28 April 1981.

32. Hall to C.A.B., 5 May 1983. The views expressed in the next sentence are from Sir Hugo Marshall to C.A.B., 24 July 1983 and Weatherhead to C.A.B., 21 September 1983.

33. Weatherhead to C.A.B., 21 September 1983. The following quotations describing Kaduna are from Niven, *op.cit.*, pp.76–8.

34. Niven, *op.cit.*, p.71.

35. Niven, *op.cit.*, pp.79–80.

36. Lady Colby to C.A.B., 28 April 1981, 8 May 1984 and 12 August 1984; Lady Colby, interview with C.A.B., 18 June 1983; Heussler, *op.cit.*, p.88.

37. Harford to C.A.B., March 1982.

38. Lady Colby to C.A.B., 12 August 1984.

39. Tallents to C.A.B., 6 July 1983; Secretary, English Bridge Union to C.A.B., 3 March 1989; *Bridge Magazine*, April 1935, p.546, and June 1935, pp.52–7.

40. Hastings *op. cit.*, p.204; see also Heussler, *op. cit.*, p.89.

41. Sharwood-Smith, *op. cit.*, pp.124–5.

42. Shillingford to C.A.B., 15 March 1982; D. A. Potts to C.A.B., 16 December 1983.

43. D. A. Potts to C.A.B., 16 December 1983.

44. Lady Colby to C.A.B., 12 August 1984 and 24 September 1987.

45. Lady Colby to C.A.B., 12 August 1984.

46. Weatherhead to C.A.B., 21 September 1983.

47. Hall to C.A.B., 25 September 1983.

48. Marcus Colby, interview with C.A.B., 26 June 1984.

49. Lady Colby to C.A.B., 12 August 1984.

50. Niven, *op.cit.*, pp.3. and 9.

51. Lady Colby to C.A.B., 28 April 1981.

52. *Colonial Office Memorandum on Financial Organisation of Colonial Government*, reproduced in *Nyasaland Government Gazette*, 1937, pp.125–7.

53. Lady Colby to C.A.B., 28 April 1981; Hall to C.A.B., 25 September 1983.

54. Lady Colby to C.A.B., 28 April 1981.

55. Sir Thomas Shankland to C.A.B., 15 February 1983. Details of the work of the supply branch are from this source, unless otherwise stated. H. T. Bourdillon to C.A.B., 6 July 1983 and 19 July 1983; Sir Kenneth Maddocks to C.A.B., 7 August 1984.

56. Hall to C.A.B., 5 May 1983; Sir Eric Tansley to C.A.B., 24 March 1983 and 28 November 1983; Mrs F. C. Cann to C.A.B., 16 October 1983; R. Varvill to C.A.B., 31 March 1983, 8 May 1983 and 17 May 1983.

57. Lady Colby to C.A.B., 15 February 1983; and an account written by Colby from Nairobi, 3 November 1942.

58. Sir Frederick Pedler to C.A.B., 8 July 1983.

59. Lady Hoskyns-Abrahall to C.A.B., 17 July 1983.

60. Hall to C.A.B., 5 May 1983 and 25 September 1983; the quotation in the following sentence is from Shankland to C.A.B., 20 November 1983.

61. Hall to C.A.B., 5 May 1983.

62. Niven to C.A.B., 8 August 1983; R. Peel to C.A.B., 21 July 1983 and 21 November 1983. See also R. Peel, *Old Sinister* (Cambridge: Piggott, n.d. [c.1985]).

63. Peel to C.A.B., 21 July 1983.

64. Lady Colby, interview with C.A.B., 19 June 1983.

65. Nigeria Government Staff List, 1945, FCO Library Ref. no. JF 1521.

66. Niven to C.A.B., 8 August 1983.

67. Peel to C.A.B., 21 July 1983.

68. Lord Grey to C.A.B., 5 February 1983.

69. Sir Hugo Marshall to C.A.B., 20 May 1983; Hall to C.A.B., 25 September 1983; Shankland to C.A.B., 20 November 1983; Peel to C.A.B., 21 July 1983.

70. Lord Grey to C.A.B., 17 August 1982; Peel to C.A.B., 21 July 1983.

71. M. Varvill to C.A.B., 8 May 1983; Peel to C.A.B., 21 November 1983.

72. Shankland to C.A.B., 20 November 1983.

73. Senior promotions are dealt with in A. H. M. Kirk-Greene, 'On Governorship and Governors in British Africa', in L. H. Gann and P. Duignan (eds.), *African Proconsuls: European Governors in Africa* (New York: The Free Press, 1979), pp.250 ff.

74. Sir Hilton Poynton to C.A.B., 21 May 1982.

75. Sir John Martin to C.A.B., 3 May 1982.

76. Sir Hilton Poynton to C.A.B., 21 May 1982.

77. A. H. M. Kirk-Greene, *The Progress of Pro-Consuls: Advancement and Migration among the Colonial Governors of British African Territories, 1900–1965* (Oxford: Institute of Commonwealth Studies, 1979).

78. Sir William Gorell Barnes to C.A.B., 14 May 1982; Sir Hilton Poynton to C.A.B., 26 April 1982; Sir George Cartland to C.A.B., 21 September 1982; M. J. Davies to C.A.B., 4 May 1982. See also Darrell Bates, *A Gust of Plumes: A Biography of Lord Twining of Godalming and Tanganyika* (London: Hodder and Stoughton, 1972), p. 182.

79. Lady Colby to C.A.B., 28 April 1981.

80. Lady Colby to C.A.B., 28 April 1981; G. D. Hayes, 'Lake Nyasa and the 1914–1918 War', *Nyasaland Journal*, vol.xvii, no.2, 1964, pp.17–24.

81. Lady Colby to C.A.B., 2 August 1981; Lady Colby, interview with C.A.B., 18 June 1983.
82. John Haslam, assistant press secretary to the Queen, to C.A.B., 17 July 1984.

Chapter 3

1. *Nyasaland Times*, 19 February 1948, p.7.
2. Lady Colby to C.A.B., 28 April 1981.
3. A. H. M. Kirk-Greene, 'On Governorship and Governors in British Africa', in L. H. Gann and P. Duignan (eds.), *African Proconsuls: European Governors in Africa* (New York: The Free Press, 1979), p.228.
4. *Ibid.*, p.227.
5. Sir Rex Niven, *Nigerian Kaleidoscope* (London: Hurst, 1982), pp.147–8.
6. Sir Alexander Grantham, *Via Ports* (Hong Kong University Press, 1965), p.63; Niven, *op. cit.*, p.237.
7. Sir Darrell Bates, *A Gust of Plumes* (London: Hodder and Stoughton, 1972), p.211.
8. Winifred Tapson, *Old Timer* (Cape Town: Howard Timmins, 1957), chapter I. Details, which follow, of the journey are from this source, unless otherwise stated.
9. Lady Colby, interview with C.A.B., 18 and 19 June 1983.
10. Ibid.
11. Ibid.
12. Lady Jenkins to C.A.B., 30 May 1983.
13. Lady Colby to C.A.B., 28 April 1981.
14. Ibid.
15. For a general account of the country, see J. G. Pike and G. T. Rimmington, *Malawi: A Geographical Study* (London: Oxford University Press, 1965).
16. C. A. Baker, 'Nyasaland, the History of its Export Trade', *Nyasaland Journal*, vol.XV, no.1, January 1962, pp.7–35.
17. C. A. Baker, *Johnston's Administration* (Zomba: The Government Press, 1970).
18. Details of the annual budgets and the size of the Civil Service are from the *Annual Estimates of Expenditure, Nyasaland* for the relevant years.
19. R. C. F. Maughan, *Nyasaland in the Nineties* (London: Lincoln Williams, 1935), p.30.
20. A. Johnston, *The Life and Letters of Sir Harry Johnston* (London: Jonathan Cape, 1929), p.130.
21. *Ibid.*, p.24.
22. L. Decle, *Three Years in Savage Africa* (London: Methuen, 1900), p.260.
23. R. B. Boeder, *Alfred Sharpe of Nyasaland: Builder of Empire* (Blantyre: Society of Malawi, 1981).
24. H. L. Duff, *African Small Chop* (London: Hodder and Stoughton, 1932), pp.23–4.
25. E. Booth Langworthy, *This Africa Was Mine* (n.p.; Sterling, 1950), p.51.
26. A. Sharpe, 'Recent Progress in Nyasaland', *Journal of the African Society*, vol.IX, no.36, July 1910, pp.337–48.

27. *Legislative Council Proceedings* (hereafter LCP followed by the Session Number) 9, May 1912, p.3. For the railway guarantee see chapter 9.
28. LCP 22, March 1920, pp.3–4.
29. Ibid., pp.7, 17.
30. LCP, Extraordinary Session, June 1920, p.4.
31. LCP 23, January 1921, p.26.
32. LCP 40, December 1929, p.3.
33. LCP 27, April 1923, p.3.
34. LCP 29, May 1924, p.5.
35. LCP 32, April 1926, pp.13–14.
36. LCP 34, May 1927, p.7.
37. Ibid., p.18.
38. M. E. Leslie to C.A.B., July 1979.
39. LCP 39, April 1929, p.6.
40. LCP 40, December 1929, pp.3–6.
41. E. C. Barnes to C.A.B., 26 July 1979.
42. M. E. Leslie to C.A.B., July 1979.
43. R. D. Martin to C.A.B., 10 August 1979.
44. LCP 44, November 1931, p.4.
45. LCP 40, December 1929, p.3.
46. LCP 41, April 1930, p.3.
47. LCP 42, September 1930, p.3.
48. LCP 41, April 1930, p.3.
49. Passfield to Thomas, 15 July 1930, National Archives of Malawi, (hereafter referred to as NAM) SI/124AI/29, 4A. Ec. 151278 *et seq.*
50. *Yearbook and Guide to the Rhodesias and Nyasaland, 1937*, unreferenced volume in NAM.
51. C. A. Baker, *The Evolution of Local Government in Malawi* (Ile Ife: University of Ife Press, 1975), Chapter 5.
52. Governor's Circular no.19/33, 8 June 1933, FCO Library, 13648, vol.I.
53. Sir Roy Welensky, interview with C.A.B., 12 June 1982.
54. *Nyasaland Government Gazette*, 1939, p.5.
55. LCP 51, October 1935, p.2.
56. LCP 45, June 1932, p.5.
57. LCP 51, October 1935, p.2.
58. NAM, SI/1404II/28.
59. LCP 56, December 1940, p.13.
60. *Nyasaland Government Gazette*, 1940, 1941, 1943, *passim.*
61. M. E. Leslie, private diary, February 1941.
62. *Nyasaland Government Gazette*, 30 November 1912.
63. M. E. Leslie to C.A.B., July 1979.
64. E. C. Barnes to C.A.B., 26 July 1979. This information was given to Barnes by Lady Richards.
65. R. W. Kettlewell to C.A.B., August 1979; Lady Jenkins to C.A.B., 26 July 1983.

Chapter 4

1. *Nyasaland Times* (hereafter referred to as *NT*), 6 January 1949, p.7 and 22 January 1950, p.5.
2. Lady Colby, interview with C.A.B., 18 June 1983.
3. *NT*, 2 December 1948, p.8; LCP 64, November 1948, Governor's opening address.
4. LCP 66, November 1950, p.9, Governor's opening address.
5. LCP 65, November 1949, pp.8–9, Governor's budget address.
6. R. W. Kettlewell, *Agricultural Change in Nyasaland: 1945–1960* (Stanford University Press, 1965), p.238.
7. LCP 64, February 1949, pp.2–3, Governor's opening address; LCP 65, November 1949, p.9, Governor's budget address.
8. Governor's reply to speech of welcome by president of Nyasaland Chamber of Commerce, 12 July 1948, reported in *NT*, 15 July 1948, pp.7ff.
9. G. F. T. Colby, 'Recent Developments in Nyasaland', *African Affairs*, vol.55, no.221, October 1956, pp.273ff.
10. Governor's reply to speech of welcome by president of Nyasaland Chamber of Commerce, 12 July 1948, reported in *NT*, 15 July 1948, pp.7ff.
11. Governor's New Year message, reported in *NT*, 27 December 1951.
12. *NT*, 13 February 1950, p.4.
13. Details of Civil Service establishment and of annual expenditure here and elsewhere in this chapter are taken from the *Annual Estimates of Expenditure*, 1948–1956. Expenditure figures are actual and not corrected for inflation.
14. Kettlewell, *op. cit.*, pp.238–9.
15. Annual Report, Department of Agriculture, 1950, part I, p.5.
16. Kettlewell, *op. cit.*, p.239.
17. Governor's address to Nyasaland African Protectorate Council, 7 July 1948, reported in *NT*, 22 July 1948, p.3.
18. Colby to senior government officers, January 1950, on subject of 'The need for greatly increased production', privately held.
19. Natural Resources (Amendment) Ordinance, no.22 of 1949; Kettlewell, *op. cit.*, pp.240–1.
20. *An Outline of Agrarian Problems and Policy in Nyasaland* (Zomba, 1955), ref. no. Sec 7368/650/4.55, paper laid on table of Legislative Council on 2 May 1955; also Kettlewell, interview with C.A.B., 5 September 1973.
21. Colby to Kettlewell, 20 January 1955, privately held.
22. R. Peel, *Old Sinister: A Memoir of Sir Arthur Richards* (Cambridge, no publisher, n.d.), p.186.
23. *Report of the Post-War Development Committee*, (Zomba, 1946), p.89; *Nyasaland Protectorate Annual Reports*, 1948, p.30 and 1956, p.87.
24. Kettlewell, *op. cit.*, pp.247–9.
25. Kettlewell, *op. cit.*, pp.247–9; Kettlewell to C.A.B., 18 February 1990.
26. T. S. Bell (former development secretary) to C.A.B., 28 December 1982.
27. *Nyasaland Protectorate Annual Reports*, 1948–1956, *passim*.
28. *Report of the Post-War Development Committee*, pp.2–3.
29. *Report on a Fiscal Survey of Nyasaland*, (Zomba, 1947), p.7.
30. LCP 63, July 1948, Governor's opening address.

31. Colby, *op. cit.*, p.279.
32. *Nyasaland Protectorate Annual Reports*, 1948–1956, *passim*.
33. *Nyasaland Protectorate Annual Report*, 1948, p.31; *Report of Standing Finance Committee, Annual Estimates*, 1954, p.*v.*
34. *Nyasaland Protectorate Annual Report*, 1951, p.56.
35. *Nyasaland Protectorate Annual Report*, 1954, p.95.
36. Lady Colby, interview with C.A.B., 18 June 1983.
37. Colby, *op. cit.*, p.280.
38. Ibid.
39. C. A. Baker, 'The Government Medical Service in Malawi, 1891–1974', *Medical History*, vol.20, no.3. July 1976, pp.296–311.
40. Lady Jenkins to C.A.B., 26 July 1983.
41. *Annual Staff Lists* 1948–56; *Nyasaland Protectorate Annual Reports*, 1949, p.54; 1950, p.67; 1951, p.82; 1952, p.106; 1953, p.115.
42. *Nyasaland Protectorate Annual Report*, 1950, p.65.
43. LCP 65, November 1949, p.8, Governor's opening address.
44. *Nyasaland Protectorate Annual Reports*, 1948, pp.43–4; 1956, pp.119–20.
45. Governor's address to the third annual conference of the Nyasaland Council of Women, 2 July 1948, reported in *NT*, 8 July 1948, p.7.
46. Governor's reply to speech of welcome by president of Nyasaland Chamber of Commerce, 12 July 1948, reported in *NT*, 15 July 1948, pp.7ff.
47. For example, from the Convention of Associations and the Council of Women; *NT*, 18 February 1948, p.6 and 8 March 1948, p.2.
48. Financial secretary's memorandum, *Annual Estimates*, 1948, p.19.
49. Financial secretary's memorandum, *Annual Estimates*, 1949, p.13. For the Aden, Gold Coast and Nigerian disturbances, see Sir Charles Jeffries, *The Colonial Police* (London, Max Parrish, 1952), Chapter 12.
50. *Nyasaland Protectorate Annual Reports*, 1952, p.98; 1953, pp.106–7.
51. Police (Amendment) Ordinance, no.21 of 1953.
52. *Nyasaland Protectorate Annual Report*, 1953, p.5.
53. *Nyasaland Protectorate Annual Report*, 1953, p.106.
54. Report of Standing Finance Committee, *Annual Estimates*, 1954–5, p.*vi* and p.*x*.
55. Executive Council (hereafter Ex. Co.), 16 September 1953, Minute 528.
56. LCP 66, November 1950, p.9.
57. Ex. Co., 14 March 1951, Minute 137; 23 May 1951, Minute 251; 4 July 1951, Minute 317; 17 July 1951, Minute 331; 2 August 1951, Minute 361; 18 October 1951, Minute 483; 24 October 1951, Minute 494.
58. LCP 67, December 1951, *passim*; *NT*, 7.1.1952, Leader, p.6; *East Africa and Rhodesia*, 31 January 1952, Leader.
59. G. Hodgson (former provincial commissioner and clerk to Ex. Co.) to C.A.B., 22 October 1981.
60. *Development Plan 1962–1965*, (Zomba, 1962), p.43.
61. C. E. Lucas Phillips, *The Vision Splendid* (London, Heinemann, 1960), pp.264–5.

Chapter 5

1. Details of Government House and Colby's work there, unless otherwise stated, are taken from correspondence with the private secretary and aide-de-camp, 1948–9, D. G. Longden, to C.A.B., 1982–7; and Mrs J. Henderson, (Government House stenographer, 1948–9) to Longden, 21 July 1982, privately held.
2. D. G. Longden to C.A.B., 26 August 1982.
3. A. H. Mell to C.A.B., 7 November 1982.
4. *Nyasaland Government Gazette*, 1948, p.52; *NT*, 15 March 1948, p.4.
5. G. Hodgson to C.A.B., 22 October 1981.
6. See, for example, Minutes of 71 Session of Convention of Associations, 22 July 1949, NAM; *NT*, 15 March 1951, p.14, reporting proceedings of the chamber of commerce.
7. G. Hodgson to C.A.B., 22 October 1981.
8. There are numerous examples of this and of the following points in the secretariat files in the National Archives of Malawi.
9. H. E. I. Phillips, interviews with C.A.B., 20 January 1989 and 31 August 1990.
10. R. W. Kettlewell to C.A.B., August 1979.
11. G. Hodgson to C.A.B., 22 October 1981.
12. H. E. I. Phillips, interview with C.A.B., 20 January 1989.
13. R. W. Kettlewell to C.A.B., 16 November 1986.
14. R. Rowland to C.A.B., 20 September 1982.
15. R. W. Kettlewell, interview with C.A.B., 8 November 1986.
16. R. W. Kettlewell to C.A.B., 18 February 1990.
17. Ex. Co., 3 June 1948, Minute 182.
18. D. G. Longden to C.A.B., 3 March 1983.
19. Ex. Co., 29 April 1948, Minute 127.
20. For example, Ex. Co., 20 May 1948, Minute 156.
21. R. W. Kettlewell to C.A.B., 16 November 1986.
22. R. Rowland to C.A.B., 21 June 1982.
23. *NT*, 6 March 1950, p.5; R. W. Kettlewell to C.A.B., 16 November 1986.
24. *NT*, 11 May 1950, p.7.
25. P. K. O'Riordan to C.A.B., 8 November 1983.
26. *NT*, 2 October 1950, p.7.
27. *NT*, 11 January 1951, p.7.
28. I. Nance to C.A.B., 4 April 1983.
29. R. Rowland to C.A.B., 21 June 1982.
30. D. A. G. Reeve to C.A.B., 9 February 1982.
31. R. Rowland to C.A.B., 20 April 1982.
32. G. Hodgson to C.A.B., 22 October 1981.
33. R. Rowland to C.A.B., 20 April 1982 and 21 June 1982; H. Eaton to C.A.B. 24 April 1984.
34. R. Rowland to C.A.B., 20 April 1982.
35. R. W. Kettlewell to C.A.B., 16 November 1986 and 18 February 1990.
36. A. H. Mell to C.A.B., 7 November 1982.
37. G. Hodgson to C.A.B., 22 October 1981.

38. H. Eaton to C.A.B., 24 April 1984.
39. J. Watson to C.A.B., 30 March 1982; I. Nance to C.A.B., 4 April 1983; D. A. G. Reeve to C.A.B., 9 February 1982.
40. See Chapter 10.
41. H. S. Norman Walker to C.A.B., 2 May 1982.
42. P. K. O'Riordan to C.A.B., 8 November 1983; R. G. M. Willan to C.A.B., 17 April 1986, 29 May 1986, 22 March 1987. Details of the Mlanje Mountain visit are from these sources.
43. D. G. Longden to C.A.B., 3 March 1983.
44. *Nyasaland Government Gazettes*, 1948–56, *passim*.
45. D. G. Longden to C.A.B., 26 August 1982; Lady Colby, interview with C.A.B., 19 June 1983; Mrs E. Apthorpe to C.A.B., 27 July 1983; R. Rowland to C.A.B., 21 June 1982.
46. P. F. C. Nicholson to C.A.B., 7 April 1982.

Chapter 6

1. The following details are from H. S. Norman Walker to C.A.B., 2 May 1982; H. Graham Jolly to C.A.B., 13 September 1982; H. Eaton to C.A.B., 24 April 1984.
2. *NT*, 9 April 1951, p.7, and 16 April 1951, p.5.
3. H. Graham Jolly to C.A.B., 19 February 1983.
4. H. Eaton to C.A.B., 24 April 1984.
5. The following details are from C. B. Garnett to C.A.B., 11 May 1982, 5 and 23 January 1985 and 26 April 1985; C. B. Garnett, interview with C.A.B., 4 February 1985; R. W. Kettlewell to C.A.B., 26 January 1985 and 16 November 1986.
6. The following details are from J. S. Lynn to C.A.B., 22 November 1985 and 23 April and 17 July 1986; J. Patterson to C.A.B., 10 July and 7 September 1986; A. C. Heathcote to C.A.B., 4 July and 26 August 1986; *Nyasaland Government Staff List*, 1948; *Nyasaland Government Gazette*, 1948; Ex. Co. 10 August 1948, Minute 221.
7. The following details are from *Nyasaland Government Staff List*, 1948; D. G. Longden to C.A.B., 3 March 1983; G. Hodgson to C.A.B., 20 June 1984.
8. R. W. Kettlewell to C.A.B., 18 February 1990.
9. The following details are from *Nyasaland Government Gazette*, 1953 and 1955; A. H. Mell to C.A.B., 7 November 1982; J. Edwards to C.A.B., 18 April 1984.
10. H. Graham Jolly to C.A.B., 13 September 1982 and 19 February 1983.
11. J. Henderson to D. G. Longden, 21 July 1982, privately held.
12. A. Dow, interview with C.A.B., 20 November 1983.
13. Details in this paragraph are from Ex. Co., 4 January 1950, Minute 14; and D. Dow, interview with C.A.B., 20 November 1983.
14. J. Patterson to C.A.B., 7 September 1986; A. C. Heathcote to C.A.B., 26 August 1986.
15. The following details are from R. W. Kettlewell to C.A.B., 23 April 1982,

26 January 1985, 18 February 1990; P. Scott to C.A.B., 8 November 1983; *NT,* 26 April 1951, p.7.

16. R. W. Kettlewell, speech at the opening of the Lilongwe Agricultural Show, reported in *NT,* 11 August 1952, p.14.
17. *Nyasaland Government Staff Lists,* 1952–5.
18. R. W. Kettlewell to C.A.B., 16 November 1986, 22 February 1987, 18 February 1990.
19. *Nyasaland Government Staff List,* 1956.
20. Colby to Cohen, 29 May 1951, Colby Papers.
21. M. J. Bennion to C.A.B., 18 September 1982.
22. W. R. Crocker, *Nigeria, a Critique of British Colonial Administration* (London: George Allen and Unwin, 1936), p.199.
23. A few years earlier, Twining, then governor of North Borneo, had made similar representations to the Colonial Office; Darrell Bates, *A Gust of Plumes* (London: Hodder and Stoughton, 1972), p.167.
24. See Chapter 10.
25. H. E. I. Phillips, interviews with C.A.B., 20 January 1989 and 31 August 1990.
26. Lady Colby, interview with C.A.B., 19 June 1983.
27. R. Rowland to C.A.B., 20 September, 1982.
28. D. G. Longden to C.A.B., 26 August 1982.
29. R. C. Robertson-Glasgow, *46 Not Out* (London: Hollis and Carter, 1948), p.61.
30. G. F. T. Colby, 'Recent Developments in Nyasaland', *African Affairs,* vol.55, no.22, October 1956, p.281.

Chapter 7

1. See Chapter 6.
2. H. W. Stevens to C.A.B., 22 May 1982.
3. See Chapter 3.
4. D. G. Longden to C.A.B., 26 August 1982.
5. H. Eaton to C.A.B., 24 April 1984.
6. See Chapter 4.
7. See Chapter 11.
8. *NT,* 5 December 1949, p.4.
9. *NT,* 4 December 1950, p.4.
10. *NT,* 24 May 1951, p.6.
11. Lady Colby, interview with C.A.B., 19 June 1983; and *Who Was Who, 1961–1970*
12. *NT,* 24 May 1951, p.6.
13. R. W. Kettlewell to C.A.B., 18 February 1990.
14. *NT, 24 May 1951, p.6.*
15. *NT,* 2 February 1950, pp.7 and 13.
16. *NT,* 13 February 1950, p.4.
17. See Colin Baker, 'Depression and Development in Nyasaland, 1929–1939', *The Society of Malawi Journal,* vol.XXVII, no.1, January 1974, pp.7–26.
18. *NT,* 13 February 1950, p.4.

19. H. S. Norman Walker to C.A.B., 2 May 1982.
20. Details in this paragraph are from: Lady Colby, interview with C.A.B., 19 June 1983; R. W. Kettlewell to C.A.B., 24 February and 8 September 1983, and 22 February 1987; and I. Schwarz, Sir Malcolm Barrow's private secretary, to C.A.B., 7 February 1983.
21. *NT*, 18 December 1953, p.1, and 22 December 1953, p.8; Lady Colby, interview with C.A.B., 18 June 1983.
22. H. S. Norman Walker to C.A.B., 2 May 1982; W. D. Lewis to C.A.B., 22 May 1982; R. W. Kettlewell, interview with C.A.B., 8 November 1986.
23. R. W. Kettlewell to C.A.B., 16 November 1986.
24. M. H. Blackwood to C.A.B., 1 February 1982.
25. Details in the remainder of this paragraph are from M. Widdas to C.A.B., 29 May 1983.
26. See Chapters 9 and 11.
27. Details in this and the following paragraph are from M. J. Bennion to C.A.B., 18 September 1982, unless otherwise stated. Bennion's Colonial Service career was spent in northern Nigeria, the Nigeria secretariat, Lagos and Nyasaland.
28. R. Rowland to C.A.B., 20 April 1982.
29. I. Nance to C.A.B., 8 August 1979.
30. This point is also made by Sir Rex Niven, *Nigerian Kaleidoscope* (London: Hurst, 1982), p.17; Sir Bryan Sharwood-Smith, *op. cit.*, p.108; and Sir Alan Burns, *Colonial Civil Servant* (London: George Allen and Unwin, 1949), p.107.
31. Reprinted in *NT*, 2 February 1950, pp.7 and 13.
32. See Chapter 5.
33. Mposa, interviews with C.A.B., 1955 to 1956; Muwamba, interviews with C.A.B., 1964 to 1970.
34. *Nyasaland Protectorate Annual Reports*, 1950, pp.72–3; 1951, p.58; 1956, p.8.
35. Ex. Co., 14 December 1949, Minute 655.
36. Ex. Co., 14 December 1949, Minute 641; September 1952, Minute 390; 22 October 1952, Minute 461; *Staff Lists*, 1953 and 1955.
37. Ex. Co., 24 March 1952, Minute 148.
38. R. C. Robertson–Glasgow, *46 Not Out* (London: Hollis and Carter, 1948), p. 60.

Chapter 8

1. For fuller details of the department's development, see Colin Baker, 'The Postal Services in Malawi Before 1900', *Society of Malawi Journal*, vol.24, no.1, 1971, pp.14–51, and 'The Administration of Posts and Telecommunications', *Society of Malawi Journal*, vol.29, no.2, 1980.
2. LCP 34, May 1927, p.19.
3. *Report of the Post-War Development Committee* (Zomba: The Government Press, 1946; hereafter referred to as RPWDC); and *Revised Report of the Post-War Development Committee* (Zomba: The Government Press, 1947; hereafter referred to as RRPWDC).

4. RPWDC, para.98.
5. RPWDC, para.100.
6. RRPWDC, paras.74 and 75.
7. RRPWDC, para.75.
8. RRPWDC, paras.76 and 77.
9. Telegraph engineer to postmaster-general, 30 October 1949, privately held.
10. W. J. Silvester to C.A.B., 4 August 1986.
11. Telegraph engineer to postmaster-general, 30 October 1949, privately held.
12. A. C. Heathcote to C.A.B., 4 July 1986.
13. Ex. Co., 10 August 1948, Minute 221.
14. 'Report of the Standing Committee on Finance', *Annual Estimates*, 1948 (Zomba: The Government Press), 1948, p.3.
15. See Chapter 6.
16. Reference to these events is found in Arthur Loveridge, *I Drank the Zambezi* (New York: Harper, 1953), p.17, and *NT*, 16 August 1948, p.5.
17. *NT*, 16 August 1948, p.5.
18. Ex. Co., 1 July 1948, Minute 192.
19. Ibid; also A. C. Heathcote to C.A.B., 26 August 1986.
20. *NT*, 16 August 1948, p.5.
21. Ex. Co., 10 August 1948, Minute 221.
22. R. C. Smith, *Rhodesia, A Postal History* (Salisbury: Marden, 1967), p.249; Ex. Co., 25 October 1948, Minute 276.
23. Ex. Co., 25 October 1948, Minute 276.
24. *NT*, 8 September 1949, p.7.
25. J. I. Patterson to C.A.B., 10 July 1986 and 7 September 1986.
26. A. C. Heathcote to C.A.B., 26 August 1986.
27. E. S. Ellis to C.A.B., 15 May 1986, and J. I. Patterson to C.A.B., 10 July 1986.
28. *Nysaland Government Gazette*, 1948, p.50.
29. Convention of Associations, 71 Session, 22 July 1949, referring to previous meeting, *NT*, 4 August 1949, p.4.
30. *NT*, 16 January 1950, p.7.
31. *NT*, 11 May 1950, p.4.
32. J. I. Patterson to C.A.B., 10 July 1986, and W. J. Silvester to C.A.B., 26 August 1986.
33. W. J. Silvester to C.A.B., 4 August 1986.
34. *NT*, 4 August 1949, p.4.
35. E. S. Ellis to C.A.B., 15 May 1986.
36. *NT*, 15 February 1951, p.2, and 16 April 1951, p.5.
37. Ibid.
38. *Protectorate Annual Reports*, 1950, p.71; 1952, pp. 109–10; 1953, p.122; and *NT*, 20 November 1950, p.1.
39. 'Report of the Standing Committee on Finance', 1952, p.3.
40. Federal constitution, 2nd Schedule, Part I, item 27.
41. *Nyasaland Government Gazette*, 1954, p.249.
42. H. Hepburn to C.A.B., 30 August 1982.
43. J. I. Patterson to C.A.B., 10 July 1986.
44. *Staff List*, 1953.

Chapter 9

1. Material on the evolution of the system is drawn from: B. Pachai, *Malawi: the History of the Nation* (London: Longman, 1973), pp.143–52; L. Vail, 'The Making of an Imperial Slum: Nyasaland and Its Railways', *Journal of African History*, xvi, 2, 1975, pp.89–112; *Report of the Commission Appointed to Enquire into the Financial Position and Further Development of Nyasaland*, Colonial No.152 (London: HMSO: 1938), pp.111–12, 282–329 (hereafter referred to as Bell Report).

2. *Central Africa Times* (hereafter referred to as *CAT*), 18 January 1908, p.4.

3. *CAT*, 11 January 1908, p.7; 18 January 1908, p.7; Bell Report, p.284.

4. The material in this and the following eight paragraphs is drawn from Bell Report, paragraphs 508–9, 516–24, 532, 548–51 and 555.

5. Nyasaland Government Annual Estimates 1937–1948.

6. Phillips, interviews with C.A.B., 20 January 1989 and 23 August 1989.

7. *Report on a Fiscal Survey of Nyasaland* (Zomba: The Government Press, 1947; hereafter referred to as *Butters Report*), para 15; CO 1015 437, Note by Central Africa Department, 31 October 1951.

8. *Report of the Post-War Development Committee* (Zomba: The Government Press, 1946), para 69.

9. CO 1015/437. Note on file CAA77/3/02 n.d. probably late 1951.

10. CO 1015/437, Lambert to Clough, 5 September 1951.

11. CO 1015/437. Referred to in Colby to Brown, 26 November 1952.

12. National Archives of Malawi (hereafter referred to as NAM), SMP.10228. Record of a Meeting Between the Nyasaland Government and the Nyasaland Railways, 8 March 1951.

13. Nyasaland Colloquium on Finance, Oxford, 23 April 1980; interviews, Phillips with C.A.B., 20 January 1989 and 23 August 1989.

14. CO 1015/437. Note on file CAA 77/3/01. n.d. probably 1952; and NAM, SMP.12664, Note of discussion, 26 April 1949.

15. Butters Report, para 19.

16. Referred to in CO. 1015 437. Lambert to Colby, 15 November 1951.

17. *Who Was Who*, 1979–80 (London: Black, 1981).

18. CO 1015 437. Lambert to Colby, 15 August 1951.

19. CO 1015 437. Gorell Barnes to Lloyd, Minute 22 December 1952.

20. CO 1015 437. Colby to secretary of state for the colonies (hereafter S.S.), 12 November 1951.

21. CO 1015 437. Nield to Crown Agents, 22 November 1951.

22. CO 1015 437. Lambert to Colby, 4 January 1952.

23. CO 1015 437. Colby to S.S., 7 January 1952 and registrar of companies, Malawi to C.A.B., 28 April 1987.

24. CO 1015 437. Lambert to Colby, 8 February 1952.

25. CO 1015 437. Colby to S.S., 14 February 1952.

26. CO 1015 437. Colby to S.S., 4 March 1952.

27. CO 1015 437. S.S. to Colby, 19 March 1952.

28. CO 1015 437. Colby to S.S., 20 March 1952.

29. CO 1015 437. Colby to S.S., 4 June 1952.

30. CO 1015 437. Codrington to Cohen, 20 November 1951.

31. Phillips, interview with C.A.B., 23 August 1989.
32. CO 1015 437. Gorell Barnes to Colby, 26 September 1952.
33. Stevens to C.A.B., 22 May 1982.
34. CO 1015 437. Gorell Barnes to Lloyd, Minute 24 December 1952.
35. M. Widdas to C.A.B., 24 May 1983.
36. Stevens to C.A.B., 22 May 1982.
37. CO 1015 437. Gorell Barnes to Colby, 26 September 1952.
38. Ibid.
39. CO 1015 437. S.S. to Colby, 19 March 1952.
40. Ibid.
41. CO 1015/437. Note of a meeting to discuss Nyasaland's financial and railway affairs, amended copy, 19 June 1952.
42. CO 1015/437. Lambert to Colby, 19 July 1952.
43. CO 1015/437. Colby to Lambert, 7 August 1952.
44. CO 1015/437. Colby to Gorell Barnes, 15 July 1952.
45. CO 1015/437. Gorell Barnes to Colby, 26 September 1952.
46. CO 1015/437. Colby to Gorell Barnes, 11 November 1952.
47. CO 1015/437. Colby to Brown and Milne, 26 November 1952.
48. CO 1015/437. Colby to Gorell Barnes, 26 November 1952.
49. CO 1015/437. Gorell Barnes to Lloyd, Minute 22 December 1952.
50. CO 1015/437. Minute by Bourdillon, 19 December 1952.
51. CO 1015/437. Colby to Gorell Barnes, 11 November 1952.
52. Colby Papers: speeches, speech at opening of LCP 68, 1 December 1952, pp.38–41.
53. *Financial Times*, London, 3 December 1952.
54. CO 1015/437. Dodds Parker to Lyttelton, 3 December 1952.
55. CO 1015/437. Minute by Gorell Barnes, 4 December 1952.
56. CO 1015/437. S.S. to Colby, 4 December 1952.
57. CO 1015/437. Minute by Gorell Barnes, 24 December 1952.
58. CO 1015/437. Marnham to Brown and Milne, 6 December 1952.
59. CO 1015/437. Sinclair to Lyttelton, 9 December 1952.
60. CO 1015/437. Referred to in Nield to Sun Life Assurance Company, 16 December 1952.
61. *Sunday Express*, London, 7 December 1952. CO 1015/437. Minute, unsigned, 9 December 1952.
62. CO 1015/437. Colby to S.S., 5 December 1952.
63. CO 1015/437. Colby to Lyttelton, 8 December 1952.
64. Stevens to C.A.B., 22 May 1982.
65. CO 1015/437. Minutes by Bourdillon, 19 December 1952; Marnham, 19 December 1952; Nield, 20 December 1952; Gorell Barnes, 22 December 1952; Lloyd, 24 December 1952.
66. CO 1015/437. Minute by Nield, 20 December 1952.
67. CO 1015/437. Gorell Barnes to Lloyd, Minute 22 December 1952.
68. CO 1015/437. Colby to Gorell Barnes, 11 November 1952.
69. CO 1015/437. Gorell Barnes to Lloyd, Minute 22 December 1952.
70. CO 1015/437. Minute by Bourdillon, 19 December 1952.
71. CO 1015/437. Gorell Barnes to Lloyd, Minute, 22 December 1952.
72. CO 1015/437. Lloyd to S. S., Minute 24 December 1952.

73. CO 1015/437. Gorell Barnes to Lloyd, Minute 22 December 1952.
74. CO 1015/437. Minute by Nield, 22 January 1953; Details of the meeting are from CO 1015/437, draft note of a meeting held at 10.30 a.m. on Friday 30 January in S.S.'s room to discuss Nyasaland railway matters.
75. CO 1015/437. Colby to Gorell Barnes, 12 March 1953.
76. CO 1015/437. Memorandum, Proposed Purchase of Nyasaland Railways and Central African Railways by the Nyasaland Government or the Federal Government (n.d. probably April 1953).
77. NAM. SMP 27308 Nyasaland and Associated Railways. 19 January 1955.
78. CO 1015/437. Nield to Bourdillon and Gorell Barnes, Minute 7 April 1953.
79. CO 1015/437. Colby to Gorell Barnes, 18 April 1953.
80. CO 1015/437. Minute by Nield, 15 May 1953.
81. CO 1015/437. Minutes by Marnham, 19 May 1953 and 27 May 1953; Gorell Barnes, 4 June 1953; Lloyd, 5 June 1953.
82. CO 1015/444. Marnham to Hillier-Fyfe, 19 June 1953.
83. CO 1015/437. Gorell Barnes to Colby, 17 June 1953.
84. CO 1015/444. Colby to Gorell Barnes, 23 September 1953.
85. CO 1015/1027. Maclennan to Clark, 27 January 1954.
86. CO 1015/1027. Clark to Maclennan, 18 January 1954.
87. CO 1015/1027. Maclennan to Clark, 27 January 1954.
88. Ibid.
89. K. Bain, interview with C.A.B., 19 January 1990.
90. CO 1015/1027. Referred to in note on file for Gorell Barnes, n.d. probably 11 June 1954.
91. Stevens to C.A.B. 22 May 1982.
92. CO 1015/1027. Referred to in note on file for Gorell Barnes, n.d. probably 11 June 1954.
93. CO 1015/1027. Robertson to Gorell Barnes, Minute 11 June 1954.
94. CO 1015/1029. Williams to Stacpoole, Minute 6 November 1954.
95. CO 1015/1029. Codrington to Lennox-Boyd, n.d. probably between 9 and 24 December 1954.
96. CO 1015/1029. Codrington to Lennox-Boyd, 26 December 1954.
97. CO 1015/1029. Referred to in Codrington to Lennox-Boyd, 1 December 1954.
98. NAM, SMP 27308. Minute by Colby, 19 January 1955.
99. Stevens to C.A.B., 22 May 1982.
100. *NT,* 27 May 1955, p.1.
101. *Malawi Hansard,* 4th session, 2nd meeting, 23 August 1966, pp.25–27.

Chapter 10

1. R. W. Kettlewell to C.A.B., 26.1.1985.
2. H. Rowley, *The Story of the Universities Mission to Central Africa* (London: Saunders, 1867), p.244.
3. Ibid., p.347.
4. W. A. Elmslie, *Among the Wild Ngoni* (London: Oliphant, Anderson and Ferrier, 1899), p.168.

5. *Colonial Annual Report for 1922: Nyasaland* (London: HMSO, 1923), pp.4–5.

6. R. W. Kettlewell, *Agricultural Change in Nyasaland, 1945–1960* (Stanford: Food Research Institute, 1965), p.239.

7. *Nyasaland Protectorate Annual Report*, hereafter *PAR*, 1948, p.26.

8. Colby to Anson, 29 May 1948, cited in J. McCracken, 'Planters, Peasants and the Colonial State', *Journal of Southern African Studies*, vol.9, no.2, April 1983, pp.172–92. See also Address to Protectorate Council, 7 July 1948, reported in *NT*, 22 July 1948, p.3.

9. Ex. Co., 3 June 1948, Minute 185. Ex. Co. Minutes are located in the National Archives of Malawi (NAM).

10. Chief secretary (hereafter C. S.) to chairman, Tea Association, 1 June 1948, reported in *NT*, 24 June 1948, p.7.

11. *PAR*, 1948, p.26.

12. C. S. to chairman, Tea Association, 1 June 1948, reported in *NT*, 24 June 1948, p.7.

13. Ibid.

14. Ibid.

15. Ex. Co., 9 September 1948, Minute 235.

16. R. W. Kettlewell to C.A.B., 16 June 1985.

17. Except where otherwise stated, material in this paragraph and the following four paragraphs is from A. P. S. Forbes to C.A.B., 1 July 1982, 7 August 1982 and 18 August 1982.

18. DC Blantyre to provincial commissioner, 4 February 1949. Except for correspondence with C.A.B., and except also where otherwise stated, correspondence is located in NAM, files nos. AFC 1/1/1, 1/3/1, 2/1/1, 2/2/1, 3/1/1, 6/4/1 and 9.

19. C. B. Garnett to C.A.B., 11 May 1982, and interview with C.A.B. 4 February 1985.

20. M. R. Chiwooka, interview with C.A.B., 28 August 1987.

21. Ex. Co., 12 January 1949, Minutes of meeting.

22. Ex. Co., 13 January 1949, Minute 32.

23. Ibid.

24. Material in this and the next paragraph is from H. S. Norman-Walker to C.A.B., 2 May 1982.

25. *Nyasaland Government Gazette*, 1949, p.19, General Notice No.22.

26. Ex. Co., 25 January 1949, Minute 60.

27. Ex. Co., 3 February 1949, Minute 70.

28. Speech to chamber of commerce, 12 July 1948 reported in *NT*, 15 July 1948, pp.7ff.

29. DC Blantyre to provincial commissioner, 3 February 1949.

30. Ex. Co., 3 February 1949, Minute 74.

31. Details of the meeting are from Colby to secretary of state, 11 February 1949 on file AFC 6/4/1.

32. Note at folio 1 on AFC 2/3/2, February 1949.

33. Ex. Co., 10 February 1949, Minute 86.

34. Ex. Co., 10 February 1949, Minute 78.

35. The following details are from Ex. Co., 3 February 1949, Minute 70.

36. H. G. Graham-Jolly to C.A.B., 19 February 1983.
37. Note on AFC 2/3/2, February 1949.
38. For attitude to free issues of food, see generally file AFC 3/1/1.
39. DC Zomba to African Foodstuffs Commissioner (hereafter AFC), 21 March 1949.
40. Notes for speech at opening of legislative council session, 28 February 1949.
41. Ibid.
42. *PAR*, 1949, p.3, and 1950, p.3
43. Ex. Co., 1 April 1948, Minute 104; and 29 April 1948, Minute 122.
44. *PAR*, 1949, p.3 and 1950, p.68; A. B. Henderson to C.A.B., 29 July 1983; G. R. Daniel to C.A.B., 3 June 1983.
45. H. G. Graham-Jolly to C.A.B., 19 February 1983.
46. Ex. Co., 1 July 1948, Minute 204, and 25 October 1948, Minute 286, H. W. Stevens to C.A.B., 22 May 1982.
47. *PAR*, 1949, p.3.
48. AFC to district superintendent, Rhodesia Railways, 25 February 1949.
49. Ex. Co., 10 February 1949, Minute 96, and 1 March 1949, Minute 128.
50. CS to AFC, 22 April 1949; DC Dowa to AFC, 7 June 1950; and DC Domasi to AFC, 12 August 1950.
51. *PAR*, 1950, p.38.
52. *PAR*, 1949, p.44, and 1950, p.54.
53. A. Westrop, *Green Gold* (Bulawayo: Cauldwell, n.d. prob.1971), p.237.
54. H. G. Graham-Jolly, interview with C.A.B., 17 June 1982.
55. W. Petrie to C.A.B., 8 May 1983.
56. Lady Jenkins to C.A.B., 30 May 1983.
57. *PAR*, 1949, p.7, and 1950, p.4; R. W. Kettlewell to C.A.B., 26 January 1985; F. Habgood, interview with C.A.B., 2 July 1983.
58. Ex. Co., 1 February 1950, Minute 63.
59. F. Habgood, interview with C.A.B., 2 July 1983.
60. Ex. Co., 3 February 1949, Minute 64.
61. Ex. Co., 16 March 1949, Minute 154.
62. Commissioner of Prisons to AFC, 29 April 1949.
63. Ex. Co., 4 January 1950, Minute 14.
64. Note at folio 4 on AFC 2/1/1, n.d. prob. March 1949.
65. Material in this paragraph is from AFC 2/2/1.
66. AFC to C. S., 6 July 1950.
67. K. A. Smith, interview with C.A.B., 10 September 1983.
68. *Nyasaland Government Gazette*, 1949, p.188.
69. Ex. Co., 10 August 1949, Minute 427.
70. Ex. Co., 14 September 1949, Minute 489.
71. Ex. Co., 31 August 1949, Minute 456.
72. *Nyasaland Government Gazette*, 1949, p.276.
73. Barnes to C. S., 17 January 1950.
74. K. A. Smith, interview with C.A.B., 10 September 1983, and M. Sabbatini to C.A.B., 25 August 1983.
75. C. S. to director of public works, 17 January 1950.

76. C. S. to Barnes, 20 January 1950, and Ex. Co., 19 January 1950, Minutes of Meeting.
77. DC Karonga to AFC, 10 May 1950.
78. Provincial commissioner to C. S., 11 February 1950.
79. Ex. Co., 19 January 1950, Minute 38.
80. Ex. Co., 1 February 1950, Minute 70.
81. AFC to DuToit and DuPreez, 17 March 1950.
82. *PAR*, 1950, p.54; M. Sabbatini to C.A.B., 25 August 1983.
83. H. W. Stevens to C.A.B., 16 July 1986; M. Sabbatini to C.A.B., 25 August 1983.
84. M. P. Barrow, LCP 65, November 1949, p.26.
85. LCP 65, November 1949, p.26.
86. Minute Colby to C. S., 22 March 1949.
87. R. W. Kettlewell to C.A.B., 22 February 1985 and 16 June 1985.
88. LCP 67, December 1951, p.3.

Chapter 11

1. A fuller account is given in Colin Baker, *Seeds of Trouble* (London: British Academic Press, 1993).
2. H. Johnston, *British Central Africa* (London: Methuen, 1897), p.32.
3. Johnston, *op. cit.*, pp.112–13.
4. The traditional system of land allocation is dealt with in J. C. Mitchell, *The Yao Village* (Manchester University Press, 1956), pp.62–3; H. Rowley, *Africa Unveiled* (London: SPCK, 1876), pp.109–10; W. H. Rankine, *A Hero of the Dark Continent* (London, Blackwood, 1896), pp.175–6. See also, T. O. Elias, *The Nature of African Customary Law* (Manchester University Press, 1956), Chapter 9.
5. Johnston, *op. cit.*, p.113.
6. Supervisor of Native Affairs versus Blantyre and East Africa Company, *Gazette*, Supplement, 30 April 1903.
7. Johnston, *op. cit.*, p.113; *Nyasaland Protectorate Legislative Council, Proceedings of the Select Committee Appointed to Consider the Position Of Natives on Private Estates* (Zomba: The Government Press), 1934, Paper 6, p.2.
8. The following details of the agreements and of the judgment in Supervisor of Native Affairs versus Blantyre and East Africa Company are from *Gazette*, Supplement, 30 April 1903, pp.1–8.
9. NAM, SMP. S/1/385/25, Land Commission Report, 6 May 1903; Pachai, *op. cit.*, pp.88–90.
10. *Ordinances of the Nyasaland Protectorate* (London: Stevens, 1913), Chapter 48: The Lands (Native Locations) Ordinance, no.5 of 1904.
11. Ibid., s.3.
12. Ibid., s.6.
13. *Blue Book 1905* (Zomba: The Government Press 1906), pp.124, 136, 137.
14. Land Commission to Pearce, 6 May 1903, cited in Pachai, *op. cit.*, p.84.
15. LCP 5, 24–26 May 1910, pp.6–10. See also LCP 10, 5–8 November 1912, pp.20–23.

16. *Report of the Commission Appointed by His Excellency the Governor to Inquire Into Various Matters and Questions Concerned with the Native Rising within the Nyasaland Protectorate*, Supplement to *Gazette*, 31 January 1916. See also, G. Shepperson and T. Price, *Independent African: John Chilembwe and the Origins, Setting and Significance of the Nyasaland Native Rising of 1915* (Edinburgh: The University Press, 1958), *passim*.

17. *Life and Work in Nyasaland*, no.3, December 1916, pp.1–3, cited in Shepperson and Price, *op. cit.*, p.393.

18. Ordinance no.16 of 1917.

19. *Gazette*, 31 July 1920, pp.191–2.

20. *Report of a Commission to Enquire into and Report on Certain Matters Connected with the Occupation of Land in the Nyasaland Protectorate* (Zomba: The Government Press, 1920; hereafter referred to as the *Jackson Report*), pp.14–15.

21. *Blue Book*, 1905, p.89, and 1920, p.O.1; *Jackson Report*, p.12.

22. *Jackson Report*, p.15.

23. Ibid., p.20.

24. CO 525/104, Bowring to S. S., 10 November 1924.

25. *Report of the Land Commission 1946* (hereafter referred to as the *Abrahams Report*) (Zomba: The Government Press, 1947), Appendix vi.

26. LCP, 35, 22 August 1927, p.4.

27. Ibid., p.9.

28. CO 525/73, Smith to S. S., 16 April 1917.

29. *Laws of Nyasaland, 1933* (London: Roworth, 1934), Chapter 43.

30. Ibid., s.21(7).

31. Select Committee Report 1934, Paper 2, p.6; Annual Report of the Provincial Commissioners, 1939 (Zomba: The Government Press, 1940), p.12.

32. Select Committee Report 1934, Paper 2, p.1.

33. Ibid., Paper 2, p.2.

34. Ibid., Paper 1, pp.1 and 8.

35. S. S. to Kittermaster, 24 October 1934, quoted in *Abrahams Report*, paras. 43 and 44. A distinguished commentator said in 1946 that the ordinance was 'an attempt to give equal treatment all round': C. K. Meek, *Land Law and Custom in the Colonies* (London: Oxford University Press 1946), p.118.

36. *Report on Native Affairs 1933* (Zomba: The Government Press, 1934), p.9. The estimate of 3124 people is calculated on the basis of 4 people per tenant family.

37. Kittermaster to S. S. 23 January 1937, quoted in *Abrahams Report*, paras. 49–52.

38. SS. to Kittermaster, 22 September 1937 referred to in *Abrahams Report*, para. 53.

39. *Bell Report*, pp.34–7. Debenham later expressed this policy point as: 'With the Government must rest the last word on what is expedient. It can claim that there is no case of injustice ... it is rather a question of policy and that is to a large extent the prerogative of the Government':

F. Debenham, *Nyasaland: Land of the Lake* (London: HMSO, 1955), p.103.

40. *Annual Report of the Provincial Commissioners, 1938* (Zomba: The Government Press, 1939), p.18. 123 applications from the Bruce Estates is the figure given in this report: White (*op. cit.*, p.196) gives a figure of 127 applications, possibly following Pachai (*op. cit.*, p.127), who gives 127 as the number of actual evictions from the whole of the Southern Province.

41. *Confidential Report on Native Administration and Political Development in British Tropical Africa* (London; HMSO, n.d. prob. 1943), pp.257–8.

42. *Memorandum on Native Policy in Nyasaland* (Zomba: The Government Press, 1939), p.19.

43. *Abrahams Report*, paras. 57–9.

44. *Abrahams Report*, para. 60. Details of the Mpezo applications for eviction are from NAM, SMP.11967, Confidential Appendix to the Draft Report of the Land Planning Committee, 1948.

45. *Gazette*, 31 July 1946, p.152, General Notice no.215.

46. *Abrahams Report*

47. *Abrahams Report*, para. 75.

48. Ibid.

49. Ibid., para. 106.

50. *Gazette*, 17 February 1947, General Notice no.56.

51. *Gazette*, 31 March 1947, General Notice no.107. Details of the reports are from NAM, SMP.11967, *Draft Report of the Land Planning Committee* (hereafter *DRLPC*), para. 8, and NAM, SMP.10521/I, *Report of the Land Planning Committee*, 1948 (hereafter *RLPC*).

52. *RLPC*, paras. 11–12.

53. Ibid., paras. 13–16.

54. Ibid., para. 17.

55. *RLPC*, para. 33; *DRLPC*, para. 35.

56. Instructions passed under the Royal Sign Manual and Signet, to the Governor and Commander-in-Chief of the Nyasaland Protectorate: Nyasaland Order-in-Council, Instruction XXXIV, *The Laws of Nyasaland, 1933* (London: Roworth, 1934), vol.II, p.1071.

57. NAM, LANCOM.14, Colby to Cohen, 28 April 1948.

58. Drafts on NAM, LANCOM.14, April 1948.

59. Sir Douglas Dodds Parker to C.A.B., 27 November 1983.

60. NAM, SMP.10521, Minute by Colby, no.48, 31 August 1948.

61. NAM, SMP.12258, McDonald to C.S., 12 December 1948. The following details are from this source.

62. NAM, SMP.10521, Minute by Colby, no.63, 12 October 1948; SMP.12258, Minute by Colby, 22 December 1948.

63. NAM, SMP.10521/I, Minute by Colby, 23 October 1948.

64. NAM, SMP.I.12664, Note of discussion with S. S. at Goverment House, 26 April 1949.

65. NAM, SMP.10521, Minute by Colby, no.87, 24 November 1949.

66. NAM, SMP.I.12501, Barrow to Colby, 24 June 1949.

67. CO.1015/707, referred to in Minute by Marnham, 14 October 1953.

68. *Nyasaland Protectorate Annual Report*, 1950, p.14.

69. *NT,* 18 December 1950; Nyasaland Protectorate Estimates for 1953, Head 22, item 106, note 2, p.69; NAM, SMP.10719, Proposed Acquisition of Freehold Land Belonging to the BSA Company: Edwards to Robbins, 9 October 1947 and Report by Rangeley, 10 April 1948.

70. Ex. Co., 22 April 1953, Minute 195.

71. Ibid.

72. *Report on the Nyasaland Protectorate for the Year 1953,* Zomba: The Government Press, 1954, p.5.

73. Ex. Co., 8 September 1953, Minute 523.

74. CO.1015/707, Colby to S.S., 2 October 1953. See also CO.1015/707, Colby to Gorell Barnes, 20 November 1953.

75. CO.1015/707, Marnham to Colby, 9 November 1953; Minute by Marnham, 13 October 1953; Gorell Barnes to Colby, 24 October 1953.

76. NAM, SMP.20767/43, Colby to S.S., 16 March 1954.

77. NAM, SMP.20767, Minute by Colby, 26 October 1953.

78. NAM, SMP.20767, Minute by Graham-Jolly, 17 June 1954.

79. The draft memorandum is in NAM, SMP.20767, folio 15, and a copy of the final version was reprinted in *East Africa and Rhodesia,* 10 June 1954, pp.1287–8.

80. NAM, SMP.20767, Colby to S. S., 16 March 1954. See also Ex. Co. Precis, Ref.26127, April 1954.

81. NAM, SMP.20767, S.S. to Colby, 16 April 1954.

82. NAM, SMP.62531, S.S. to President, Nyasaland Protectorate African Council, n.d. (probably late May 1954).

83. CO.1015/847, Minute by Marnham to Gorell Barnes, 18 March 1954.

84. *East Africa and Rhodesia,* 27 May 1954, p.1219.

85. CO 1015/707, Colby to S.S., 2 October 1953.

86. *East Africa and Rhodesia,* 27 May 1954, p.1219.

87. NAM, SMP.25282.K, and CO.1015/847, Dixon to S. S., 1 May 1954. Details of the memorandum are from this source.

88. Ordinances No. 19 of 1948 and No. 34 of 1952; *NT,* April–September, 1952, *passim;* LCP 66, 17 December 1952; and LCP 68, November 1953.

89. NAM, SMP.25282.A and CO 1015/847, Record of a meeting held at Government House on 6 May 1954. See also CO 1015/849, Colby to S. S., 7 May 1954.

90. NAM, SMP.20767/43, Colby to S. S., 16 March 1954.

91. CO 1015/847, Footman to Gorell Barnes, 22 May 1954.

92. CO 1015/707, Gorell Barnes to Footman, 16 August 1954; NAM, SMP.25282.A, *passim;* CO 1015/848, Minute, Marnham to Gorell Barnes, 20 October 1954; NAM, SMP.25282.A, Footman to Gorell Barnes, 7 September 1954.

93. NAM, SMP.25282.A, Gorell Barnes to Footman, 27 May 1954.

94. NAM, SMP.25282.A, and CO 1015/847, Record of discussion in Ex. Co., 9 June 1954. See also NAM, SMP.25282.A, Minutes 14, 21, 25, 54, 115, 116, 119.

95. Ex. Co., 10 December 1954, Minute 561.

96. CO 1015/848, Minute, Williams to Gorell Barnes, 9 February 1955.

97. CO 1015/851, Colby to SS, 6 April 1955; NAM, SMP.25282, Colby to SS, 6 April 1955.
98. V. L. Oury to C.A.B., 30 October 1987, enclosing extract from the chairman's statement in BCA Company's Annual Report for 1953.
99. CO 1015/851, Colby to S.S., 20 November 1954.
100. CO 1015/848, S.S. to Colby, 5 April 1955; CO 1015/851 and CO 1015/848, Note of a Meeting in S.S.'s Room, 4 May 1955.
101. CO 1015/848, Colby to Footman, 29 April 1955.
102. CO 1015/851 and CO 1015/848, Colby to Brook, 11 May 1955; CO 1015/848, Colby to SS, 20 June 1955.
103. Chairman's Statement, BCA Company Annual Report for 1955.
104. CO 1015/848, Colby to S.S., 7 October 1955.
105. CO 1015/848, Colby to SS, 7 October 1955 and S.S. to Colby, 28 December 1955.
106. L. V. Oury to C.A.B., 30 October 1987, enclosing extract from the chairman's statement in BCA Company's Annual Report for 1956.
107. CO 1015/1337, Armitage to S.S., 24 January 1958, and Armitage to S.S., 25 February 1959.
108. LCP 76, 29 May–1 June 1962, pp.266 *et seq*. Details of the bill and of the debate on it are from this source.

Chapter 12

1. *Nyasaland Protectorate Annual Report*, 1951, p.98.
2. Ibid., pp.106–7.
3. Local Government (District Councils) Ordinance, no.48, 1953.
4. The Chilembwe rising in 1915 was the only marked exception to the peaceful internal conditions: G. Shepperson and T. Price, *Independent African* (Edinburgh, 1958), Chapter 6.
5. *NT*, 8 July 1948, p.7.
6. *NT*, 15 July 1948, p.7ff.
7. Lady Colby, interviews with C.A.B., 18 and 19 June 1983.
8. NAM, SMP 10282, vol.I, Circular Despatch, Creech-Jones to Colby, 2 April 1948.
9. NAM, SMP 10282, vol.II, Paper by Colonial Information Policy Committee, n.d. (prob. August 1949).
10. NAM, SMP 10282, vol.I, Creech-Jones to Colby, 31 March 1949.
11. NAM, SMP 10282, vol.I, Colby to Creech-Jones, 27 June 1949; A. Dow, interview with C.A.B., 20 November 1983.
12. NAM, SMP 10282, vol.II, Creech-Jones to Colby, Despatch no.15 of 20 September 1949.
13. NAM, SMP 10282, vol.II, Note of discussion held on 31 October 1949.
14. NAM, SMP 10282, vol.II, Colby to Creech-Jones, 12 December 1949.
15. NAM, SMP 10282, vol.II, Creech-Jones to Colby, Despatch no.15 of 20 September 1949.
16. NAM, SMP 10282, vol.II, Creech-Jones to Colby, 9 February 1950.
17. Native Development and Welfare Fund Ordinance, no.29 of 1949.

18. R. Niven, *Nigerian Kaleidoscope* (London: Hurst, 1982), pp.191 and 193; M. J. Bennion to C.A.B., 14 September 1983.
19. Rene Philip to C.A.B., 4 January 1983; Sir Rex Niven to C.A.B., 29 August 1983.
20. Lady Colby, interviews with C.A.B., 18 and 19 June 1983; Rene Philip to C.A.B., 4 January 1983; R. Peel to C.A.B., 21 November 1983.
21. *Nyasaland Government Gazette*, 1949, p.87.
22. *Nyasaland Government Gazette*, 1950, p.4.
23. Rene Philip to C.A.B., 3 February 1983. Mrs Philip was born in 1910 and her home was The Grange, Kildwick near Skipton in Yorkshire, some 12 miles from Lady Colby's family home at Hanlith Hall, Kirkby Malham. Her maiden name was Senior and she married an RAF officer, Howard, before the Second World War. In 1949 she was public relations officer at Enugu in Nigeria when the 'Enugu Massacre' occurred. During a strike at Enugu the European officer in charge of the police detachment ordered his men to open fire and they killed 21 strikers. In the ensuing commission of enquiry the police officer responsible for the shootings was adjudged to have acted honestly but to have made an error of judgement which fell short of the standard expected of one of his rank and seniority. That officer was Ricky Philip and he joined Rene in Nyasaland at the latest in December 1951 when he was appointed printer at the African Press, and they set up home together on a 500-acre tobacco farm at Neno with her parents. Rene had a number of interesting political acquaintances. Lord Milverton (formerly Sir Arthur Richards) introduced her to Sir Winston Churchill at the House of Lords; Barbara Castle – whom she knew through her husband, a Fleet Street colleague, Ted Castle – introduced her to Michael Foot; and James Callaghan – whom she first met when he was on a fact-finding mission in Nigeria – entertained her, with his wife, to dinner at the House of Commons.
24. K. Smith, interview with C.A.B., 10 September 1983; and Rene Philip to C.A.B., 3 February 1983.
25. Ex. Co., 14 March 1951, Minute 137; and Rene Philip to C.A.B., 3 February 1983.
26. Rene Philip to C.A.B., 4 January 1983 and 3 February 1983.
27. Ex. Co., 23 May 1951, Minute 251.
28. NAM, SMP 12385, Colby to Marshall, president of chamber of commerce, 11 February 1949; and NAM, SMP 12930, Brown to Lilley, 4 March 1949; Note of meeting held at Government House, Zomba, 15 March 1949; Hess to Colby, 15 March 1949, in a Note on the Policy, Responsibility and Conduct of the Nyasaland Times.
29. Ex. Co., 23 May 1951, Minute 251.
30. Ibid.
31. Native Development and Welfare Fund Ordinance, No.29 of 1949.
32. Ex. Co., 23 May 1951, Minute 251.
33. Ibid. Fletcher's salary as chairman was £2000 a year, the same as the chief secretary's, and Mrs Philip's salary was £1000, the same as most heads of government departments.

34. Ex. Co., 16 May 1952, Precis no.138/52; K. Smith, interview with C.A.B., 10 September 1983.
35. Ex. Co., 23 May 1951, Minute 251.
36. Rene Philip to C.A.B., 3 February 1983.
37. Rene Philip to C.A.B., 4 January 1983.
38. Rene Philip to C.A.B., 22 May 1983.
39. Ex. Co., 23 May 1951, Minute 251.
40. Ex. Co., 4 July 1951, Minute 317.
41. H. G. Graham-Jolly, interview with C.A.B., 17 June 1982.
42. Ex. Co., 17 July 1951, Minute 331.
43. Ex. Co., 2 August 1951, Minute 361; Register of Companies, Nyasaland, 1951, List of Shareholders, and Registrar of Companies to C.A.B., 17 March 1987, from which sources later details of directorships and shareholdings are derived.
44. Ex. Co., 2 August 1951, Minute 361.
45. Rene Philip to C.A.B., 22 May 1983.
46. *NT,* 10 April 1952, p.7; 28 April 1952, p.7.
47. *NT,* 16 June 1952, p.7; 19 June 1952, p.8.
48. *NT,* 17 April 1952, p.8.
49. *NT,* 2 June 1952, p.6.
50. *East Africa and Rhodesia,* 27 March 1951, reproduced in *Nyasaland Times,* 17 April 1951, p.8.
51. *East Africa and Rhodesia,* 1 May 1951, reproduced in *NT,* 12 May 1951, p.7.
52. LCP 67, 17 December 1951; *NT,* 3 January 1952, p.12; Registrar of Companies to C.A.B., 17 March 1987.
53. LCP 67, 17 December 1951; *NT,* 3 January 1952, p.12.
54. *NT,* 17 April 1952, p.9; 12 May 1952, p.7; 15 May 1952, p.7.
55. Official Secrets Ordinance, no.3 of 1913, s 4.
56. *NT,* 12 June 1952, p.9, and 10 December 1951, p.7.
57. *NT,* 10 July 1952, p.8.
58. *NT,* 12 May 1952, p.7.
59. *NT,* 31 July 1952, p.2.
60. *NT,* 1 September 1952, p.7.
61. *NT,* 11 September 1952, p.7.
62. *NT,* 29 September 1952, p.12.
63. The minutes of the chamber of commerce and Convention of Associations lodged in NAM contain no reference to Barrow's statement at the meeting of 17 September 1952.
64. *NT,* 23 April 1953., p.11.
65. Ex. Co., 25 June 1953, Minute 374.
66. Nyasaland Protectorate Annual Report, 1953, p.125; and NAM, SMP 22658, Note by Morris on visit by the brothers Paver, n.d. (probably early 1953).
67. LCP 67, 17 December 1951; *NT,* 7 January 1952, p.1.
68. *NT,* 14 June 1951, p.4.
69. *NT,* 22 November 1951, p.6.
70. *NT,* 15 July 1948, p.7ff.

71. Lady Colby felt that Fletcher had let Colby down very badly and had spent a great deal of money unwisely (Lady Colby, interview with C.A.B., 19 June 1983); it appears also that when addressing the chamber of commerce, Fletcher was unsteady on his feet (H. W. Stevens to C.A.B., 12 March 1987).
72. Lady Colby, interviews with C.A.B., 18 and 19 June 1983.

Chapter 13

1. See Chapter 11.
2. For compact accounts of the background to closer association, see T. M. Frank, *Race and Nationalism* (London: George Allen and Unwin, 1960), Chapter 3; A. J. Wills, *An Introduction to the History of Central Africa* (London: Oxford University Press, 1964), Chapter 9; G. Jones, *Britain and Nyasaland* (London: George Allen and Unwin, 1964), Chapter 6; and J. R. T. Wood, *The Welensky Papers: A History of the Federation of Rhodesia and Nyasaland* (Durban: Graham Publishing, 1983), Chapters 1–3. The following account draws on these sources.
3. LCP Extraordinary Session, 6 June 1933, pp. 4–8.
4. NAM, SMP 14452, acting governor to secretary of state, 11 March 1948.
5. NAM, SMP 14452, S.S. to acting governor, 19 March 1948.
6. Colby to Cohen, 4 June 1948, Ref. No. GH.149. Colby Papers. (In 1990 Colby's daughter deposited a number of files, which Colby had retained, in Rhodes House Library, Oxford. These are referred to as Colby Papers.)
7. NAM, SMP 14452, Gore Browne to Colby, 22 October 1948.
8. Colby Papers, Colby to Milverton, 23 December 1948.
9. *NT*, 21 February 1949, p.1. Material in the remainder of this paragraph is from this source. See also Wills, *op.cit.*, p.315.
10. Colby Papers, Colby to Barker (provincial commissioner) 24 March 1949.
11. *NT*, 25 April 1949, p.5.
12. Ibid.
13. *NT*, 28 April 1949, p.7.
14. Referred to in NAM, SMP 12248. Barnes (provincial commissioner) to Brown (chief secretary) 23 June 1949.
15. Ibid.
16. Ibid.
17. *NT*, 25 April 1949, p.5, and 2 May 1949, p.5.
18. NAM, SMP 12968, extract from minutes of the eleventh meeting of the Central African Council, 25 January 1950.
19. NAM, Benson to Thornton (chief secretary, Northern Rhodesia) and Brown (chief secretary, Nyasaland), Ref.No. S.3/300C/50 of 18 January 1950.
20. Referred to in NAM, SMP 12968, Colby to Cohen, 13 January 1950.
21. Ibid.
22. NAM, SMP 12968, Colby to Cohen, 13 January 1950. Details in this and the following three paragraphs are from this source.
23. NAM, SMP 12529, Colby to Rennie, 6 January 1950; Benson to Brown,

14 January 1950; and SMP 12968, extract from the minutes of the eleventh meeting of the Central African Council, 25 January 1950.

24. NAM, Benson to Secretary of State, 10 December 1949, Ref. S.26/300C; SMP 12968, Colby to secretary of state, Rennie and Benson, 13 January 1950; Benson to Thornton, Brown and Lambert, 18 January 1950.

25. *NT,* 29 August 1949, p.7.

26. *NT,* 6 February 1950, p.1.

27. *NT,* 13 February 1950, p.4.

28. NAM, SMP 13772II enclosed with chief secretary, Central African Council, to secretary for African affairs, 31 October 1950.

29. See Wills, *op. cit.,* p.316.

30. See Chapter 12.

31. *NT,* 14 September 1950, p.1.

32. *NT,* 11 September 1950, p.6.

33. Sir Peter Smithers to C.A.B., 8 July 1983.

34. *NT,* 16 November 1950, p.6.

35. *NT,* 4 January 1951, p.9.

36. Ex. Co., 21 February 1951, Minute 77.

37. *NT,* 8 January 1951, p.7, and 8 March 1951, p.1; details of the conference proceedings, from the Nyasaland delegation viewpoint, in the following paragraphs are from W. J. R. Pincott to C.A.B., 10 December 1992 and 28 January 1993.

38. Cmd 8233 (London: HMSO, 1951). See also *NT,* 18 June 1951.

39. Nyasaland Colloquium on Finance, Oxford, 23 April 1980, Sir Henry Phillips. Report privately held.

40. *NT,* 14 June 1951, p.7.

41. NAM, SMP 20808, no date, probably early July 1951; and *NT,* 3 September 1951, p.10.

42. *NT,* 18 June 1951, p.1.

43. Ibid.

44. *NT,* 9 July 1951, p.5.

45. *NT,* 23 August 1951, p.1.

46. *NT,* 3 September 1951, p.1, and 6 September 1951, pp.1–3 and p.9; *Rhodesia Herald,* 25 August 1951.

47. R. W. Kettlewell to C.A.B., 1 June 1987. See also J. R. T. Wood, *op. cit.,* pp.209–10.

48. *NT,* 30 August 1951, p.1; 3 September 1951, p.2.

49. *NT,* 3 September 1951, p.10.

50. K. A. Smith, interview with C.A.B., 10 September 1983.

51. Kettlewell to C.A.B., 1 June 1987.

52. *Nyasaland Protectorate Annual Report, 1951* (London: HMSO, 1952), p.1. For details of the conference, see Wood, *op. cit.,* pp.213ff.

53. *NT,* 17 September 1951, p.1.

54. J. M. Greenfield to C.A.B., 23 July 1983.

55. Cmd. 8573 (London: HMSO, 1952), pp.37–8.

56. *NT,* 20 September 1951, p.1.

57. Ibid. See also Wood, *op. cit.,* p.219.

58. *NT,* 24 September 1951, p.1.

59. *NT*, 27 September 1951, p.6.
60. *NT*, 22 November 1951, p.1.
61. *NT*, 8 October 1951, p.1.
62. Welensky, interview with C.A.B., 12 June 1982.
63. Smithers to C.A.B., 8 July 1983.
64. Colby Papers, Colby to secretary of state, 30 November 1951.
65. Colby Papers, Cohen to Colby, 3 December 1951.
66. *NT*, 3 January 1952, p.11.
67. *NT*, 14 January 1952, p.5.
68. Cmd. 8573, *op.cit.*, p.3.
69. *NT*, 31 January 1952, p.6.
70. *NT*, 6 March 1952, p.1., report of Labour Party motion criticising the British government decision to proceed with federal proposals.
71. Cmd. 8573, *op.cit.*, p.3.
72. Colby Papers, Colby to secretary of state, 19 March 1952. Material in this and the following three paragraphs is from this source.
73. R. Welensky, *Welensky's 4000 Days* (London: Collins, 1964), p.23.
74. *NT*, 21 April 1952, p.1.
75. *NT*, 21 April 1952, p.1.; *Nyasaland Protectorate Annual Report, 1952* (London: HMSO, 1953), p.5; Wood, *op.cit.*, p.249.
76. *NT*, 19 June 1952, p.8.
77. *NT*, 10 July 1952, p.8.
78. *East Africa and Rhodesia*, 7 August 1952, p.1; and *NT*, 14 August 1952, p.9.
79. *NT*, 18 August 1952, p.6, and 25 August 1952, p.8.
80. *East Africa and Rhodesia*, 7 August 1952, p.1.
81. *NT*, 28 August 1952, p.9.
82. *NT*, 14 August 1952, p.1, 18 August 1952, p.1 and 21 August 1952, p.1.
83. *NT*, 14 August 1952, p.1.
84. A. Campbell to C.A.B., 1 September 1983.
85. Sir John Marnham to C.A.B., 26 August 1983.
86. *NT*, 1 September 1952, p.1.
87. A. Campbell to C.A.B., 1 September 1983.
88. See Chapters 9 and 11.
89. Sir Peter Smithers to C.A.B., 25 July 1983.
90. *NT*, 1 September 1952, p.7.
91. R. I. Rotberg, *The Rise of Nationalism in Central Africa*, (Cambridge, MA: Harvard University Press, 1967), pp.246–247.
92. Ex. Co., 17 December 1952, Minute 552.
93. Ibid.
94. LCP 68, 1 December 1952, reported in *NT*, 4 December 1952, p.5.
95. *The Times*, London, 24 February 1953, p.7.
96. *NT*, 15 December 1952, p.1.
97. *NT*, 5 January 1953, p.1.
98. NAM, SMP 4–11–3F, 8846, Ref.No. 20, 787A, December 1952.
99. *NT*, 8 January 1953, pp.1 and 9, and 12 January 1953, p.1.
100. *The Times*, London, 24 February 1953.
101. Reported in *NT*, 15 January 1953, p.1.

102. Cmd. 8753 (London: HMSO, 1953), p.7.
103. Rotberg, *op. cit.*, p.248.
104. *NT,* 9 April 1953, p.1, 16 April 1953, p.1; Wood, *op. cit.*, p.362.
105. *NT,* 16 April 1953, p.1.
106. Ex. Co., 16 April 1953, Minute 181.
107. LCP 68, 20 April 1953.
108. *NT,* 23 April 1953, p.1.
109. NAM, SMP 4–11–3F, 8846, n.d.
110. Ex. Co., 21 February 1951, Minute 77.
111. NAM, SMP 4–11–3F, Note on Report of the Fiscal Commission, n.d., probably late September 1952.
112. Ex. Co., 22 October 1952, Minute 452.
113. NAM, SMP 21576, a series of minutes from 6 March 1953 to 14 September 1953; Ex. Co., 11 March 1953, Minute 107.
114. NAM, SMP 21576, Barrow to Welensky, 21 May 1953.
115. NAM, SMP 21576, Minute by Colby to chief secretary, 6 March 1953; Barrow to Welensky, 21 May 1953.
116. NAM, SMP 21576, Minute by Colby to chief secretary, 6 March 1953.
117. Ex. Co., 11 March 1953, Minute 107.
118. Referred to in NAM, SMP 21576, Colby to Lloyd, 23 April 1953.
119. Ibid.
120. NAM, SMP 21576, Colby to Lloyd, 23 April 1953.
121. NAM, SMP 21576, Gorell Barnes to Colby 11 May 1953.
122. Referred to in NAM, SMP 21576 Lloyd to Colby 5 June 1953.
123. NAM, SMP 21576, Lloyd to Colby, 5 June 1953.
124. NAM, SMP 21576, Barrow to Welensky, 21 May 1953.
125. Ibid.; Colby to secretary of state, 21 July 1953.
126. NAM, SMP 21576, secretary of state to Colby, 9 June 1953.
127. Ibid.
128. NAM, SMP 21576, Phillips to Strachan, 22 July 1953.
129. NAM, SMP 21576, secretary of state to Colby, 25 August 1953.
130. D. Taylor, *Rainbow on the Zambezi* (London: Museum Press, 1953), p.82.
131. Ex. Co., 22 April 1953, Minute 196.
132. Ex. Co., 18 October 1951, Minute 469.
133. Ex. Co., 22 April 1953, Minute 196.
134. Ibid.
135. Ex. Co., 22 April 1953, Minute 195.
136. Ex. Co., 28 April 1953, Minute 207.
137. Ex. Co., 28 April 1953, Minute 218.
138. Ibid.
139. *NT,* 18 May 1953, p.1.
140. Ex. Co., 7 May 1953, Minute 245.
141. Ex. Co., 13 May 1953, Minute 249.
142. Ex. Co., 27 May 1953, Minute 292.
143. *NT,* 25 May 1953, p.1.
144. *NT,* 28 May 1953, p.1.
145. Ex. Co., 27 May 1953, Minute 292.
146. *NT,* 1 December 1953, reporting speech by Colby to legislative council.

147. *NT,* 2 July 1953, p.1.
148. *NT,* 13 July 1953, p.6.
149. Ex. Co. 13 July 1953, Minute 406.
150. *NT,* 20 July 1953, p.1.
151. Ex. Co., 9 July 1952, Minute 291.
152. *NT,* 30 July 1953, p.5; and Cap. 64, *Laws of Nyasaland,* 1957.
153. *NT,* 20 August 1953, p.1.
154. *NT,* 24 August 1953, p.1.
155. *NT,* 27 August 1953, p.1.
156. Ex. Co., 8 September 1953, Minute 523.
157. *NT,* 27 August 1953, p.1.
158. *NT,* 31 August 1953, p.1.
159. Ibid.
160. Ibid.
161. *NT,* 24 September 1953, p.6.
162. *NT,* 31 August 1953, p.1.
163. *NT,* 7 September 1953, p.1.
164. *NT,* 7 September 1953, p.7.
165. P. Short, *Banda* (London: Routledge and Kegan Paul, 1974), p.77.
166. Colby's address to legislative council, reported in *NT,* 1 December 1953, p.1.
167. *NT,* 17 September 1953, p.9.
168. *NT,* 8 October 1953, p.1.
169. *NT,* 7 September 1953, p.1.
170. *NT,* 14 September 1953, p.8.
171. D. Taylor, *op. cit.,* pp.78 and 82.
172. *East Africa and Rhodesia,* 10 September 1953. Joelson's anti-African progress pronouncements long continued: in his publication of 7 April 1955 he wrote, 'Mr James Johnston M.P. evidently expects black Africans to rule Nyasaland. We expect nothing of the kind and can conceive nothing worse for the territory.'
173. Sir Hugh Norman-Walker to C.A.B., 2 May 1982.
174. Ex. Co., 1 September 1953, Minute 505.
175. *NT,* 8 October 1953, p.8.
176. Ibid.
177. Ex. Co., 16 September 1953, Minute 528.
178. Ex. Co., 8 September 1953, Minute 523.
179. Ex. Co., 1 September 1953, Minute 505; and 16 September 1953, Minute 528.
180. Ex. Co., 16 September 1953, Minute 528.
181. Ex. Co., 24 September 1952, Minute 535.
182. *NT,* 9 November 1953, p.7.
183. Kettlewell to C.A.B., 21 June 1986 and 1 June 1987.
184. *NT,* 18 December 1953, pp.7 and 11.
185. K. A. Smith, interview with C.A.B., 10 September 1983.
186. *NT,* 18 December 1953, p.1, and 22 December 1953, p.8.
187. Lady Colby, interview with C.A.B., 18 June 1983.
188. Kettlewell to C.A.B., 1 June 1987.

189. *Nyasaland Protectorate Annual Report, 1954* (London: HMSO, 1955), p.1.
190. C. A. Baker, *The Development of the Civil Service in Malawi 1891–1972*, Chapter V (London University, unpublished PhD thesis, 1981).
191. Ex. Co., 12 August 1953, Minute 485.
192. *NT,* 7 September 1953, p.7.
193. *NT,* 5 October 1953, p.7.
194. NAM, SMP 25867, Minutes by Colby to chief secretary, 20 December 1953, 20 January 1954, 21 February 1954, 18 April 1954.
195. NAM, SMP 25867, Huggins to Colby, 18 January 1954.
196. NAM, SMP 25867, Colby to Huggins, 20 December 1953.
197. *Nyasaland Government Gazette, 1954* (Zomba: The Government Press, 1954), pp.138 and 301.
198. Colby Papers, Colby to Benson, 30 December 1954.
199. Colby Papers, draft of a letter Colby to Huggins, n.d., probably early December 1954; it is this letter which is referred to in the following paragraph.
200. Colby Papers, Colby to Benson, 30 December 1954.
201. Colby Papers, Minute by Footman to Colby, 3 January 1955.
202. Colby Papers, Colby to Gorell Barnes and to Benson, 17 January 1955, Ref.No. F.8/55.
203. Colby Papers, Colby to Benson, 30 December 1956.
204. Ibid.
205. Ibid.
206. Colby Papers, Marnham to Colby, 27 January 1955, and Gorell Barnes to Colby, 29 March 1955.
207. Colby Papers, Gorell Barnes to Colby, 29 March 1955.
208. Colby Papers, Colby to Welensky, 27 June 1955, Ref.No. F.8/55.
209. Welensky, interview with C.A.B., 12 June 1982.
210. Kettlewell to C.A.B., 1 June 1987.
211. Colby Papers, Welensky to Colby, 14 July 1955.
212. See Chapter 10.
213. Colby Papers, Welensky to Colby, 14 July 1955.
214. Colby Papers, Colby to Welensky, 15 August 1955, Ref.No. F.8/55.
215. Kettlewell to C.A.B., 8 September 1983.
216. J. M. Greenfield to C.A.B., 9 and 23 July 1983, and Sir John Coldwell to C.A.B., 22 August 1983. The point in these letters is that federal ministers acknowledged that Colby faithfully implemented federation.
217. H. W. Stevens to C.A.B., 22 May 1982.
218. Diary of Dr McIntosh of Rockefeller Foundation; copy supplied by Foundation, privately held.
219. Sir Ronald Prain to C.A.B., 20 June 1983.
220. Welensky, interview with C.A.B., 12 June 1982.
221. Federation of Rhodesia and Nyasaland (Constitution) Order in Council, 1953, *Laws of Nyasaland*, 1957, vol.vi, Appendix 4.
222. Ex. Co., 8 September 1953, Minute 523.
223. NAM, SMP 27987, Richards (director of public works) to acting chief secretary, 10 October 1955.
224. NAM, SMP 27987, Minute by Colby to chief secretary, 29 May 1955.

225. NAM, SMP 27987, Minute by Colby to chief secretary, 19 August 1955.
226. NAM, SMP 27987, Minute by Colby to chief secretary, 14 February 1956.
227. NAM, SMP 27987, director of public works to acting chief secretary, 10 October 1955.
228. Ibid.
229. Ibid.
230. Caldicott to C.A.B., 18 November 1983; and NAM, SMP 25410, note on discussion at Government House, Zomba, on 28 January 1954.
231. Ibid.
232. *NT*, 15 March 1955, p.4; 26 April 1955, p.5; 3 May 1955, p.1; 14 June 1955, p.4; and 4 November 1955, p.1.
233. *NT*, 15 March 1955, p.4.
234. Kettlewell to C.A.B., 18 February 1990.
235. *NT*, 15 April 1955, p.5.
236. *NT*, 14 October 1955, p.5.
237. Colby to Kettlewell, 20 June 1955, privately held.
238. Welensky, interview with C.A.B., 12 June 1982.
239. Welensky to C.A.B., 28 May 1982.
240. NAM, SMP 260931, Minutes by Colby, 25 August 1955 and 2 October 1955.
241. NAM, SMP 26422, Minute by Colby, 18 November 1955.
242. Colby Papers, Colby to Lennox-Boyd, 24 January 1956.
243. LCP 70, 12 July 1955, p.1.
244. *NT*, 30 December 1955, p.1.
245. Colby to Lennox-Boyd, 24 January 1956, Ref. No. 20976/7; copy enclosed in Armitage to C.A.B., 9 May 1982.
246. Colby Papers, Colby to Lennox-Boyd, 24 January 1956.
247. Colby to Armitage, March 1956, privately held.
248. Ibid.
249. Welensky, interview with C.A.B., 12 June 1982.
250. Colby Papers, Colby to Welensky, 15 August 1955, Ref. No. F.8/55.
251. Colby Papers, Colby to Lennox-Boyd, 24 January 1956.

Chapter 14

1. LCP 42, September 1930, p.3.
2. See Chapter 7.
3. See Chapter 13.
4. See Chapter 11.
5. See Chapter 12.
6. W. D. Lewis to C.A.B., 22 May 1982.
7. See Chapter 9.
8. *NT*, 19 June 1952, p.8.
9. See Chapter 9.
10. *NT*, 7 January 1952, p.6.

11. See Dixon's speeches in legislative council and elsewhere on the issue of the African Press; see Chapter 12.
12. *NT,* 22 December 1952, p.10.
13. H. C. Duncan to editor, *NT,* 8 January 1953, p.2.
14. Sir Robert Armitage to C.A.B., 9 May 1982, enclosing Dixon to Armitage, 21 April 1956.
15. Ibid.
16. E.g. *NT,* 5 January 1953, p.9.
17. Welensky, interview with C.A.B., 12 June 1982.
18. *NT,* 22 November 1951, p.6.
19. Ex. Co., 21 February 1951, Minute 77.
20. LCP 68, 1 December 1952, governor's opening address.
21. See Chapter 4.
22. LCP 68, 1 December 1952, governor's opening address.
23. LCP 67, 7 April 1952, financial secretary's address.
24. Colby Papers, secretary of state to Colby, n.d., probably mid-1952.
25. *NT,* 1952 and 1953, *passim.*
26. Colby Papers, Colby to Mitchell, 29 June 1949.
27. Colby Papers, Colby to Cohen, 29 May 1951.
28. Sir John Martin to C.A.B., 26 August 1983.
29. Colby Papers, Colby to Lennox-Boyd, 24 January 1956.

Chapter 15

1. C.A.B.'s diary, privately held, from which details of the departure from Limbe are taken.
2. C. A. Baker, *Johnston's Administration* (Zomba: The Government Press, 1970), p.95.
3. Lady Colby, interview with C.A.B., 19 June 1983.
4. H. W. Stevens to C.A.B., 22 May 1982.
5. J. H. Illingworth, *The Malham Story* (Lymington: Nautical Publishing Company, 1972), p.19.
6. Illingworth, *op.cit.,* p.9.
7. Lady Colby, interview with C.A.B., 18 June 1983.
8. N. Tallents to C.A.B., 6 July 1983.
9. E. Apthorpe to C.A.B., 27 July 1983.
10. *African Affairs,* vol.55, no.221, October 1956, pp.273–82.
11. R. W. Kettlewell to C.A.B., 16 August 1983, and interview with C.A.B., 8 November 1986.
12. Marcus Colby, interview with C.A.B., 26 June 1984.
13. Lady Colby, interview with C.A.B., 19 June 1983.
14. Marcus Colby, interview with C.A.B., 26 June 1984.
15. *Yorkshire Herald and Pioneer,* 24 December 1958.
16. W. Monk, *Dr Livingstone's Cambridge Lectures* (London: Deighton Bell and Company, 1858), p.24.
17. J. Goodall, *Goodbye to Empire: a Doctor Remembers* (Edinburgh: Pentland, 1987), p.78.
18. N. Tallents to C.A.B., 7 September 1983.

19. Marcus Colby, interview with C.A.B., 26 June 1984.
20. Colby to Kettlewell, 3 March 1958; R. W. Kettlewell to C.A.B., 16 August 1983.
21. Colby to Kettlewell, 3 March 1958.
22. N. Tallents to C.A.B., 19 August 1983 and 7 September 1983.
23. E. Apthorpe to C.A.B., 27 July 1983.
24. Lady Colby to M. and R. W. Kettlewell, 11 January 1959; and R. W. Kettlewell to C.A.B., 8 November 1986.
25. Marcus Colby, interview with C.A.B., 26 June 1984.
26. Lady Colby to M. and R. W. Kettlewell, 11 January 1959.
27. R. W. Kettlewell, *Food and Cash Crops, Nyasaland, September 1983*, document in Overseas Development Research Project papers, Rhodes House Library, Oxford.
28. G. F. T. Colby, 'Recent Developments in Nyasaland', *African Affairs*, vol.55, no.221, October 1956, pp.273–82.
29. *NT*, 23 December 1958, p.8.
30. *NT*, 23 December 1958, p.1.
31. *The Times*, London, 24 December 1958, p.9.

Index